W9-ADZ-504

WITHDRAWN

Rethinking the *Romance of the Rose*

University of Pennsylvania Press
MIDDLE AGES SERIES
Edited by Edward Peters
Henry Charles Lea Professor
of Medieval History
University of Pennsylvania

A listing of the available books in this series appears at the back of this volume

Rethinking the *Romance of the Rose*

Text, Image, Reception

Edited by Kevin Brownlee
and Sylvia Huot

upp

University of Pennsylvania Press

Philadelphia

Library of Congress Cataloging-in-Publication Data
Rethinking The romance of the Rose : text, image, reception / edited by Kevin Brownlee
and Sylvia Huot.
    p.   cm.—(Middle Ages Series)
Includes bibliographical references and index.
ISBN 0-8122-3115-5
1. Guillaume, de Lorris, fl. 1230. Roman de la Rose. 2. Jean, de Meun, d. 1305—Criticism
and interpretation. 3. Love poetry, French—History and criticism. 4. Literature, Medieval—French influences. 5. Manuscripts, Medieval—France. 6. Courtly love in literature.
I. Brownlee, Kevin. II. Huot, Sylvia Jean. III. Series.
PQ1528.R48   1992   92-10510
841'.1—dc20   CIP

Contents

Acknowledgments

Many debts have been acquired in the preparation of this volume and it is a pleasure to acknowledge them. First of all, the editors would like to thank Ben Semple for his invaluable help as an editorial assistant and proofreader, especially during the busy period when he was finishing his Ph.D. thesis at the University of Pennsylvania and preparing to undertake his current position as Assistant Professor in the Department of French at Yale. Among the many colleagues whose support and advice was precious to us, we would like to single out Professors Marina Brownlee, Douglas Kelly, Eberhard König, Stephen Nichols, and Nancy Regalado. In addition we would like to thank Professors Heather Arden, Michael Camille, and Sandra Hindman. We have greatly benefited from the critical perspective and astute comments of our editor at the University of Pennsylvania Press, Jerome Singerman.

The idea for this volume originated at the 1987 Newberry Library Renaissance Conference, where the initial versions of many of the essays contained here were first given. The conference was made possible by the sponsorship of the Newberry Library's Center for Renaissance Studies, Northern Illinois University, Dartmouth College, and the Ramon Guthrie Fund. We wish to express our thanks for this generous support. For their help in the logistics of conference organization and production, we would also like to thank Ann Roberts of the Center for Renaissance Studies and Deborah Booth of Northern Illinois University, both of whom were always a pleasure to work with.

Two of the essays contained herein, those by Kevin Brownlee and Lee Patterson, were originally published in *Romanic Review* 79 (1988): 199–221, and *Speculum* 58 (1983): 656–95 respectively. We would like to thank the editors for permission to reprint the revised versions of these essays.

Finally, we wish gratefully to acknowledge the University of Pennsylvania and Northern Illinois University for subventions granted in support of the publication of this volume.

All translations not otherwise indicated are by the authors of the individual chapters. The editors would like to thank the University Press of New England for permission to use the English translation of the *Roman de la Rose* by Charles Dahlberg.

Philadelphia/DeKalb   K.B.
June 1991   S.H.

Kevin Brownlee and Sylvia Huot

Introduction: Rethinking the *Rose*

The *Romance of the Rose* is generally recognized as the single most significant work in the Old French literary tradition. Written between 1225 and 1275, the *Rose*'s success among medieval readers was extraordinary: well over two hundred manuscripts are extant, dating from a period of nearly three hundred years. Its influence was pervasive in late-medieval works both in and outside France. By the close of the fourteenth century, it had been translated into Italian, into Dutch, and into English. It was one of the only medieval vernacular texts to be cited and glossed in learnèd monastic treatises. Furthermore, its influence continued into the Renaissance. The *Rose* was one of the few medieval works of vernacular literature to be printed in both fifteenth- and sixteenth-century editions. It was singled out for praise by the humanist Joachim du Bellay, in his *Deffence et Illustration de la Langue Françoyse* of 1549, as the preeminent poem of the French Middle Ages.

The *Rose* has been a controversial text since it was written. There is evidence for radically different readings as early as the first half of the fourteenth century. It provided inspiration for both courtly and didactic poets. Some read it as a celebration of human love; others as an erudite philosophical work; still others as a satirical representation of social and sexual follies. It was praised as an edifying treatise and condemned as lascivious and misogynistic. Several manuscripts contain glosses, sometimes in Latin, a most unusual feature for a vernacular poem. In addition, the *Rose* was the first medieval vernacular text to provoke an extended literary debate, thus figuring as the subject of literary critical essays. Indeed, several of these essays are included in an early fifteenth-century manuscript of the *Rose* (Paris, B.N. fr. 1563), possibly the first truly "critical edition" of a medieval vernacular text ever produced.

The *Rose* has remained controversial in the modern period, playing a central role in—even generating—a variety of literary debates. This has been particularly true over the course of the last thirty years, during which the *Rose* has been the focus of some of the most intensive and innovative scholarship in the field of Medieval Studies. This scholarly activity has been characterized by a wide variety of critical approaches and methodologies, from neo-patristics and history of ideas to intertextuality and reception theory. This striking heterogeneity has been extremely fruitful.

Three major "orientations" have emerged with regard to the interpretation of the poem itself. First is the neo-patristic perspective, which reads the *Rose* as Christian allegory, focusing on questions of moral content and didactic intention. This has been a predominantly American "school," growing out of the earlier work of D. W. Robertson (1962). Its most comprehensive spokesman has been John V. Fleming in his two books, *The "Roman de la Rose": A Study in Allegory and Iconography* (1969) and *Reason and the Lover* (1984). Second is the philosophical perspective, which situates the *Rose* in the context of medieval neoplatonist poetics and mythography. The complex implications of this dimension of the poem have been explored by Winthrop Wetherbee in *Platonism and Poetry in the Twelfth Century* (1972) and in subsequent articles by Thomas D. Hill (1974) and Wetherbee (1976). The third major perspective is a more purely literary one, placing primary emphasis on questions of rhetorical organization, narrative structure, literary genre, and poetic discourse. Daniel Poirion's *Le "Roman de la Rose"* (1973) reflects all these concerns, as does the work of Stephen Nichols (1967), Douglas Kelly (1978), Karl D. Uitti (1978), and Nancy Freeman Regalado (1981). Within this context, Kevin Brownlee (1982a, 1982b, 1985, 1991) and David Hult (1981, 1982, 1986) have focused on the problematics of writing and interpretation, while Sylvia Huot (1985, 1987) has addressed issues of voice and textuality.

At the same time, there has been renewed interest in the reception of the *Roman de la Rose*. The important question of the *Rose*'s influence on subsequent medieval French literature has been brilliantly reformulated by Pierre-Yves Badel in his groundbreaking and magisterial study, *Le "Roman de la Rose" au XIVe siècle: Étude de la réception de l'œuvre* (1980). Kevin Brownlee (1984) has investigated the literary uses to which the *Rose* is put in the œuvre of Guillaume de Machaut. A new and comprehensive perspective on the fifteenth-century "Quarrel of the *Rose*" has resulted from Eric Hicks's *Le Débat sur le "Roman de la Rose"* (1977). Stephen Nichols (1966–67) has examined the literary dimension of the sixteenth-century "adaptation" by Clément Marot; Sylvia Huot (1987) has explored the *Rose* manuscript tradition, studying interpolations, abridgments, and *remaniements* as evidence for medieval readings of the poem. New interpretations of the literary "career" of the *Rose* in fourteenth-century Italy have been formulated by Luigi Vanossi (1979) and E. Jeffrey Richards (1981), and the reception of the *Rose* in the Low Countries has been studied by Dieuwke E. van der Poel (1989). The extremely rich scholarly tradition devoted to the *Rose*'s reception in medieval England—especially, in the works of Chaucer—has recently been expanded by the innovative work of Lee Patterson (1983), Winthrop Wetherbee (1984), and John V. Fleming (1985).

Finally, the importance of the illuminations of the many *Rose* manuscripts is being reconsidered in the light of—indeed, as linked to—literary interpretation. Fleming's 1969 study was pioneering in this regard, going far beyond the initial survey of Alfred Kuhn (1913–14) in the treatment of the relationship between courtly and sacred iconography and the role of the artist as reader of texts. Rosemond Tuve (1966) discussed *Rose* illustrations in the context of medieval allegory. Much additional work remains to be done in this extremely rich field. Further investigations of the interaction between text and illustration in *Rose* manuscripts, and the literary implications of codicological organization, are currently under way in the work of Eberhard König (1987), Sylvia Huot (1987), Stephen Nichols, and Lori Walters.

Two striking features emerge from this brief survey of recent work on the *Romance of the Rose*. First, a wide range of academic disciplines have been involved: philosophy, theology, history, art history, and codicology, as well as literature. This is not only a function of the medieval work of art itself, but also the result of our postmodern focus on "culture" from a cross-disciplinary perspective. Second, the methodological heterogeneity of the past three decades of *Rose* research has been extremely fruitful.

The present volume grows out of both of these developments. We feel it is time for a new and wide-ranging collaboration among the various individual approaches and disciplines within which *Rose* scholarship has flourished until now. Thus the contributors represent all the major areas of current work on the *Romance of the Rose*, both in America and in Europe, while the volume as a whole involves an attempt at a new kind of intellectual interaction and "cross-fertilization." A double orientation is at issue: This volume offers a collective reevaluation of past work during a particularly rich period, a critical taking stock of where we stand now. It also represents the breaking of new ground, the suggestion of new connections and new syntheses.

The overall focus of the book is on problems of reading and interpretation in the *Rose*, and it is informed by several broad themes, the exploration of which contributes to a new understanding of the *Rose* and its place in medieval literary culture. First, there is the analysis of the *Rose* itself, really two poems in one: that of Guillaume and that of Jean. Emmanuèle Baumgartner and Daniel Poirion both examine aspects of Guillaume's poetics, focusing on narrative temporalities and the use of rhyme, respectively; Poirion additionally contrasts Guillaume's aesthetics with those of Jean. Several other essays treat the important question of the literary sources of the *Rose*. The relationship between the *Rose* and the Latin tradition is addressed by John Fleming, David Hult, and Stephen Nichols, each of whom, from different perspectives, examines the implicit and explicit presence in the *Rose* of classical and medieval Latin models. Sylvia Huot's essay, in turn, includes a consideration of the ways in which medieval *remanieurs* responded to, and revised, Jean de Meun's use of Latin authors. The vernacular sources of the *Rose* are treated by Karl Uitti, whose essay demonstrates the importance of the romances of Chrétien de Troyes as a context for Guillaume de Lorris's innovative poem.

Equally important is the medieval reception of the *Rose*, addressed by a variety of literary and codicological approaches. Stephen Nichols, Lori Walters, and Sylvia Huot examine the evidence of the manuscript tradition: illustrations, manuscript format, and reworkings of the text itself. Robert Harrison and Dieuwke E. van der Poel describe the translation/ adaptations of the *Rose* in Italian and Flemish, respectively; Lee Patterson examines a particular instance of Chaucer's reworking of *Rose* material; and Kevin Brownlee treats Christine de Pizan's ongoing dialogue with the *Rose* in the context of her literary career as a whole. Pierre-Yves Badel, finally, traces the posthumous reputation of the *Rose*'s second and more famous author, Jean de Meun. Scholars have long been concerned with the medieval interpretation of the *Rose*, but most of the evidence presented here is previously untapped, affording both new perspectives on the *Rose* and new methods for the study of medieval literary interpretation.

An important issue that emerges from the essays collected here is that of the relationship between *remaniement*, continuation, translation, and other kinds of literary responses to the *Rose*. As is often noted, the *Rose* contains an explicit discussion of authorship, identifying the poem as the joint work of two French poets who are placed in a tradition of Latin elegiac poets. The Appendix to this volume, prepared by Walters, shows that the scribes and illuminators who produced manuscripts of the *Rose* employed rubrics and miniatures to highlight both the moment of transition from Guillaume de Lorris to Jean de Meun and the discussion of authorship itself: the fact of dual authorship was central to medieval perceptions of the *Rose*. The poem was further reworked by scribal editors and remanieurs, whose treatment of the important authorship passage reflects their own concerns as poets of the *Rose*; its translators sometimes inserted their own names into the discussion of authorship, usurping the role of poet/protagonist for themselves. The *Rose* and the tradition that it generated thus provide extraordinarily fertile ground for the examination of late-medieval notions of authorship and literary authority. The impact of the *Rose* as an authoritative text extends not only to poets who imitated, countered, or reworked it in their own writings, but also to those who chose to work on the *Rose* itself.

Most fundamentally, the *Rose* is a poem about love, one in which, to cite Guillaume de Lorris's famous formulation, "l'art d'Amors est tote enclose" [the art of love is completely enclosed (ed. Lecoy, v. 38)]. A reading of the poem's exposition of love is central to many of the essays in this volume. Baumgartner relates her analysis of the poem's temporal play to its representation of desire and its status as the story of an erotic dream; while the thematic of desire and the erotic gaze is treated by Nichols from a different perspective, that of the rhetorical trope of ekphrasis. Uitti's analysis of Guillaume's allegory focuses on the centrality of the couple that is formed in the course of the narrative. Fleming, in turn, offers a reading of Jean de Meun's continuation and expansion of the "art of love" begun by Guillaume, with particular emphasis on Jean's moral critique of sensual gratification as a form of idolatry. The interpretive process becomes more complicated when the evidence of illustrations, translations, and *remaniements* is brought to bear, for these can transform the *Rose* into a poem with a message other than the one it originally had. Huot, for example, shows that the poem's treatment of erotic love and its place in the natural and the cosmic orders differs considerably in the various recensions of two thirteenth-century *remaniements*, those of Gui de Mori and the *B* redactor; while Harrison and van der Poel explicate the very different ways in which the Italian and Flemish translators respectively adapted the allegory of love. It is clear that medieval readers approached the *Rose* from a variety of perspectives, focusing on different aspects of the poem and reshaping it to conform to their ideas of what it was or ought to be.

The essays collected here thus present a range of medieval and modern readings of the *Rose*: as an art of love; as a poetic compendium combining political, philosophical, and amorous doctrine; as a reinterpretation of Latin and vernacular literary traditions; and as a meditation on the very concepts of language and signification, of poetry, and of authorship. The volume as a whole is organized into three general topics: first, literary approaches to the poem; second, the iconographic tradition; and third, the reception of the *Rose* among medieval readers in France, Italy, the Low Countries, and England.

The collection begins with Emmanuèle Baumgartner's essay, which focuses exclusively on the first *Roman de la Rose*—that of Guillaume de Lorris—and addresses the elusive dynamics of this narrative that defies easy analysis or classification. Guillaume took the highly innovative step of situating his narrative outside of chronological time, in the imaginative time of dream; furthermore, most of the narrative takes place in a space, the garden, from which Old Age, hence the passage of time, has been excluded. Baumgartner examines the various strategies by which Guillaume creates a narrative temporality *ex nihilo*. She further analyzes the tensions inherent in this self-generated construct: between the immobility of Narcissus and the circular, repetitive movements of the dancers on the one hand and the succession of narrated events on the other; between paratactic and fragmentary description and chronological order; between the impulse to suspend time's passage in order to create an eternal present and the need for narrative progression; between a sense of timelessness and a proliferation of many different times—historical, literary, mythical, and so on—that intersect in the privileged space of the dream.

For Baumgartner, the Fountain of Narcissus is the locus at once of fixation and of narrative renewal; the Perilous Mirror is a figure for the power of narrative description to impose an order, to present a comprehensive vision that, in turn, situates the Lover in his setting and makes subsequent narrative action possible. Generations of *Rose* critics have returned to the spellbinding image of the rosebud reflected in the crystals at the bottom of the Fountain, without ever exhausting the mysteries of this passage; the perspective elaborated by Baumgartner sheds new light on the important and complex role of Fountain and Mirror, vision and desire, and time and timelessness in the poetic economy of Guillaume's text.

The points that Baumgartner raises intersect with those touched on elsewhere in this volume. The importance in the *Rose* of description and vision, for example, is taken up by Nichols who, in his essay on ekphrasis and desire, delineates the distinction between "vision" and "gaze." Nichols's comments on the conflict between history and erotic desire further complement Baumgartner's discussion of temporality in Guillaume's poem of love. Baumgartner's analysis of the poem's generation of narrative time, in turn, and its definition of a time that is more a function of internal psychology than of the external calendar, complements Karl D. Uitti's discussion of Guillaume's *Rose* as a story of growth, in which the slow but inevitable unfolding of the rosebud not only marks the passage of time but also parallels the Lover's own psychological maturation. As Uitti demonstrates, the Lover is not initially so very different from Narcissus: when he first sees the Rose at the Fountain of Narcissus, the bud on its stem is an image less feminine than masculine, indeed phallic. As the narrative progresses, the slowly opening rose becomes an increasingly feminine image: the Lover is learning to recognize, and make contact with, a feminine Other.

Uitti's emphasis on the importance of the allegorized couple formed by the Lover and the Rose is central to his reading of Guillaume's *Rose* as an instance of romance *dépassement*: that is, as a poeticization, and a going beyond, of the conventions established by twelfth-century verse romance. These conventions include the importance of naming; the inscription of classical models, at once identified with and differentiated from medieval poetic figures; and the central importance of the romance couple, conjoined through love, shared adventure, or marriage.

With Daniel Poirion's essay, the focus moves to Guillaume's poem in the larger context of the conjoined *Rose* that includes Jean de Meun's continuation. Poirion examines the complex function of rhyme in the conjoined *Rose* text in order to explore the work's "disunity": the artistic originality and coherence of Guillaume's poem. Poirion sees the different uses of rhyme in the two parts of the *Rose* as the sign of two different aesthetics. The systematic valorization of rich rhyme in Jean de Meun thus indicates a more "rhetorical" conception of poetry, which is both discursive and logical. Guillaume de Lorris's significantly less frequent use of rich rhyme is linked to a more purely lyric conception of verbal art, which valorizes sonorous, musical effects. At the same time, there is a corresponding difference in the semantic function of rhyme in the two *Rose* poets. What emerges is nothing less than the fundamental opposition between Guillaume's Platonic and Jean's Aristotelian concepts of language and signification.

Poirion's analysis of Guillaume's distinctness from Jean in terms of literary aesthetics has several important implications in the realm of codicology. First and foremost, it provides a new perspective for one of the major problems in the *Rose* manuscript tradition: the fact that while Jean's "continuation" is relatively homogeneous, aside from easily recognizable interpolations and abridgments, the significant variants occurring in Guillaume's poem have made it difficult to establish the authentic version of the text. Poirion sees this situation as the result of a progressive and irregular transformation of the poetic values inherent in Guillaume's text, from the standpoint of the very different poetics ultimately embodied by Jean de Meun. Rhyme, due to its stability, provides a privileged means both for recuperating Guillaume's aesthetics and for reestablishing the text of his poem.

With John Fleming's essay, the emphasis of the volume's literary analysis of the *Rose* moves from Guillaume de Lorris to Jean de Meun. Fleming considers Jean's intertextual use of authoritative Latin models in the context of a serious reevaluation of Jean's status—his literary identity—as poet. First, Fleming argues for Jean's self-conception as a "Latin" rather than a French poet, that is, as a translator identified with the classical tradition rather than a romance poet contributing to the vernacular tradition. The corollary of this self-conception is that Jean's employment of specific classical subtexts involved an informed selectivity and intentionality—a highly developed awareness of the literary context of the passages he cites from the *auctores*, as well as a systematic will to remotivate, to reinterpret these passages within the poetic economy of the *Rose*. For Fleming, this economy involves the relationship, both moral and poetic, between pagan past and Christian present and the transformation of this problematic disjunction into a central poetic theme.

Three Latin authors central to Jean's *Rose* serve to illustrate and nuance these general points. First, there is Ovid: in Fleming's view, Jean took over and "completed" the first-person Ovidian didactic stance of Guillaume de Lorris by incorporating the perspective of the *Remedia amoris* into the Ovidian erotics of the first *Rose* text. In this way he made good on Guillaume's stated intention (in vv. 37–38) that the *Rose* contain the *entire* art of love. Second, there is Jean's use of Boethius as a "catalytic agent" that contributes moral and philosophical weight to Ovidian eroticism. For Fleming, Jean's basic literary strategy here involved a critical rereading of Ovid through the perspective of the *Consolation of Philosophy*. Finally, Fleming considers the heretofore largely neglected area of Jean's Virgilianism, analyzing two important citations of the Latin poet that function in the concluding episode. Stressing the importance of their Virgilian context, Fleming interprets Jean's allusions to these passages as part of a master strategy that undercuts the *Rose*'s first-person narrator-protagonist and his idolatrous pursuit of sexual gratification.

David Hult also addresses the relationship of Jean de Meun to a Latin tradition, but from an entirely different perspective. Focusing on the debate about obscenity that is argued by the Lover and Reason, Hult examines a particular thematic nexus created by Jean de Meun: "the condition of fallen man; human justice; procreation; proper language use; and erotic desire" (p. 113). Hult notes the link established between obscenity, the disjunction of word and thing, and castration: the appearances of the fateful word *coilles* are in connection with the castration of Saturn, of Abelard, and of Origen. Yet if the primal act of castration is to be associated with the fall of the Golden Age, and the imperfect relation of word and thing with censorship, repression, and a disorder at once linguistic and erotic, nonetheless, as Hult points out, the castration of Abelard and that of Origen both had as result the furtherance of scholarship. Also, the dissociation of words and things opens up new possibilities for linguistic figuration. In a very real way, the birth of erotic desire and of figurative discourse is what makes poetry possible.

As Hult shows, Jean's text contains numerous instances of wordplay—some of them operating across the linguistic boundary between French and Latin—generated by the discussions of castration, of testicles, and of the words used to name them, and, in general, of the processes of dis-membering and re-membering both the physical and the textual body. Jean's insistent thematization and problematization of language and interpretation call attention to the materiality of words as the basis of poetic production: ultimately, as Hult shows, "Jean's *Rose* represents less of a speculation *on* language than a performance *of* language as orchestrated through what itself pretends to be a meta-discourse" (p. 110, emphasis his).

Stephen Nichols's essay opens the section dealing with the interrelation between text and image in the *Rose* manuscript tradition. Nichols provides a new literary theoretical context for this subject by considering the rhetorical, ideological, and iconographic implications of ekphrasis. In this connection, he focuses on the key ekphrastic moment in *Aeneid* 1—Aeneas before the Temple of Juno in Carthage—as a model for the ekphrasis that opens Amant's initiation into the love experience in Guillaume de Lorris's *Rose*: the portraits on the wall of Déduit's garden.

First, Nichols analyzes the way in which the Virgilian text opposes the imperative of political history with that of private (erotic) affect in a way which problematizes figural art, particularly that which "theatricalizes the body" (p. 141). Within the poetics of the *Aeneid*, therefore, this ekphastic scene, with its indictment of rhetorical and visual images, initiates an ongoing dialectic between art and history, portrayed as ideologically incompatible. Nichols next considers how medieval commentaries on the *Aeneid* worked to undo Virgil's attempt to subordinate image to the rational, Platonic model. In particular, Bernardus Silvestris's *Commentum super sex libros Eneidos Virgilii* played a crucial role, interpreting the images not in terms of material referentiality but as the figuration of desire. This emphasis on the psychology of perception in turn "opens the space of the medieval manuscript to explore the rhetoric of perception as sensual event" (p. 149).

In Nichols's view, this is how Guillaume's ten ekphrastic portraits work. Their overall effect is to open the text of the *Rose* to an elaborate play of image production and image reception, operating through both the verbal text and the illustrations. First, the portraits function qua verbal text both to recall and to transform their Virgilian model. Thus, they establish an allegorical discourse that is figurative, corporeal, and self-reflexive: it both represents the body and mirrors the viewing/reading subject in an ideological context outside the scope of Virgilian political history. Second, the frequent manuscript illuminations of this scene involve a privileged kind of metacommentary, resulting from the juxtaposition of rhetorical and visual image; they oblige the reader to imitate the scopic and interpretive activity both of the protagonist and of the narrator. Nichols illustrates the way in which text and image here constitute a complex dual system by considering specific manuscript examples.

Lori Walters's study of *Rose* iconography in turn focuses on the analysis of a particular manuscript, the important copy of the *Rose* preserved in Tournai. This redaction of the remaniement of Gui de Mori, the most extensive rewriting of the *Rose* that survives today, is endowed with an illustrative program that departs in many ways from standard *Rose* iconography and was most likely designed especially for this particular version of the text. In a discussion that complements the textual analysis of Gui's work offered by Huot, Walters examines Gui's authorial persona and surveys some of the more important modifications that he introduced in his recasting of the *Rose*; she then discusses ways in which the Tournai manuscript, with particular attention to its illustrations and its elaborate colophon, constitutes a response to this rewritten *Rose* and to the figure of Gui himself as he is inscribed in the text.

By focusing on the related problems of literary reception, iconography, and *mise en livre*, Walters raises important, and thorny, problems of critical interpretation. The analysis of the codex requires the identification of successive layers of creative and interpretive activity: the original poetic work of Guillaume de Lorris; the transformation and continuation of

Guillaume's poem at the hands of Jean de Meun; the further transformations realized by Gui de Mori; possible scribal revision of the resulting triple-authored poem; and the resulting manifestation of the poem in this particular codex, a construct that includes not only the text itself but also such elements as illustrations, rubrics, marginal annotations, and colophon. These successive textual and codicological layers must be at once distinguished and then placed in their proper relation one to another.

Walters's study thus provides an interesting focal point for issues raised in several other essays: Poirion's suggestion that Guillaume's text may have been revised by Jean; the studies of Flemish and Italian recastings of the *Rose* offered by van der Poel and Harrison; and Huot's study of the reception of the *Rose* by medieval remanieurs. Huot focuses on two rewritings of the text: that of Gui de Mori, and the version transmitted in Langlois's *B* family, which, though more widespread in the Middle Ages than Gui's version of the text, is less known today. Both the *B* text and that of Gui represent significant revisions of the *Rose*. For example, both remanieurs sought to impose a linear order on Jean de Meun's discursive, indeed kaleidoscopic, style; the *B* remanieur additionally wished to recast Jean's text in the image of Guillaume's romance. The study of these rewritings of the *Rose* shows some of the difficulties that medieval readers experienced in their encounter with Jean's enormously varied poem. In addition to opening up medieval perspectives on the *Rose* that can help us in our efforts to interpret the poem today, the investigation of remaniements and manuscript variants is invaluable for any study of the influence of the *Rose* on subsequent poets, who may have known the text in a version that differs slightly or even considerably from that of the modern editions.

Huot also discusses the fate of remaniements in critical tradition, which betrays considerable uncertainty about the phenomenon of revision and variant readings. Is the remanieur an author? Is the remaniement a text in its own right? To what extent should critical editions account for divergent versions that clearly postdate a poem's original author? Scholars today are deeply concerned with questions of canon formation and with the definition, or range of possible definitions, of an author. Medievalists in particular are debating the important questions of how best to edit texts—how, if at all, to incorporate into the critical edition information about the full range of manuscript variations. As is shown by both Huot's study of remaniement and Walters's analysis of an individual codex, the rich manuscript tradition of the *Rose* is a fertile ground for the exploration of these important questions.

Kevin Brownlee's essay shifts the examination of *Rose* reception from the poem's own manuscript tradition to the responses elaborated by medieval authors in their own literary corpora. Brownlee examines Christine de Pizan's polemical reactions to the *Rose* in the context of her own evolving authorial identity. For Christine, because the *Rose* constituted the single most authoritative work in the vernacular French literary canon, her self-definition as a new kind of (woman) author required an explicit coming to terms with the dominant discourses and ideologies that she viewed as embodied in the *Rose*. Brownlee focuses on three of Christine's early works, in which he sees a progression.

In the *Epistre au Dieu d'Amours* (1399), Brownlee views Christine as representing the inadequacies of both the courtly and the clerkly registers of the *Rose*, on that poem's own terms. She thus speaks "through" the mouth of a corrected version of the *Rose*'s structurally central authoritative character, Cupid; there is no explicit self-figuration at the diegetic level. In Brownlee's reading of the *Dit de la Rose* (1402), Christine employs an exclusively courtly discourse simultaneously to critique and to renew the courtly register of the *Roman* by recontextualizing it. Here, it is the central metaphor of the earlier poem that is transformed, that is, the rose itself. The *Dit* is recounted directly in the first-person by Christine's courtly persona; Christine as character, figured as a courtly writer, plays a key role on the level of the plot. In the *Epistres sur le Débat du "Roman de la Rose"* (1401–02), Brownlee sees Christine adopting an exclusively clerkly discourse to confront the clerkly arguments and authority of the *Rose*. Here, she speaks entirely in her own voice, dispensing with fictional frames and constructs altogether. She presents herself as a learnèd female *clerc* directly engaged in interpretive activity in a contemporary sociohistorical context. Here, it is the central author figure of the *Rose* that is at issue, as Jean de Meun is both undermined and exploited.

Brownlee thus sees three "stages" in Christine de Pizan's engagement with the *Roman de la Rose* as dominant literary predecessor. In the *Epistre au Dieu d'Amours*, Christine confronts and displaces the *Rose*'s Ovidian Cupid with a corrected Cupid of her own. In the *Dit de la Rose*, she confronts and displaces Guillaume de Lorris both as poet and as protagonist with a fictionalized version of herself as poet-protagonist. In the dossier of the *Epistres sur le Débat du "Roman de la Rose,"* she confronts and displaces Jean de Meun as authoritative vernacular clerk with a historically "real" self-representation as learnèd woman author.

Pierre-Yves Badel's study of the long-standing association of the *Rose* with the alchemical tradition brings the discussion of reception up into the fifteenth and sixteenth centuries; indeed, his analysis demonstrates that a sixteenth-century alchemical reading of the *Rose* forms the basis for all subsequent interpretations of alchemical symbolism, real or imagined, in the poem. Badel surveys the existing literary and codicological evidence for the growth of Jean de Meun's posthumous reputation as an alchemist and for the eventual articulation of an alchemical reading of the *Rose*. That the *Rose* should have come to play such a role in the history of alchemical writings is in part simply a manifestation of the tendency of late-medieval and Renaissance writers to appropriate literary texts of all kinds as vehicles for the elaboration of an increasingly philosophical, even mystical, alchemical science. Nonetheless, the *Rose* was particularly well suited to such appropriation because of its encyclopedic nature, whereby the topics of spiritual salvation, natural philosophy, astrology, and even alchemy itself are explicitly addressed.

Badel's study touches on crucial interpretive problems, whose relevance extends well beyond the narrow question of whether or not Guillaume or Jean had alchemical processes in mind when writing the *Rose*. The critic seeking to evaluate an "alchemical thematics" brings to the text a certain conception of alchemy or of an alchemical code. The critic carries as well a sense, whether tacit or explicit, of what constitutes a literary thematics and of what must come together in order for a series of suggestive images to form a coherent program. As Badel shows, attempts to discern an alchemical program in the *Rose*, whether of the sixteenth or the twentieth century, have ascribed to alchemy a moral and spiritual dimension that it had not yet acquired in the thirteenth century. Moreover, such critical efforts turn on the identification of certain key elements—symbols, motifs, colors, numbers—as inherently alchemical because of their appearance in genuine alchemical treatises. Yet these very elements were originally appropriated by alchemical writers from the domain of literature. When is an image literary, when is it alchemical? What are the limits of interpretation of sustained allegory and metaphor—a type of poetic discourse that is, by its very nature, tantalizingly open-ended? By exploring these important questions in a well-defined context, Badel provides an exemplary investigation of a complicated critical problem, the larger implications of which concern any study of medieval literature and its critical reception.

With Robert Harrison's essay, the volume's consideration of the reception of the *Rose* moves from an exclusively French to a broader Western European context. Harrison studies the thirteenth-century Italian adaptation of the *Rose* entitled *Il Fiore* by its nineteenth-century editor. Bracketing the long and inconclusive controversy over Dante's possible authorship of this anonymous poem, Harrison focuses on the significance of the *Fiore* as an Italian literary response to the magisterial French model: for him the question of provenance, rather than authorship, assumes central importance.

Harrison's approach is threefold. First, he considers the *Fiore*'s privileging of narrative particularly interesting in light of the fact that, formally speaking, the Italian poem is a lyric collection—a sonnet sequence. It is in this context that its status as abridgment is most significant: the discrepancy in length between the *Rose* and the *Fiore* is largely accounted for by the Italian author's reduction of the text to its essential narrative content. Second, Harrison analyzes the *Fiore*'s poetic "landscape," revealing a strategy of radical minimalism: a barren, wintry shore; a single flower; the starkness of January rather than the lush greenery of May. In terms of figurative language, "poverty of resource" thus emerges as the primary element that distinguishes the *Fiore* from the *Rose*. Finally, Harrison relates both the *Fiore*'s "narrative essentialism" and its figural minimalism to the poem's fundamental identity—its provenance—as Italian. It thus reflects, even emblematizes, the absence of a coherent cultural, linguistic, and political context that characterized nascent Italian literature. At the same time, the *Rose* emerges as a kind of canonical vernacular standard which transcends national boundaries, provoking simultaneously imitation and differentiation.

From a different perspective, Dieuwke E. van der Poel continues the examination of translation and remaniement in her study of a Flemish adaptation of the *Rose*. The Flemish *Rose* is evidence for the circulation of the *B* text, some version of which lies at the basis of the Flemish poet's work. Van der Poel's work thus illustrates the necessity of taking scribal redactions, variants, and remaniements into account when considering the impact of the *Rose*, or any medieval work, on subsequent literary tradition. Her study, moreover, serves to remind scholars of medieval French literature of an important dimension of the reception of Old French texts: as she points out, Dutch and Flemish adaptations of these texts provide us with responses and interpretations that are in many cases virtually contemporary.

As van der Poel shows, the *Rose*—an unusual text by any standards—required some recasting to render it appropriate for its new northern European audience. By describing his encounter with the narrating

"I" of the *Rose*, the Flemish poet seems almost to be offering a poeticization of his own experience of reading the *Rose*: he has absorbed the story of the Lover's quest, and he relays it to his Flemish audience. The introduction of Florentine as a figure for the lady, all but eclipsing Bel Acueil, suggests a desire to temper pure allegory with a certain degree of realism. One can see a similar impulse in the manuscript tradition of the Old French *Rose* itself. It was not uncommon for artists to portray Bel Acueil as a maiden, at least in scenes of intimacy with the Lover or in the company of la Vieille; one manuscript even alters the text to give Bel Acueil a female gender during the discourse of la Vieille (Rennes, Bibl. Mun. 15963). The concerns of the Flemish poet thus intersect with those of certain French readers of the *Rose*. A more exhaustive study of the reception and manuscript tradition of the *Rose* and its adaptations, both in and outside France, would no doubt yield many more such parallels, greatly enriching our knowledge of the status of the *Rose* in the later Middle Ages and its meaning for medieval readers.

Lee Patterson's essay moves from the field of translation and remaniement to investigate a different kind of literary adaptation of the *Rose*: the relationship between the Wife of Bath in Chaucer's *Canterbury Tales* and Jean de Meun's character, la Vieille. For Patterson, these two key figures offer particularly illuminating examples of the profound ambivalence that characterizes the medieval idea of the feminine as it functions in literary discourse. This ambivalence is related to the fundamental tensions—even contradictions—with which both the *Canterbury Tales* and the *Rose* grapple: those between, for example, "history and apocalypse, character and vocation, nature and grace." In this context, la Vieille and the Wife of Bath play important parallel roles as both agents and paradigms of resolution: each appears at a crucial moment in the poem, allowing Jean de Meun and Chaucer, respectively, to review and clarify the central issues of the work as a whole.

Patterson reads la Vieille's long speech both as itself structured by programmatic deferral and as thematizing deferral in terms relevant to the structure (and the ideology) of the *Rose* as a whole. In this way, la Vieille provides the strategy that can lead to resolution, anticipating and authorizing the speech of Nature, where the erotic dialectic of delay and fulfillment gives way to one of human action and providential vision. The temporality introduced in la Vieille's autobiographical discourse provides an important nexus for the conjoining of the poem's diverse themes, both amorous and philosophical.

This textual fact is Patterson's point of departure for analyzing la Vieille as a model for the Wife of Bath. It is the crucial role played by la Vieille in the *Rose*'s progressive meditation on identity, authorship, and closure that suggests why Chaucer should introduce the figure of the old woman at a crucial revisionary moment of his own poem. Like la Vieille, the Wife of Bath serves to reorient the narrative dynamic, to set it on a new critical path. Within the context of the present volume, Patterson's detailed reading of the Wife of Bath as a "rewriting" of Jean de Meun involves a new kind of reception of the *Rose* in the mainline tradition of late-medieval English literature. Chaucer reacts to the French text of Guillaume de Lorris and Jean de Meun as if it were the product of a Latin *auctor*.

The volume concludes with an Appendix, prepared by Lori Walters, which offers an overview of the ways in which the dual authorship of the *Rose* was handled in fourteenth-century manuscripts, charting the presence or absence of author portraits or rubrics concerning authorship at the break between Guillaume and Jean and at the midpoint of the conjoined *Rose*, where the poem's authorship is explicitly discussed. As noted above, the survey indicates that the dual authorship of the *Rose* and the precise identification of the break between the two parts of the text were of great importance for medieval readers: the *Rose* was indeed two poems in one.

References

Badel, Pierre-Yves. 1980. *Le "Roman de la Rose" au XIVe siècle: Étude de la réception de l'œuvre.* Publications Romanes et Françaises 153. Geneva: Droz.

Baumgartner, Emmanuèle. 1974. "De Lucrèce à Héloïse: Remarques sur deux exemples du *Roman de la Rose* de Jean de Meun." *Romania* 95, 433–42.

———. 1984. "'L'Absente de tous bouquets...'." In *Études sur le "Roman de la Rose" de Guillaume de Lorris*, pp. 37–52. Ed. Jean Dufournet. Collection Unichamp 4. Paris: Champion.

Blumenfeld-Kosinski, Renate. 1980. "Remarques sur songe/mensonge." *Romania* 101, 385–90.

Brownlee, Kevin. 1982a. "Orpheus' Song Resung: Jean de Meun's Reworking of *Metamorphoses* X." *Romance Philology* 36, 201–09.

———. 1982b. "Reflections in the *Miroër aus Amoreus*: The Inscribed Reader in Jean de Meun's *Roman de la Rose*." In *Mimesis: From Mirror to Method*, pp. 60–70. Ed. John D. Lyons and Stephen G. Nichols. Hanover, NH: University Press of New England.

———. 1984. *Poetic Identity in Guillaume de Machaut*. Madison: University of Wisconsin Press.

———. 1985. "Jean de Meun and the Limits of Romance: Genius as Rewriter of Guillaume de Lorris." In *Romance: Generic Transformation from Chrétien de Troyes to Cervantes*, pp. 114–34. Ed. Kevin Brownlee and Marina S. Brownlee. Hanover, NH: University Press of New England.

———. 1991. "The Problem of Faux Semblant: Language, History, and Truth in the *Roman de la Rose*." In *The New Medievalism*, pp. 253–71. Ed. Marina S. Brownlee, Kevin Brownlee, and Stephen G. Nichols. Baltimore: Johns Hopkins University Press.

Fleming, John V. 1969. *The "Roman de la Rose": A Study in Allegory and Iconography*. Princeton, NJ: Princeton University Press.

———. 1984. *Reason and the Lover*. Princeton, NJ: Princeton University Press.

———. 1985. "'Smoky Reyn': From Jean de Meun to Geoffrey Chaucer." In *Chaucer and the Craft of Fiction*. Ed. Leigh Arrathoon. Rochester, MI: Solaris Press.

Hicks, Eric. 1977. *Le Débat sur le "Roman de la Rose."* Paris: Champion.

Hill, Thomas D. 1974. "Narcissus, Pygmalion, and the Castration of Saturn: Two Mythographic Themes in the *Roman de la Rose*." *Studies in Philology* 71, 404–26.

Hult, David F. 1981. "The Allegorical Fountain: Narcissus in the *Roman de la Rose*." *Romanic Review* 72, 125–48.

———. 1982. "Vers la société de l'écriture: Le *Roman de la Rose*." *Poétique* 50, 155–72.

———. 1986. *Self-Fulfilling Prophecies: Readership and Authority in the First "Roman de la Rose."* Cambridge: Cambridge University Press.

Huot, Sylvia. 1985. "From *Roman de la Rose* to *Roman de la Poire*: The Ovidian Tradition and the Poetics of Courtly Literature." *Medievalia et Humanistica* n.s. 13, 95–111.

———. 1987a. *From Song to Book: The Poetics of Writing in Old French Lyric and Lyrical Narrative Poetry*. Ithaca, NY: Cornell University Press.

———. 1987b. "The Medusa Interpolation in the *Romance of the Rose*: Mythographic Program and Ovidian Intertext." *Speculum* 62, 865–77.

———. 1987c. "The Scribe as Editor: Rubrication as Critical Apparatus in Two Manuscripts of the *Roman de la Rose*." *L'Esprit Créateur* 27, 67–78.

———. 1987d. "Vignettes marginales comme glose marginale dans un manuscrit du *Roman de la Rose* au quatorzième siècle (B.N. fr. 25526)." In *La Présentation du livre: Actes du colloque de Paris X-Nanterre (Dec. 4–6, 1985)*, pp. 173–86. Ed. Emmanuèle Baumgartner and Nicole Boulestreau. Littérales: Cahiers du Département de Français, 2. Nanterre: Centre de Recherche du Département de Français de Paris X.

Kelly, Douglas. 1978. *Medieval Imagination: Rhetoric and the Poetry of Courtly Love*. Madison: University of Wisconsin Press.

König, Eberhard. 1987. *Der Rosenroman des Berthaud d'Achy: Codex Urbinatus Latinus 376*. Codices e Vaticanis Selecti . . . 71. Facsimile edition with commentary volume. Belser Verlag.

Kuhn, Alfred. 1913/14. "Die Illustration des Rosenromans." *Jahrbuch der kunsthistorischen Sammlungen des allerhöchsten Kaiserhauses* 31, 1–66.

Nichols, Stephen G. 1966/67. "Marot, Villon, and the *Roman de la Rose*: A Study in the Language of Creation and Re-Creation." *Studies in Philology* 63 (1966), 135–43; and 64 (1967), 25–43.

———. 1967. "The Rhetoric of Sincerity in the *Roman de la Rose*." In *Romance Studies in Memory of Edward Billings Ham*, pp. 115–29. Ed. Urban T. Holmes. Hayward: California State College.

Patterson, Lee. 1983. "'For the Wyves love of Bathe': Feminine Rhetoric and Poetic Resolution in the *Roman de la Rose* and the *Canterbury Tales*." *Speculum* 58, 656–95.

Poirion, Daniel. 1973. *Le "Roman de la Rose."* Paris: Hatier.

———. 1983. "De la signification selon Jean de Meun." In *Archéologie du signe*, pp. 165–85. Ed. L. Brind'Amour and E. Vance. Recueils d'études médiévales 3. Toronto: Pontifical Institute of Mediaeval Studies.

Regalado, Nancy Freeman. 1981. "'Des contraires choses': La fonction poétique de la citation et des exempla dans le *Roman de la Rose* de Jean de Meun." *Littérature* 41, 62–81.

Richards, E. Jeffrey. 1981. *Dante and the "Roman de la Rose": An Investigation into the Vernacular Context of the "Commedia."* Tübingen: Niemeyer.

Robertson, D. W. 1962. *A Preface to Chaucer: Studies in Medieval Perspectives.* Princeton, NJ: Princeton University Press.

Tuve, Rosemond. 1966. *Allegorical Imagery: Some Medieval Books and Their Posterity.* Princeton, NJ: Princeton University Press.

Uitti, Karl D. 1978. "From *Clerc* to *Poète*: The Relevance of the *Romance of the Rose* to Machaut's World." In *Machaut's World: Science and Art in the Fourteenth Century*, pp. 209–16. Ed. M. Cosman and B. Chandler. New York: New York Academy of Sciences, 1978.

Van der Poel, Dieuwke E. 1989. *De Vlaamse "Rose" en "Die Rose" van Heinric: Onderzoekingen over twee Middelnederlandse bewerkingen van de "Roman de la Rose" (avec un résumé en français).* Middeleeuwse Studies en Bronnen, 13. Hilversum: Verloren.

Vanossi, Luigi. 1979. *Dante e il "Roman de la Rose": Saggio sul "Fiore."* Florence: Olschki.

Wetherbee, Winthrop. 1972. *Platonism and Poetry in the Twelfth Century: The Literary Influence of the School of Chartres.* Princeton, NJ: Princeton University Press.

———. 1976. "The Theme of Imagination in Medieval Poetry and the Allegorical Figure of 'Genius.'" *Medievalia et Humanistica* 7, 45–64.

———. 1984. *Chaucer and the Poets: An Essay on "Troilus and Criseyde."* Ithaca, NY: Cornell University Press.

Part I

Reading the *Rose*: Guillaume de Lorris

Emmanuèle Baumgartner

1. The Play of Temporalities; or, The Reported Dream of Guillaume de Lorris

> "... tout laisser dans l'instant de l'apparition."
> [to leave everything in the moment of its appearance]
> —Marguerite Duras, *Emily L.*

In the three volumes of *Time and Narrative*, Paul Ricoeur has presented a philosophical summa, a comprehensive body of thought, that comes at an opportune moment to remind literary specialists of a long-recognized but still underexploited phenomenon: the essential link between narrative, historical or fictional, and time.[1] For Ricoeur has shown how narrative—in his words, that "guardian of time"—is the privileged medium by which the writer shapes, and the reader reshapes, "our confused, unformed, and at the limit mute temporal experience";[2] and how it permits us to delimit more accurately, if perhaps not fully to master, the "mystery of time."

It would be impossible here to apply Ricoeur's ambitiously far-reaching method to the *Roman de la Rose* of Guillaume de Lorris. Not only does this method involve the temporal structures of narrative, which fall within the domain of literary specialists, but also it seeks to "reconstruct the set of operations by which a work lifts itself above the opaque depths of living, acting, and suffering, to be given by an author to readers who receive it and thereby change their acting."[3] This quotation, however, suffices to show to what extent theoretical and philosophical reflection coincides with the project of the narrator in the first segment of the *Roman de la Rose*: to shape his earlier dream of love in order to represent, for himself and for the beloved lady to whom he initially addresses his narrative, the experience that he had five years earlier.

Nevertheless, unlike the "traditional" narratives that could have provided Guillaume with a model, this one does not set out to translate into narrative the time of a real-life experience or of a story taken from Arthur-

Translated by Benjamin Semple

ian legend or other legends. Through the task of anamnesis, there is an attempt to reconstruct, and to narrate, a spatiotemporal setting that differs a priori from that provided by either the perceivable world or literary tradition: the space and time of dreams. The primary object of this essay will therefore be to study, without claiming to be exhaustive, several of the ways in which the "dream fiction" influences the representation of time or dimensions of time in the first part of the *Rose* and to examine the special status that this "dream fiction" confers on the narrator.[4]

The Time of Desire

One of the first and most difficult problems facing the writer of romances or the historian is that of delimiting a time and of establishing a point of origin for the narrative. Where, or when, should one begin, once one has eliminated the facile solution of beginning *in medias res*? The solution adopted by the universal histories of the Middle Ages is well known: they endeavor to start—or start over—at the very beginning, *a principio*, to recapitulate Genesis, perhaps because of a reluctance to divide history into periods, to cut into the heart of time.[5] In the domain of literature, the twelfth-century *Roman de Troie* offers a prime example of this return to a very distant past, the expedition of the Argonauts: a voyage not only back in time, but also back through the chain of causes that set the war in motion. Several years later, Chrétien de Troyes cut this Gordian knot when he placed Arthur and his kingdom at the beginning of *Erec et Enide*, as a space and time of reference that preexist the narrative. The cleverness of this solution goes far to explain the favor with which later romance authors adopted this prefabricated framework without substantial modification.[6]

By situating the time of the narrated event within that of the dream, Guillaume broke with narrative tradition and established a beginning for himself; at the same time, he anchored his narrative to a moment impossible to locate or to situate in historical time because it does not exist, nor did it ever exist except in the consciousness or subconscious of the dreamer.[7] Thus Guillaume established a triple beginning, for the awakening of the dreamer in the middle of the night coincides with the awakening of nature one spring morning, and causes the narrative to "awaken," to begin its course.

To open a narrative, or a narrative segment, with the lyric motif of the *reverdie* is not an absolute innovation. The springtime awakening of the dreamer in the *Roman de la Rose* is in many ways similar to the departure of young Perceval, and to Perceval's awakening as he comes into contact with the beauty of the world; and one could cite numerous other examples of this type of beginning, or renewal, in texts of the twelfth century.[8] What does appear novel in the case of the *Roman de la Rose*, however, is the ability of this dream fiction to infuse new meaning into the motif and to dispense with the connection between the actual return of the "beautiful season" and the renewal of poetic song, a connection that the troubadours and trouvères felt obliged either to evoke or to denounce.[9]

In the dream, the *reverdie* is no longer presented as a predictable, expected moment in the calendar of seasons and days. It no longer functions merely as a point in time known to all.[10] It becomes a psychological predisposition on the part of the dreamer, a palpable image of the erotic impulse that is the sole source of the dream and of the narrative inaugurated by the dream. The cause and effect relationship between *reverdie* and desire is thus inverted and internalized, and the chronological primacy of the time of desire over the time of the world is affirmed.

The Lover

The dream fiction thus permits us to link the activation of the narrative to its ultimate origin in the time of desire, to situate its birth in a time that is, without further specification, that of youth, of the *joven* celebrated by the troubadours. But simultaneously the dream fiction establishes a narrative voice, an "I" who speaks in the present, rewrites his past, and projects himself into the future, always eluding our attempts to situate the story in space and time.

To date the narrative and the voice that delivers it, there are still, of course, external criteria such as form, language, underlying literary traditions, concrete historical details, and so on: elements that are easily verified, and all of which situate the text in the literary and cultural milieu of the thirteenth century. But without Jean de Meun's information, which could well be misleading or doctored, what could one know about Guillaume de Lorris, about the *leal sergent* [loyal servant] of the God of Love—much less about the "I" who undertakes the narrative?[11]

Furthermore, this voice that speaks for itself, this implicated narrator, is doubled: five years separate the "I" of the dreamer from the "I" who reports the dream and who takes on most of the functions and the status of the narrator—five years that must be added on to the twenty years of the dreamer, thus making the narrator, if not the author, a young man twenty-five years of age. But these five years, this precise lapse of time—the number five does not seem to have any clear symbolic value here—function as a "free vector," without any identifiable origin on the axis of time.

The many advantages and possibilities of the time lag created in this manner have often been described. It has been shown how this distance tends to close, especially toward the end of the narrative, and how the voices of the dreamer and the narrator begin to overlap;[12] or, from another standpoint, how each of the narrative voices can be related to a different persona, with the lyric "I" of the dreamer being transmuted into the "I" of the clerk, of the master of the narrative.[13]

One can also note that the distancing thus effected is unprecedented in that it does not seem to have any antecedent in literary tradition. In principle, any dream immediately becomes the object of a narrative or of an attempted gloss. This haste can easily be explained by the prophetic character of dreams and visions, which are often obscure, sometimes disturbingly so.[14] In this case, however, the delay in narrating the dream is not a passage to oblivion, nor is it a sign of insignificance.[15] The delay allows for, without necessarily exhausting, the time in which the content of the dream has come about ("avenu," v. 29) in its entirety. The time elapsed between the dream and the narrative, a period during which a "real" love story supposedly took place, thus restores to the dream its classic status as prophetic revelation. This lapse of time confers on the dream its measure of truth. A dream, even if it is based simply on the desire to love, could not be a lie. . . . But this "truth" is, of course, unverifiable: it is not the subject of a narrative, nor is it authenticated by anything except the assertions of the narrator. We will never know any more of the love story than the moment outside of historical time that is constituted by the dream.

Another advantage, or consequence, of the framework adopted is to render not only the dreamer but the narrator himself less real. As narrator of a dream, he does not need to burden himself with the demands of realistic fiction in order to authenticate this experience by definition individual, indeed incommunicable except by a profound effort of reconstruction. Far from it: everything transpires as if the writer had carefully avoided all points of reference such as name, place of origin, historical period, social condition, and so on, in order to present of himself only the timeless image of a man twenty to twenty-five years of age who unites, in a single impulse of desire, his love for a woman with the emblematic name of Rose—taking the *senhal* to its limits—and his literary endeavor, an Art of Love intended to entertain his readers, male and female, and to win over the woman he loves.

It goes without saying that medieval literature presents many other examples of anonymous authorship, intentional or otherwise. It suffices to refer the reader to a body of texts more or less contemporaneous with the *Roman de la Rose*, the prose Grail romances, which almost systematically practice authorial anonymity or pseudoepigraphy. Nevertheless, here again there does not seem to be any text prior to the *Rose* of Guillaume de Lorris that combines anonymity with the textual presence of an "I" who, by telling his own story, simulates the conditions of the autobiographical pact even as he eliminates the basis of this pact: the unveiling of the narrator and, especially, of the author.[16] Nothing, except the bloom of youth and the integrity of his desire, individualizes the narrator, much less the author.

The technique of effacement employed in this simulacrum of autobiography goes even further in that the "I" who takes responsibility for the act of writing, who puts the dream into verse, cannot be assimilated to any of the existing figures of the medieval writer, while nonetheless drawing on each of these figures. The narrator is related to the figure of the clerk proud of his skill, of his *letreüre* [learning]; he quotes Macrobius and asserts the superiority of his talents over those of his predecessors.[17] This same "I" also brings to mind the figure of the troubadour who finds inspiration in his personal experience of love; indeed the style and stance of the troubadour are adopted in several passages. Nor is there any reason to exclude from this rapid survey of narrative masks the more recent figure of the noble, of the love-struck knight who, like Renaut de Bagé in *Le Bel Inconnu*, writes to please his lady, and who claims no other qualification for his undertaking than the sincerity of his desire. But Renaut de Bagé stops short of the experiment conducted by Guillaume: it is through creating another, the ancestral figure of Guinglain, son of the fairy, that he dreams his own passion, the incompleteness of his desire.[18]

In the *Roman de la Rose*, in turn, the novel figure of a dreamer/narrator imposes itself as a sort of common denominator for the "I" of Guillaume's text: this dreamer/narrator appears first, if not solely, in the form of the Lover and claims no other source of existence, no other source for his writing, than a dream of love. It is therefore no accident that both rubrics and critical tradition,[19] though not the poem itself or its characters, designate as "Lover" that being who is not allegorical but who, through the mediation of the dream and of the irreality that it authorizes, can combine the fiction of an individual experience with that of an experience presented as essential, atemporal, and independent of any referent.

The Time of the Garden

What I will call the garden sequence—that portion of the narrative leading from the arrival of the dreamer in front of the spot "tot clos de haut mur bataillé" [all enclosed with a high fortified wall (v. 131)] to the revelatory vision of the Rose in the crystals of the Fountain—is of great importance for the play of temporalities with which the narrative proper experiments. As we know, one of the vices exposed to contempt on the garden wall is Old Age. Within the description devoted to Old Age (vv. 339–404) is enclosed (vv. 361–86 or thereabouts: there is, for good reason, no clear break) a meditation on the passing of time, on its destructive powers, and on our inability to conceptualize the present except in its flight:

> que l'en ne puet neïs penser
> quel tens ce est qui est presenz,
> sel demandez a clers lisanz,
> qu'ençois que l'en l'eüst pensé
> seroient ja .III. tens passé.
> (vv. 368–70b)

[So that one cannot even conceive what time this is which is now present; ask a learned clerk: three instances of time would have passed before one could have conceived of it.]

The reference to the "clers lisanz" [learned clerk] draws the reader's attention, should it be necessary, to the fact that this is a topos learned at school, of which the ultimate source is surely the famous meditation on time in Book II of Saint Augustine's *Confessions*—indeed, the meditation with which Paul Ricoeur's study begins. The important point, in the perspective adopted here, is that this digression, this *amplificatio* grafted onto the description, attempts to signify the continually renewed flow of the waves of time through rhythm, syntax, and rhetorical figures, especially anaphora; and to concretize the capacity of writing to seize and contain the present. Even if it is only a paltry attempt, whereby the aging of Old Age is arrested for some twenty-four lines, nonetheless her disappearance from the text, her approaching death, are put off.

This meditation on the course of time, denied and defied through writing, serves as a prelude to the primary goal of the garden sequence: to describe a space where one spends time pleasantly without ever feeling or perceiving its passage. Therefore Old Age, and passing time, are excluded from this space.

The figure and the name of Oiseuse [Idleness], the role of guide that she momentarily assumes for the dreamer, and the gestures and frivolous activities that she tirelessly repeats (vv. 583–86) establish from the beginning a universe in which one "passes time" but in which nothing, in the end, commits one to any action, to any substantial modification of one's state. The procedures used in subsequent descriptive passages also contribute to this effect of time suspended, fixed in an eternal present.

It would not be possible to offer here a global analysis of this thematics; such a study would in any case replicate many earlier works. For our purposes the important points are the technique of accumulation and the succession of descriptive sequences. Under the gaze of the dreamer, directed by the narrator, the space of the garden becomes increasingly populated, and the accumulating catalogs of birds, animals, flowers, and allegorical figures or objects, as well as the abundance of characteristics applied to them, draw out the time of description and the time of reading to the limits of what can be tolerated.

Unlike the vices, fixed and isolated on the garden wall, the courtly "virtues" form a circle dance, or carol, a chain that moves as a continuous line through space. But in fact, this carol seems almost stationary, and the description breaks it up effortlessly, cutting out each allegorical figure and separating it from the others by the repetition of *delez* [next to], of *après* [after], without devising any transition, literal or figurative, from one allegorical figure to the next, except perhaps for the discontinuous movement of the dreamer's eyes as they observe the scene. We are, moreover, familiar with the ambiguity of this image of the carol and with the risk of oblivion to the world and to the passage of time that threatens the sense-less person who surrenders to its charms.[20]

Fragmentation and discontinuity are equally characteristic of the dreamer's movements, punctuated by the repetition of the adverb *lores* [then]. The disordered and delirious manner by which he acquaints him-self with the garden allows him to discover all of its nooks and crannies, from one *destor* [corner] to the next; but, up to the intervention of the crystals in the Fountain, it prevents him from having an overview. And he remains unaware of the essential element, the rosebush: "Mes j'alai tant destre et senestre, / que j'oi *tot l'afere et tot l'estre* / dou vergier cerchié et veü" [but I turned so often to the right and to the left that I sought out and saw *the entire layout and substance* of the garden (vv. 1415–17, emphasis mine)]; and yet. . . .

The simultaneous description of the garden and of the dreamer's movements, as presented by the narrator, thus accomplishes the rhetorical tour de force that was heralded by the digression on time and the exclusion of Old Age. Through the interplay of repetitions and of the vision and movement of the dreamer, this description isolates an eternal present and fixes it in the space of the text: the present of the dream-made-present, of which the "tableteresses" [women *tablete* players (v. 751)] and "timbe-resses" [women tambourine players (v. 752)], as well as the ".II. demoi-selles mout mignotes" [two very gracious young ladies (v. 757)] are an appropriate image, for they repeat their acrobatic movements like au-tomata. It is also in this dream-present that all possible temporalities con-verge and coexist.

In this vein, we can note—to cite only a few examples—the refer-ences and evocations in the text to the mythical time of the God of Love and of the story of Narcissus; to the historico-epic time of Alexander, Charlemagne, and Pepin; to the "literary" time of the knight to whom Largesse gave her hand and who is "dou lignage / le bon roi Artu de Bretaigne" [of the lineage of good King Arthur of England (vv. 1174–75)]; to "historical" time, with the jarring allusion to the wealth of Arras or to the "filz au seignor de Guindesores" [son of the Lord of Windsor (v. 1226)]; and, finally, to the permanently open time of the reception of the text with its enigmatic *envoi* to the ladies who are to reflect on the death of Narcissus. We must add to this list the "living present" of the narrator, who forthrightly punctures the temporal fiction he himself estab-lishes, thus revealing its precarious nature.[21]

The garden sequence thus strains to the breaking point descriptive techniques that are already well established, principally by the *romans antiques*, and reveals what is truly at stake in such descriptions. Here, as in other works, the immediate goals of description are to ornament the narrative and to give proof of the creative *inventio* of the writer. In this particular case, this *inventio* may well seem too redundant, too prolix, and especially too predictable. But profusion itself, *copia*, as it will later be called, shows even more clearly the ambition to create time, to spend and expand narrative time and, as in the digression on time, to capture the present moment in order to shape, through writing, our confused and unformed temporal experience, to overcome our inability to express or conceptualize the present.

The Fountain of Love or the Time of the Unmediated Vision

This experiment, however, could not be prolonged in literary form without bringing about the death of the narrative. A paratactic narrative, stripped of orientation and sense, must give way to a directed narrative. Once stabilized and caught in the perilous mirror of description, time must resume its course; the narrator must recuperate the ecstatic vision of the dreamer, order it in linear fashion, project it (chrono)logically, and loose the eternal grip that the time of the garden has on him: "Tot ensemble dire ne puis, / mes tot vos conteré par ordre, / que l'en n'i sache que remordre" [I cannot tell you everything all at once, but I will tell you everything in order, in a way that no one will be able to criticize (vv. 696–98)].

This transformation takes place at the Fountain, with the selection of the rosebud as an object of desire and with the wound dealt by the arrow of Love. The God of Love's speech creates, for a time, another detour, a narrative within a narrative, and lists the range of possible narratives with which the Lover might find himself engaged; with which he might lose, or spend, his time. But beginning around v. 2798, the thorny quest "par ronces et par esglantiers" [through thorns and briars (v. 2798)] that the dreamer undertakes brings us back to the usual regimen of fictional narrative. Scenes and summary alternate; duration is condensed by the use of frequentatives such as "sovent me semont d'approchier" [repeatedly he bids me approach (v. 2855)], and by the locution, so common in medieval narratives, "tant que" [until (v. 2956)], which provides for an ellipsis in time even as it renews the narrative. Passing time is even more precisely

noted, and we see, for example, the inevitable process of the opening of
the rosebud:

La rose auques s'eslargissoit
par amont, si m'abellissoit
ce qu'el n'iere pas si overte
que la graine fust descovierte;
ençois estoit encor enclose
entre les fueilles de la rose
qui amont droites se levoient
et la place dedenz emploient,
si ne pooit paroir la graine
por la rose qui estoit pleine.

(vv. 3343–52)

[The rose was expanding somewhat at the top, but it pleased me
that it was not yet open enough to reveal the seed; rather, the seed
was still enclosed between the petals of the rose, which were rising
straight up and which enveloped what was inside, so that the seed
with which the rose was full could not appear.]

From this point on the narrative and the dreamer are immersed and
enveloped in chronological time. Like the arrow loosed by Ulysses, the
arrow of Love, piercing first the eye and then the heart of the Lover, knits
together all the stitches of time; it thus unites in a single trajectory, in a
single projection, the dreamer and the narrator, the reconstructed past and
the living present where the speaking subject is born:

par mi l'ueil m'a ou cuer mise
sa saiete par grant roidor
et lors me prist une froidor
dont je desoz chaut peliçon
ai puis sentu mainte friçon.

(vv. 1692–96)

[Through my eye he shot his arrow into my heart, brutally, and at
that moment I was seized by a coldness that has since caused me many
a chill even beneath a warm fur-lined coat.]

And at the Fountain, the play on time that once took place there is reproduced but also inverted, like an image in a mirror. The story of Narcissus, as the narrator relates it, is in fact the narrative of a disordered hunt, of a man who is immobilized and dies from an unquenchable thirst next to a fountain, at the moment when he has finally identified his desire:

> Narcisus par aventure
> a la fontaine clere et pure
> se vint soz le pin ombroier
> un jor qu'il venoit de chacier,
> qu'il avoit soffert grant traval
> de corre et amont et aval,
> tant qu'il ot soif por l'aspreté
> dou chaut et por la lasseté
> qui li ot tolue l'alaine.
>
> (vv. 1467–75)

[Narcissus, by chance, came to seek shade under the pine tree next to the clear, pure fountain, one day when he had been hunting, and had exerted himself a great deal by running up and down hills, so much so that he was thirsty because of the keenness of the heat and because of the fatigue which had made him out of breath.]

One could indeed set as epigraph to a large portion of medieval literature the poetic theme illustrated by the well-known line of Charles d'Orléans: "Je meurs de soif auprès d'une fontaine" [I die of thirst next to a fountain]. Yet it is at this same fountain—whose name, however, has already undergone a metamorphosis—that the dreamer, who gazes into the fountain without even seeking to quench his thirst in it and thus preserves intact the force of his desire, throws himself, a hunted beast wounded by the arrow of Love, into the open time of the quest. This springtime dream, like Arthur's court in another fiction, is thus the space and time in which beginnings are elaborated and without which nothing could take form. But the Fountain of Love is the crucial locus where the narrative refreshes itself and begins anew, setting out on a course that will henceforth be oriented and directed by the vision of the rosebud.

We should note, moreover, that the vocabulary and stylistic features used for the description of the Fountain and for the description of its effects on dreamer and narrative alike are identical. The verb *sourdre* [surge] and the adjective *novel* [new] qualify both the water "tot jorz fresche et novele, / qui nuit et jor sort a grant ondes" [always fresh and renewed, which surges out day and night in great waves (vv. 1528–29)], and the surging, continually renewed wells of desire:

> Ci sort as genz noveile rage,
> ici se changent li corage,
> ci n'a mestier sens ne mesure,
> ci est d'amer volenté pure,
> ci ne se set conseiller nus.
>   (vv. 1581–85)

[Here a new fury surges up in people, here inner sentiments are transformed, here neither good sense nor moderation has a place, here is a pure will to love, here no one can help himself.]

The anaphora here marks not the irrepressible flow of time but the sudden and ever-renewed transformation brought about by the force of love.

It remains to be seen, however, why the Fountain ceases to exert its power to immobilize and becomes the locus of dynamism in the narrative, where time pursues its course. One explanation is that the Fountain itself, from the moment of Narcissus's discovery of it, is immersed in time. The Fountain of Narcissus, which keeps the marks of his passing and guards his memory in the inscription engraved on its rim, is also the Fountain covered by the seed of love, sown by Cupid; and around the lip of the Fountain, nourished by this living spring,

> croist l'erbe menue,
> qui vient por l'eve espesse et drue
> ne en yver ne puet mourir,
> ne l'eve sechier ne tarir.
>   (vv. 1531–34)

[. . . grows the tender grass, which becomes thick and lush because of the water; nor does the grass itself die in winter, nor does the water dry up or exhaust itself.]

The narrator, as we know, does not speak of Narcissus's transformation into a flower, of the metamorphosis with which the Ovidian text concludes. It is as though a sort of transfer or displacement were taking place in the medieval text: the pale flower of the narcissus is replaced by the crimson splendor of the rosebud, which suddenly appears to the dreamer's eyes. But the miracle of the Fountain is not simply that it fixes or crystallizes a desire that heretofore has remained "unformed and mute," to use once again the words of Paul Ricoeur cited at the beginning of this chapter: the Fountain is, in a single revelatory moment, the locus at once of unmediated vision and of an experience of possession.

In the crystal that has formed in the depths of the Fountain are mirrored the dispersed narrative fragments that the previous descriptions have evoked: an ordered world, perceived in its entirety, is reflected there. At the Fountain of Love, precisely that which the narrative seeks is produced:

> Si est cil cristaus merveilleus,
> une tel force a que li leus,
> arbres et flors, et quan qu'aorne
> le vergier, *i pert tot a orne.*
> > (vv. 1547–50, emphasis mine)

[This crystal is so marvelous, it has such force that the locality, with trees and flowers and everything that adorns the garden, *appears there, each thing in its place.*]

The difference between the vision in the crystal and the narrative, however, is crucial. The narrative announces the disclosure of totality without ever achieving it, and projects it into the future:

> Por la graine qui fu semee
> fu ceste fontaine apelee
> la Fontaine d'Amors par droit,
> dont plusor ont en maint endroit
> parlé en romanz et en livre.
> Mais ja mes n'oroiz mielz descrivre
> la verité de la matere,
> quant j'avré apost le mistere.
> > (vv. 1593–1600)

[Because of the seed that was sown, this fountain was named, accordingly, the Fountain of Love, of which many have spoken in numerous passages in books and romances. But you will never hear the truth of the matter better explained than when I shall have revealed its mystery.]

The vision reserved for the dreamer, on the other hand, permits him to perceive, from the very beginning, the manifestation ("demontrance," v. 1567) of "tot l'estre dou vergier" [the totality of the garden (v. 1559)], to penetrate its "mistere" [mystery] to the fullest:

> tot autresi vos di por voir
> que li cristaus sanz decevoir
> tot l'estre dou vergier encuse
> a celui qui en l'eve muse;
> . . . .
> si n'i a si petite chose,
> tant soit reposte ne enclouse,
> dont demontrance ne soit feite.
> (vv. 1557–60, 1565–67)

[Just so, I tell you truly that the crystal, without deception, reveals the total state of the garden to him who muses in the waters of the fountain; . . . and there is not the smallest thing, however hidden or enclosed it might be, that should not be made manifest.]

To set out in quest of the Rose, to strive to spread its petals, patiently, in order to penetrate its mystery: this could thus be understood as a search to recover in the object of desire—to grasp again in the flow of time—the essential moment that the dream alone granted, when the entire universe of this garden paradise, the entire universe of love, was offered to the eyes of the dreamer, forever haunted by this lost vision:

> Adés me plot a demorer
> a la fontaine remirer
> et as cristaus, qui me mostroient
> mil choses qui entor estoient.
> Mes de fort eure m'i miré.
> Las! tant en ai puis soupiré!
> Cil miroërs m'a deceü:
> se j'eüsse avant coneü
> quex ert sa force et sa vertuz
> ne m'i fusse ja enbatuz.
> (vv. 1601–10)

[Therefore it pleased me to remain there, looking at the Fountain and at the crystals, which showed me a thousand things that were around me. But it brought me bad fortune to gaze there. Alas! I have sighed much for it since! This mirror deceived me: if I had known before-hand what its strength and power were, I would never have betaken myself there.]

It has become almost a cliché to compare the Rose and the Grail. The two quests do, in fact, organize themselves around a search for the *veraie semblance* [true semblance], as Bohort says in the *Queste del saint Graal*,[22] or for the nakedness of the Word, as Umberto Eco implies at the end of the *Name of the Rose*: "Stat rosa pristina nomine, nomina nuda tenemus" [the pristine rose remains in name, we grasp the naked names]. The *Queste* is, in fact, a narrative about a progressive unveiling, a vision that becomes more and more penetrating and is finally granted to the chosen person, even if it remains ineffable. In Guillaume's narrative, the vision is granted, but in the "time outside of time" of the dream and in the space of the Fountain. The vision is the "matire...bone et nueve" [new, excellent subject matter (v. 39)] at the source of desire and at the source of the desire to write, but the vision cannot incarnate and renew itself in chronological time, in the normal course of seasons and days. The narrative attributed to Guillaume de Lorris ends with the lament of the dreamer, now fused with the narrator; it is no accident that he compares himself to the peasant who, like him, has been unable to bring about the metamorphosis of the seed, the harvest of his desire:

> Je resemble le païsant
> qui giete a terre sa semance
> et a joie grant ou comance
> a estre bele et drue en herbe;
> mes avant qu'il en cueille gerbe,
> l'empire, tel eure est, et grieve
> une male nue qui lieve
> quant li espi doivent florir,
> si fet le grain dedenz morir
> et l'esperance au vilain tost,
> qu'il avoit eüe trop tost.
>   (vv. 3932–42)

[I am like the peasant who casts his seed upon the earth, and rejoices when the grain begins to become beautiful and thickens in the blade; but before he gathers a single sheaf of grain, such is fate that a disastrous cloud disappoints and afflicts him, a cloud that comes just when the ears of grain are about to flower, and, causing the grain within to die, strips the peasant of the hopes he had formed too soon.]

The Biblical image that Chrétien de Troyes appropriates in the prologue to the *Conte du Graal*, that of the sower casting his seed on fertile soil where it will be able to grow and multiply, is thus reappropriated here, even in the rhymes *semance* / *comance*. But inverted, abased, rendered sterile, the image signifies from this point onward both the failure of love and the impotence of the writer who cannot master, except in the moment outside of time provided by the dream, the fruitful course of time and its mystery.

Notes

1. Paul Ricoeur, *Temps et récit*, 3 vols. (Paris: Seuil, 1983–85). Translated by Kathleen McLaughlin and David Pellauer as *Time and Narrative* (Chicago: University of Chicago Press, 1984).

2. *Time and Narrative*, vol. 1, p. xi ("notre expérience temporelle confuse, informe et à la limite muette," vol. 1, p. 13).

3. *Time and Narrative*, vol. 1, p. 53 ("reconstruire l'ensemble des opérations par lesquelles une œuvre s'enlève sur le fond opaque du vivre, de l'agir et du souffrir pour être donnée par son auteur à un lecteur qui la reçoit et change ainsi son agir," vol. 1, p. 86).

4. I cite the *Roman de la Rose* in the edition by Félix Lecoy, 3 vols., Classiques Français du Moyen Âge 92, 95, 98. The bibliography of works devoted to the text of Guillaume de Lorris is immense. Only those works that have made a particular contribution to this study are listed here: Roger Dragonetti, *Le Mirage des sources* (Paris: Seuil, 1987), pp. 200–23; Michelle A. Freeman, "Problems in Romance Composition: Ovid, Chrétien de Troyes, and the *Romance of the Rose*," *Romance Philology* 30 (1976–77): 158–68; David F. Hult, "The Allegorical Fountain: Narcissus in the *Roman de la Rose*," *Romanic Review* 72 (1981): 125–48; Hult's *Self-Fulfilling Prophecies: Readership and Authority in the First "Roman de la Rose"* (Cambridge: Cambridge University Press, 1986); Sylvia Huot, *From Song to Book: The Poetics of Writing in Old French Lyric and Lyrical Narrative Poetry* (Ithaca, NY: Cornell University Press, 1987), pp. 83–105; J. Kessler, "La Quête amoureuse et poétique: la Fontaine de Narcisse dans le *Roman de la Rose*," *Romanic Review* 73 (1982): 133–46; Christiane Marchello-Nizia, "La Rhétorique des songes et le songe comme rhétorique dans la littérature française médiévale," in *I Signi nel Medioevo*

(Rome: Edizioni dell'Anteneo, 1985), pp. 245–59; Rupert T. Pickens, *"Somnium and Interpretation in Guillaume de Lorris,"* *Symposium* 29 (1974): 175–86; Jean Rychner, "Le Mythe de la Fontaine de Narcisse dans le *Roman de la Rose* de Guillaume de Lorris," in *Le Lieu et la formule: Hommage à Marc Eigeldinger* (Neuchâtel: Éditions de la Baconnière, 1978), pp. 33–46; Paul Strohm, "Guillaume as Narrator and Lover in the *Roman de la Rose,*" *Romanic Review* 59 (1968): 3–9; Paul Zumthor, "Récit et anti-récit: le *Roman de la Rose,*" in his *Langue, texte, énigme* (Paris: Seuil, 1975), pp. 249–64.

5. In this respect, one might note the change that takes place when we go from universal histories to historical chronicles: Wace in the *Roman de Rou*, Robert de Clari, and Villehardouin, to cite a few examples, begin their chronicles with a date that makes a clean cut into time. For Wace, this date is the moment when he begins to write; for the other chroniclers, it is the date of the beginning of the Fourth Crusade.

6. On this point, see my "Temps linéaire, temps circulaire et écriture romanesque (XIIe–XIIIe siècles)," in *Le Temps et la durée dans la littérature du Moyen Âge et de la Renaissance*, ed. Yvonne Bellenger (Paris: Nizet, 1985), pp. 7–21.

7. We should note here, once and for all, that this dream, unlike most literary dreams—a notable exception is Iseut's dream in Béroul's *Tristan*—is not sent or inspired by an entity external to the dreaming subject, by a figure of authority such as God or some other divine messenger; this dream has no other acknowledged "source" than the dreaming subject himself.

8. The motif of the "reverdie" is similarly linked to the desire to write and to the activation of the narrative in *Partenopeu de Blois* and to the renewal of the act of writing in the prologue of *Guiron le Courtois*; the motif returns at key moments in the *Roman de Troie*, among others.

9. On the motif of the "reverdie" in lyric poetry, and the explicit rejection of that motif by certain trouvères and troubadours, see Roger Dragonetti, *La Technique poétique des trouvères dans la chanson courtoise: contribution à l'étude de la rhétorique médiévale* (Bruges: De Tempel, 1960), pp. 169–93; and my "Remarques sur la poésie de Gace Brulé," *Revue des Langues Romanes* 88 (1984): 1–13.

10. A point in time that is described in this manner by the narrator, vv. 48–93.

11. Without adopting the extreme position of Dragonetti, who, in *Le Mirage des sources*, makes Guillaume de Lorris's name a pseudonym for Jean de Meun, we can nevertheless note that this "I" does not name himself at all in the part of the romance traditionally attributed to Guillaume. This goes beyond the habitual reticence of the troubadours and trouvères, who often sign and dedicate their poetic works in the *envoi*, thus partially escaping from the anonymity of the lyric "I."

12. See especially Strohm, "Guillaume as Narrator"; Zumthor, "Récit et anti-récit"; Armand Strubel, "Écriture du songe et mise en œuvre de la 'senefiance' dans le *Roman de la Rose* de Guillaume de Lorris," in *Études sur le "Roman de la Rose"*, ed. Jean Dufournet, Collection Unichamp 4 (Paris: Champion, 1984), pp. 145–79.

13. See Freeman, "Problems in Romance Composition."

14. There is, however, a remarkable exception in the *Queste del saint Graal*, ed. Albert Pauphilet, Classiques Français du Moyen Âge (Paris: Champion,

1967): the vision of Lancelot relayed by the dream of Mordrain (pp. 130–31, 134–35). Both vision and dream are, in many respects, visions of the origin or source from which the lineage of Lancelot and Galahad, and that of the Grail, arises and unfolds.

15. See, for example, in both verse and especially prose Arthurian romances, fomulas such as "he rode for a day, for a year, for years . . . without finding any adventure worthy of being related."

16. See Philippe Lejeune, *Le Pacte autobiographique* (Paris: Seuil, 1975).

17. For example, with respect to the description of the Fountain of Love (vv. 1593–1600).

18. The hero of the *Bel Inconnu* is known to bear the same arms as the "author" of the narrative, identified as Renaut de Bagé, whose mythical ancestor he thus becomes. See A. Guerreau, "Renaut de Bagé, *Le Bel Inconnu*, structure symbolique et signification sociale," *Romania* 103 (1982): 28–82; Michèle Perret, "Atemporalités et effet de fiction dans le *Bel Inconnu*," in *Le Nombre du temps: en hommage à Paul Zumthor* (Paris: Champion, 1988).

19. See Huot, *From Song to Book*, pp. 90–95.

20. As does Lancelot, who is caught in the trap of the magical carol in the prose *Lancelot*, ed. Alexandre Micha, vol. 4, p. 234. In the *Rose*, the songs of the birds, however pleasant they are to listen to, are nevertheless compared to the songs of the Sirens (vv. 667–70).

21. See, for example, vv. 1606–12, where the distance between the time of the dream and the time of the narration of the dream is abolished.

22. Ed. Pauphilet, p. 167.

Karl D. Uitti

2. "Cele [qui] doit estre Rose clamee" (*Rose*, vv. 40–44): Guillaume's Intentionality

Entre ces boutons en eslui
Un si trés bel qu'envers celui
Nul des autres rien ne prisai,
Puis que je l'oi bien avisé,
Car une color l'enlumine
Qui est si vermeille e si fine
Con Nature la pot plus faire.
De fueilles i ot quatre paire,
Que Nature par grant maistire
I ot assises tire a tire;

La queue est droite come jons,
Et par desus siet li boutons
Si qu'il ne cline ne ne pent.
L'odor de lui entor s'espant:
La soatume qui en ist
Toute la place replenist.
Et quant jou senti si flairier,
Je n'oi talent de repairier,
Ainz m'aprochasse por le prendre,
Se j'i osasse la main tendre . . . .

(vv. 1655–74; emphasis mine)[1]

[One of these buds I chose, so beautiful that in comparison none of its mates I prized at all; and I was well advised for such a color did illumine it—so fine was its vermilion—that it seemed that in it Nature had outdone herself. Four pairs of leaves had she in order set about the bud with cunning workmanship. The stalk was straight and upright as a cane, and thereupon the bud was seated firm, not bending or inclined. Its odor spread, the sweetness burdening the air about. Now when I smelled the perfume so exhaled I had no wish to go, but drew more near, intending to (grasp) the tempting bud if I dared stretch my hand . . .][2]

On first reading these lines do not appear to impress the reader as seriously problematic. They merely recount how the Lover, having gazed into Narcissus's "perilous fountain" in the Jardin de Déduit and been wounded by Cupid's arrow, first sees and fixes upon what would be the object of his amorous passion, the rosebud. Yet, the undeniable indeterminacy with respect to the object of our lover-protagonist's passion underscores a certain emptiness that appears to characterize this object, at least at this juncture in Guillaume's poem. This is quite jarring; readers conventionally speak of the Lover's obsession with *a* rose. In the passage just cited, however, the rose in question is, to put it mildly, odd. Moreover, the term *rose* never appears in this section of the poem in the sense of a specific flower. At first, the young Lover speaks of plucking "one of them [i.e., roses]" on the bush: "Se assailliz ou mesamez / Ne cremisse estre, j'en cuillisse / Au moins une, que je tenisse / En ma main" [vv. 1630–33: Had I not feared to be assailed or scorned, one of them, at least, I would have picked in order to grasp it in my hand]. Elsewhere the *masculine* term *bouton(s)* 'bud' is invariably used. Gender-specificity is strikingly absent from this early description of the "rose." What is emphasized here is hardly the rose as flower; it is, rather, the straight, stiff stem, on the top of which the *bouton* is seated; and the protagonist desires first and foremost to reach out and hold it (*le prendre*) in his hand. (In fact, earlier the narrator had stated his—the Lover's?—preference for rosebuds over full-fledged flowering roses: "Les roses overtes et lees / Sont en un jor toutes alees, / Mais li bouton durent tuit frois / A tot le moins deus jorz ou trois" [vv. 1645–48: For roses spreading wide within one day will all be gone; but fresh the buds will still remain at least two days or three.]) Such a "rose" as appears clearly to be preferred by our amorous hero strikes me, when I think of roses as feminine metaphors, as a perfect counterpart, an exact mirroring, of what Ovid had called Narcissus's *imago mendax*, or of what, somewhat earlier, Guillaume de Lorris's *Rose* (= *Rose I*) refers to as the "enfant bel a desmesure" with whom Ovid's pathetic youth falls so hopelessly in love. One cannot conceive of a more phallic, masculine sort of rose, in my judgment, than the rose described here as it reposes, closed in its budlike shape, on its long and stiffly upright stem.

What is Guillaume up to in this passage? How do these lines fit into the system of intentions making up his poem? Or, more interesting, how might these lines lead to a fuller grasp of Guillaume's intentionality? In many respects, of course, Guillaume's lover-protagonist assimilates the Narcissus story; indeed, his fear of the Fountain extends to the very name it carries. Consequently, this story is both his own story and, for him, a classic cautionary tale. *His* narrative contains and, so to speak, *mirrors* that of Narcissus. Or, perhaps more accurately, Guillaume's narrative *gazes intently into* the story of Narcissus and reflects upon it.

Although much critical scholarship has been devoted to the Narcissus Episode in *Rose I*, to my knowledge nobody has as yet examined the implications of the "phallic rose" described in such detail by Guillaume de Lorris. Indeed, I am not aware of its even having been noticed before.

Perhaps this is due to its not conforming with the scholarly or critical schemes to which Guillaume's poem has variously been accommodated.

The Critical Background

No Old French (OF) poetic text has come close to enjoying the kind of ongoing, and controversial, success one associates with the *Romance of the Rose*. This *summa*-like poem, begun, as Jean de Meun informs us,[3] by a certain Guillaume de Lorris (around the year 1230), and both "continued" and "brought to conclusion" by Jean himself approximately a half-century later, was read, copied, translated, amplified, imitated, decried, studied, counterfeited, edited, and explicated for almost half a millennium. Following upon their late-medieval- and Renaissance-poet and critic predecessors, scores of nineteenth- and twentieth-century scholars representing varying disciplinary interests have sought to articulate its meanings, to pin it down. Indeed, the truths ascribed to it by early and modern commentarists alike appear to illustrate the aptness of Ernest Renan's somewhat disabused *boutade*: "Le malheur quand on cherche la vérité, c'est qu'on finit par la trouver."

We know some things about the *Romance of the Rose*; however, much of what many of us assume we know is but a matter of more or less well-informed conventional opinion and/or personal conjecture. That the poem attracts the attention of learnèd readers even today is evidenced in this jointly written volume and in the ever-expanding list of publications devoted yearly to it. The artifact is certainly something that we can be scholarly about, as are its many ramifications. We are constantly redrawing the boundaries between what we really do know and either what we feel impelled to accept as what we know or what we merely—or triumphantly—affirm we know. Unlike numerous other poems, the *Rose*, along with the scholarly commentary generated by it, seems to invite attack and defense, and, of course, to favor the construction of arguments designed to strengthen one's plans of assault and of resistance. We choose to ignore what we might otherwise learn because, perhaps, to know what we choose to ignore could well turn out to be embarrassingly inconvenient to our general schemes and plans. From the times of Dante, of Machaut, and of Christine de Pizan down to our own day, the *Rose* has consistently functioned as a marvelously rich pretext.

Ideally, one would prefer to proceed like Descartes from the known to the less certain (but highly plausible) and only in the last resort to more problematical and hypothetical matters. But discrete tiers of this sort do not turn out to be wholly feasible when one discusses the *Rose*. Even setting aside momentarily the vast issue of critical ground rules affords little comfort. Great gaps in areas where we otherwise possess a fair degree of certainty occur with disheartening frequency. For instance, "Guillaume de Lorris" is a tag applied by Amors (i.e., Love personified) to the poet-Lover figure whose story (and work) will, Amors informs us at the approximate midpoint of the conjoined texts of Parts I and II of the *Rose*, be "continued" by a certain "Jehans Chopinel" who is yet to be born, on the banks of the Loire River, at Meung. Our ignorance with respect to this individual is complete, at least as far as hard data are concerned. Whatever "Guillaume de Lorris" has become for us results from our reconstruction of him—pure inference. And this reconstruction has every bit as much to do with our scholarly requirements and poetic tastes as it does with the types of concern articulated by our text.

Quite predictably, then, *Rose* commentary and analysis are replete with rules and strictures: "Do this; above all *don't* do that! " and so forth. Thus, given the work's temporal context, such and such "*must* mean this, and *not* that." By extension the sheer magnitude of the poem—its length, its complexity, its extraordinary fortune and undeniable historical importance—has often invited totalitarian responses: seen as a *system* of one kind or another, the work has engendered systematic critical (and poetic) reactions, and this in turn has contributed to a narrowing of possible agreements as well as to a certain deadening, or stifling, of the poem. I for one cannot believe that the *Divine Comedy* constitutes even in part a reaction to a *Rose* understood by Dante simply as a kind of versified system. However, it strikes me as plausible that in order for the *Divine Comedy* to be what it was destined to be, it (on several levels) *systematized* the *Rose*. Unlike the purely scholarly systematizations, however, a poetic one manages, or can manage, also to celebrate the poem in which it finds whatever it has subverted in this fashion. Is not this celebration in fact one of the chief lessons of the *Romance of the Rose* itself? The single poem of Guillaume de Lorris and Jean de Meun overrides in many significant ways the works, respectively, by Guillaume and Jean—what we have accustomed ourselves to call Parts I and II.

Surely, then, we can all agree that the *Rose* is at once an intriguing and a demanding poem, and that it virtually dares us to attempt to "understand" it. Other significant areas of agreement also suggest themselves. For example, the work was undertaken at a time when French narrative in octosyllabic rhyming couplets had been subjected to severe criticism of the type "Rhymed discourse is inherently mendacious because the choice of words depends more on rhyme than on sense," or, "Romances cannot be serious—at best they can aspire merely to entertain, at their worst they serve up noxious tales of adultery and other immoralities." Truly serious, and seriously true, French narrative is necessarily historical, and in prose. Indeed, much early thirteenth-century verse romance—for example, the epigonal and formally playful *Bel Inconnu, Aucassin et Nicolette*, or *Fergus*[4]—appears to reject historical seriousness, while prose recastings of older stories couched in verse such as the *Prose Tristan* and the *Prose Lancelot* seem, precisely, to have been devised in order to "historicize" earlier verse romance *matières*. The central issue is truth.

This issue is directly addressed, of course, in the opening lines of the *Romance of the Rose*;[5] we remember the *songe : mençonge* rhyme of vv. 1–2, here reversed with respect to its common usage in OF romance: dreams are *not* invariably untruthful, and the estimable Macrobius (who "wrote down" [*sic*[6]] the dream of Scipio) is called upon to substantiate this affirmation. The classic format of the OF romance prologue, we note, prevails here: the general statement, or *sententia*, followed by an appeal to unimpeachable authority, leads to a matter of particular relevance in regard to the narrative at hand. A first-person narrator is speaking. The stage is set for a story—for a romance specifically like those epitomized by Chrétien de Troyes; a romance, like many others of the first quarter of the thirteenth century, that seems to proclaim its epigonality.

But what is the "narrative at hand"? And who is our narrator? In the name of whom and to what purpose does he speak? These questions are not easy to answer.

A thesis is advanced, namely, the truth of dreams. Those who disbelieve this thesis may well decide, though incorrectly, to dismiss our narrator as a fool, but our narrator remains nonetheless convinced that "songes est senefiance / Des biens as genz e des enuiz" (vv. 16–17). A thesis advanced in this manner is rather unusual in romances up to this time.[7] Thesislike *sententiæ* more commonly introduce, and shore up, the material recounted in the romance that follows;[8] here a reversal of this pattern obtains: the romance narrative appears to support, rather, the validity of the thesis.[9]

A kind of transitional narrative ensues. In support of his thesis—his belief concerning the *senefiance*, or prophetic meaningfulness, of dreams—the narrator tells, in a kind of "second" Prologue (vv. 21–44), that when he was in his twentieth year he dreamt a dream which was very beautiful and pleasing to him; but nothing in this dream, he declares, *failed actually to take place.* I repeat: What he had dreamt soon happened *just as* the dream had foretold! Is this assertion literally accurate? If it is accurate, when and under what conditions did the dream actually come to pass? If it is not accurate, to what purpose was the assertion made?

Let me recapitulate. (1) A narrative "I" advances a thesis concerning the veracity of dreams—a veracity by no means universally granted, but guaranteed, seemingly, by a reputed classical author (the same Macrobius, incidentally, who "taught Chrétien how to 'describe'" [10]). (2) The truthfulness of dreams is linked to their "significance"—to their acting as "signifiers" of the good and of the bad things that (eventually) come to affect people [11]—and to their prophetic value (what is dreamt of "covertly" often is later "seen overtly"). (3) Proof of the foregoing is provided by the first-person narrator's own past experience: when he was about to turn twenty, that is, at that canonically "historical" time of life when Love exacts his toll of young men, he had a beautiful and pleasing dream while sleeping soundly, and everything that he dreamt soon came to pass exactly as the dream had stated it. Can we agree that what I have just said outlines accurately, though very summarily, what the initial thirty lines of the *Rose* say?

A number of questions arise, however. First, what is the nature of the relationship between "dreaming" and "seeing" (vv. 18–19)? When one sees what one has previously dreamt, does one witness a "real" event or is seeing an exclusively mental activity more or less equivalent to understanding? Can it be somehow both of these? (It is worth remembering that OF *senefiance* also denotes "witness". [12]) Might it not be that dreaming and seeing provide a context for each other and that, in complementarity, they impart meaning to each other?

"Now," so our narrator informs us, "I wish to put *that* dream into rhyme, in order to cheer up your hearts, for Love, at present, asks and commands it of me." Is this command yet another avatar of the "toll" required of young men in their twentieth year? Is it merely a reiterative formulation of that earlier exaction?

The experience recounted in vv. 21–30 to buttress the thesis advanced earlier in the Prologue, now becomes, we observe, the subject matter of a rhymed *romanz* (v. 35)—a vernacular narrative—which the narrator at present undertakes at the behest of Amors for the purpose of bringing pleasure and joy (*esgaier*) to the hearts of those who are depicted vocatively as listening to him. The story will be called *The Romance of the Rose*, and it will encompass an unabridged—the *entire*—"Art of Love" ("Ou l'Art d'Amors est *toute* enclose"). Its "matter" is both "good" and "new" (MS *Za: bele e voire* 'beautiful and true'). One is led to speculate as to whether the wholeness—the completeness—of this Art of Love might not have something important to do with its "goodness" and "newness" (or "truth" and "beauty") and with the poet-narrator's obvious pride in his workmanship.[13]

The romance itself is to be "received" by her "por cui je l'ai empris" ('on account of whom I have undertaken it'); may she receive it willingly! To be sure, the enterprise responds to Amors's command; however, it is *occasioned* by *cele*—a Lady—whose merit is so outstanding and who is so worthy of being loved that she fully deserves to be proclaimed "Rose." The inspiration emanating from the Lady to the person of the first-person narrator causes the entire complex set of relationships involving dreaming and reality to fall into place. Her pertinence to our narrator—he loves her—acts as his primary *motivation*. No longer is he merely the nineteen-year-old who routinely is paying dues to Love. No longer is he serving, so to speak, the idea of love, or narcissistically loving himself and manifesting crudely and exclusively the physical ardor characteristic of red-blooded nineteen-year-old males.[14] Meanwhile, she, as he loves her and by virtue of his hope that she will reciprocate his love, will stimulate him to render the "goodness" and the "newness" of his "matter" (*bone et nueve*)—of the Art of Love—contained in his *Roman de la Rose*. Conversely, his prophetic dream, as he will recount it, predicts and informs the Lady; the dream, its signifying power, names her: she must be proclaimed *Rose* ("el doit estre Rose clamee" [v. 44]). If God grants that she accept his gift to her of his poem-dream-experience, they, in consequence, as conjoined couple, will achieve completeness as themselves *in their relationship to, and with, one another.* What has hitherto remained virtual, or latent, in the dream (its *senefiance*) will in fact have come to pass. The dream will have undergone validation, that is, it will have fulfilled itself as prophecy (which is the nature of dreams), and the Art of Love will have been authentically articulated within a proper context. All this, in turn, will bring about the further benefit of a society newly rid of sadness and unhappiness: there is presumably no room for jealous *losangiers* in a world made up of "gay hearts."

Unlike Ovid's *Art of Love* and the amusing treatiselike late-twelfth-century repertory by Andreas Capellanus, *The Romance of the Rose* constitutes an Art of Love that depends entirely on the truthfulness of the personal experience that provides its foundation. What happened then in the canonically construed lifetime of the lover-protagonist was dreamt and only given value, significance, within the subsequent and new context of that protagonist who meanwhile became the poet-initiator of the *Rose*.

Intertextual Considerations: OF Romance Narrative

Like the Perceval of Chrétien's *Conte du Graal* (ca. 1190) who, as it were, dreams of becoming a knight and who, we are sure, is quite capable of achieving this goal, but who initially confuses genuine chivalry with its exterior trappings, the young disciple of Love in the *Rose* clearly has in him considerable natural ability. He has what it takes to achieve the status of an authentic lover, that is to say, to participate fully (and humbly) in the Couple formed of Man and Woman, but not before he outgrows the limitations of his adolescent lack of *sen*. Analogously, the two central experiences of Perceval, his coming to love Blanchefleur and his failure at the Grail Castle, similarly transform an incomplete and unpolished, albeit naturally gifted, youth, whose ambition is confined to imitating the famous and sophisticated, but hollow, Gauvain, into a complex and fully individualized knight truly to be reckoned with. Perceval's knightliness eventually stands with respect to the chivalry of Gauvain as the charity of Count Philip of Flanders compares with Alexander's vainglorious liberality.[15] The artful polishing of native ability constitutes, then, in both *The Romance of the Rose* and the *Conte du Graal* a material theme of very great importance. Indeed, the recounting of adventures is largely the articulation of this basic theme in the two works.

Chrétien's *Graal* itself takes up values previously explored by the same romancer in his *Le Chevalier de la Charrette (Lancelot)*, composed over a decade earlier (contemporaneously with *Le Chevalier au Lion* [*Yvain*]). If, in the front matter to the *Charrette*, what Chrétien de Troyes labels the *san* (provided to him by his patroness, Countess Marie de Champagne) may properly be understood as the *fact* of Lancelot's loving devotion to Queen Guenevere (opposed, say, to the attitude displayed toward both by Gauvain in Chrétien's romance and by the hero of the Middle High German *Lanzelet*—a text that may well, in this regard, reproduce the now lost French source of the *Charrette*), then the contrast between Gauvain and Lancelot on the one hand and, on the other, the "growth" from a Lanzelet-type protagonist to Chrétien's Lancelot may be seen as foreshadowing, even authorizing, one's expectation that the *Rose* lover-protagonist, in his development from nineteen-year-old callowness to twenty-five-year-old poet-Lover, will undergo a similar process. The example of Perceval who, after achieving parity with Gauvain at the Blood Drops scene, eventually outshines Gauvain in maturity and understanding reinforces this expectation. (Lancelot, of course, also "grows" from his initial, though very slight, hesitation in climbing aboard the Infamous Cart to a deeper awareness of *all* the implications of his love, especially in regard to honor.) Does Guillaume's Lover move on from the "Gauvain stage" to a "Lancelot/Perceval stage," and, if so, in terms of what model or pattern?

Also, as in several of Chrétien's romances, *naming* lies at the heart of *The Romance of the Rose*. To name someone or something is less, however, a matter of exercising a kind of Adamic control over what is named than a form of identification that incorporates, even creates, that which is named into the economy of the poem. By naming Vieillece, for instance, or the Fountain of Narcissus, the protagonist establishes a pertinent relationship between that personification or that object and himself. The act of naming implies recognition and intent. The name corresponds to the poet-narrator-Lover's desire ("I wish the romance which I am undertaking to be called . . . the *Romance of the Rose*"); the name expresses his understanding in terms of what he intends that his poem do. Finally, naming appears to objectify—to make real—what otherwise might legitimately be construed as an arbitrary and capricious, or unordered, presentation of what simply appears worthwhile or interesting to say. Within the text of the poem, a link of truth is established between the name and what is named; and this link confers authenticity upon whatever undergoes this process of being named. Vieillece *exists*, so to speak, in her own right because she is so named in the poem and described there as she is seen by the poet-protagonist.

Another antecedent comes to mind, that of Chrétien's naming his *Le Chevalier au Lion* as this tale comes to a close, that is, as it reaches its completion and its truth:

Del *Chevalier au Lion* fine
CRESTIIENS son romanz einsi;
Qu'onques plus conter n'an oï
Ne ja plus n'an orroiz conter
S'an n'i viaut mançonge ajoster.[16]

Thus, the *Rose* poeticizes an old and peculiarly romance narrative convention, that of the crucial significance accorded the naming-revelation of characters, places, and poetic works. To put the matter another way, in giving his work the title *Romanz de la Rose*, the poet-narrator adheres to the tradition we find already fully exploited in Chrétien's *Lancelot*, *Yvain*, and *Perceval*. (Jean de Meun's recourse to this same tradition at the approximate midpoint of the conjoined two parts of the *Rose* shows that he too is fully aware of the centrality of this device in Guillaume's poem.) By virtue of following this tradition (among other things), the poet-narrator identifies his work as a romance. In this fashion he acquires, and can utilize for his own ends, the rich resources of vernacular romance narrative in verse, despite the fact that, in most other respects, his work appears to depart both radically and self-consciously from romance tradition (for example, oft-told stories about Arthur and the Round Table, or about Tristan, and so forth[17]). Whatever pertains to, or derives from, the set of possibilities we associate with vernacular romance narrative lends itself, like the contents of a vast warehouse, to the uses our poet wishes to make of these possibilities. Guillaume's imagination is a *romance* imagination.

In the verses that have concerned us so far, the poet-narrator takes a basically lyric situation to be found in countless *chants courtois*: the poet offers a song (an artifact) to the Lady he loves in the hope that she will willingly accept this gift and, one supposes, respond to his love. Like the angles of an equilateral triangle, the poetic "ego," the song, and the love experience are equal to one another and, to a considerable degree, interchangeable. The poet rephrases this lyric situation in romance narrative terms, however. (Meanwhile, verse remains, of course, a "natural medium" for his enterprise; our poet thus simply disarms those who criticize verse discourse.) The Beloved is she for whom he has composed his work (as Chrétien's *Charrette* was composed at the behest of Countess Marie de Champagne). The substance of the narrative, namely, the first-person protagonist's amorous adventure, is also lyric, but treated in a narrative manner: the narrator is *both* the "same person" as his protagonist and a "different person." The former underwent the adventure, we recall, in his twentieth year; the latter is recounting the story five or more years later.[18] One is reminded of Chrétien's Calogrenant, in *Yvain*, and of Enéas's tale to Dido of the Fall of Troy, in the *Roman d'Enéas* (ca. 1150), two romance characters who tell a story concerning a central past event in their lives. "Guillaume de Lorris" is thus *both* the knightly, lyric-type protagonist *and* the clerkly, romance-style narrator; he is at once, so to speak, Lancelot *and* Chrétien.

The question of identification and difference is, of course, fraught with complexity. Chrétien himself, we recall, plays with this question repeatedly in the author/narrator relationship he sets up, and modifies constantly, in each of his romances. The "author" of *Yvain* is most pertinently *not* to be confused with the narrator (who does not achieve complete clerkly status until the very end of the romance, when, appropriately enough, "Crestïens" is finally named); "Godefroi de Leigni" and "his" role in the *Charrette* remains a question mark; the narrator of *Cligés* is a kind of authorial foil. And what must one conclude from the curious identification of Chrétien's absolutely devoted clerkly service to his Lady (i.e., patroness) in the Prologue to the *Charrette* and the chivalric service provided by Lancelot to his beloved queen? In *Rose I* temporality furnishes an important key (and it is also borrowed, but with significant modification, by Jean de Meun in his above-mentioned elegaic *translatio* of poets in the service of Venus). The extended (and marvelous) meditation on time included in the description of the portrait of Vieillece (vv. 339–406) deserves quotation in respect of the problem of identification and difference. This meditation, strategically located at the start of the Lover's quest, indicates Guillaume's acute awareness of the issue:

Li Tens qui s'en vait nuit et jor,
Senz repos prendre e senz sejor,
E qui de nos se part e emble
Si celeement qu'il nos semble
Qu'il s'arest adès en un point,
E il ne s'i areste point,
Ainz ne fine de trespasser,
Que l'en ne puet neïs penser
Queus tens ce est qui est presenz,
Sel demandez as clers lisanz;
Car ainz que l'en l'eüst pensé
Seroient ja troi tens passé.

(vv. 361–72)

[Time is forever fleeting, night and day, without sojourn, and taking no repose; but as he goes he steals away from us so secretly that he appears to stand, although he never rests, nor stays his course; so that no man can say that time is now. Ask of some learned clerk; ere he can think three times will Time already have passed by.]

Interestingly, Calogrenant and Enéas both tell their sad stories of failure at the pressing request of queens—Guenevere and Dido—though neither willingly does so, since the two autobiographical stories cause pain to their narrators. Enéas's tale contributes much to fan the flame of Dido's passion; Guenevere, however, almost glaringly shows no such interest in Calogrenant. Told for the first time some seven years after the events recounted in it, however, the latter's narrative, like that of Guillaume de Lorris, offers a perfect model of professional clerkly romance story-telling, with a well-wrought prologue and significant midpoint, a veritable web of intertextual references, and flawless courtly diction. In both *Yvain* and the *Enéas* the failures are redeemed: Yvain avenges his cousin's humiliation and marries the Dido-like Laudine; Enéas will resuscitate Troy on the banks of the Tiber and, with Lavine, the daughter of King Latinus, will found a new chivalric lineage.

Does a similar pattern apply in the case of the *Rose*? Will the adolescent Lover's lack of chivalric success be compensated for by the twenty-five-year-old's poetic (and amorous) achievement in conjunction with "Cele [qui] doit estre Rose clamee"? In any case, the situation of the Lover-Dreamer in his twentieth year is profoundly different from that of the poet-Lover of the *Rose*, and the poem's truth largely derives from its exploration of this difference.

The story is not "vain and pleasant" as are—to take up the formulation by Jean Bodel—the Breton fables of King Arthur. It is a true story (or it is presented as such) and an integral part of the biographical dynamics of the lyrically focused writer-witness who is telling it. On the other hand, the kind of narrative "objectivity" provided by typical third-person romances protects what is being told (or confessed) from accusations of insincerity. After all, the poem contains the entire Art of Love; it is addressed to an audience "por voz cuers plus faire esgaier"—an audience, I venture to guess, not unlike the noble lords referred to by Godefroi de Leigni at the close of *Lancelot*.

The protagonist experiences (in his twentieth year) initiation into love: he loves, and desires, one of the roses in Déduit's Orchard. The story stops, however, before the problems facing him are entirely resolved. He has not yet possessed what he yearns for. (Or, if "in fact" he *had* possessed it and thereby had brought the adventure to a "successful" conclusion, the poet-Lover did not choose to say so. Of course, one can think of various quite cogent reasons, given his *present* situation, why he would have preferred not to dwell on this "triumph.") The question remains. Was it in fact conceivable, given who and where the narrator was, that a narrative conclusion resolving the Lover's problems could plausibly take place? A Jean de Meun, *continuing* the tale of a Guillaume de Lorris and identified as so doing, could, and did, resolve the plot: the rosebud is plucked, and the story *as narrative* abruptly ends, as we very well know.

I confess that what makes sense to me, given what I have been trying to say so far, is that the plot *not* being brought to a conclusion by the poet-narrator we know as Guillaume de Lorris constitutes a particularly effective means of closure: that, in other words, Guillaume's poem has truly ended. Why might one justifiably think this?

The importance of midpoints to the architecture and structure of meanings of many OF romances has been frequently noted in scholarship over the past several decades. Often the midpoint of a romance has bearing on matters of identity, naming, and/or title. It is thus at the (approximate) midpoint of *Le Chevalier au Lion (Yvain)* that Yvain receives his new name (the Lion Knight) and, in the *Charrette*, that Lancelot's name is revealed. At the midpoint of the conjoined texts of Parts I and II of the *Rose*, we recall, Jean de Meun introduces the names of the authors as well as a new title. Consequently, if only "experimentally," it would seem justifiable to take a look at the approximate midpoint of the some 4058 lines generally attributed to Guillaume de Lorris (around v. 2000 and a bit beyond). Here we find Love's instructions to the Lover-protagonist (Love, we remember, is also speaking at the midpoint of the conjoined texts). The twenty-five-year-old poet-narrator summarizes these instructions in terms strikingly reminiscent of the Prologue:

> Li deus d'Amors lors m'encharja,
> Tot ensi con vos orroiz ja,
> Mot a mot ses comandemenz:
> Bien les devise cist romanz.
> Qui amer viaut or i entende,
> Que li romanz des or amende;
> Des or le fait bon escouter,
> S'il est qui le sache conter,
> Car la fin dou songe est mout bele
> E la matire en est novele;
> Qui dou songe la fin orra,
> Je vos di bien que il porra
> Des jeus d'Amors assez aprendre,

Por quoi il vueille tant atendre
Que j'espoigne e que j'enromance
Dou songe la senefiance:
La verité, qui est coverte,
Vos sera lores toute aperte
Quant espondre m'orroiz le songe,
Car il n'i a mot de mençonge.
(vv. 2057–76)

[The God of Love then gave to me the charge which you will soon hear, and word by word the ordinances he set forth of love. Well does this romance state these points. May he who wishes to love pay close heed; for, from now on, the romance will get better. It is good now to listen carefully, for he who tells this tale his business knows. The end of all this dream is very fine; its subject matter is new (renewed). He who shall hear the story from beginning to end quite well will understand the game of love, provided that he will have the patience to await the dream's signification, which I expound in the vernacular language: the truth of it which now is hidden will open itself up to you after you have heard me expound it, for there is not a word of lying in it.]

Admittedly, all this is a matter of conjecture. However, from virtually every point of view this text smacks of the sort of discourse one finds, indeed *expects* to find, at the midpoint of an OF romance narrative. The reader's architectural expectations are satisfied. One is strongly tempted to conclude that Guillaume never intended to write more than the 4058 lines we ascribe to him. What might, then, the "end" (*fin*) of the dream actually be? Not, surely, the harvesting of the rosebud, which does not take place in the narrative. What, instead, does take place is the writing of the romance itself—obedience to Love's injunction *as occasioned by* her who is so worthy to be loved that she "must be proclaimed Rose." This, I believe, is the *fin*, or finality, of the dream, the *senefiance* of which, previously hidden, is now brought out into the open. Like Villon's *Testament*, Guillaume's *Rose* is outwardly circular.[19]

Also, successfully picking the flower does not jibe with the nature of the poetic intentionality that governs the poem. Let me explain. If the Lady who inspires the poet does so because she is worthy of being proclaimed "Rose," the opposite is hardly true—the rosebud itself, or its being plucked, would have brought everything to a dead end. The rose is no Lady, no woman. The flower, like that into which Ovid's Narcissus is metamorphosed as it becomes the symbol of that story, is merely the very passive *object* upon which the twenty-year-old's passionate and self-centered obsessions are caused to fix. It is merely the goal to which one accedes after overcoming a series of more or less serious obstacles (e.g., the thorns that protect it). Meanwhile the Lady, beloved of our twenty-five-year-old poet, who must be proclaimed Rose is *there*; she is a woman, and *as such* understandable to us (in part) thanks to her metaphorical association with the flower. The poet-Lover *sees* in her, in this Lady, the "Rose," because he loves *her*; thus his seeing her is diametrically opposed to his "seeing" the bunch of roses reflected in the Fountain's two crystals, even though "seeing roses" is *ostensibly* common to both instances.

Ovidian Subtextuality and the Mirror [20]

When Ovid's reader contemplates the flower into which Narcissus has been transformed,[21] and when he understands the great pity of this transformation, that flower comes in his mind metaphorically to stand for the passionately narcissistic self-love that arguably represents the greatest possible impediment to love: narcissism is the negative, destructive "mirror-image" of love. Part of the heavy toll levied on vigorous, but immature, young men by Love is precisely the narcissist danger Love exposes them to.

　　The news, however, is not all bad in our poem. The poem is supposed to cheer up our hearts, and it succeeds in doing so, I think. *The Romance of the Rose I* celebrates growth. Just as Chrétien's Perceval learns and understands more, and more perfectly, as his story of successes and failures progresses, until he learns to "read" the three drops of blood on the snow as metaphorically designating the face of the Lady who, thanks perhaps mainly to this act of reading, becomes his Beloved, so our Lover experiences the purification of failure and the problematic relativity of certain kinds of "success." To put the matter briefly, he manages, though with great difficulty and even despair,[22] to learn to handle metaphor—to designate his Lady as Rose, more accurately to see her, and to confer upon her this name because of his forming with her the authentic couple of his romance and life. In other words he *genuinely*, not routinely, articulates his, and, he hopes, *their* love. He sees ("discovers" or "invents") and celebrates the Rose in her. This articulation is the *Art of Love* that, as he says, his poem *contains*, and which, I venture to guess, he would not have been able to formulate had he not chosen to tell the story of his dream-vision. Ovid's Narcissus story thus undergoes a thorough reversal at the hands of "Guillaume de Lorris."

Much more deserves to be said about this reversal, but it is time to conclude. Let me comment upon a few mirrors and upon the OF verb *soi mirer* 'to gaze intently, to look as though into a mirror [at oneself or upon another object]'.[23]

There is no doubt that Ovid's Narcissus sees himself reflected in the water. Although he does not at first realize it, *we* know that he is smitten with his own reflection; the twelfth-century OF Narcissus and the Narcissus of our poet-narrator are also presented in this way. But Guillaume's Narcissus does not *soi mirer*; he sees his own face, nose, and mouth in the water (vv. 1483–84) and believes it to be that of a beautiful *enfant* (vv. 1487–88): his own reflection (*ses ombres*) has betrayed him. When the narrative is repeated in the context of our poet-protagonist's summary of the Fountain's power, the "proud Narcissus" once again "mira sa face e ses iauz vairs" (vv. 1572–73). The Fountain has become "li miroers perilleus," against which there is no sure protection, not even for the "wisest" or for the most "valiant" of men if he chooses to "se mire[r]" in "cel miroer" (v. 1575). The seeds of love sown in the Fountain by Cupid inevitably infect whoever runs the risk of looking in it with a kind of madness (*rage*) that knows no "measure" or "sense." This madness is "d'amer volenté pure" (v. 1586), which I construe to mean 'unbridled desire to love and to possess—physical and mental compulsion, without regard to a choice of the object of love [like an animal in heat]' and which corresponds to Cupid's purpose. This last is, quite simply, to trap as many youths and maidens as he can; Cupid wishes to extend his own power. Who or what one loves is beside the point.

Things turn out badly for Narcissus, or so Guillaume seems to be telling us, because (1) Narcissus had scorned Echo (thereby meriting punishment), and (2) he looked intently into the Perilous Fountain. His seeing himself reflected there, believing the reflection to be that of another, falling in love with that false Other, and his discovery of his error make up the story of the revenge taken upon him. Narcissus is the victim of his self-centered libido. The fact is that the object of his love, himself, as it turns out here, was determined by Cupid (and chance); he had no voice in the matter. Because of the Fountain, all he was interested in was, as it were, indiscriminate amorous self-expression, a particularly virulent form of illness.

Both Ovid and our poet-protagonist point out the falseness of Narcissus's position and the despair that eventually brings about his death.[24] Ovid's Narcissus ironically fulfills the prophecy made by Tiresias to his mother upon his birth: he does, in a way, come to know himself. However, this self-knowledge consists merely in a clear sense of *part of* his predicament. He does not so much bewail his infatuation with himself as he laments his inability to split himself in two, so that corporeally he might possess the Other that he at present imprisons within himself. He regrets the impossibility for him of the *reality* of love, the frustration of his libido. What he loves is, literally, a *mirage*, a mirror effect; the mirror produces an untrue image (the *imago mendax* referred to at the start of this chapter), a false vision. Yet, his passion supports this lie to the very end; he addresses his reflection in these pathetically touching words: "Nunc duo concordes anima moriemur in una" (v. 473) [now we two shall die together in one breath].

At the center of *both* the Ovidian story and *Rose I*, there appears to be an inherent mendacity dwelling in an obsession focused merely on the "shadow," or self-projection, of a nonexistent Other. Narcissus's *imago mendax*—rendered by Guillaume de Lorris as *ses ombres*—shares the falsely objective character Guillaume's lover-protagonist projects upon the rose-bud. Narcissus's disdain of love, it is suggested, brings about his pathetic entanglement in Cupid's nets; it is our protagonist's (at least potentially) empty quest for love (the "mirror image" of Narcissus's disdain) that launches him on a similarly dangerous path. Narcissus is thus predisposed to "misread" the mirror, and *his* misreading conditions the reading performed by our protagonist, creating the likelihood for him of a similarly sterile and lamentable fate. But, because he knows Narcissus's story, he, unlike Ovid's protagonist, is aware of the danger. Narcissus, he tells us, approached the Fountain one day, after hunting, in order to cool off and to quench his thirst (vv. 1470–77); he had no idea of what would happen to him. Our nineteen-year-old would-be lover is thus in a position to reconstruct Narcissus's *imago mendax* into a new and pertinent truth. Of course, he chooses to gaze into the Fountain anyway ("por folie") where he observes the two crystals that, as he puts it, perform just like a mirror (v. 1555), reflecting the entire contents of Déduit's Orchard. His own adventure, as I noted above, will mirror that of Narcissus. Consequently, what he sees and chooses to focus on in the reflection provided by the two crystals, namely the rose bushes "chargiez de roses" (v. 1616), in particular "la graignor tasse" (v. 1622), mirrors—corresponds to—the reflection that came to obsess Narcissus, acquiring in the process the same characteristics of futility and non-Otherness.

The rose undergoes (in the Lover-protagonist's experience of it and as he benefits from Love's teaching) a process of growth which is noted in the poem, as, for example, when the hero obtains a kiss. By this time he has absorbed Love's lessons and has made the acquaintance of his allies (and enemies). This process of growth coincides, I believe, with the rose's slow transformation and feminization.[25] His growing into maturity as the Lover accompanies the flower's becoming increasingly womanlike. This evolution, of course, is a prerequisite for the "happy ending" announced at the start of the poem and for the metamorphosis of the Lover-protagonist into the Lover-poet, as well as for his eventually "seeing" his Lady as worthy of being proclaimed "Rose." However, what we have just observed in respect of the integration of the Narcissus story into that of our poem, its being "mirrored" there and our Lover's "looking intently at himself" *in* Narcissus, acts as an indispensable prelude for the eventual reversal of the Narcissus story *by* our poem. It, and the mirror, underlie the formation of the Couple that the poem celebrates.

Mirrors in early OF literature are at times significantly associated with couples. Space permits here the citing of but two examples. The first is part of the Bride's *planctus* that follows upon the discovery of Saint Alexis's dead body in the Latin *Vita sanctii Alexii*:

> Heu me, quia hodie desolata sum et apparui vidua. Jam non habeo in quem aspiciam nec in quem oculos levem. *Nunc ruptum est speculum meum* et periit spes mea. Amodo coepit dolor qui finem non habet.

> [Alas! For today I have been reduced to desolation, and have taken on the widow's state. No longer do I have him upon whom I might gaze or direct my sight. My mirror has now been broken and my hope has perished. Thus begins the pain that has no end.]

The OF *vie* glosses this passage as follows:

> Ore sui jo vedve, sire, dist la pulcela,
> Ja mais ledece n'avrai, quar ne pot estre,
> *Ne ja mais hume n'avrai an tute terre . . .* (MS L)

["I am now widowed, lord," said the maid. "Never will I have joy, for it is not to be, never will I have a man anywhere on earth . . ."]

MS *P* rather more explicitly stresses the corporealness of the dead Husband: ". . . leece . . . charnel," and, also like MSS *A* and *S*, "charnel home."[26] Alexis has been his Bride's mirror; *speculum* and *charnel home* are equivalent. He was her counterpart in the construct making up their couplehood. His death, she is saying, provokes and confirms her own fragmentation. The case of Chrétien's *Erec et Enide* is even more striking. At the point where Enide is introduced, just before she sees Erec (and he, her) for the first time, the narrator describes her flawless beauty. He goes on to tell us:

Ce fu cele par verité,
Qui fu feite por esgarder;
Qu'an li se poïst an mirer
Aussi com an un mireor.[27]

[In truth she was the woman who was created to be looked upon; for upon her one might gaze as intently as one looks into a mirror.]

Enide was so worth gazing upon that one could look as deeply upon her as one would look into a mirror. In fact: "Erec d'autre part s'esbahi / Quant an li si grant biauté vit" [vv. 448–49: Erec for his part was struck dumb when in her he saw such great beauty]. He immediately falls rapturously in love (and she reciprocates this love); the initial step of their *conjointure* is on the verge of being articulated. She was made to be admired, and one could look at her with the intensity and thoroughness one usually reserves for fixing one's gaze upon a mirror. In the *Vita* that is devoted to him, Alexis is for the Sponsa the mirror that Enide is to Erec in Chrétien's romance. Seeing the Other in the Couple just as one looks at a mirror thus constitutes a high degree of authentic self-knowledge and a key to self-realization, in love. The image reflected upon one by the Other is both perfect and entire.

It is no longer merely a matter of rendering service to Love, according to rules and regulations.[28] Service is rendered to the Other; and in this service, a form of devotion, one's very self is transfigured in conformity with the Other. Like a mirror, the Other absorbs one—one's gaze is assimilated—and, in turn, the Other allows itself to be absorbed. In many respects resembling a poem (which, to use our poet-narrator's phrase, *contains* what "it is about"), the self achieves the highest potential a human being can hope for on this earth, and, with this achievement, it supersedes and vanquishes the isolation—Narcissus's isolation—of unmitigated, childish self-centeredness without abandoning the passion and drive typical of young masculine energy.

I contend, finally, that in Part I of *The Romance of the Rose*, as in certain other thirteenth-century texts (e.g., *The Quest of the Holy Grail*), we possess a striking example of romance narrative illustrating the power of what I have elsewhere called romance *dépassement*. The *Rose* utilizes romance in order to justify romance and, concomitantly, to transcend it. It thematizes untruth, for example, and by glorifying growth it depicts a likely victory of truth. Its rhymed discourse possesses the mysterious truth of dreams. To be sure, the *Rose contains* the whole Art of Love, but by virtue of being the container of this Art, it is necessarily larger than it. No more and no less, Guillaume de Lorris's poem reveals the meanings of romance to *persons*, Man and Woman, at the same time that it discloses *their* meanings thanks to the exemplarity of the individual persons, the poet-Lover and his Lady, who constitute the Human Couple (Martianus Capella's *copula sacra*) that both initiates and closes it, in time and in timelessness. Consequently, it too is a mirror, a mirror quite *intentionally* held up to the romance tradition from which it derives and whose convert truths it opens up, for our pleasure and for our joy.

Notes

1. Quotations from *The Romance of the Rose* are taken from *Le Roman de la Rose par Guillaume de Lorris et Jean de Meun*, ed. Ernest Langlois, 5 vols., Société des Anciens Textes Français (Paris: Firmin Didot/Édouard Champion, 1914–24).

2. Translation by Harry W. Robbins, *The Romance of the Rose by Guillaume de Lorris and Jean de Meun*, ed. Charles W. Dunn (New York: E. P. Dutton, 1962), p. 34. English translations of the *Rose* given in the text are taken from this work; I have at times modified them in the interests of as literal a version as possible. (English-language versions of other texts cited here are my own.)

3. Jean de Meun presents "Guillaume de Lorriz" in a long speech attributed to Amors as the latest in the "lineage" of poet-lovers (starting in antiquity) who have served Venus, at the approximate midpoint of the conjoined texts of Parts I and II of the *Rose*. He is first introduced (v. 10526) as the lover-protagonist of the poem who is victimized by Jalousie. One day, Amors declares, Guillaume will die, and he will construct a beautiful tomb to contain his remains. Then "Johans Chopinel" will be born, at Meung, on the River Loire; he will so love the *romanz* that

"quant Guillaumes cessera, / Johans le continuera" [vv. 10587–88: Where William stops, Jean will continue it].

4. The question of "epigonal" (i.e., post-Chrétien de Troyes) verse romances, dated usually during the first third or so of the thirteenth century, has begun to interest scholars anew. See, for example, Michelle A. Freeman, "*Fergus*: Parody and the Arthurian Tradition," *French Forum* 8, 3 (1983): 197–215.

5. Here is the text of Guillaume's first, or general, Prologue:

> Maintes genz dient que en songes
> N'a se fables non e mençonges;
> Mais l'en puet teus songes songier
> Qui ne sont mie mençongier,
> Ainz sont après bien aparant;
> Si en puis bien traire a garant
> Un auctor qui ot non Macrobes,
> Qui ne tint pas songes a lobes,
> Ançois escrist l'avision
> Qui avint au roi Scipion.
> Quiconques cuide ne qui die
> Que soit folor e musardie
> De croire que songes aveigne,
> Qui ce voudra, por fol m'en teigne;
> Car endroit moi ai je fiance
> Que songes est senefiance
> Des biens as genz e des enuiz;
> Car li plusor songent de nuiz
> Maintes choses covertement
> Que l'en voit puis apertement.
>
> (vv. 1–20)

[Many a man holds dreams to be but lies, all fabulous; but there have been some dreams no whit deceptive, as was later found. Well might one cite Macrobius, who wrote the story of the Dream of Scipio, and was assured that dreams are ofttimes true. But, if someone should say or think 'tis fond and foolish to believe that dreams foretell the future, he may call me a fool. Now, as for me, I have full confidence that visions are significant to man of good and evil. Many dream at night of things covertly that subsequently are seen overtly.]

6. Of course, Macrobius did not "write" (in the modern sense of "compose") *The Dream of Scipio*; OF *escrivre* is not entirely coterminous with MF *écrire*; it means, essentially, 'to perform the physical act of writing, to copy'. Moreover, as Professor David F. Hult helpfully reminds us, the text of Cicero's *De Re Publica*, which contains the "fable" of Scipio's Dream, was available to the Middle Ages only in a highly truncated form (*Self-Fulfilling Prophecies: Readership and Authority in the First "Roman de la Rose"* [Cambridge: Cambridge University Press, 1986],

p. 115). Our poet-narrator may be forgiven for having made an "improper" attribution. Meanwhile, however, Macrobius's *Commentary* fits very nicely into the
sense and compass of *escrivre*.

    7. I am tempted to apply the term "allegory," a word I confess to finding
myself often very ill at ease with, to this process.

    8. The beginning of Chrétien de Troyes' *Conte du Graal* offers a case
in point:

> Ki petit semme petit quelt,
> Et qui auques requeillir velt,
> En tel liu sa semence espande
> Que Diex a cent doubles li rande;
> Car en terre qui riens ne valt,
> Bone semence seche et faut.
> CRESTIENS semme et fait semence
> D'un romans que il encomence,
> Et si le seme en si bon leu
> Qu'il ne puet [estre] sanz grant preu,
> Qu'il le fait por le plus preudome
> Qui soit en l'empire de Rome.

[Who sows little, reaps little, and he who wants to harvest something must
sow his seed in such a place that God return to him two-hundred fold; for in
worthless land good seed dries up and dies. CHRÉTIEN sows and makes
seed of a vernacular story which he here is beginning, and he sows it in so
good a place that it cannot fail to be of great profit, for he is composing it
for the wisest knight to be found in the Empire of Rome.]

Chrétien de Troyes, *Le Roman de Perceval ou le Conte du Craal*, ed. William Roach.
Textes Littéraires Français 71 (Geneva-Paris: Droz-Minard, 1959), vv. 1–12.

    9. Something of this sort happens at the start of Chrétien's *Le Chevalier au
Lion (Yvain)* (ca. 1180). There the narrator states his conviction that the "good old
days" of King Arthur were a time when, unlike those of today, knights and ladies
were genuinely courteous and knew everything about Love. Subsequent events,
we remember, shockingly fail, however, to support this contention of the *Yvain*
narrator.

    10. Macrobius, we recall, was the *auctor* who taught Chrétien de Troyes how
to *descrivre*. See *Erec et Enide*, ed. Wendelin Foerster, *Christian von Troyes, Sämtliche
Werke*. 3. Reprt. (Amsterdam: Éditions RODOPI, 1965), vv. 6736–43; see my "Ver-
nacularization and Old French Mythopoesis, with Emphasis on Chrétien's *Erec et
Enide*," in *The Sower and His Seed*, ed. Rupert T. Pickens, French Forum Monographs 44 (Lexington, KY: French Forum Publishers, 1983), pp. 101–03. Macrobius, especially in regard to applications made of his notion of *narratio fabulosa*,
was second only to Martianus Capella in his contribution to the theoretical elaboration of OF romance and its claims to truth.

    11. The predictive, or omenlike, value of *senefiance* should not be underesti-

mated. The idea of *sign* is involved. This meaning may be found as late as Froissart: "dont on tint che a grant senefiance de bien" (see Karl Bartsch and Leo Wiese, *Chrestomathie de l'ancien français* [*VIIIᵉ–XVᵉ siècles*], 12th ed. [New York: Hafner Publishing Co., 1951], §87b, 102).

12. Confer the "De vidua" attributed to Marie de France, *Fables*, as given by Bartsch and Wiese, *Chrestomathie*, §51d, vv. 37–39: "Par iceste signefiance / pöum entendre quel creance / deivent aveir li mort es vis" [By this sign we can understand what kind of faith the dead may have in the living].

13. Here is the text of vv. 21–44:

> Ou vintieme an de mon aage,
> Ou point qu'Amors prent le paage
> Des juenes genz, couchiez m'estoie
> Une nuit, si con je soloie,
> E me dormoie mout forment;
> Si vi un songe en mon dormant
> Qui mout fu biaus e mout me plot;
> Mais en cel songe onques rien n'ot
> Qui trestot avenu ne soit
> Si con li songes recensoit.
> Or vueil cel songe rimeier,
> Por voz cuers plus faire esgaier,
> Qu'Amors le me prie e comande.
> E se nus ne nule demande
> Coment je vueil que li romanz
> Soit apelez que je comenz,
> Ce est li *Romanz de la Rose*,
> Ou l'Art d'Amors est toute enclose.
> La matire en est bone et nueve;
> Or doint Deus qu'en gré le reçueve
> Cele por cui je l'ai empris;
> C'est cele qui tant a de pris
> E tant est dine d'estre amee
> Qu'el doit estre Rose clamee.

[When I had attained the age of twenty—the age when Love exacts his toll upon young men—as I was wont, one night I went to bed and soundly slept. But then there came a dream which much delighted me, it was so sweet. No single thing which in that dream appeared has failed to find fulfillment in my life, with which the vision well may be compared. Now I'll recount this dream in rhymed verse, to make your hearts more gay, as Love commands and wills; and if any person shall ever ask the name of the romance I am starting, it is the *Romance of the Rose*, and it enfolds within its compass all the Art of Love. The subject is both good and new [renewed]. God grant that she for whom I have undertaken it receive it with favor. She is the one whose worth is such and who so merits being loved that she must be proclaimed Rose.]

14. One is led to wonder, or speculate, as to the resonances of Latin AMORE(M) > OF *ameur* 'rutting, animal mating (or copulation)' upon the elegant Provençalism *amo[u]r* in OF usage. Did there prevail a situation of equivocation analogous to, say, Modern French *baiser*? Tobler-Lommatsch do not document *ameur* (which, however, is fully attested to in the *FEW*, 1, sv. *AMOR*). There is surely a strong presence of what Antoine Thomas (in *Romania* 44, 321) called the "ardeur amoureuse des animaux" in the toll levied upon our lover-protagonist by Amors. One is given to understand that animals practice little discrimination in their choice of partner when they are under the sway of *ameur*; like our nineteen-year-old Lover, they are "turned on."

15. See the Prologue to the *Conte du Graal*, vv. 13–59.

16. *Der Löwenritter (Yvain)*, ed. Wendelin Foerster, *Christian von Troyes, Sämtliche Werke*. 2. Reprt. (Amsterdam: Éditions RODOPI, 1965), vv. 6814–18: Concerning *The Lion Knight* Chrétien thus finishes his romance; I never heard anything more told of it nor will you ever hear anything more about it unless it were to add lies to it.

17. The departure is not entirely complete, however; see n. 28.

18. "Avis m'iere qu'il estoit mais, / Il a ja bien cinc anz ou mais, / Qu'en mai estoie..." [vv. 45–46: I believe that it was in May, a good five years or more ago—that I was in the month of May...].

19. See my "A Note on Villon's Poetics," *Romance Philology* 30, 1, The Jean Frappier Memorial Issue (August 1976): 187–92.

20. Let me declare my indebtedness at this point to the pioneering essay by Michelle A. Freeman, "Problems in Romance Composition: Ovid, Chrétien de Troyes, and the *Romance of the Rose*," *Romance Philology* 30, 1, The Jean Frappier Memorial Issue (August 1976): 158–68.

21. *Metamorphoses*, Bk. 3. Quotations in the present article are taken from *Les Métamorphoses*, ed. Joseph Chamonard. 2 vols. (Paris: Garnier, 1953).

22. The lover-protagonist's despair is echoed in the poet-narrator's commentary on the former's experience of gazing into the two crystals at the bottom of the Fountain of Narcissus: "Las! tant en ai puis sospiré! / Cil miroers m'a deceü. / Se j'eüsse avant coneü / Queus sa force iert e sa vertuz, / Ne m'i fusse ja embatuz, / Car maintenant ou laz chaï / Qui maint ome a pris e traï" [vv. 1608–14: Alas, how often therefore I have sighed! That mirror has deceived me. Had I but known its power and its strength, I would not have approached it with such alacrity, for now I am fallen in the snare which has captured and betrayed many a man].

23. *Soi mirer* is by no means invariably reflexive (i.e., 'to look, gaze, at oneself'), in fact its far more usual meaning is 'to look, gaze intently, single-mindedly'. Mistranslations of this verb have cropped up in scholarly analyses of the *Rose*, for example, Frederick Goldin, *The Mirror of Narcissus in the Courtly Love Lyric* (Ithaca, NY: Cornell University Press, 1967), p. 57, n. 10: "*se mire* [as in *Rose*, v. 1607: *m'i mirai*]...obviously...[means] 'se regarder, se contempler'." The Lover-protagonist did *not* gaze upon himself in the crystals of the Fountain of Narcissus! He stared fixedly into the Fountain and saw, reflected in the Fountain's two crystals, the garden of Déduit.

24. Let us not forget that Narcissus's tale is recounted within the broader context of Juno's wifely jealousy of Jupiter's dalliance with the nymph, Semele, and of the banter between Juno and Jupiter concerning which—the male or the female—derives more pleasure from lovemaking (the question is referred to Tiresias, who is in a position, presumably, to answer). Narcissus's pathetic story constitutes both part of Juno's revenge against the talkative Echo and the answer to the prayers of a male admirer whose love Narcissus had spurned and who had called upon Nemesis for vengeance.

25. By the time the Lover, after absorbing what Amors has taught him, is able (with the assistance of Venus herself) to kiss the Rose, the flower has blossomed into an increased female maturity:

Si con j'oi la rose apressiee,
Un poi la trovai engroissiee,
E vi qu'ele estoit puis creüe
Que je ne l'oi de près veüe;
La rose auques s'eslargissoit
Par amont; si m'abelissoit
Ce qu'el n'iere pas si overte
Que la graine fust descoverte;
Ançois estoit encore enclose
Entre les fueilles de la rose,
Qui amont droites se levoient
E la place dedenz emploient,
Si ne pooit paroir la graine,
Por la rose qui estoit pleine.
Ele fu, Deus la beneïe,
Assez plus bele espaneïe
Qu'el n'iere avant e plus vermeille.

(vv. 3357–73)

[When I approached the Rose, I found it grown a little larger than it was before; a little greater height the bush had gained. But I was pleased that the unfolding flower had not yet spread so as to show the seed, which still was by the petals well concealed, that stood up straight and with their tender folds hid well the grains with which the bud was filled. And, thanked be God, the bud's maturer curves were redder hued and comelier than before.]

26. I have taken these texts from W. Foerster and E. Koschwitz, eds., *Altfranzözisches Übungsbuch*. 6th ed. (Leipzig: Reisland, 1921), and have added the necessary punctuation myself.

27. Vv. 438–41; emphasis mine. Quotations from *Erec et Enide* have been taken from Foerster's above-cited edition.

28. It is interesting to note that in his strictures to the lover-protagonist concerning authentically courtly behavior, Love exemplifies unacceptable discourse by referring to Keu ("Qui jadis par son moqueïz / Fu mal renomez e haïz"); Gauvain,

meanwhile, provides the model of the knight who is "bien apris" (vv. 2091–98). The presence of these "Breton" knights proves that, from Love's point of view, we are indeed in stylish Arthurian romance territory, with all the "vain and pleasant" rules and regulations, and limitations, which that venue implies! Once again our poet's *consciously recognized* debt to Chrétien de Troyes looms large.

Daniel Poirion

3. From Rhyme to Reason: Remarks on the Text of the *Romance of the Rose*

Fascinated by the mirror in the "fountain of Narcissus," critics compete in ingenious attempts to unveil its philosophical implications. The *Romance of the Rose* has thus become a key text for the definition of unhappy self-consciousness. However, this medieval poem teaches us at the same time how to turn away from contemplating an empty consciousness in order to examine those things without which consciousness is nothing: the "malady" induced by analyzing subjectivity should be healed by a healthy dose of objectivity. That which Guillaume de Lorris's text suggests, Jean de Meun's demonstrates explicitly, by multiplying references to concrete objects within his poetic language. There, perhaps, lies an indication of the route to follow in order to return the critical enterprise to common sense.

This attention to "things" leads us back to the problem of editing the text. Fitted into Jean de Meun's book, Guillaume de Lorris's poem reaches us in diverse manuscripts with significant variants that leave us uncertain regarding the authentic version. Jean's "continuation" itself poses few problems, as noted by Félix Lecoy, who edited the joint text.[1] This contrast gives rise to several thoughts. The difficulties begin with the first words, as some manuscripts have: "Aucunes genz dient qu'en songes" [Some people say that in dreams]; and others: "Maintes gents dient que en songe" [Many people say that in dreams]. Editors have rarely paid attention to this divergence that does not change the meaning of the sentence. It is, nonetheless, worth noting, given the importance accorded to the first, often decorated, letter of a manuscript.[2] In addition, it could involve a nuancing of the identification of *songes* [dreams] with *mensonges* [lies]: *aucunes* [some] would here designate people who could be named, and who would have used this maxim, this dictum, like the author of the *Voie de Paradis*, who encloses his allegorical voyage between these two

Translated by Kathy M. Krause

words (vv. 1 and 1028), transforming Raoul de Houdenc's formula from the beginning of the *Songe d'Enfer*: "En songes doit fables avoir" [In dreams one must have fictions]. *Maintes* [many] would refer to a more general saying and not to a citation. The version with *aucunes*, common to the Florence manuscript (Biblioteca Riccardiana 2775) and the Paris manuscript B.N. fr. 1573, owes its value to the latter, which gives us an independent version of Guillaume de Lorris's text, one separated codicologically from the transcription of Jean de Meun's text.[3] The first part is, in fact, transcribed in the first thirty-four folios, that is to say four gatherings plus one additional folio, with Jean de Meun's text starting with a new gathering at folio thirty-five. Thus, paradoxically, manuscript 1573, considered one of the best, provides us with the largest separation of the two authors of the *Romance of the Rose*: the first section was not necessarily revised by the author of the second. Other manuscripts, on the contrary, may demonstrate evidence of such a revision. In addition, such a hypothesis may allow us to establish a semblance of order among the variants without waiting for an exhaustive inventory of the codicological facts, which modern technology allows us to envision.

The split that becomes apparent from the first words grows into an opposition, already noted by Ernest Langlois, between two groups of manuscripts: the first group is headed up by MS B.N. fr. 1573 (H), dating from the end of the thirteenth century, while the second would be represented, in my opinion, by MS B.N. fr. 1559, also from the end of the thirteenth century. If the instances of agreement between these two groups cataloged by Langlois allow a critical edition of Jean de Meun's text to be established with reasonable certainty, no such solution has yet been discovered for the text of Guillaume de Lorris's section. An examination of the variants should be taken up again. Langlois's use of "errors" as criteria, in fact lumping together a heterogeneous mass of MSS in a third group, is ill-founded: one must define the literary aesthetic according to which editorial values are to be established.

Thus certain variants seem to result from a planned transformation of the poetic values first established by Guillaume de Lorris, whether he revised the text himself or whether, as is more probable, a continuator such as Gui de Mori or Jean de Meun himself altered the text that he transcribed before finishing it, taking into account the demands of a different poetics. It is clearly a matter of reconstructing the relationships between two or three different stages of the text, separated from one another by several decades, with the initial stage having been poorly disseminated. However,

in the study of those vestiges that can be spotted amidst the general re-
modeling, we can begin by considering the most stable element, the one
defined by the rhymes. Does not its solidity appear, in contrast with the
instability of the first words, beginning with the poem's opening verses,
with the first rhyme word pair: *songes* / *mensonges* [dreams / lies] which is
reduplicated by the following pair: *songier* / *mensongier* [to dream / to lie]?

The "richness" of the rhymes is a particular sign of poetic language.
For Langlois, who cataloged Guillaume de Lorris's and Jean de Meun's
use of rhyme,[4] "la rime masculine de Jean de Meun est plus riche que celle
de Guillaume de Lorris; elle commence, même avec les monosyllabes et les
noms propres, à la voyelle qui précède la syllabe accentuée"[5] [the masculine rhyme of Jean de Meun is richer than that of Guillaume de Lorris; it
begins even in monosyllables and proper names with the vowel preceding
the accentuated syllable]. We can, in effect, continue from this general
impression and say that in Jean de Meun there exists a tendency to "enrich" the rhyme, using leonine or even equivocal rhymes.

We might thus ask ourselves if this tendency appears in the variants
of those manuscripts where Guillaume de Lorris's text may well have been
submitted to the influence of this phonetic, or graphic, aesthetic of richness. Guillaume does not neglect this resource of rhyme, as we can see
from the first four lines. But in his section richness measured from the
penultimate syllable is not consistently the rule. There is room for a possible "enriching" by the copyist or continuator. Thus an editor of the text
hesitates to choose the "richest" variant; we can even consider it suspect
on account of that very richness, which is potentially an enriching. In this
way, the principle Langlois uses to establish his corrections alternates between the exigencies of logic and those of rhyme. Thus in verses 23–24,
". . . couchier m'aloie / une nuit, si con je souloie" [I lay down one night,
as usual], he corrects *aloie* with *m'estoie* to establish a more rigorous temporal coherence, "impoverishing" the rhyme. On the other hand, in verses
331–332, "il ne li tenoit d'envoisier, / de quaroler ne de dancier" [she had no
part of merrymaking, of caroling nor of dancing] he corrects *dancier* with
baisier [embracing], which improves the rhyme a bit but breaks the figure
of chiasmus created by verse 335: "de dancier ne de quaroler." We cannot,
then, decide on the value of a rhyme without taking into consideration the
respective values of the manuscripts. Langlois does not have any clear ideas
concerning the rhymes. His vocabulary is approximative, and his study
contains several contradictions. In his 1910 study, Langlois states: "Guillaume de Lorris a cherché la rime riche," and he corrects verses 1257–58

(Lecoy 1255–56) "... qu'ele m'ovri / l'uis dou vergier, seue merci," [... that she opened for me the door to the garden, by her grace] with "le guichet dou vergier flori"[6] [the gate of the flowering garden]. The rhyme is better, but one must also consider style ("seue merci" has the appearance of padding, of being there only to rhyme with "ovri" and to fill out the meter) and vocabulary: one might hesitate between "uis" [door] and "guichet" [gate]. For verse 516, the manuscripts are divided between "guichet" and "huisset"; in verses 519 and 575 they use "uis"; in verse 690 it is "le guichet dou vergier ramé" [the gate of the wooded garden]. But what can justify the correction is Jean de Meun's vocabulary, which in verse 20280 (Lecoy 20250) uses: "... du biau jardin quarré / clos au petit guichet barré" [of the lovely square garden, closed with a little barred gate]. This is a true "reading" by Jean de Meun that must be taken into account in classifying the versions of the text.

It must also be admitted, of course, that there are accidental or personal modifications due to the intervention of diverse copyists. But we may suppose the influence of an aesthetic approximating that of Jean de Meun—and that might indeed be his own. It would be characterized by greater dialectic subtlety, more rhetoric, and greater interest in rich rhyme. The versions deriving from this aesthetic transformation finally win out in the manuscript tradition of the fourteenth and fifteenth centuries. But it is already found in the manuscript B.N. fr. 1559, from the thirteenth century, which follows the manuscript B.N. fr. 25523 (published by Garnier-Flammarion), not without referring as well to the other tradition for certain recurrences of a version closer to that of Guillaume de Lorris.

The art of the first author of the *Romance of the Rose* could, thus, be understood by comparing it with other versifiers of the beginning of the thirteenth century. Take for example the other *Roman de la Rose,* that of Jean Renart. It is apparent that he still wrote under the influence of the troubadours, whose art was essentially musical. What is necessary for song is a sonority based on vowels, somewhat like assonance. Rhyme develops through an awareness of the surrounding consonants, starting with poems in medieval Latin and their grammatical homophony. But truly musical poetry does not seek rich rhymes, "ce bijou d'un sou" as Verlaine says. This is apparent in the songs inserted by Jean Renart in his narrative. He rhymes *moutons* [sheep] with *compegnons* [companions] without a second thought, as well as all the infinitives in *-er* with *mer.* As for his own octosyllables, their system is fairly simple: he extends the rhyme to the last accented vowel for feminine (*rose/chose*) as well as for masculine (*romans/chans*) rhyme words. But there are richer rhymes, and to be more precise in our surveys we should indicate the gradations as follows:

feminine:	m	en	s	onges
masculine:	m	a	m	ort
degree:	4	3	2	1

An initial survey of Jean Renart gives us:

feminine 1:	22%	masculine 1:	36%
feminine 2:	12%	masculine 2:	30%

Moving to Guillaume de Lorris we find, in a provisional survey from Lecoy's edition:

feminine 1:	33%	masculine 1:	4%
feminine 2:	20%	masculine 2:	25%
feminine 3:	6%	masculine 3:	10%
feminine 4:	1%	masculine 4:	1%

Compared to Jean Renart, the number of rich rhymes (degree 2 or greater) has doubled. Masculine poor rhymes (degree 1) involve only monosyllables, or suspect cases. Above all, we see that the enriching involves the number of phonemes contained in the rhyme. In Jean de Meun the enriching again doubles, in terms of both the quality of "rimes riches" and the number of phonemes concerned. We have then, with these three texts, three examples, each deriving from a different aesthetic. The verse narrative is evolving toward a more graphic conception of rhyme, toward a "rhetorical" conception of poetry, which will triumph, appropriately, with those poets known as "les grands rhétoriqueurs." But there is another tendency—represented as late as the fifteenth century by Charles d'Orléans—which resists this enriching. Here the lyrical and musical tradition wins out: very rich rhyme is only occasional, rarely exceeding the couplet and never extending itself to an entire stanza (the multiplication of similar rhymes in lyrico-narrative verse does not encourage the use of rich rhymes).

With Guillaume de Lorris we are dealing with an aesthetic in transition between the two schools of lyric and rhetoric. In his work, there are even sequences, groups of verses that form a unit, with proportions analogous to lyric poems. This may have to do with the basic units of poetic creation. The beginning of these sequences, or paragraphs (whose demarcation should be redefined according to the manuscript tradition), is the object of particular care. There the rhymes are particularly rich as in the beginning of the work itself. Similarly, rich rhymes reappear in the closing of these passages. It is in the middle of the passages that the weakening of the rhymes is apparent, and the same holds true for the accumulation of problems posed by the variants, as if scribes had wanted to correct this weakness.[7]

Guillaume de Lorris, however, does not search for rich rhymes. He uses them to adjust the contours, as a figure of rhetoric, which is, in fact, what rhyme is for the rhetoricians. Aside from this, the quality he demands from his rhymes derives from other principles. What in fact strikes the reader in his text is the variety, both of sonority and of vocabulary. If we take, for example, the portrait of the God of Love in lines 863–906 of Lecoy's edition, only one rhyme is reused, in a less rich form:

| 879 / 880 | escuciaus / lionciaus
[little shields / lion cubs] |
| 899 / 900 | oisiaus / rosigniaus
[birds / nightingales] |

In the second case we encounter a well-known motif of lyric poetry, and we find the rhyme word pair appearing in the form of *rosignolez / oiselez* in lines 607–608. It is a lyric ornament, associated with the portrait of the *damoiseau* [young man]. But aside from the insertion of this ornament, the creation of sonority is accomplished by the variety and the unusualness of the rhymes.

In fact, sonority contributes to the impression of beauty, with its nuances of fear or of pain intended by the poet, as at the end of the text attributed to Guillaume de Lorris, with the recurrence of the letter "r" in the majority of the rhymes:

> car j'en sueffre la penitance
> plus grant que nus ne poroit dire.
> Par un poi que je ne fons d'ire
> quant il me menbre de ma perte
> qui est si grant et si aperte;
> si ai poor et desconfort,
> qui me donront, ce croi, la mort.
> N'en doi ge bien avoir poor,
> quant je sai que losengeor
> et traïtor et envieus
> sont de moi nuire curieus?
>   (vv. 4008–18)

[for I suffer a greater penance for it than anyone could tell. I almost melt with anger when I remember my loss, which is very great and apparent. And I experience fear and pain which will, I think, cause my death. Should I not indeed be afraid when I know that slanderers and envious traitors are eager to harm me?]

Since we are considering these aspects of a poetics of rhyme, it is appropriate to note (in addition to the overall effects perceptible in these sequences or units) the semantic association of words joined by rhyme, which creates true poetic syntagms where the most proud aesthetic intention is inscribed. Thus the poetic commentary on the words *demoisiaus / oisiaus* in verses 817–18 comes in the following passage, which was discussed just above. In that commentary the entire atmosphere of Oiseuse's garden and all its symbolism are summarized, deepening the significance of the ornamental topos of "lyric joy." Certain verbal associations, such as this one, are inherited from tradition and reproduce traditional stylistic effects. Thus the pair *cote / mignote* evokes the atmosphere of dance songs while *courtois / serventois* comes from a more elevated style, and *melodie / reverdie* refers us to a specific genre. We can note, then, that the lyric insertions in the first *Romance of the Rose*, that of Jean Renart, belong among these elliptical references, in the form of sonorous echos.

Associated with this lyric intertextuality are other references: the pair *vermeilles / merveilles* (vv. 1403–04) recapitulates the symbolism of Chrétien de Troyes. Other associations derive more generally from the aesthetic of the twelfth century, such as *brune* / *lune* / *estoilles* / *chandailles* from verses 995–98, in a passage which displeased Gui de Mori, according to the manuscript Copenhagen G.K.S. 2061-4°. Exotic images reinforce the description of a *table* / *delitable* (vv. 1343–44) before other, more domestic ones, appear. Thus, throughout the passage, odd rhymes are sought out: *guernades* / *malades*, *mugades* / *fades*, *espice* / *ricalice*, *novele* / *canele* [seeds / sick, nutmeg / tasteless, spice / licorice, new / cinnamon (vv. 1329–42)], *domesches* / *pesches*, *gros* / *fos*, *fresnes* / *chesnes* [domestic / peaches, large / beeches, hazel / oak (vv. 1345–58)]. The association of words by rhyme replaces discourse (which would establish a logical relationship), as with the *faintes* / *saintes* [feigned / saints], the *escrites* / *hypocrites* [written / hypocrites (vv. 423–24, 405–04)] that represent the figures painted on the wall of the garden, and which Jean de Meun will remember when he reconstructs the discourse and the dramatic developments suggested by these lexical signs. The pair *escritures* / *pointures* [inscriptions / paintings (vv. 133–34)] truly characterizes allegorical description, associating written poetry with painting, which already has a positive aesthetic connotation: "il resembloit une pointure / tant estoit biaus et acesmez" [he ressembled a painting, he was so handsome and full of grace (vv. 810–11)]. The rhyme in *-ure* is like a leitmotif in the text, the musical key of a poetry whose rhyming lexicon contains sixty or so words in *-ure*, such as *creature*, *aventure*, *nature*, *dure*, *ardure*. We will find this tonality again in Jean de Meun with, according to Langlois's inventory (p. 179), 142 rhymes in *-ure*, *urent*, *ures*. This is truly the signature of the allegorical poem. It is there that the symbolism that the twelfth century had bestowed upon image-objects, and which is now reduced by grammatical alchemy to a relationship between sounds and letters, finds its place in a narrative setting.[8]

In passing, it is appropriate to note the discriminatory function filled by the enriching of the rhymes in the case of suffixes or verb endings. These categories could involve tedious lists of words rhyming in *-er*, in *-ir*, or in *-ent*, for example, which would deprive the word-groupings of any value. Rich rhymes, on the other hand, because they include the root, establish subsets which emphasize the full range of associations between words: *florir* / *morir*, *loisir* / *desir* [to flower / to die, leisure / desire]. This strengthens the symbolic function of rhyme, which was to be lost with the lyric poets of the fifteenth century (though it was then that the entire allegorical construction of the poem was again to be charged with concrete symbolism).

We could thus reformulate the definition of literary art on the basis of the limited but highly significant feature of poetic rhyme. This would not be a simple enterprise, since it would have to take into account some rather subtle effects: everything depends on nuance. But there are some convincing details. Thus, the generative rhyme, the master-rhyme that defines the theme and represents the symbol of Guillaume de Lorris's book, is, indeed, the rhyme *rose* / *enclose* of verses 37–38. It links to the natural and geometric symbol of the desired body the closure inherent in hermeticism: an art of love and an art of writing simultaneously. This involves both echoing and modulating Jean Renart's formula, "en cestui Romans de la Rose / qui est une novele chose" [in this Romance of the Rose / which is a new thing (vv. 11–12, ed. Lecoy)]. The copyists took up Guillaume's phrase to designate the work as a whole, for example in the *explicit* of the Yale manuscript number 592, folio 175, "explicit le Rommant de la Rose / ou l'art d'amours est toute enclose" [here ends the Romance of the Rose / where the art of love is completely enclosed]. The story that it tells is defined by the encounter with the enemies of desire who have succeeded in *enclosing* the rose. In similar terms, Jean de Meun alludes to Jealousy, who has caused the roses to be enclosed (vv. 3593–94), as he foretells the future break-in: "si porrez lors cuillir la rose / ja si fort ne l'avront enclose" [then you will be able to cut the rose no matter how strongly they have enclosed it (vv. 8225–26, Langlois 8255–56)]. And it is well known that Guillaume de Lorris's text ends with the image of this enclosure, inside Jealousy's castle:

> Je n'oi bien ne joie onques puis
> que Bel Acueil fu em prison,
> que ma joie et ma guerison
> est toute en li et en la rose
> qui est entre les murs enclose.
>   (vv. 3966–70)

[I experienced neither happiness nor joy ever since Fair Welcome was put into prison, for my joy and my cure are entirely in him and in the rose that is enclosed within the walls.]

This is the hostile aspect of the citadel, to which the idea of intimate shelter is opposed: "qu'encor ai ge ou cuer enclose / la douce savor de la rose" [I still have enclosed in my heart the sweet fragrance of the rose

(vv. 3759–60)]. This leitmotif of imprisoning, of closure, leads us to doubt that Guillaume wanted to leave his work open or unfinished. The meaning and the destiny of passion tended toward closure: the idea of the death of the poet, advanced by Jean de Meun, substitutes an anecdotal ending for the logical ending of the narrative; but Jean will himself effect narrative closure at the end of a long process of unveiling. With Guillaume, rhyme is the instrument of a hermetic aesthetic, it is a result of the poetic research in which certain troubadours who practiced the *trobar clus* were engaged. By substituting for the idea of closure that of *glose* [gloss] in order to rhyme with *rose*, however, Jean de Meun returns to the *trobar leu*.

Let us return now to the problem of establishing the text. Lecoy was right to prefer the manuscript that he edited, but he did not specify the problems inherent in that version—certainly one of the oldest—on account of various weaknesses, notably in the transcription of rhyme words. Langlois was right to attempt to resolve these difficulties, but he did so using a very debatable principle of scribal error. His classification of the manuscripts suffers from this weakness. Even in his critical treatment of key passages like the enumeration of the guardians of the roses (who numbered three or four depending on the version [vv. 2835–67]), Langlois does not see the reasons that might lead, in the context of another aesthetic, or another reading, to the initial choice of three guardians, before the intervention of Fear, who is not yet a personification in verse 3032. The same holds for the version that substitutes one crystal for the two seen in the Fountain of Narcissus (though here we are dealing with objects rather than images). We must reconsider these divergences in light of the hypothesis we formulated in our study of the rhymes. Guillaume de Lorris's text underwent two types of transformation, one banal, corresponding to the habits of copyists, and which Langlois analyzes fairly well; the other, specific to this work and tied to the evolution of taste, in terms of its *reception* by succeeding generations. It is unlikely that Guillaume reworked a text that he appears not to have finished. But we discover two stages of modernization through the enriching of the rhymes and through the modification of the meaning of certain passages. One stage (represented in MS B.N. fr. 1559) seems anterior to Jean de Meun, and may be tied to the intervention of Gui de Mori; the other would be the result of Jean de Meun himself, whose textual legacy was however revised by copyists who had at their disposal the earlier version transmitted in MS B.N. fr. 25523.

If we reconsider the question of variants from this perspective, it becomes clear that we must not search systematically for the version that gives us the rich rhyme, but for the one whose meaning agrees with what we know of the text as a whole, and of the signifying function of rhyme. We can even distinguish between the vocabulary of Guillaume and that of Jean de Meun, even though they both come from the same region. Thus Guillaume is astounded at the departure of the God of Love because he does not know how the god has left, "...je ne soi mot / que il se fu esvanouiz; / et lors je fui mout esbahiz [I could not say a word before he vanished: and I was then quite astonished (Lecoy, vv. 2750–52)]. Langlois corrects this according to another version: "si en fui mout essaboïz" [then I was greatly stupefied (v. 2768)]. A little further on Guillaume is "tot esbaïz" (v. 2936) at the departure of Bel Acueil, and Langlois again corrects the text: "Lors s'en est Bel Accueil foïz, / E je remés essaboïz" [Then Fair Welcome fled, and I remained stupefied (vv. 2951–52)]. In the two cases the correction improves the rhyme (which passes from degree 1 to degree 2), but in doing so it reintroduces an uncommon word which had been used by Jean de Meun in verse 20553 with regard to paradise where the sun's rays do not dazzle the eyes of those who look at it:

> que de cestui soleill li rai
> ne troblent pas ne ne retardent
> les euz de ceus qui les regardent
> ne ne les font essabouir
> mes ranforcier et resjouir.
>   (vv. 20550–54)

[the rays of that sun do not harm or weaken or dazzle the eyes of those who look at them, but they strengthen and delight.]

It is Jean de Meun, or one of his copyists, who would have reintroduced this term into Guillaume de Lorris.[9] The placing of Guillaume's text into that of Jean de Meun has thus led to all sorts of transformations at the level of textual detail, and the manuscripts indicate the history of these transformations.

And now, what does Narcissus see in the fountain? The *figure* [figure (v. 1485)] or the *faiture* [form] (MS B.N. fr. 25523) of a child "bel a demesure" [lovely to excess]? In this variant two aesthetics are opposed: on the one hand, the aesthetic of the geometric *figure*, which the mirror reflects, in all its purity:

ausi con li mireors montre
les choses qui sont a l'encontre
et i voit l'en sanz coverture
et lor color et lor figure.

(vv. 1553–56)

[Just as the mirror shows things that are in front of it, and one sees there without cover both their colors and their shapes.]

This is Guillaume de Lorris's aesthetic, the aesthetic of a Platonically conceived nature. As for the *faiture*, on the other hand, we recognize the work of the artisan, of the artist, whose myth is the story of Pygmalion that Jean de Meun will recount in order to oppose it to that of Narcissus.[10] Guillaume de Lorris knew the word *faiture*. He uses it in verse 159 precisely to characterize the work of the artist, painter and sculptor, who made the *images* (painted statues) seen on the wall of Déduit's garden. He does not use it to designate natural beauty. It is Jean de Meun who wants us to glimpse, in Narcissus' reflection, the *faiture* of the woman sculpted by Pygmalion: another aesthetic, the one whose influence on the text and iconography of Guillaume de Lorris's part serves to justify the belated unity of the text, defined by the subtle analysis of certain critics. But we should free the originality of the first 4028 verses from this illusory unity, which is due to the reworking of the text: Guillaume's is an originality that is amply demonstrated by a careful study of the rhymes, whose beauty is in no sense illusory.

Notes

1. Guillaume de Lorris and Jean de Meun, *Le Roman de la Rose*, ed. Félix Lecoy, vol. 1. Classiques Français du Moyen Âge 92 (Paris: Champion, 1965), pp. xxxv–xliii.

2. Thus the first page of the Yale manuscript number 592 (dated 1446) develops the two curves of the letter M, very ornately, in two scenes showing Guillaume lying down and Guillaume washing his hands, under two arches of the same curve.

3. Ernest Langlois, *Les Manuscrits du "Roman de la Rose": description et classement* (Lille: Tallendier / Paris: Champion, 1910), pp. 29–32.

4. *Le Roman de la Rose par Guillaume de Lorris et Jean de Meun*, ed. Ernest Langlois, vol. 1, Société des Anciens Textes Français (Paris: Firmin-Didot, 1914), pp. 55–184.

5. Langlois, 1914, p. 58.

6. Langlois, 1910, p. 264, p. 334.

7. See also the units constituted by vv. 1–20, 21–44, 45–102, 129–28, etc. In this context, let us note, at the beginning of a sequence characterized overall by fairly poor rhymes, the following series of rich rhymes (with only one poor rhyme among them): *escrite / hypocrite, apelee / recelee, garde / coarde, marmiteus / piteus, criature / aventure* (vv. 405–14).

8. See Daniel Poirion, *Résurgences: mythe et littérature à l'âge du symbole* (Paris: PUF, 1986).

9. See Tobler-Lommatzsch, *Altfranzösisches Wörterbuch* (Wiesbaden: Franz Steiner Verlag), p. 1283. There is a variant, *esbloïr*, in verse 20553.

10. Daniel Poirion, "Narcisse et Pygmalion dans le *Roman de la Rose*," in *Essays in Honor of Louis Francis Solano*, ed. Raymond J. Cormier and Urban T. Holmes (Chapel Hill: University of North Carolina Press, 1970), pp. 153–65.

Part II

Reading the *Rose*:
Jean de Meun

John V. Fleming

4. Jean de Meun and the Ancient Poets

My subject is Jean de Meun and the ancient poets—the great poets of Latin antiquity—and I approach this subject in what I take to be the spirit of this volume, a volume dedicated to *re*thinking the *Roman de la Rose*. There are many questions concerning the poem, including in my opinion a number of the most important ones, which are not yet ripe for *re*thinking for the simple reason that they have never been much thought about in the first place, but this is hardly true of the subject of what is usually called Jean de Meun's "classicism." Even before the poem received its great modern edition, the editor, Ernest Langlois, had established in his preliminary study of the *Origines et sources du Roman de la Rose* (1890) a number of the basic assumptions that have directed investigations of Jean's debt to the antique past. Among these assumptions are the following three. First, that Jean's poem is radically vernacular in its aspirations, a work of *vulgarization* midway between the English and the French connotations of that word. Second, that it is fundamentally encyclopedic in nature. Third, that—how to put it—Jean de Meun did not have a poetic bone in his body.

I have formulated these assumptions in unsubtle or intentionally facetious form because it is in unsubtle or unintentionally facetious form that they have often directed the scholarly pursuit of Jean's "humanism." I shall not pursue an extensive review of the criticism of the *Roman*, nor indeed make specific examination of the work of individual scholars, but it does seem to me potentially useful to begin *re*thinking our subject by questioning these assumptions, or by at least drawing attention to certain intellectual infelicities that may follow from their plenary acceptance. I say "plenary acceptance" in speaking of these three assumptions because there is probably general scholarly recognition that these assumptions, including the third, contain a certain amount of truth in each of them. I take it that the task of the *re*thinker should be to explore these "limitations" rather than to applaud adequacies and to subject the tried and true to retrial upon appeal. Such, at any rate, is the premise behind my own essay.

At first blush the assumption of the *vernacular* status of the *Roman de la Rose* hardly needs defense. The poem is, indisputably, written in the French language. Furthermore Jean's literary career, as defined by himself in the elegant, extensive, and self-conscious passage in the prologue to the *Boece*, is that of a vulgarizer, a translator from the learned to the lay tongue. These are, certainly, facts, but facts of a different order that even before Langlois's time had become rather unusefully confused.

What I suggest is that it is one thing to write in a vernacular language, but quite another to be a vernacular writer—that is, one whose artistic vision is substantially controlled by an extant body of vernacular literature. One of the things I find most remarkable in Jean's poem when one compares it with a broad spectrum of French compositions from the *romans d'antiquité* of the twelfth century to the poetic doxographers of the mid-fifteenth is precisely its studied reluctance to enroll itself in the vernacular tradition implicit in Guillaume's poem. Jean de Meun cites by name or transparent allusion several dozen literary authorities, including many poets, and all of them, with a single exception to which I shall in a moment return, are *auctores*, which is to say *Latin* writers.

This phenomenon by no means necessarily goes with the turf. One of the few genuine antecedents of the *Roman de la Rose* as a serious philosophical and theological poem in the form of a vernacular allegory is the *Tornoiement Antichrist* of Huon de Meri. Though little read today, it was possibly known to Guillaume de Lorris and certainly known to Jean de Meun.[1] For all his considerable conceptual and poetic crudity, Huon shared with the authors of the *Roman de la Rose* the worthy ambition of pursuing the distinctively Christian mode of literary allegory in "romance," which is to say in French.

What interests me most in the present inquiry is the nearly embarrassing way in which Huon tries to make his poem what it is not and never could be, namely, a chivalric fiction in the tradition of Chrétien de Troyes. Huon starts out in the forest of Broceliande—at the magic fountain from *Yvain*, to be precise—and never quite manages to make it home to the *Psychomachia* of Prudentius. Jean de Meun, on the other hand, studiously leaves us with the impression that the only books he has ever read in French are his own translations and the truncated essay of Guillaume de Lorris. To take Jean de Meun seriously is to humor his implicit claim to be a classical writer who happens to write in the vernacular, like Dante Alighieri of the *Divine Comedy* or Geoffrey Chaucer of *Troilus and Criseyde*, to mention two of his soul mates, the one a possible, the other a certain imitator.

Rethinking the second assumption, namely, that the design of Jean's

Roman is fundamentally encyclopedic, is a briefer exercise only because the implications of the assumption for Jean's classicism are more sharply obvious. If the *Roman* is ordered according to a principle of eclectic inclusiveness, it should follow that no particular priority can be assigned to the materials present in the poem. Virgil, Horace, and Ovid are to some extent present in the *Roman de la Rose* in the same way that optics, meteorology, and political philosophy are there—as parts of an *omnium gatherum* of liberal education. But since *everything* is there, there can be no special significance to any one particular thing. It is still often said that what Jean meant by the proposed title *Miroër aus Amoreux* was an encyclopedic "Mirror of Love," a vernacular *speculum* that systematically dealt with all aspects of love as that subject was understood in the western Middle Ages. I fear that I myself have said that in the past.

The virtue of the encyclopedic assumption has been that it offers comfort to the reader faced with the exasperations of nearly ten thousand couplets of less than inexorably structured poetry: Such and such is here because *everything* is here. But the assumption also has serious deficiencies, the chief of which is that *everything* is *not* in the poem. For example, vast chunks of the introductory liberal arts curriculum are not there. Far from being a complete encyclopedia of love, Jean's poem fails to touch upon entire topics that are *de rigeur* in real medieval encyclopedias of love, which exist in fairly impressive number. I have in mind such topics as sexual physiology, the "degrees" of love, secular or profane, the theology of marriage, or those aspects of the sociology of sexual love in which Andreas Capellanus invests such interest and effort. I conclude from this that Jean's "use" of the Latin poets is more likely to have an individual rather than a general significance, and that his poetic strategies are probably better understood by an examination of discrete instances of textual citation and allusion than by a general field theory of encyclopedic intention.

Finally I come to the idea that Jean is after all not much of a *poet*—as opposed, perhaps, to a satirist, a misogynist, a sensualist, a sexual communist, or a political utopian—the list could go on. We should note two things about this assumption. The first is that it has often been as friendly to Jean as it has been hostile. That is, it has often been advanced or harbored by readers who have applauded Jean's perceived modernism, his perceived materialism, and his perceived secularism. The second is that it has grown out of an intellectually dubious critical procedure, recognized as such at least as early as the time of Pierre Col, and that is the positivist identification of the historical and empirical Jean de Meun with the agenda of various fictional *personae* in his poem.[2]

So far as my own argument is concerned, the aspect of the assumption most in need of rethinking pertains to Jean's sensitivities as a *reader* of poetry rather than as a *writer* of poetry. Jean's poetic abilities, or lack thereof, have inevitably been discussed in the critical tradition in terms of his relationship with Guillaume de Lorris. Since Jean is widely supposed to have been an "anti-Guillaume," one way of characterizing his poetic achievement has been to do so in terms of a schedule of antitheses. Guillaume is subtle and courtly, Jean crude and bourgeois. Guillaume is spiritual and ambiguous, Jean earthy and direct. I have no wish to beat this horse further, but I do want to make the point that, contrary to what might be the belief of many serious readers of the poem, the horse is not yet dead. It remains a fundamental assumption of a good deal of writing about the *Roman de la Rose* that Jean de Meun's enterprise rests squarely upon a fundamental and gross misreading, whether intentional or unintentional, hostile or indifferent, of the poem of Guillaume de Lorris. The implications of such an assumption for the purposes of this chapter are serious though oblique, indeed often merely implicit. The chief of them is that we can hardly look to Jean for a more defensible reading of Virgil or Ovid than of Guillaume de Lorris.

I propose, for the purposes of "rethinking" the *Roman de la Rose*, three tentative modifications, or perhaps even anti-assumptions, that might usefully guide future study of Jean's commerce with the ancient poets. The first is that Jean considers himself to a considerable and quite self-conscious degree to be a translator working in the classical tradition rather than a romance *poet* augmenting a vernacular corpus. The second is that Jean's inclusion of specific classical materials within his poem is in general less satisfactorily explained by encyclopedic ambition than by definite and local intellectual intention. The third is that Jean was a careful and gifted reader of poetry—by which word he himself would primarily have understood *Latin* poetry—and that we may expect his classicism to reveal a certain amount of intellectual subtlety and not merely the random pillage described by Ernest Langlois.

In my most recent book on the *Roman de la Rose, Reason and the Lover*, I tried to lay the foundations of a double argument concerning Jean's preoccupations with the Latin classics of pagan and Christian antiquity. One strand of the argument relates to the third anti-assumption just formulated: that Jean de Meun was a careful reader of antique Latin texts, and that he brought to them much more than the mere antiquarian appetites of the "medieval humanist" of conventional literary history. Specifically, he brought to them a considerable degree of cultural sensitivity and contextual understanding. My second argument is that he actually takes as a principal poetic theme the moral and poetic relationship between the pagan past and the Christian present. Once again I would point to a fundamentally analogous enterprise, only superficially masked by conspicuously differing stylistic visions and generic options, in Dante's *Commedia* and Chaucer's *Troilus*—the latter of which bears the stains of its happy contagion by Jean's poem on its every page. That relationship as posited by the great Christian humanist poets of the Middle Ages, among whom in my opinion Jean deserves not merely a place but a place of pride, was a particularly complex one, involving on the one hand the sincere submission of the Christian poet before an artistic achievement he could hardly dream of rivaling and on the other an equally sincere moral superiority of the farther-seeing dwarf on the back of the giant.

So much by way of conceptual framework. The questions posed are large ones, and however they are to be resolved they would demand a kind of protracted attention far beyond the scope of the present chapter. While I do indeed hope to turn to them in a larger work in progress, my current agenda must be far more limited, local, and specific, though I hope validly relevant to the prevailing ethos of Jean's *Roman*. What I want to suggest is the manner in which two classical poets provided Jean de Meun with the central intellectual tension of his poem, and to offer some readings from a third representative of others who offered him occasional elegant emblems of literary iconography. The major models are Ovid and Boethius; the supporting role will be Virgil's.

The one vernacular poet mentioned by Jean de Meun is, of course, Guillaume de Lorris. As students of the *Roman de la Rose* we should remind ourselves, whenever considering certain fundamental questions about Guillaume de Lorris, such as whether in point of fact he ever existed, that Jean de Meun's single reference to him makes up his entire biographical dossier. All we know or can ever know about Guillaume is that, roughly in the middle of the *Roman*, the God of Love, in a passage that elaborately imitates the ninth elegy of the third book of Ovid's *Amores*, bewails the demise of Guillaume and finds consolation in the prophecy of the advent of Jean de Meun, destined to complete Guillaume's unfinished work, a work that is coterminously a poem and a seduction.

There is nothing in this reference except the implied presence of Guillaume's text that would make the reader guess that Guillaume is a vernacular poet. On the contrary, he is catalogued as the fifth in a list of well-known Latin elegists beginning with Tibullus, including Gallus and Catullus, and ending with the greatest of them all, Ovid. Ovid is the fourth, Guillaume himself the fifth. As another scholar has pointed out, Jean de Meun here seems to be inventing the topos of the first-person poetic voice who places himself sixth in the poetic academy—a topos most famously exemplified in the fourth canto of the *Inferno*.[3]

Among the several implications of the fact that Jean de Meun first assigns to "Guillaume de Lorris" and then to himself the first-person voice of Ovidian erotic pseudoautobiography are two of particular interest. The first and more obvious is that Jean unquestionably understood Guillaume's own Ovidian gesture in offering a kind of creative imitation of the *Ars amatoria*:

> ce est li *Romanz de la Rose*,
> ou l'art d'Amors est tote enclose.
> La matire est et bone et nueve . . .
> (vv. 37–39)

[this is the *Romance of the Rose*, where the art of Love is completely enclosed. The material is both good and new . . .]

Within the context of thirteenth-century literary culture, the phrase "art of love" has to be a sharp allusion rather than a vague commonplace, and Guillaume, with his insistence that his material is "new," is true to the third of D. A. Russell's elegantly stated laws of creative imitation in classical literature: he will make the ancient work his own.[4] A second implication will perhaps be less obvious, except to scholars who have spent time with the copious medieval *scholia* to Ovid's erotic poetry. The latter presented the pseudo-autobiographical voice of the *Roman* as what was usually called an *amator fatuus*—a *foolish* lover. This is of course the technical term rendered into French as *fol amoureux* by the defenders of Jean de Meun at the time of the Quarrel.

How did Jean set out to pursue an "Ovidian" art of love? In 1977 a scholar named Thérèse Bouché published an article, which unfortunately has apparently been lost in the great bibliographical sea, entitled simply "Ovide et Jean de Meun."[5] This excellent essay, a work of good old-fashioned positivist French philology, is innocent of any interpretive claims or, for that matter, of any particular interest in interpretation. What Bouché did was simply—not that such an achievement is really simple—

collate the text of Jean de Meun's *Roman* with the pages of the *Ars amatoria* of Ovid. Her results, codified in a convenient table at the end of the article, are extremely enlightening. In the first place, Jean de Meun turns out to be more Ovidian by several miles than Guillaume de Lorris if we judge such things by specific textual parallels, of which Bouché found well over a hundred, many of them extensive.

Three of Bouché's other findings, however, seem to me even more important. I summarize them briefly as follows. (1) There is a definite dramatic structure in the erotic dialogues of Jean's poem, a structure that Bouché actually analyzes in terms of its three "acts" and its subordinate "scenes." (2) There is systematic correlation between Jean's doxographic narrative voices and the three books of the *Ars*; that is, all the best lines in Amis's long speech come from the first two books of the Ars, and they do so in sequential order. Jean's verses 7400 through 7700 in the *Roman* correspond to Ovid's first book, verses 7700 through 10000 to his second. The best lines in the long speech of la Vieille, who is very insistently a woman, come from Ovid's third book, the woman's book. (3) Jean rarely alters Ovid's sense, but he does subject it to a kind of cultural *aggiornamento*, placing the advice within the context of a recognizably medieval as opposed to antique social setting. One obvious example has to do with slaves, a group from whom Ovid frequently recruits his knowing go-betweens. Slaves did not exist in thirteenth-century Paris and had to be replaced by various kinds of courtly "familiars."

Like many fine literary demonstrations, this one seems rather obvious once it has been made; although there is nothing in it very surprising, there is much in it that is *bone et nueve* for our understanding of Jean's larger design. My one criticism of Bouché's work is that it approaches Ovid's *Ars amatoria* from the vantage point of a modern classicist rather than from that of a medieval reader of Ovid. In the school-tradition of the twelfth and thirteenth centuries, the three books of the *Art of Love* were generally taken to be incomplete without a fourth—the book that Ovid had published separately under the title of the *Remedia amoris*. In that work the pseudoautobiographical "Ovid" turns to sexual passion as a genuinely serious physical and mental pathology and offers practical poetical medicaments for its relief and cure. It was the four-book "art" that gained a permanent place in the copious medieval antimatrimonial and antierotic library. We see its trace in the structure of Andreas's *De amore*, and we actually find it bibliographically present in Jankyn's "Book of Wykked Wyves."

Whatever else Guillaume's stated intention of supplying the *whole* art of love (*tote*) might imply, it had to imply the presence of the antieroticism of the *Remedia*. And that is precisely what Jean de Meun supplies with such imaginative originality in the cardinal presence of his character Reason and in his persistently ironic manipulation of his erotic plot. The devices used to supply the wanting remedial Ovid from Guillaume's text are many, but the most original and satisfying is his introduction into the poem of perhaps the greatest poet of Christian antiquity, Boethius. I hope that in light of the wide variety of often brilliant work recently done on Boethius I may simply state, rather than elaborately argue, the fact of the *Consolatio*'s essentially poetic character.[6]

So far as Jean's literary strategy was concerned, the *Consolation of Philosophy* was the absolutely indispensable catalytic agent that could make the subject of Ovidian eroticism both philosophically and morally weighty. Here was the Christian criticism of the false goods of "love," a criticism powerfully advanced not in terms of a biblical theology but in terms of the most venerable traditions of pagan moral philosophy, a book so apparently pagan in its assumptions and procedures that several distinguished scholars have denied that its author could possibly have been a Christian. Jean had no such doubts, of course; but in inviting his readers to make moral adjudications within the world of the *Roman*, his implicit appeal is not in the first instance to the Pentateuch or to Pennyfort but to Socrates and to Cicero. Thus he needs must inscribe within his own book the book of Boethius, and this he does with panache as well as with reverence.

Jean was the pioneer whose invention, as obvious and even as crude as it must now seem when compared with, for example, Chaucer's refinement of it in the *Troilus*, alone offered an accessible path to his desired end: a fiction responsive both to the demands of the historical imagination and to the impulses of the socially responsible moralist, a fiction that could transform the problem of the disjunctions of ancient and modern, pagan and Christian, into a central poetic theme. Jean had inherited, in the poem of Guillaume de Lorris, a major if incomplete monument of thirteenth-century Ovidiana, a work in which the author did his best to maintain the façade of an allegorical world secular and erotic to its core, in which the only social concerns were those supplied by Ovidian decorum or stratagem (such as the way lovers should behave) and the only history was Ovidian history (such as the story of Narcissus). Guillaume's thirteenth-century Christian culture is, of course, the very backdrop against which his Ovidian miming was played out, but throughout his poem it maintains the courteous unobtrusiveness of the obvious.

Things are very different with Jean de Meun, for among the many differences between the two parts of the *Roman*, Jean's vast increment of ambition is conspicuous. What has usually been taken by scholars to be his critique of Guillaume de Lorris is more accurately described, in my view, as his critique of Ovid, or rather of one voice of Ovid, the deadpan pedagogue of the *Ars amatoria*, the book that Guillaume had explicitly identified as the model for his own enterprise. Jean's first and most powerful move is to subject this "Ovid" to the scrutiny of Boethius, which is the effect of the long dialogue between Reason and the Lover that begins Jean's continuation of the poem. He thus examines sexual love from the perspective of a Boethian analysis, treating love as one of the goods of Fortune. The literary possibility here exploited was already explicit in the *Consolatio* itself, in the second prose of the third book, and it had found embryonic development in the Latin school poetry of the twelfth century. From the introductory portrait of Reason in the *Roman de la Rose*, a portrait that conflates scriptural Wisdom with Boethian Philosophy, we may licitly deduce that Guillaume de Lorris himself was entirely aware of it, as Chrétien, among others of his vernacular forebears, had been before him. But to Jean de Meun must go the credit, or perhaps the blame, of being the impressario who arranged the pugilistic contest between Love and Reason that was to be the main event in a good deal of European erotic poetry until the time of Shakespeare's sonnets and beyond.

For Jean as for his readers, Boethius was a Christian theologian of nearly unimpeachable authority, the most happily literary of the Fathers of the Church, even if he had chosen to write his *Consolatio* not as a dogmatic theologian but as a "philosopher," a lover of wisdom. Jean could thus internalize within his poem the Christian corrective to Ovidian erotic doctrine, and he did so in a manner decorously appropriate for a poem ruled over by the Ovidian deities, Venus and Cupid. Boethius had written a book in which the moral theology of the Christians was submerged in the wisdom of the antique philosophers, a book that made obligatory claims not merely on the baptized but on all men endowed with reason. Jean transposed its claims to the Ovidian never-never land of Guillaume's dreamscape. Amant, vassal to Cupid and votary to Venus, is nowhere held accountable for his ignorance of the book of Leviticus or the Epistle to the Galatians; but he is repeatedly and schematically lampooned for his unwillingness to accept the literary lessons of Lady Reason, a guide as highly esteemed by the pagan world of Socrates or Cicero as by the Christian world of Thomas Aquinas.

Another feature of the *Consolation of Philosophy* that Jean must have prized was the fashion in which Boethius had appropriated in lyric expression a number of rich moral emblems from the ancient poets, such images as those of the Golden Age, Hercules, and Orpheus. It is Boethius, I believe, who provides us with our clearest analogy to Jean's philological strategies of moral allegory and subversive allusion. Jean's increment of parody, of the grotesque, and of clerical comedy decisively removes his poem from Boethian *style*, but his techniques are based on a very similar sharp and scrupulous Latinity.

Some specific Magdunian classical "readings" may help guide our appreciation of the range of Jean's philological and moral understanding of ancient Latin poetry. I shall take two examples of explicit citations of Virgil, since, so far as I know, Jean's Virgilianism remains largely unexplored.

Genius, in a passage of classical misogyny, speaks thus:

> Mes, san faille, il et voirs que fame
> legierement d'ire s'anflame.
> Virgiles meïsmes tesmoigne,
> qui mout connut de leur besoigne,
> que ja fame n'iert tant estable
> qu'el ne soit diverse et muable.
> Et si rest trop ireuse beste.
>   (vv. 16293–99)

[But it is also true, without fail, that a woman is easily inflamed with wrath. Virgil himself bears witness—and he knew a great deal about their difficulties—that no woman was ever so stable that she might not be varied and changeable. And thus she remains a very irritable animal.]

The sting in this passage is in its tail, and specifically in the word *beste*. Jean would appear at first blush to be attempting to palliate a rather gross and gratuitous expression of medieval clerical misogyny with an irrelevant invocation of classical poetical authority. I shall not speculate on Jean's social motives, or rather those of Genius, but I should point out that the passage provides a very sensitive reading of a specific Virgilian text, namely the oracle of Mercury to the somnolent and uxorious Aeneas of the fourth book.

Aeneas must abandon his life of carnal ease in Carthage and sail to

Italy! He must follow the immutable decrees of destiny, not the shifting moods of a passionate woman!

> heia age, rumpe moras. varium et mutabile semper
> femina.   ed. Pease, (4.569−70)

[up then, break off delay. Woman is always fickle and changeable.]

There is a shocking misogyny in the Virgilian text, but it is grammatical rather than lexical. The adjectives *varium* and *mutabile* are neuters, not feminines. "The neuter . . . is here clearly contemptuous: woman is viewed less as a person than as a physical phenomenon."[7] This is the textual truth recognized by Jean de Meun and "translated" by the insulting word *beste*. The passage in the French text commits Jean to no particular interpretive position, but it does commend him as a scrupulous Latinist.

Jean also invokes Virgil by name, among other places, in the climactic scene of the storming and firing of the castle. As the forces of antieroticism flee in confusion, Courtoisie counsels her son Bel Accueil to give himself over to Love in the following terms:

> Biau filz, Amour vaint toutes choses,
> toutes sunt souz sa clef ancloses.
> Virgiles neïs le conferme
> par santance courtaise et ferme;
> quant *Bucoliques* cercheroiz,
> "Amors vaint tout" i trouveroiz
> "et nous la devons recevoir."
> Certes il dit et bien et voir;
> en un seul ver tout ce nous conte,
> n'i peüt conter meilleur conte.
>   (vv. 21297−306)

[O fair son, Love conquers everything; everything is held in by his key. Even Virgil confirms this idea in a powerful and courtly saying. When you look through the *Bucolics* you will find that "Love conquers all" and that "we should welcome it." Indeed he spoke well and truly when he tells us all this in a single line; he could not tell a better tale.]

The citation, of course, is that of a famous line in the tenth eclogue: *omnia vincit Amor: et nos cedamus Amori*. It is a line often removed from context;

but for Jean, a poet of contexts, its setting is more powerful than the line. Here, in an emphatic terminal moment of the *Eclogues*, we find restated Virgil's essential erotic pessimism. The power of "Love" levels human cultures, making Ethiopians of Arcadians and beasts of men.[8]

What unites Jean's use of the two Virgilian passages, in my opinion, is a consistent moral vision. Sexual passion is regarded as a dehumanizing insult to rational human nature that, in effect, reduces a human being to the level of the beasts. Stated thus baldly, the idea may sound "medieval" and "clerical." In fact it is ancient and humanistic, a commonplace of the Stoic antieroticism that characterizes Virgil's attitude toward sexuality.[9] Jean de Meun is frequently presented as a revolutionary figure, but I can agree with such an assessment only insofar as it speaks to Jean's technical artistry. At least my own protracted study of Jean has left me convinced that he is a Horatian poet, brilliantly original in his artistic expression, deeply traditional in his moral vision. For him, as for a later brilliant, satirical mediator of the classical tradition, the burden of true wit is "what oft was thought, but ne'er so well expressed." And on the topics of love and sex the classical poets had thought, and expressed, quite a good deal.

I therefore seek to defend the view that Jean's moral and literary attitudes, and especially his attitude toward the Christian poet's appropriation of the pagan past, are essentially conservative and even conventional. Jean is a writer of moral allegory, and his classicism is that of the Christian allegorist in the tradition of Boethius and John of Salisbury. Such a view certainly needs defense, since the counterarguments have by now been so often repeated and so widely accepted. In essence there are two such arguments, both related to the great work of the late Beryl Smalley. The first is that the main thrust of Christian biblical exegesis, generally seen as related in unspecified ways to "fable moralization" of Ovidian and other antique texts, shifted directions after the twelfth century from an interest in allegory to literal, historical, and philological concerns. The second is that the advanced humanistic thinkers of the thirteenth and fourteenth centuries working with "secular" materials—Smalley's humanist friars, for example—exhibit a parallel shift in scholarly taste and practice.

I do not believe that either of these arguments can stand up to examination, but this chapter is not the place to pursue the issue at a theoretical level. What I seek to do instead is to examine a concrete example of the way such assumptions can cloud our understanding of Jean de Meun's commerce with the ancient poets. I turn to some remarks by Alastair Minnis, who seeks to place Jean squarely in the camp of the new secular literalists as opposed to that of the old clerical allegorists exemplified, in textual form, by the respective commentaries on the *Consolation of Philosophy* of Nicholas Trevet and William of Conches. William indulges in the moral exegesis of mythological fables but Trevet eschews them. So, according to Minnis, does Jean de Meun.

Speaking of the mythological materials in the *Roman de la Rose*, Minnis claims that Jean's "own attitude was unflinchingly literal, and on occasion we may even detect him regarding the procedure of moralization with amusement."[10] Really? The particular passage in which we are invited to observe Jean's unflinching literalism and his possible amusement at the moral interpretation of classical fable comes at the very end of the *Roman de la Rose* in the veiled description of sexual intercourse that concludes the Lover's quest. Paraphrasing and condensing somewhat, I find that the Lover says roughly this: "I kissed the statue. Then I tried to ram my pilgrim's staff into the aperture in the wall between the pillars. I worked very hard to get by an obstruction blocking the path—rather as Hercules worked hard to get past the stone blocking the way to Cacus' cave. When I got in, I shook the rose." Now in order to believe that this is an unflinchingly literal description of sexual coition one would have to have, I suggest, rather peculiar notions about the nature of language or even more peculiar notions about the mechanics of sexual intercourse. But that is not Minnis's point. The point is that "Like Chaucer after him, Jean eliminated the 'wonder-element' of the story of Hercules, ignored any possible allegory which could be derived from it, and related its incidents in an earthy way."[11] Minnis contrasts the treatment of the story of Hercules and Cacus as he finds it in the Boethius commentary of William of Conches, where it "formed part of an elaborate allegory about the moral progress of the wise man" (p. 16).

I want to suggest a fundamentally different approach. Let us recognize that Jean de Meun is writing a *poem*, not a philosophical commentary, and that his techniques and strategies are in the first instance more likely to be illuminated by the practice of poets than by that of scholiasts. To begin with, Jean de Meun and his narrator (the Lover) are two very different people. That the Lover is at times (though not at this time) unflinchingly literal is certain. This is the principal point of his truculent ignorance of poetic integuments:

Mes des poetes les sentances,
les fables et les methaphores
ne bé je pas a gloser ores.
(vv. 7160—62)

[But as for the sentences, fables, and metaphors of the poets, I do not now toe to gloss them.]

As all major commentators of this passage agree, the words *sentances* and *metaphores* refer to what Reason has called the *integumenz*—which in turn is defined in Lecoy's glossary as "interprétation allégorique des poètes." Hence, no less apparent to me than the fact of the Lover's attitude of unflinching literalism is its poetic meaning. The Lover's attitude, which is jovially stupid in its context, stands in stark opposition to the literary attitudes of Reason. Common sense alone would suggest that the authorial Jean de Meun, a poet, is more likely to mock than to embrace such an attitude; but of course there is considerable contextual evidence to demonstrate the same truth.

When we examine the Lover's invocation of the story of Hercules and Cacus in its context, we find he says this:

Se bohourder m'i veïssiez,
por quoi bien garde i preïssiez,
d'Herculés vos peüst mambrer
quant il voust Cacus desmambrer:
.iii. foiz a sa porte asailli,
.iii. foiz hurta, .iii. foiz failli,
.iii. foiz s'asist en la valee,
touz las, por ravoir s'alenee,
tant ot soffert peine et travaill.
(vv. 21589–97)

[If you had seen me jousting—and you would have had to take good care of yourself—you would have been reminded of Hercules when he wanted to dismember Cacus. He battered at his door three times, three times he hurled himself, three times fell back. His struggle and labor were so great that he had to sit down three times in the valley, completely spent, to regain his breath.]

I find nothing notably "earthy" in Jean's mode of narration here, any more than in the Virgilian text he certainly had before him as he wrote.

Ter totum fervidus ira
lustrat Auentini montem, ter saxea temptat
limina nequiquam, ter fessus ualle resedit.
(*Aeneid* 8.230–32)

[In a boiling rage he circled the Aventine Mount three times. Three times he tried the stone-blocked entrance way, but in vain. Three times down in the valley he sank back in weariness.]

There is a fine metaphysical—or, perhaps, Pythagorean—wit in the Virgilian passage that describes Hercules' triplex assault with three uses of the adverb *ter* in three lines. Jean acknowledges his appreciation of Virgil's wit even as the Lover, with an excess decorous to his poetic character, adds a fourth "trois fois," thus violating the text even as he violates the woman.

That we here discover Jean de Meun regarding the procedure of moralization with amusement strikes me as most unlikely, except insofar as the Lover's mock heroics amusingly deflate his pretentions. Jean depends upon his reader, at least any reader learned enough to be worried about whether he is or is not moralizing classical fable in the first place, to recognize and to apply the Virgilian context. Aeneas has arrived in Latium, where he finds his way challenged by Turnus. At an appropriate narrative point Virgil describes how Aeneas assisted at the festival established by the grateful Arcadians in honor of Hercules' triumph over Cacus, a three-headed, fire-breathing monster who had ravished their countryside. It is nearly impossible to read the eighth book of the *Aeneid* without seeing in it the "procedure of moralization": there is an obvious thematic and moral parallel between the heroes Hercules and Aeneas, both of whom arrive from foreign parts to cleanse Italy of malign forces.

Many critics have sought to discover more or less specific allegories, the most obvious and tropological of which depend upon the observation that "Cacus" is a Latin form of the Greek word meaning "evil."[12] This etymological observation was not the inspiration of the twelfth century; it came from the ancient schools, as of course did the long tradition of the "moralized" Hercules, of which the philosopher Seneca was a powerful advocate.[13] It did not require the obscure commentator William of Conches to "allegorize" Boethius's treatment of Hercules in *Consolation of Philosophy* (4m7); it should be obvious to any reader of that poem that Boethius had already "allegorized" the hero himself.[14] For Boethius, Hercules is indeed the just mythological analogue for the *vir sapiens* that Lady Philosophy would have "Boethius" become in 4p7—the man, that is, who is not a cat's paw of Fortune. (This meter, incidentally, is noisy with echos of Seneca's *Agamemnon*.)[15]

Are we really to believe that Jean de Meun chuckled with secular amusement over the folios of William of Conches that dealt with *Hercules sapiens*? In that case, one presumes, he absolutely howled with laughter at the tragedies of Seneca. I must say that I doubt that he did either. Whether he agreed with Seneca that Hercules was a moral philosopher of the caliber of Cato (*Dialogues*, II, 21, 1) I cannot say, but he certainly presents Seneca himself as a philosopher of the caliber of Socrates, a *preudhom* untouched by the treachery of Fortune (6145ff.)

I am far from believing that Jean wants an amused attitude as he writes this passage or that he would deprive the reader of amusement in its perusal; I conclude, however, that the objects of amusement are not the procedures of allegorical moralization but the Lover's sexual and rhetorical grotesqueries. Once again the critic is aided by poetic context. Jean's introduction of the myth of Hercules and Cacus at the end of his poem is in fact a thematic reprise. The story is first introduced midway through the formal psychomachia (vv. 14778ff.) that is the poem's military centerpiece and that prepares the definitive rout of the forces of Chastity. Braggadoccio Seurtez takes on Paor in single combat and derides her for her cowardice:

> Avec Chacus vos anfoïstes,
> quant Herculés venir veïstes
> le cours, a son col sa maçue;
> vos fustes lors toute esperdue
> et li meïstes es piez eles,
> qu'il n'avoit onques eü teles,
> por ce que Chacus ot emblez
> ses beus et les ot assemblez
> an son receit, qui mout fu lons,
> par les queues a reculons,
> que la trace n'an fust trovee.
> (vv. 15543−53)

[You fled with Cacus when you saw Hercules come running, with his club at his neck. You were quite completely distracted then, and you put wings on his heels, wings such as he had never had before. Cacus had stolen Hercules' cattle and brought them together into his cave, a very deep one, by leading them backward by the tail, so that no trace of them was found.]

This part of the story prepares and complements its fugal reprise at the end, but even so it anticipates its audience's independent awareness of the Virgilian text. (If we do not realize that Cacus's "door" is in fact a vast boulder we shall not fully appreciate the Lover's sexual stamina in breaking through a maidenhead.) [16] Of the several amusing aspects of Jean's text, one of the most delightful is that Fear is not the least bit fearful in taking on the forces of lubricity, which she does so effectively that Cupid fears he is about to lose the whole campaign. In this situation Jean de Meun orchestrates an elaborate mythographic joke. Cupid treacherously arranges a truce to give him time to send off for his Doomsday Weapon, Venus Cytherea.

It is on Mount Cytheron that Cupid's messenger discovers Venus, who has just returned from a tumble in the hay with Adonis down below.[17] Jean prepares the meeting with a summary précis of the story of Venus and Adonis from the *Metamorphoses* of Ovid, followed by a brief but memorable *moralization* of the same from the Lover. The story, briefly, is this. Young Adonis loved to hunt. Venus loved young Adonis and feared lest a hunting accident do him damage and hence deprive her of her own sexual pleasure. She therefore instructed him never to hunt *audaces* (bold animals that defend themselves against the hunter) but only timorous *fugaces* (Robertson's "little, furry creatures"). Adonis ignored his lover's warnings, however, and he was killed in the chase by a ferocious boar. It is true that the critical tradition of the Middle Ages and the Renaissance is unanimous in attributing to Adonis a moral heroism in his preference for the "hard hunt" over the "soft hunt." Once again, however, such "moralization" is clearly continuous with ancient tradition, as we find it for example in the amusing verse epistle of Ausonius called the "Cupido crucifixus." Jean's own Lover is far from regarding the story "simply as a story," and he offers the following moralization of it:

> Biau seigneur, que qu'il vos aviegne,
> de cest example vos souviegne.
> Vos qui ne creez voz amies,
> sachiez mout fetes granz folies;
> bien les deüssiez toutes croire,
> car leur diz sunt voirs conme estoire.
> S'el jurent: "Toutes somes vostres,"
> creez les conme paternostres;
> ja d'aus croire ne recreez.
> Se Reson vient, point n'an creez;
> s'el vos aportoit croicefis,
> n'an creez point ne quel je fis.
> Se cist s'amie eüst creüe,
> mout eüst sa vie creüe.

(vv. 15721–34)

[Fair lords, whatever happens to you, remember this example. You who do not believe your sweethearts, know that you commit great folly; you should believe them all, for their sayings are as true as history. If they swear "We are all yours," believe what they say as if it were the *paternoster*. Never go back on your belief in them. If Reason comes, do not believe her at all. Even if she brought a crucifix, believe her not one bit more than I do. If Adonis had believed his sweetheart, his life would have grown much longer.]

That we have here unflinching literalism I take to be obvious; that it is Jean de Meun's I utterly deny. This passage, too, is a thematic reprise, and in it the Lover plays out his deadpan and doltish role of one who explicitly despises the *sentances*, the *fables*, and the *metaphores* of the poets. In proposing as the moral of the story of Venus and Adonis that the whole duty of man is the absolute credence of woman (except for the woman Dame Reason, *bien entendu*), the Lover echoes, thematically and verbally, his earlier and equally preposterous opinion (in Guillaume's part of the poem) that the moral of the story of Narcissus is that the whole duty of woman is sexual generosity to man:

Dames, cest essample aprenez,
qui vers vos amis mesprenez;
car se vos les lessiez morir,
Dex le vos savra bien merir.
(vv. 1505–1508)

[You ladies who neglect your duties toward your sweethearts, be instructed by this exemplum, for if you let them die, God will know how to repay you well for your fault.]

Thus where Minnis finds in the *Roman de la Rose* an amused rejection of "the procedure of moralization," I find artistic manipulations made possible by the stability of the traditional exegetical associations of Virgilian and Ovidian myth. Far from following Jean de Meun into alleged attitudes of literalism, Minnis followed him into a number of the more sophisticated techniques of Gothic allegory. What we often detect in Jean de Meun and in Chaucer is a certain surface inappropriateness or incongruity of what we too simply call "classical allusion." The adjective that best describes the phenomenon is, I think, "Ovidian." The great secular writers of the vernacular Middle Ages learned so much from Ovid's grandeur and his high style that we may neglect the fact that they learned also from him much of their impishness. When Jean de Meun reports the labored progress of his Lover's penis in the language of Virgilian epic,

> .iii. foiz a sa porte assailli,
> .iii. foiz hurta, .iii. foiz failli,
> .iii. foiz s'asist en la valee

he exercises his taste for robust and baroque parody, not an unflinching literalism. One distinguished classicist has written thus of Ovidian parody: "Parody is of two kinds: in one the writer derides the thing parodied, in the other himself or his theme. Parody of the second kind delights by its incongruity: when Ovid writes hoc opus, hic labor est, primo sine munere iuni (*Ars amatoria* 1, 453) he is mocking not so much Virgil (*Aeneid* 6, 129) as his own pretentions."[18] Thus also does Jean de Meun deride "himself" (that is, his first-person narrator) and his theme—the pursuit of sexual gratification as an idolatrous religion. As so often, Jean de Meun found that he could be most modern by applying himself with attention to the study of the ancients.

Notes

1. So far as I know it has not been noticed that Jean took one of his most celebrated phrases—"la diffinitive santance" as delivered by Genius, 19474—from Huon (*Le Tornoiement Anticrist*, ed. Margaret O. Bender [University, MS: Romance Monographs no. 17, 1976], p. 129, line 2746). In Huon, of course, the authoritative *santance* comes from the mouth of Reason in opposition to the forces of Venus and Cupid. Quotations in this essay are from the *Roman de la Rose*, ed. Félix Lecoy, 3 vols. Classiques Français du Moyen Âge 92, 95, 98 (Paris: Champion, 1965–70).

2. See *Le Débat sur le "Roman de la Rose,"* ed. Eric Hicks (Paris: Champion, 1977), pp. 89ff.

3. David Wallace, "Chaucer and Boccaccio's Early Writings," in *Chaucer and the Italian Trecento*, ed. Piero Boitani (Cambridge: Cambridge University Press, 1983) p. 151.

4. D. A. Russell, "De imitatione," in *Creative Imitation and Latin Literature*, ed. David West and Tony Woodman (Cambridge: Cambridge University Press, 1979), pp. 1–19.

5. Thérèse Bouché, "Ovide et Jean de Meun," *Le Moyen Âge* 83 (1977): 71–87.

6. See especially Seth Lerer, *Boethius and Dialogue* (Princeton, NJ: Princeton University Press, 1985).

7. Thus comments A. S. Pease in his encyclopedic edition, *Publii Vergilii Maronis Aeneidos Liber Quartus* (Cambridge, MA: Harvard University Press, 1935), p. 460.

8. See O. Tescari, "Amor omnibus idem," *Studi Romani* 1 (1953): 121–23.

9. See John O'Meara, "Virgil and Augustine: The Roman Background to Christian Sexuality," *Augustinus* 13 (1968): 307–26.

10. A. J. Minnis, *Chaucer and Pagan Antiquity* (Cambridge: Cambridge University Press, 1982), p. 16.

11. Minnis, pp. 16–17.

12. See, e.g., Gerhard Binder, *Aeneas und Augustus: Interpretationen zum 8. Buch der Aeneis* (Meisenheim am Glan: A. Hain, 1971), pp. 141ff.

13. "Novimus autem malum a Graecis kakon dici"; Servius, II p. 227. Servius's gloss, incidentally, is both "demythologizing" and "allegorizing." Salutati quotes it at length in *De laboribus Herculis* (pp. 335–43). This book, usually regarded as one of the greatest works of classical scholarship of the Italian Renaissance, would be rendered old-fashioned and retrograde by the phantom demise of moral allegory and "fable moralization" in the late Middle Ages.

14. See Joachim Gruber, *Kommentar zu Boethius de Consolatione Philosophiae* (Berlin and New York: De Gruyter, 1978), pp. 372–74.

15. See Tarrant, p. 324n, where, however, the relationship seems to me to be too cautiously suggested.

16. Individual lines once again show that Jean has the Virgilian text specifically in mind:

fugit ilicet ocior Euro
speluncam petit, pedibus timor addit alas (8.223–24).

"et li meïstes es piez eles" (v. 15547).

17. I think this approximates Jean's tone: "L'un se geue a l'autre et deduit" (v. 15735).

18. E. J. Kenney, "Nequitiae Poetae," in *Ovidiana*, ed. N. I. Herescu (Paris: Champion, 1958), p. 201.

David F. Hult

5. Language and Dismemberment: Abelard, Origen, and the *Romance of the Rose*

Virtually from the time of its composition in the late thirteenth century, Jean de Meun's continuation of the *Romance of the Rose* has been an object of controversy: its wit and its style have been celebrated; some of its more adventurous moral or social views have been condemned. The epistolary exchange in which Christine de Pizan participated was the first extended realization of such debates, but this exchange was itself preceded by evidence we can glean from literary works modeling themselves on the *Rose* allegory as well as from scribal manipulation of the text itself.[1] While the plethora of manuscripts copied in the fourteenth century—nearly unprecedented for a vernacular work of the time—bespeaks a wide-ranging and intensely committed audience, the variety of marginal notations, abridgments, deletions, expansions, moralizations, and so forth suggests that debate germinated even as the text was reaching its first readers. One of the troublesome aspects of the poem's formal presentation resides in its being both a continued narrative poem and an encyclopedia, a work of fiction and a compilation of learned (philosophical, scientific, and ethical) pronouncements. The justly celebrated midpoint of the romance, with its curiously provocative discussion of the poem's authorship inserted within the fiction, proposes both of these possibilities. First, the God of Love identifies Jean de Meun as his faithful servant, the author who will come along to complete the romance left unfinished by his predecessor Guillaume de Lorris, now deceased:[2]

> Cist avra le romanz si chier
> qu'il le voudra tout parfenir . . .
> et dira por la meschance,
> par poor de desesperance
> qu'il n'ait de Bel Acueill perdue
> la bienvoillance avant eüe:

"Et si l'ai je perdue, espoir,
a poi que ne m'en desespoir,"
et toutes les autres paroles,
quex qu'els soient, sages ou foles,
jusqu'a tant qu'il avra coillie
seur la branche vert et foillie
la tres bele rose vermeille
et qu'il soit jorz et qu'il s'esveille.
(vv. 10554–55, 10561–72)

[He (Jean de Meun) will be so fond of the romance that he will want to finish it right to the end . . . and through the despairing fear that he may have lost the good will that Fair Welcoming had shown him before, he will say, "And perhaps I have lost it. At least I do not despair of it." And he will set down all the other speeches (lit.: words), whatever they may be, wise or foolish, up to the time when he will have cut the most beautiful red rose on its green, leafy branch, to the time when it is day and he awakes. (pp. 187–88)]

Within this passage is circumscribed the entire narrative program of the bipartite *Rose* bringing the Lover's quest to fulfillment, from the direct quotation of Jean de Meun's putative first words to the rhyme that repeats the romance's famous final couplet some ten thousand lines later:

Ainsint oi la rose *vermeille*.
Atant fu jorz, et je m'*esveille*.
(vv. 21749–50)

[Thus I had the red rose. Straightway it was day, and I awoke. (p. 354)]

Second, in this same central section of the romance, the God of Love will rename the romance in accordance with the new subject matter, his own doctrine or "sciance" expressed in the vernacular ("selonc le langage de France" [v. 10613]):

car tant en lira proprement
que tretuit cil qui ont a vivre
devroient apeler ce livre
le *Miroër aus Amoreus*.
(vv. 10618–21)

[For he will read (or instruct) so fittingly that all those alive should call this book *The Mirror for Lovers*. (p. 188)]

As has been pointed out on numerous occasions, this *Miroër* is a French translation for the Latin *Speculum*, a term that was applied to the encyclopedic collections so popular in the thirteenth century and after, the most illustrious examples of which were Vincent of Beauvais's enormously successful *Speculum historiale* and *Speculum naturale*, written scarcely a generation before Jean.

It is fairly straightforward that, as dictated from within the poem, there are two modes of reading the work: continuous or disjunctive, totalizing or episodic, as predicated upon the superimposition of two titles and the authorizing fiction of two poets. It is endemic of the critical tradition, however, that one or the other model should be used to read the work. Thus Christine de Pizan's attack on the *Rose*'s immorality and misogynist rhetoric will take virtually no account of the work's form or fiction, ascribing all opinions expressed in it to the author. She admits that not all in the book is objectionable: "je ne reppreuve mie *Le Rommant de la Rose* en toutes pars, car il y a de bonnes choses et bien dictes sans faille"[3] (p. 21). ["I do not condemn the *Roman de la Rose* entirely, for it does indeed contain some good things, and its style is poetically pleasing" (p. 54).] However, only a few lines later, she calls for it to be burned: "mieulx lui affiert ensevelissement de feu que couronne de lorier" (Ibid.). ["I consider it more fitting to bury it in fire than to crown it with laurel" (p. 55).] In objecting to Reason's foul speech, Christine merely echoes the Lover's objections to Reason's loose tongue, a fact pointed out by her most astute opponent, Pierre Col:

En verité l'Amant, ou chapistre de Raison, fait plus d'argumens et de plus fors la moitié que tu ne fais: auxquelx Raison respons: et toutevoies tu ne respons pas aux raisons d'icelle meisme, laquelle chose tu deusses fere avant que tu la reprisses. (p. 91)

[In fact, in this chapter of Reason, the Lover himself offers a broader and more forceful argument against naming the secret members than you do. And Reason responds to this argument, and yet you do not address yourself to this response at all, as you should have done before you criticized her. (p. 94)]

The nature of allegorical personification as an expository mode becomes increasingly implicated in the criticism of the poem's doctrinal message. Most notably, Jean Gerson's attack in the vernacular (he also inveighed against the *Rose* in a couple of Latin sermons) takes the form *not* of a treatise but of an allegorical dream sequence focusing on the denunciation of the poem in the court of Justice by Theological Eloquence. Not only does Gerson thereby attempt to undermine the allegory by means of its own discursive strategy, but he then, somewhat disingenuously, condemns this strategy, declaring that it does not make any difference *who* is speaking. Heretical doctrines, he tells us, must be proscribed in any context:

> Lequel est pis: ou d'ung crestien clerc preschier en la persone d'ung Sarrasin contre la foy, ou qu'il amenast le Sarrazin qui parlast ou escripst? Toutefois jamais ne seroit souffert le segond oultraige; si est toutefois pis le premier (c'est a dire le fait du Crestien), de tant que l'ennemy couvert est plus nuisable que l'appert . . ." (p. 73)

> [What is worse: for a Christian clerk to assume the character of a Saracen preaching against the Faith, or for him to introduce a real Saracen speaking or writing against the Faith? Never indeed should the second disgrace be tolerated. Nevertheless, the first, the deed apparently of a Christian, is worse. How much more injurious the secret enemy than the open . . . (pp. 80–81)]

Gerson's frustration initially seems to arise from the fact that the text never speaks its own voice in favor of, or against, a particular doctrine. However, he continues,

> Tout semble estre dit en sa persone; tout semble estre vray come Euvangille . . . et, de quoy je me dueil plus—tout enflamme a luxure, meismement quant il la samble reprouver. (p. 74)

> [Everything seems to be said in his own person; everything seems as true as the Gospel . . . And I regret to say, he incites the more quickly to lechery, even when he seems to reproach it. (p. 81)]

As with Christine's awareness of "good" passages in the *Rose*, which nonetheless do not justify portions to which she objects, Gerson here shows that even when Jean does express a laudable attitude (or especially when he does so) the moral or doctrinal effect is essentially negative. Who indeed is responsible for a text that has an effect upon its readers opposite to its stated intention? More important, perhaps, how does a poem convey such an effect?

Pierre Col's affinity with Jean de Meun is evident not only from his skillful defense, but also from his deep understanding of the problematics of expression and intention raised by the *Rose* author. His defense involves two strategies, both arguably inspired by Jean de Meun's fiction, that attack the opponents from different angles. On the one hand, he justifies Jean's illustrative use of personifications for the purpose of edification, stressing their similarity to Biblical examples of shocking behavior (such as Sodom and Gomorrah) or to those used in sermons. He suggests that it is naive to believe that an author's intention is necessarily to be read into the speeches mouthed by fictional characters:

> Je respons a dame Eloquance et a toy par ung meisme moyen, et dy que maistre Jehan de Meung en son livre introduisy personnaiges, et fait chascun personnaige parler selonc qui luy appartient: c'est assavoir le Jaloux comme jaloux, la Vielle comme la Vielle, et pareillement des autres. Et est trop mal pris de dire que l'aucteur tiengne les maulx estre en fame que le Jalous, en faisant son personnaige, propose. (p. 100)

> [I answer Lady Eloquence and you by the same means, and I say that Master Jean de Meun in his book introduced characters, and made each character speak according to his nature, that is, the Jealous Man as a jealous man, the Old Woman as an old woman, and similarly with the others. And it is wrongheaded to say that the author believes women to be as evil as the Jealous Man, in accordance with his character, declares. (p. 103)]

As with the Bible, according to Col, one must go beyond any superficially objectionable details and read the text *in bono*, by way of extracting positive messages and useful illustrations. By implication, to cleave to the surface is merely to project one's own depraved interests or misconceptions.

On the other hand, Pierre Col subtly unseats the discursive assurance of Christine de Pizan and Jean Gerson. First, as we have seen, he enfolds Christine's own objections back into the romance fiction itself, highlighting the superficiality or unoriginality of her argument. He goes on to impugn the piety of their very gesture—the faith that both maintain in the reliability of their own writings—by suggesting that even the intent of their letters might be turned to an opposite effect. After bemusedly considering and then dismissing possible reasons for their excessive dislike of the *Rose* (personal hatred for Jean de Meun, envy of his success, or simple ignorance) he arrives at a final, more cynical possibility:

> Par aventure faingnés vous blasmer le dit livre pour cause de l'essaucer par esmouvoir les escoutans les paroles a le lire, et vous savés bien que qui le lira, il trouvera le contraire de vos escrips et tous ensaingnemans tres notables: et

en ce cas les repreneurs devroient estre tenus assés pour excusés, car la fin et
leur entencion seroit bonne, quelque moyen qu'il y eust. (p. 109)

[Perhaps you merely pretend to blame the said book in order to exalt it, that
is, by causing your hearers to read it. And you know well that he who reads
it will find there much worthy teaching, the opposite of your criticism. And
if this is your intent, you and the critics of the work should be held excused.
For such purpose would be good, whatever the means. (p. 112)]

A brief glance at the literary event known as the *Rose* Quarrel can
prove potentially helpful for understanding what is surely one of the most
unsettling and yet fascinating aspects of the work. Just as the narrative
stages in the future its own writing and the birth of the individual author
who will perform that act, it also manages to anticipate in an uncanny
fashion, through its manipulative and indecisive debate structure, any response we are likely to make, either by including that response within the
text or by deferring responsibility (which is to say, pronounced authorial
intention) through vocal or verbal chicanery. What I have termed the romance's debate structure is only the most superficial formal indication of the
stylistic phenomenon that Bakhtin has termed "dialogism," which is to say
the interpenetration within a single discourse (not necessarily an actual
dialogue) of two or more socially or ideologically charged codes.[4] It could
be what Bakhtin calls an "alien word" assimilated into a particular conceptual system, or a discrete speech event contrasted with a specific linguistic
code that it only purports to realize. One possible effect of this style in the
novel would be, as Bakhtin says of Tolstoy, one of disharmonization,
"while at the same time polemically invading the reader's belief and eval-
uative system, striving to stun and destroy the apperceptive background
of the reader's active understanding."[5] Furthermore, the dialogic use of
words is narrowly associated with an ambivalent authorial presence, as
Kristeva has noted. The author uses "le mot d'autrui pour y mettre un sens
nouveau, tout en conservant le sens que le mot avait déjà."[6] It is not an
appropriation of another's word, an imitation that takes the word in its
original context seriously, nor is it a simple opposition to that word, which
typically results in parody. Rather, it is that duplicity that refuses to pronounce: "l'auteur exploite la parole d'autrui, sans en heurter la pensée,
pour ses propres buts; il suit sa direction tout en la rendant relative."[7] One
need only adduce as evidence that Jean de Meun was aware of this fundamental discursive feature, the well-known passage that Nancy Regalado
has so persuasively pinpointed as enunciating an important poetic principle governing the *Rose* as a whole:[8]

Ainsinc va des contreres choses,
les unes sunt des autres gloses;
et qui l'une an veust defenir,
de l'autre li doit souvenir,
ou ja, par nule antancion,
n'i metra diffinicion;
car qui des .ii. n'a connoissance,
ja n'i connoistra differance,
san quoi ne peut venir en place
diffinicion que l'an face.
                (vv. 21543–52)

[Thus things go by contraries; one is the gloss of the other. If one
wants to define one of the pair, he must remember the other, or he
will never, by any intention, assign a definition to it; for he who has
no understanding of the two will never understand the difference between them, and without this difference no definition that one can
make can come to anything. (p. 351)]

If traditional critical motivations, which in most cases have scarcely
changed since the time of Christine de Pizan, consist in the articulation of
a unified meaning or message lying behind or beneath the cover of the
letter of the text, Jean's poetics operates continual reversals between the
two such that readers can never definitively exult in the mastery they might
desire. The outrageous posture of Jean's authorial persona must be viewed,
at least in part, as a defensive strategy aimed at the abuse one can suffer at
the hands of intolerant misinterpretation, as in the following passage
where Jean objects to potential disapproval of his portrayal of religious
hypocrites in the persona of Faus Semblant:

qu'onques ne fu m'antancion
de parler contre home vivant
sainte religion sivant
ne qui sa vie use en bone euvre,
de quel que robe qu'il se queuvre;
ainz pris mon arc et l'antesoie,
quex que pechierres que je soie,
si fis ma saiete voler
generaument por affoler . . .
si tré seur eus a la volee;

et se, por avoir la colee,
avient que desouz la saiete
aucuns hom de son gré se mete,
qui par orgueill si se deçoive
que deseur soi le cop reçoive,
puis se plaint que je l'ai navré,
courpe n'an oi ne ja n'avré,
neïs s'il an devoit perir.
                    (vv. 15222–30, 15245–53)

[It was never my intention to speak against any living man who follows holy religion or who spends his life in good works, no matter
what robe he covers himself with. Instead I take my bow and bend it,
sinner that I may be, and let fly my arrow to wound at random . . .
Therefore, I fire on them in the pack, and if it happens that any man
is pleased to put himself in the way of an arrow and receive a shot, if
he so deceives himself with his pride that he gets shot, and then complains because I have wounded him, it is not my fault and never will
be, even if he should perish as a result. (pp. 259–60)]

Here Jean most effectively attributes moral guilt to the beholder rather
than to the creator of art, one of the best arguments against intolerance
or censorship in any form. In this regard, it is important to take account,
at least anecdotally, of the probable context in which Jean de Meun wrote
his poem.

It is well attested that Jean was a resident of Paris, and the extent of
his erudition, while not necessarily revealing a subtle philosophical mind,
suggests that, if not a student, he at least had ties with the university community.[9] The recently formed University of Paris was undergoing a series
of conflicts as of the middle of the century; the intellectual foment resulting from the large-scale introduction of Aristotelian thought and Thomism
was met with occasionally intense opposition from conservative members
of the Theology faculty. The most significant crystallization of the conflict
appeared in the two condemnations issued by Etienne Tempier, the bishop
of Paris—the first in 1270 and the second, listing 219 forbidden propo-
sitions, in 1277. It is not so important in the present context to ascertain
whether Tempier actually had the *Romance of the Rose* in mind when he
drafted his condemnation, as to take note of the type of repression and
censorship that was beginning to taint the study of the liberal arts. Jean de

Meun's work is very much a polemical response, albeit not direct and certainly not political, to a particular way of thinking that involved a univocal
approach to the relationship between word and thought. To couch such a
response within an erotic allegory, to write it in the French language and
in rhymed octosyllabic couplets (a form that was at this point unambigu-
ously associated with frivolous fictional composition), are both important
and typically undervalued factors in Jean's ambiguous gesture of defiance.
This forceful conjunction should further remind us that the analogical relationship between mastery, interpretation, and sexuality is not a modern
invention.

The preceding reflections on the *Rose* and a hypothetical context for
dealing with its complexities, contradictions, and tortuous verbal entan-
glements are meant to serve as a suggestive preamble to the major focus of
this chapter, the debate between Reason and the Lover regarding proper
language use. The passage has commanded a considerable amount of attention in the past few years, a fact that can be explained by the avid
interest in semiotics and hermeneutics among literary scholars.[10] As an
indication of the evolution in academic interests, and by way of contrast,
Alan Gunn, who in 1952 published what remains, at nearly 600 pages, the
longest book devoted to the *Romance of the Rose*, considers the discussion
in a brief parenthetical remark: "(Raison here buttresses her argument by
reference to a familiar linguistic phenomenon.)."[11] Whereas on most other
topics we are willing to allow Jean de Meun the full force of his comic, or
at least ironic, vision, discussions of language tend to become deadly serious; they attempt to extract a coherent theory or philosophy of language
out of the debate that would then be adjudged *the* theory attributable to
Jean de Meun. Thus, for John Fleming, Reason's essentially noble, rational, and theologically orthodox (i.e., Augustinian) view of language and
of most other things points up the Lover's triviality, and her dismissal sets
the stage for the global poetic irony of the Lover's ignoble quest. Approaching the question from a quite different direction, Daniel Poirion
arrives at a similar conclusion, espousing Reason and her linguistic nominalism as Jean de Meun's response to the Lover's (and thus to Guillaume
de Lorris's) iconic courtly "realism." As far as the character Reason is concerned, however, Tom Hill has convincingly advanced the suggestion that
Reason's own position is seriously compromised by the irony of her inability to comprehend man's condition after the Fall, including its direct
linguistic result, the appearance of obscenity.[12]

What both sides of this broad polemic tend to relegate to the margins of their argumentation is the fact that language is Jean de Meun's primary tool, and rather self-consciously so. Words and things are not simply a topic of idle speculation, nor are they, conversely, a key to metaphysics in the broadest sense. Words in their materiality, taken as objects in their own right, are for Jean the very basis of poetic construction and metaphoric association. Whereas, in a primary sense, we all know that things precede words, that common language is predicated upon the existence of worldly realities, I would submit that Jean is functioning at a second level where, taking the world of language and texts as a given, further sense (or nonsense) is produced by the operations of language and not by the prior existence of things. To put the problem in slightly different terms, Jean's *Rose* represents less of a speculation *on* language than a performance *of* language as orchestrated through what itself pretends to be a meta-discourse. By adamantly reversing linguistic priorities in theory and in practice, Jean is surreptitiously providing one of the most astonishing examples of intertextuality the Middle Ages has to offer: the production of meaning within verbal behavior and beyond the narrow constraints of a specific locutionary intent.[13]

A brief outline of the encounter between Reason and the Lover is appropriate at this point. The scene is virtually the first of Jean's continuation, beginning a scant 160 lines after the above-mentioned lines pinpointed by Jean himself and extending to some 3000 lines in all, approximately one sixth of the entire continuation. Reason's appearance to the pining Lover is actually a reappearance, insofar as she had already figured, somewhat briefly (vv. 2955–3082), in Guillaume de Lorris's composition. In her attempt to win the Lover to her side, Reason initiates an attack on the God of Love and, when that fails, she attempts to convince the Lover that there are other, preferable, forms of love: friendship; and brotherly love, or charity. The Boethian aspects of Lady Reason are accentuated as she advocates the development of inner strengths over and against the acquisition of fleeting external things (such as wealth or power), thus leading to a prolonged animadversion upon Fortune. The Lover raises the question of Justice in a fallen world and its relation to love. "Which is worth more?" he asks her. Curiously, her answer is that love is more important, for whereas it is self-sufficient, justice cannot operate without love. She advances as proof—and this will become the impetus, direct and indirect, for the balance of the dialogue—the mythological exemplum of Jupiter's castration of Saturn, which resulted in the birth of Venus and the flight of Justice, both of which are symptoms of the end of the Golden Age. If Justice were to come back, Reason affirms, people would still need to love each other for, without love, Justice would exercise a cruel reign.

Jean passes under silence any potential inconsistencies of Reason's illustrative tale, the simultaneously negative (as a symptom of the Fall) and positive (as the implicit foundation of justice) facets of love, as Reason turns to a story borrowed from Livy concerning the miscarriage of justice on a Roman maiden, Virginia. The Lover then reproaches Reason for having used a dirty word in telling about Saturn's castration, "coilles." Reason asks to respond at a later time and launches into a protracted condemnation of Fortune, which entails the relation of three more anecdotes: the account of Nero and his cruelty, principally drawn from Suetonius; the tale of Croesus and his daughter Phanie; and a contemporary historical event, Charles of Anjou's conquest of Sicily. After summarizing her argument, Reason is reproached once more by the Lover for her use of dirty language, and the dialogue ends with a lively debate over the relation between words and things, literal and figurative language, and the question of the use of exemplary narrative in philosophical discourse. The Lover finally insists that he is not interested in interpretation and only wants the rose; Reason instantly departs.

The episode is extremely diverse and wide-ranging, and this overly dutiful résumé has been included by way of forestalling certain common misapprehensions. John Fleming, for instance, asserts, "In the *Roman de la Rose* the discussion of language between Reason and the Lover introduces the allegorical 'history' of the castration of Saturn, a history that is a major idea in the poem."[14] This is indeed the order in which Fleming's argument proceeds, but in the poem it is exactly the reverse. The history of the castration of Saturn in fact introduces, or at least provokes, the linguistic debate that itself concludes the episode. Perhaps by sheer necessity, but unfortunately so, the *Rose* is particularly given to lacunary or partial readings. The aforementioned tome by Alan Gunn, which contains a massive forty pages of indices, including such diverse and curious entries as "Beethoven, Ludwig van," "*Maya*, Hindu concept of," and "clouds," refers neither to Nero nor to Charles d'Anjou. Nor does Fleming's book, which is devoted exclusively to Reason's discourse. As I will be attempting to show, an important facet of Jean's "rational" argument is conveyed through seemingly unrelated lexical and imagistic elements contained in the interpolated stories.

The discussion of language is itself astonishingly dense, not because of the difficulty of the essentially Augustinian variations on the interrelationships between words and things, between language and the world (both spiritual and sublunary), but rather because of the intensity with which poetic and material images radiate within the episode and beyond it, throughout the rest of the immense poem. The occasion for the discussion of language, Jupiter's castration of Saturn, does not really prove Reason's allegation concerning Justice and in fact very nearly undermines it, as I suggested above, since Venus, the mythical personification of passionate love, is Reason's sworn enemy and the agent of the Lover's conquest of the rose at the end of the poem. The mythological tale does, however, let in through the back door, as it were, a number of topics of central importance to the *Rose*. The very fact that passionate love is associated with this archetypal dismemberment should alert us to some of the paradoxes inherent in the erotic quest. It might be added that Venus's appearance out of the sea is first summoned by a poetic, almost incantatory, suggestion:

> Joutice, qui jadis regnot,
> au tens que Saturnus regne ot,
> cui Jupiter coupa les coilles,
> ses filz, con se fussent andoilles,
> (mout ot ci dur filz et *amer*)
> puis les gita dedanz *la mer*,
> donc Venus la deesse issi,
> car li livres le dit issi.
>
> (vv. 5505–12)

[If Justice, who reigned formerly at the time when Saturn held power—Saturn, whose testicles Jupiter, his hard and bitter son, cut off as though they were sausages and threw into the sea, thus giving birth to Venus, as the book tells. (p. 113)]

The rhyming couplet "amer"/"la mer" ("bitter" and "the sea"), a well-known pun, or paronomasia, inherited from the Tristan legends, would automatically have evoked its third, unstated term, the verb *amer* ("to love"), realized textually in the following line by Venus. The fact that the excised part, the hitherto unspeakable instrument of sexual desire, is later remotivated in all of its obscene fullness, ends up short-circuiting dialogue and consequently provokes an un-reasonable association between eroticism and obscenity. The seemingly innocent anecdote (and innocence is here part of Jean's artifice) viewed in its extended context provides a brilliant thematic nexus that far surpasses anything in Jean's sources: the condition of fallen man; human justice; procreation; proper language use; and erotic desire.

Daniel Poirion has pointed out that a form of the word *coille* occurs in several episodes of Jean's *Rose*: in Reason's speech, as we have just seen; during Ami's speech, in evoking the story of Abelard and Heloise following upon a discussion of marriage; and in Nature's speech, nearly 9000 lines after that, in dealing with the early church father Origen's self-inflicted castration. It should be stated initially that Jean's careful highlighting of the word at its first mention as an obscenity—that is, as an illicit or socially inappropriate linguistic usage—necessarily induces us to attend to, and associate, these three moments.[15] Furthermore, again as Poirion has noted, all three occurrences of the word are used to signify the absence of the thing, its separation from the body, its nonexistence.

At this point, a few words could be said about the nature of Reason's verbal gesture, which is typically considered, if it is considered at all, as a puerile dirty joke unworthy of further commentary. The nature of obscenity as a linguistic phenomenon is very much at issue here. Both Hill and Fleming have discussed the significance of a passage from Augustine's *City of God*, Book XIV (chapters 9–26) for an understanding of the moral implications of sexuality after the Fall. Augustine's stance on the matter of obscenity is itself paradoxical, as Hill pointed out in his review of Fleming's *Reason and the Lover*.[16] Augustine is attempting to explain that shame in all matters sexual, including the language used to denote the act, resulted from the Fall. An important component of Augustine's proof of man's fallen nature as itself a type of punishment is the imaginary portrait of the world before the Fall, where "marriage . . . would not have given rise to any lust to be ashamed of"[17] and where "discussion could then have free scope, without any fear of obscenity, to treat of any idea that might come to mind when thinking about bodily organs of this kind. Nor would there be any reason for calling the actual words obscene."[18] Augustine can articulate man's fallen nature by imagining what it is *not*, but he cannot put it into words. This attitude toward obscenity would seem to contradict Augustine's statements concerning the conventionality of linguistic signs in his *De Doctrina Christiana*, but it is substantiated by another text that Fleming adduces from the *De Dialectica*:[19]

When, however, a word moves a hearer both on its own account and on account of what it signifies, then both the statement itself and that which is stated by means of it are attended together. Why is the chastity of the ears not offended when one hears 'He had squandered his patrimony by hand, by belly, and by penis (*pene*)'? It would be offended if the private part of the body were called by a low or vulgar name, though the thing with a different name is the same. If the shamefulness of the thing signified were not covered over by the propriety of the signifying word, then the base character of both would affect both sense and mind. Similarly, although a harlot *is* no different, she nonetheless looks different because of the clothes she wears when she stands before a judge than she looks when she lies in her dissolute bedchamber.

One can in fact suggest that Jean de Meun is in this scene articulating a paradox of obscenity with which Augustine is incapable of dealing (or unwilling to deal). How does one represent obscene things verbally, if it is improper to speak properly of the eradication of the improper? The problem is that the obscene word is both a thing and a sign, but what makes the word-thing obscene is the gesture of condemnation that fetishizes it only to repress it. Obscenity is itself predicated upon a duality, the existence of the word and its subsequent elimination or glossing: It is, in short, situational and, as a gesture, nonreferential. Reason's offhand articulation of the obscene "proper" word to tell the very myth of the Fall that explains the existence of obscenity and lust, aside from its being a marvelous example of a linguistic *mise-en-abyme*, is itself the gesture that Augustine refused to make in his discussion of prelapsarian sexuality. Jean de Meun is staging for our benefit the socially determined mechanism of obscenity already internalized in Augustine's self-censoring discourse when the Lover uses the word as a taboo thing, with no reference save to the relation between the two interlocutors. What this suggests is that the Lover's wrenching of the word out of context, his obscene cover-up, is itself a figurative replication of the primal castrating moment, and thus not merely a symptom or result, anecdotal at best, of man's fallen condition. Where Jean de Meun will go one step further, and this I will turn to in a moment, is that even after the member is cut off, it can still be present in language.

It is of no little significance that in each of the cases of dismemberment to which Jean de Meun alludes, a new sense of fullness or productivity results. The case of Saturn, from whose castration Venus, the passionate sexual drive, is born, has already been mentioned. If we pursue the analogy between the mythological account and the idea of obscenity, we might find expressed something that the modern world has come to take for granted, at least since the Marquis de Sade: The repressive gesture that in effect creates obscenity is itself a (or perhaps *the*) source of lasciviousness while casual repetition of any word dulls its scandalous effect.[20] Likewise, Roland Barthes's "pleasure of the text" is aroused by the suggestively exposed yet covered interstices of clothing or of language.

As far as Origen and Abelard are concerned, in both cases castration allows for a philosophical or pedagogical development. The only texts by Abelard that Jean de Meun certainly knew (and indeed translated), the *Historia Calamitatum* and the subsequent epistolary exchange with Heloise, could with little exaggeration receive the moralizing subtitle "How castration makes for a better philosopher and an even better teacher." Abelard himself cites Origen several times in his letters as an exemplary figure, a model of the "pure" philosopher-teacher unencumbered by worldly concerns. He even turns his own story, retrospectively, into an *exemplum* insofar as his castration becomes the pivotal moment directly preceding the turn to writing and teaching about the Christian faith:[21]

> [T]he hand of the Lord had touched me for the express purpose of freeing me from the temptations of the flesh and the distractions of the world so that I could devote myself to learning, and thereby prove myself a true philosopher not of the world but of God.

What is more interesting is that as Abelard amplifies his own exemplarity he is led to reduce Origen's. Thus he will in a subsequent letter call his castration a cleansing ("mundavit") and not a deprivation of "those vile members which from their practice of utmost indecency are called 'the parts of shame' and have no proper name of their own."[22] As if that were not enough, and here is I think another possible inspiration for Jean's linguistic discussion, Abelard, following Eusebius's account, attributes Origen's crime of self-mutilation to a misreading of the Biblical text:[23]

> The great Christian philosopher Origen provides an example, for he was not afraid to mutilate himself in order to quench completely this fire within him, as if he understood literally the words that those men were truly blessed who castrated themselves for the Kingdom of Heaven's sake . . . as if he interpreted as historic fact, not as a hidden symbol, that prophecy of Isaiah in which the Lord prefers eunuchs to the rest of the faithful.

Jean de Meun's unrelenting fascination with castration and, in broader terms, physical dismemberment radiates outward in a number of figurative ways related to the poetic treatment of the obscene verbal gesture. To begin with, the use of the "proper" word for Saturn's severed member as a point of contention with regard to the arbitrary nature of language, the dislocation between word and thing, is hardly accidental. What it suggests is not simply the importance of unfettered linguistic play, the creation of things from words, but also a mind extremely attentive to the suggestive qualities of literal objects, the physicality of the world as a producer of meaning beyond the traditional bonds of *acoutumance* (v. 7107) or, as we would say, linguistic convention. And all the while we are transfixed by the interesting linguistic facets of the argument between Reason and the Lover, we are likely to miss a number of transgressive linguistic gestures dependent upon the slippage between word and thing, the stretching of the limits of linguistic convention. One overt example of this occurs at the point of the Lover's accusation of Reason:

> Si ne vos tiegn pas a cortaise
> quant ci m'avez coilles nomees,
> qui ne sunt pas bien renomees
> en bouche a cortaise pucele.
>
> (vv. 6898–901)

> [Moreover, I do not consider you courteous when just now you named the testicles; they are not well thought of in the mouth of a courteous girl.(p. 133)]

Fleming's explanation of this passage is, I think, typical of the way most readers construe it: "[The Lover] first suggests that it is the *coilles* themselves that are unworthy . . . but then fudges the matter with qualification . . . [What he later says] seems to suggest that as a word *coilles* is an inappropriate conventional sign for a woman of Reason's social station."[24] Bloch's assertion that there is here a "playful hint of nonreproductive sexuality (oral copulation)"[25] gets closer to the gist of the passage but does not quite capture the fullness of the joke. Jean has in fact made use of the ambiguous relationship between a word-object and its referent—the very topic of discussion—in order to place, quite suggestively I might add, one *or* the other in the mouth of a courtly damsel. Grammatically speaking, the plural verb form ("ne *sunt* pas renomees") points toward the referent as grammatical subject (there is in fact only one word) but the reader's squeamish desire to avoid forming such an image (analogous to the Lover's own prudishness) points in the other direction. However, both are present thanks to Jean's verbal trick predicated upon the linguistic nominalism directly under interrogation. There is of course a further layer of irony, given that it is the Lover himself who unwittingly creates out of words alone an obscene image that turns out to be considerably more objectionable than the crime of which he accuses Reason. This little passage demonstrates most effectively the concomitant innocence and provocation of the verbal arts.

Another example that depends more on the rhetorical manipulation of parts of speech is Reason's argument in favor of the basic innocence and arbitrariness of words as a way of countering the Lover's obsessive fixation on the specific verbal icon:

> se je, quant mis les nons aus choses
> que si reprendre et blasmer oses,
> coilles reliques apelasse
> et reliques coilles clamasse,
> tu, qui si m'en morz et depiques,
> me redeïsses de reliques
> que ce fust lez moz et vilains.
>
> (vv. 7079–85)

[If, when I put names to things that you dare to criticize thus and blame, I had called testicles relics and had declared relics to be testicles, then you, who here criticize me and goad me on account of them, would reply that "relics" was an ugly, base word. (p. 135)]

Jean's immediate intention is fairly straightforward, expressing the linguistic relativism of words denoting obscene or sacred objects. When those readers who have already gotten to the end of the poem realize, however, that the term *reliques* becomes a faintly veiled metaphor for the female genitals, then it becomes clear that Reason's suggestions of a substitute word is far from arbitrary or that it is even motivated solely by a taste for the sacrilegious—that in fact a sexual transposition is being hinted at. The chiasmus "coilles reliques/reliques coilles," a favored rhetorical figure of Jean's, further suggests in its verbal intertwining either an image of copulation, the two members being poetically joined, or even of androgyny—a being possessing two sets of genitals.[26]

An extension of the initial joke is to be found in what is probably an interpolated passage, found nonetheless in a surprising number of manuscripts,[27]

> E quant pour reliques m'oïsses
> Couilles nomer le mot preïsses
> Pour si bel e tant le prisasses
> Que par tout couilles aorasses
> E les baisasses en eglises
> En or e en argent assises

[And if you had heard me provide the name *coilles* for *reliques* you would take the word for such a beautiful one and would so prize it that you would everywhere venerate *coilles* and would kiss them in churches, enshrined in gold and in silver. (translation mine)]

What Jean de Meun is in effect showing us is language getting very much out of hand. In this regard, both Reason and the Lover are being victimized, and their common bond resides in the fluid situational link between words and things. Reason's stance is clear: God might have created an earlier language but he subsequently left it to her to attach names to things:

> mes il vost que nons leur trovasse
> a mon plesir et les nomasse
> proprement et conmunement
> por craistre nostre entendement.
>   (vv. 7061−64)

[(God) wanted me to find names at my pleasure and to name things, individually and collectively, in order to increase our understanding. (p. 135)]

Reason's position here is intriguing, for however much her statement that she named things at her pleasure might seem to betoken an admission of arbitrariness in the relation between word and thing, the fact that she is, allegorically speaking, the mythical founder of human language—the language faculty itself—endows her gesture with the same sort of originary status that would have characterized God's own putative language. Furthermore, and although we might think otherwise, it is this belief alone that can explain the Lover's behavior. Whatever he claims in his illogical defense ("Even if God did make the things, he did not make the words"), his disapproval of the word necessarily stems from his disapproval of the thing. Where Reason and the Lover differ is on moral, and not linguistic, grounds. This difference is neatly encompassed in a word that occurs several times in the discussion, *propre*—which, like the modern English "proper," can play on both sides of the issue. A dirty word can be linguistically proper but morally improper. Furthermore, and here is where one must appreciate Jean's aplomb, his jokes based on the reader's own familiarity with language are only operative when *we* accept the necessary connection in common language between word and thing, its referential function. Jean is thus not simply asserting, but demonstrating, the interpenetration of common conceptions and erudite formulations and, along with it, the bad faith that consists in their artificial separation.

Reason's own originary stance is, however, also placed into question in the narrative. Her discussion of literality and propriety in naming could recall the rhetorical definition of *proprietas*, as for example found in Quintilian: "Propria sunt verba cum id significant, in quod primo denominata sunt" [Words are proper when they signify that for which they were first named].[28] But when Reason goes on to detail the sorts of euphemisms used by women in France ("borses, harnais, riens, piches,[29] pines" [v. 7113]) ["purses, harnesses, things, spades, pine cones" (translation mine)] she inadvertently undercuts her own "proper" word *coilles*. From this series in particular, the word *harnais* is taken up at the end of the poem as one of the pilgrim's instruments, along with the scrip, the staff, and so on. But a look at the Latin etymon for *coilles*, *culleus*, shows us that it too is a figure, whose literal meaning is "sheath" or "small bag."[30] Jean's own poetics undoes reasonable language use by dissecting metaphorical constructs and forging new ones. Reason's static vision of language simply cannot accommodate the diachronicity implicit in Jean's wide-ranging metaphoric production, the basis of one of the Middle Ages' favorite rhetorical tools: etymology.

Jean de Meun's play with obscenity is, in addition, based upon a type of verbal contagion. We have already noted the recurrence of the offensive word culminating in Genius's verbally obscene avalanche (cf. notes 15 and 20). Consistent with Jean's deployment of a poetics of contraries, however, *coille* echoes *cueillir*, the act of deflowerment toward which the poem inevitably leads—thus effecting a paradoxically symbolic assimilation between castration and penetration, male and female principles. Indeed, in the manuscript edited by Lecoy, B.N. fr. 1573, the scribe writes the following:

. . .
jusqu'a tant qu'il avra *coillie*
seur la branche vert et foillie
la tres bele rose vermeille
et qu'il soit jorz et qu'il s'esveille.

(vv. 10569–72)

This passage, as I mentioned above, strategically serves to circumscribe the entire poetic project but, as is visible through the scribal gesture in this isolated instance, it also reveals the verbal network subtly at work even when it is no longer a question of outright obscenity. Jean de Meun manages, *in practice*, to prove Reason's nominalist point. The scribal mark suggests another unexpected extension of the verbal play: Bel *Acueil*—that character who, as a masculine allegory of female presence, embodies the work's sexual enigma. Thus, the verbal nexus *coille—coillir—cueillir—Acueil*, disseminated throughout the text, can be seen to subtend the complex sexual agenda developed elsewhere in more explicit, and objectionable, terms.

A further terrain that has been little explored in the context of etymology is Jean's position as a writer in the vernacular.[31] First of all, Jean draws attention to the opposition between Latin and the vernacular at a couple of moments during the episode: Initially, when Reason mentions that someone who would translate Boethius's *Consolatio* would be doing lay people a great service, and later when he has the Lover reply to Reason: "Now tell me, not in Latin, but in French, what you want me to serve" (vv. 5809–11; p. 117). This outright linguistic self-consciousness suggests that if there are linguistic plays, they might be occurring across language barriers, such as in the etymological undermining of Reason that I have just proposed.[32] Judging by Jean de Meun's translation of Abelard's *Historia Calamitatum*, which might or might not have preceded his composition of the *Rose*, the word *coillon* translates the Latin *testiculum* while the versatile French *escoillez* replaces the cumbersome Latin *amputatis testiculis*.[33] These words are of course clustered at the moment when Abelard tells of his castration, following which he is brought back to an even more successful life of teaching. It is in this context also that Origen is first recalled, not because of his castration, but as the greatest Christian philosopher, one who attracted students from the study of secular literature to that of the Bible. Abelard will speak of his "use" of secular texts as a kind of lure, or fishhook ("quasi hamum quendam fabricavi"), that is to say a seduction technique that clearly compensates for his missing virility.[34] What is already an overdetermined moment of conversion, a wavering between power and impotence, a reverse emasculation of the students he has hooked, is further emphasized and reconnected by Jean de Meun within his translation when he uses a word that reverberates in this crucial passage, his French word for "student": *escollier*. By the time we reach the phrase for Abelard's teaching in school, "doctrine escolliere,"[35] we might wonder whether we are not in fact, to borrow Carolyn Dinshaw's apt phrase, dealing instead with a "eunuch hermeneutics."[36]

If Jean's manipulation of the French language brings out resonances that were not available in Latin, it might in turn be suggested that in the *Rose* there are perhaps figures based upon a knowledge of Latin. One might wonder, for instance, why the several exemplary tales recounted by Reason seem to involve decapitation. Virginius cut off the head of his daughter Virginia ("tantost a la teste coupee" [v. 5607]) in order to preserve her virginity (could this be an unarticulated pun?) from an unwanted suitor. Charles of Anjou took the head ("prist la teste" [v. 6628]) of Conrad and, later, of the greatest men of Sicily: "prist des plus granz de la vile / les testes" (vv. 6703–04). Most telling, perhaps, is Nero, who just before killing himself, asks that his head never be found: "Si s'ocist, mes ainz fist requeste/que ja nus ne trovast sa teste" (vv. 6419–20). If we consider that the Latin counterpart of our key word in Reason's speech, *testiculum*, can be interpreted by a false etymology as the diminutive of "head," *testa*, we could read into these multiple occurrences a surreptitious attempt to proliferate a linguistically determined image that is otherwise declared unspeakable. The connection between decapitation and the dissolution of linguistic bonds (and hence of understanding) is painstakingly underscored by Jean when he provides Nero's reason for his remarkable request: "por ce qu'il ne fust queneüz, / se ses cors fust enprés veüz" ["So that if afterward his body were seen it would not be recognized" (vv. 6421–22) p. 126].

It might at this point be useful to summarize the preceding discussion. Initially through a seemingly fortuitous lexical association, Jean de Meun effects a direct figurative relationship between castration or bodily dismemberment and linguistic functions as they are predicated upon the tenuous yet commonly accepted bond between word and thing. The negative aspects of man's fallen condition seem nonetheless to find their positive counterparts: from Saturn's castration, Venus is born. From those of

Abelard and Origen, scholarship is advanced. Similarly, the loosening of ties between words and things betokens the possibility of figuration in a variety of dimensions. Obliquely, Jean de Meun's writing can be qualified as a poetics of dismemberment, allowing at once for the free play of words in their material sense and, correspondingly, for the assimilation of concrete objects—the very basis of metaphor. The dismemberment of language is only to be regretted when measured against the fullness of an originary language that would have respected semiotic propriety. The resultant release is itself positive insofar as it makes possible figuration in all of its forms.

Jean further effaces the expository contours of his discussion (by which I mean the careful distinction between linguistic theorist and practitioner) by identifying the offensive member with the offensive word in such a way that in order to critique the former, you must *use* the latter. Inherent in the conceptual problem is a theme to which I alluded at the beginning and that takes on increasingly greater proportions in Jean's poem: the profound interdependence between censorship and obscenity.

The freedom of meaning production that Jean is here advocating is of course directly related to the larger discursive frame he has adopted from his model and pre-text: the allegorical poem. Reason comments thus on the transference of meaning necessary in certain discourses:

> Si dit l'en bien en noz escoles
> maintes choses par paraboles,
> qui mout sunt beles a entendre;
> si ne doit l'en mie tout prendre
> a la letre quan que l'en ot.
> (vv. 7123−27)

[In our schools indeed they say many things in parables which are very beautiful to hear (or: to understand); however, one should not take whatever one hears according to the letter. (p. 136)]

The hermeneutic confusion Reason elicits in the Lover is surely not merely intended to demonstrate his stupidity or critical naïveté. Jean is in some sense alerting us to the capriciousness of the interpretive faculty. Thus, as Fleming has aptly pointed out, the verb *gloser* has two opposite meanings in the mouth of Reason and the Lover. It can denote activity meant to clarify the meaning of an obscure text but also activity meant to cover it up, as when the Lover uses it to speak of euphemism.[37] This would replicate the distinction in modern English between "to gloss" and "to gloss over." This doubleness, or duplicity, of hermeneutic activity is clearly at the center of Jean's text. When the Lover finally dismisses Reason by saying that he does not have the time to learn how to gloss (in her sense) he is at the cutting edge of this duplicity, for has he not himself become a character within an allegorical fiction—participant *in* a gloss and simultaneously worthy of being glossed? [38]

The relation between glossing and interpretation had already been explored by Reason in her tale of Croesus and his daughter Phanie (vv. 6459–592). Ostensibly an illustration of man's helplessness before Fortune's wheel, it is in fact articulated around dream interpretation. Phanie provides what turns out to be a correct allegorical exegesis of her father's dream. He scoffs at her interpretation, insisting that hers was a "false gloss" (v. 6579) and that the dream must be understood literally, "a la letre" (v. 6580). Not only does the debate between Croesus and Phanie foreshadow the essence of virtually all debate that has accrued around the larger dream account, the *Rose* itself as figurative poem, but a passing comment by Reason suggests that the very appeal to reason in such debates is quite possibly an indispensable illusion of the interpreter's own folly:

> mes fols ne voit en sa folie
> fors que sen et reson ensemble,
> si conme en son fol queur li semble.
> (vv. 6564–66)

[but a fool sees nothing in his folly, as it seems to him in his foolish heart, except sense and reason together. (p. 128)]

If Jean de Meun seems to be stressing language's independent expressivity outside the bounds of specific authority or intentionality, I would simply say that this is a broader ideological preoccupation within the *Rose* as a whole. When he has the Lover state that even though the God of Love had forbidden him the use of obscene language he can speak this word because he was not the one to originate it, he is articulating an important principle of accountability that characterizes the authorial stance as a whole:

> Donc le ramentevré je voir,
> dis je con remanbranz et vistes,
> par tel mot con vos le deistes.

> Si m'a mes mestres deffendu,
> car je l'ai mout bien entendu,
> que ja mot n'isse de ma boiche
> qui de ribaudie s'aproiche.
> Mes des que je n'en sui fesierres,
> j'en puis bien estre recitierres;
> si nomeré le mot tout outre.
>   (vv. 5680−89)

["Indeed, I will remind you," I said, with a lively memory, "of the very word you used. My master has forbidden me—I heard him very clearly—ever to let fall from my mouth any word approaching ribaldry. But as long as I didn't use the word originally, I can easily repeat it; I will name it right out without restriction." (p. 115)]

Aside from the Lover's comic eagerness to pronounce the word he is in the process of condemning, one must jump forward to a passage several thousand lines later in order to understand fully this assertion; here the Narrator makes a rare appearance in order to justify himself before detractors, real or imagined. He states:

> s'il vos samble que je di fables,
> por manteür ne m'an tenez,
> mes aus aucteurs vos an prenez
> qui an leur livres ont escrites
> les paroles que g'en ai dites,
> et ceus avec que g'en dirai;
> ne ja de riens n'an mentirai,
> se li preudome n'en mentirent
> qui les anciens livres firent. . . .
> je n'i faz riens fors reciter,
> se par mon geu, qui po vos coute,
> quelque parole n'i ajoute,
> si con font antr'eus li poete,
> quant chascuns la matire trete
> don il li plest a antremetre;
> car si con tesmoigne la letre,
> profiz et delectacion,
> c'est toute leur entencion.
>   (vv. 15186−94, 15204−12)

[if it seems to you that I tell fables, don't consider me a liar, but apply to the authors who in their works have written the things that I have said and will say. I shall never lie in anything as long as the worthy men who wrote the old books did not lie. . . . I do nothing but retell just what the poets have written between them, when each of them treats the subject matter that he is pleased to undertake, except that my treatment, which costs you little, may add a few speeches (or words). For, as the text witnesses, the whole intent of the poets is profit and delight. (p. 259)]

The use of the word *reciter* here suggests not that it is a matter of who invented the word, as Fleming has affirmed,[39] but rather of voicing what someone has already said. In the second example, the intent is clear. If someone else has said it, then I cannot be accused for I am merely calling upon their writing, which is to say, their authority. In the case of Reason and the Lover, the latter is saying that since Reason has broached the subject and voiced the word, he cannot be condemned for quoting it in a statement of censure. The important point here is the context in which the word is used and, along with that, the discursive mode of quotation that allows one to express ideas without being responsible. I would further suggest—and this is an additional irony attendant upon the Lover and his curious counterpart, the Narrator—that the Lover is here contradicting his own statement of principle when he pronounces what he himself declares to be inherently objectionable. Even if we agree with Poirion that the Lover's abhorrence for the obscene word demonstrates a "mentalité magique"[40] that fetishizes select terms independently from their denotation, his willingness to echo the word once it has been used suggests a short-circuiting of this magical force by the inscrutable defensive power of quotation.

A further example of what might be called Jean's authoritative deferral is, of course, his statement concerning the poem's authorship, which, by submerging the creative instance within the erotic myth and chronologically placing that instance in some prophetic future time, effectively endows the work with an aura of divine inspiration.

I will conclude with a final image provided by Reason, whose speech is larded with indications of how we are supposed to read, or misread, the poem. Among the many details she includes in her ample account of Nero, Reason describes perhaps the Emperor's most despicable crime, the dismemberment of his mother:

si rot bien queur plus dur que pierre
quant il fist occierre son frere,
quant il fist desmembrer sa mere
por ce que par lui fust veüz
li leus ou il fu conceüz.
                    (vv. 6162–66)

[indeed, he had a heart harder than stone when he had his brother
killed, when he had his mother dismembered so that he might see the
place where he was conceived. (p. 122)]

The interpreter's quest for meaning—in a sense, a search for his own
oneiric origins—ends up, we might say, with a blank space, an empty
womb, denoting the very illusion of that mystical meaning. An alternate
quest is, however, suggested in the lines that follow:

et puis qu'il la vit *desmenbree,*
selonc l'estoire *remenbree,*
la beauté des *menbres* juja.
                    (vv. 6167–69)

[after he saw her dismembered, according to the story as it is remembered, he judged the beauty of her limbs (or members). (p. 122)]

As the rhyme insists, the body dis-membered attains beauty through the
story re-membered (literally, "put back together"). Thus the interpreter's
alternate quest, aesthetic in this case, should perhaps be directed to those
material parts we might otherwise have discarded—for Jean, the matter of
language itself.

Notes

    1. On the critical fortune of Jean de Meun's work in the Middle Ages, see
Pierre-Yves Badel's indispensable *Le "Roman de la Rose" au XIVe siècle: Étude de la
réception de l'œuvre,* Publications Romanes et Françaises 153 (Geneva: Droz, 1980).
    2. The *Roman de la Rose* is quoted from Félix Lecoy's three-volume edition,
Classiques Français du Moyen Âge 92, 95, 98 (Paris: Champion, 1965–70), line
numbers in the body of the paper. The English translation is Charles Dahlberg's
(Princeton, NJ: Princeton University Press, 1971), referenced by page number.
    3. The *Rose* correspondence is quoted from the edition by Eric Hicks, *Le
Débat sur le "Roman de la Rose,"* Bibliothèque du XVe siècle 43 (Paris: Champion,
1977), page numbers in text. The English translation, also indicated by page num-

ber in text, is by Joseph L. Baird and John R. Kane, *La Querelle de la Rose: Letters and Documents*, North Carolina Studies in the Romance Languages and Literatures 199 (Chapel Hill: University of North Carolina Press, 1978).

4. See for instance Bakhtin's "Discourse in the Novel," included in *The Dialogic Imagination*, ed. Michael Holquist, trans. Caryl Emerson and Michael Holquist (Austin: University of Texas Press, 1981 [orig. 1934–35]), pp. 259–422; and the chapter of his earlier *Problems of Dostoevsky's Poetics* (ed. and trans. Caryl Emerson, Theory and History of Literature, vol. 8 [Minneapolis: University of Minnesota Press, 1984 (1929)]) entitled "Discourse in Dostoevsky" (pp. 181–269).

5. *The Dialogic Imagination*, p. 283.

6. Julia Kristeva, *Semeiotike: Recherches pour une sémanalyse* (Paris: Seuil [Coll. "Points"], 1969), p. 93.

7. Kristeva, pp. 93–94.

8. "'Des contraires choses': la fonction poétique de la citation et des exempla dans le 'Roman de la Rose' de Jean de Meun," *Littérature* 41 (Feb. 1981): 62–81.

9. Jean de Meun's familiarity with the mendicant controversies of the 1250s is abundantly clear from his explicit reference to Joachim di Fiore's *Eternal Gospel* and the mid-century scandal it caused in Paris, as well as from his extensive cribbing from Guillaume de Saint-Amour's *De Periculis*. On scholastic resonances in Jean's continuation, see Gérard Paré, *Le Roman de la Rose et la scolastique courtoise*, Publications de l'Institut d'Études Médiévales d'Ottawa 10 (Paris: Vrin; Ottawa: Institut d'Études Médiévales, 1941); and Gisela Hilder, *Der scholastische Wortschatz bei Jean de Meun: Die Artes Liberales*, Beiheft zur Zeitschrift für Romanische Philologie 129 (Tübingen: Max Niemeyer, 1972).

10. See, most notably, Daniel Poirion, "Les mots et les choses selon Jean de Meun," *L'Information Littéraire* 26 (1974), pp. 7–11, and "De la signification selon Jean de Meun," in *Archéologie du signe*, ed. Eugene Vance and Lucie Brind'amour, Recueils d'études médiévales 3 (Toronto: Pontifical Institute of Mediaeval Studies, 1983, pp. 165–85; Marc-René Jung, "Jean de Meung et l'allégorie," *Cahiers de l'Association Internationale des Études Françaises* 28 (1976), pp. 21–36; Gustav Ineichen, "Le discours linguistique de Jean de Meun," *Romanistische Zeitschrift für Literaturgeschichte* 2 (1978), pp. 245–53; Maureen Quilligan, "Allegory, Allegoresis and the Deallegorization of Language: The *Roman de la Rose*, the *De planctu naturae*, and the *Parlement of Foules*," in *Allegory, Myth and Symbol*, ed. Morton W. Bloomfield, Harvard English Studies 9 (Cambridge, MA: Harvard University Press, 1981), pp. 163–86; R. Howard Bloch, *Etymologies and Genealogies: A Literary Anthropology of the French Middle Ages* (Chicago: University of Chicago Press, 1983), pp. 137–41; and John V. Fleming, *Reason and the Lover* (Princeton, NJ: Princeton University Press, 1984), pp. 97–135.

11. Alan M. F. Gunn, *The Mirror of Love: A Reinterpretation of "The Romance of the Rose"* (Lubbock: Texas Tech Press, 1952), pp. 231–32.

12. "Narcissus, Pygmalion, and the Castration of Saturn: Two Mythographical Themes in the *Roman de la Rose*," *Studies in Philology* 71 (1974): 404–26.

13. See, for instance, Michael Riffaterre, *Semiotics of Poetry* (Bloomington: Indiana University Press, 1978).

14. Fleming, p. 113.

15. A form of the word proliferates in one final section, Genius's reiteration of Saturn's castration and the resultant end of the Golden Age (cf. lines 20006, 20009, 20010, 20020, 20021, 20022, 20028, 20031, 20037, 20039, 20050).

16. *Speculum* 60 (October 1985): 973–77.

17. "[I]llae nuptiae . . . pudendam libidinem non haberent." (*De Civitate Dei*, Corpus Christianorum [Turnhout, 1955], XIV, p. 23). English translation by Henry Bettenson (Harmondsworth: Penguin, 1972), p. 585.

18. "[S]ed in omnia, quae de huius modi membris sensum cogitandis adtingerent, sine ullo timore obscenitatis liber sermo ferretur, nec ipsa verba essent, quae vocarentur obscena." (Ibid.) Trans., p. 587.

19. "Cum autem simul et secundum se verbum movet audientem et secundum id quod significat, tunc et ipsa enuntiatio et id quod ab ea nuntiatur simul advertitur. Unde enim, quod non offenditure aurium castitas, cum audit manu ventre pene bona patria laceraverat? Offenderetur autem, si obscena pars corporis sordido ac vulgari nomine appellaretur, cum res eadem sit cuius utrumque vocabulum est, nisi quod in illo turpitudo rei quae significata est decore verbi significantis operitur, in hoc autem sensum animumque utriusque deformitas feriret: veluti non alia meretrix, sed aliter tamen videtur eo cultu, quo ante iudicem stare adsolet, aliter eo quo in luxuriosi cubiculo iacere." (Augustine, *De Dialectica*, ed. Jan Pinborg, trans. B. Darrell Jackson [Dordrecht, Holland: D. Reidel, 1975], VII, pp. 100–103). This passage is discussed by Fleming, pp. 110–11. In pushing for a comic reading of the Lover's prudish stance, however, Fleming seems to misapply this quotation, for the potential propriety in speaking of vulgar things that Augustine here advocates (by avoiding words that are inherently objectionable) more closely resembles the criticism that the Lover levels at Reason. From his point of view, she could have told her exemplum properly had she simply avoided the vulgar term *coilles*. If the Lover's attempt to "tart up his harlotry" is adjudged comic or parodic, then so is the Augustinian strategy, which appears to endorse similar euphemistic cover-ups.

20. The concluding repetition of forms of the obscene word in Genius's speech, *coillons, escoilleür, escoillier*, and so forth (see n. 15 above) functions in a manner similar to the Lover's graphic penetration of the castle, effectively desensitizing the reader's censoring impulses through familiarity.

21. "[E]t ob hoc maxime dominica manu me nunc tactum esse cognoscerem, quo liberius a carnalibus illecebris et tumultuosa vita seculi abstractus studio litterarum vaccarem, nec tam mundi quam Dei vere philosophus fierem." Abelard, *Historia Calamitatum*, ed. J. Monfrin, 4th printing (Paris: Vrin, 1978), p. 81. English translation by Betty Radice, *The Letters of Abelard and Heloise* (Harmondsworth: Penguin, 1974), p. 77.

22. "[M]embris his vilissimis, quae pro summae turpitudinis exercitio pudenda vocantur, nec proprium sustinent nomen" ("The Personal Letters between Abelard and Heloise," ed. J. T. Muckle C.S.B., *Mediaeval Studies* 15 [1953]: 47–94 [89]). *Letters of Abelard and Heloise*, p. 148.

23. "In exemplo est magnus ille Christianorum philosophus Origines qui, ut hoc in se penitus incendium exstingueret, manus sibi inferre veritus non est; ac si illos ad litteram vere beatos intelligeret, qui se ipsos propter regnum coelorum

castraverunt . . . quasi illam Isiae prophetiam ad historiam magis quam ad mysterium duceret, per quam ceteris fidelibus eunuchos Dominus praefert." ("The Personal Letters," pp. 89–90). *Letters of Abelard and Heloise*, p. 148. The story is told by Eusebius in his *Ecclesiastical History*, VI, p. 8.

    24. Fleming, p. 105.

    25. *Etymologies*, p. 138.

    26. One could adduce as further evidence of Jean's attempt to conflate or confuse sexual figures the ambiguous womanly advice of la Vieille addressed to the hitherto masculine Bel Acueil; and, in the same speech of Reason, the transformation of one of the attributes of the rose—feminine symbol par excellence—, the thorn, into an unmistakably masculine member:

> ausint con ce fussent espines;
> mes quant les sentent bien joignanz,
> els nes tienent pas a poignanz.
>
> (vv. 7114–16)

[as though they [male sexual organs] were thorns; but when the ladies feel them nicely inserted, they do not consider them sharp. (translation mine)]

Jean de Meun was certainly embroidering upon a suggestive image cluster already available in Guillaume de Lorris's poem, lines 1675–78. For an astute commentary on the hermaphroditic qualities of Jean's pre-text, see Marta Powell Harley, "Narcissus, Hermaphroditus, and Attis: Ovidian Lovers at the Fontaine d'Amors in Guillaume de Lorris's *Roman de la Rose*," *PMLA* 101 (1986): 324–37.

    27. Taken from Ernest Langlois, ed., *Le Roman de la Rose par Guillaume de Lorris et Jean de Meun*, vol. III, SATF (Paris: Champion, 1921), note to line 7120, p. 31. Translation mine.

    28. *Institutio oratoria*, ed. and trans. H. E. Butler, Loeb Classical Library (Cambridge, MA: Harvard University Press, 1980 [1920]), I, v, 71.

    29. This list of common euphemisms illustrates quite appropriately the proper/improper theme in question. The origin of "piches" is obscure, but what counts is the series within which it is found. For the medieval Latin word *piga*, which could have given *piche* in Old French, du Cange provides the following definition: "nates, vel bursa, mentula" ("buttocks, or even pouch, penis"). This suggests the relative unimportance of the actual referent next to the obscene application of the word. Furthermore, the blankness of the word *riens* ("thing") unmistakably implies that obscenity is contextual and not a quality of certain lexical items. On the question of euphemistic and metaphorical extensions of sexual and scatological terminology, see J. N. Adams's richly documented *The Latin Sexual Vocabulary* (Baltimore: Johns Hopkins University Press, 1982).

    30. Cf. Fleming, p. 106.

    31. On the question of Latin/vernacular diglossia in the thirteenth and fourteenth centuries in France, see Serge Lusignan, *Parler vulgairement: Les intellectuels*

et la langue française aux XIIIe et XIVe siècles (Montréal: Les Presses de l'Université de Montréal, 1986).

32. The Lover also alludes to the native French speaker's automatic understanding of Reason's vulgar terms, as something apart from the latter's intellectualizing stance:

> Dame, bien les i puis entendre,
> qu'il i sunt si legiers a prendre
> qu'il n'est nus qui françois seüst
> qui prendre ne les i deüst,
> n'ont mestier d'autres declarances.
> (vv. 7155–59)

[Lady, I can indeed understand them; they are so easy to perceive that no one who knows French ought not to perceive them. They have no need of other clarifications. (p. 136)]

33. Jean de Meun, *Traduction de la première épitre de Pierre Abélard* (*Historia Calamitatum*), ed. Charlotte Charrier (Paris: Champion, 1934), p. 104.

34. Abelard, and perhaps Jean, would not have ignored Isidore of Seville's etymological connection between (*h*)*amus* and *amicus*: "amicus ab hamo, id est, a catena caritatis; unde et hami quod teneant." ["The word 'friend' (*amicus*) comes from 'fish-hook' (*hamus*), that is, from the bonds of charity; and also from whatever these hooks might hold."] *Etymologiarum sive Originum*, ed. W. M. Lindsay (rpt. Oxford: Oxford University Press, 1957 [1911], X, p. 5.

35. Jean de Meun, *Traduction*, p. 111.

36. Carolyn Dinshaw, *Chaucer's Sexual Poetics* (Madison: University of Wisconsin Press, 1989), pp. 156–84.

37. Fleming, p. 105.

38. On Jean de Meun's recontextualization (and resultant fictionalization) of Guillaume de Lorris's first-person narrator, see my "Closed Quotations: The Speaking Voice in the *Roman de la Rose*," *Yale French Studies* 67 (1984): 248–69.

39. Fleming, p. 102: "The prohibition against uttering dirty words applies only to new words—that is, I presume, to words that one makes up oneself. As long as you are not the maker (*fesierres*) of a dirty word, but only its reporter, you have committed no sin against Cupid." The difference being marked between Reason and the Lover in this instance is not that between mythical inventor of language and user of said language, but between a denotative and a metalinguistic usage—a distinction made by Augustine in the *De Dialectica*, chapter V, when he differentiates between words as signs of things and words as signs of other words. It is the former that the Lover designates by *fesierres* and the latter by *recitierres*.

40. "Les mots et les choses," p. 8.

Part III

The Illuminated *Rose*

Stephen G. Nichols

6. Ekphrasis, Iconoclasm, and Desire

Introduction

Ekphrasis no longer enjoys the name recognition it once did. In the terminology of classical rhetoric, ekphrasis "was the elaborate 'delineation' (ἔκφρασις, *descriptio*, description), of people, places, buildings, works of art. Late antique and medieval poetry used it lavishly" (Curtis, 69). But, along with figurative language generally, it fell victim to the hostility toward classical rhetoric manifested by literary movements from romanticism to modernism. Indeed, one history of rhetoric still in use claims authoritatively: "ekphrasis . . . perverts descriptions because it frustrates narrative movement; [and] . . . confirms a decadent habit of literature" (Baldwin, 19). The good news is that ekphrasis is making a comeback.

The renewal of interest in rhetoric and allegory within the last decade includes epideictic discourse—praise of gods of men—and thus embraces ekphrasis, description being a form of praise. Recent uses of the term, by Wendy Steiner, W. J. T. Mitchell, Murray Krieger, Michael Riffaterre, and others, however, suggest considerable agreement to take the term in the more limited sense: the description of a visual art work. My own concern focuses on the contribution of ekphrasis in two areas: the *paragone*, or conflict between word and image in Western cultural history generally, and, more particularly, the role of that conflict in defining the tension between classical and medieval forms of representation, what we might call, the Roman in the romance.

Figural language places the image in the service of the word, thereby privileging the sensual and immediate over the rational and conceptual. Rhetoric has thus been at the heart of a fundamental conflict in the Western theory and practice of representation since Plato: the conflict between figural versus rational language. In this conflict—seen, to take but two examples, in Plato's *Timaeus* and in Augustine's critique of Virgil's *Aeneid* in the first three books of *Confessions*—the images of figural language serve as deictics pointing to the presence of the body in the word. Images evoke sensual responses, as Augustine noted disapprovingly, that signal the presence of the body as other, the body as a signifier rather than a referent. Over against this model, Plato seemingly, and Augustine certainly, would set the discourse of reason, the abstract knowledge of language that effaces the presence of the body by eliding the speaking subject as a psychosomatic entity. In this model, the body is referent or, preferably, absent, rather than signifier or agent, as we see in this anecdote about a law professor's daughter from Christine de Pizan's *Livre de la Cité des Dames*:

> Quant a sa belle et bonne fille que il tant ama, qui ot nom Nouvelle, fist apprendre lettres et si avant es loys que quant is estoit occupez d'aucun essoine par quoy ne povoit vacquier a lire les leçons a ces escolliers, il envoyoit sa fille en son lieu lire aux escolles en chayere. *Et adfin que la biauté d'elle n'empeschast la penssee des ouyans, elle avoit une petite courtine au devant d'elle.* (Curnow, § 185, p. 875)

> [Giovanni Andrea, a solemn law professor in Bologna not quite sixty years ago, was not of the opinion that it was bad for women to be educated. He had a fair and good daughter, named Novella, who was educated in the law to such an advanced degree that when he was occupied by some task and not at leisure to present his lectures to his students, he would send Novella, his daughter, in his place to lecture to his students from his chair. *And to prevent her beauty from distracting the concentration of her audience, she had a little curtain drawn in front of her.* (Christine de Pizan, trans.: II.36.3, p. 154)]

Christine's anecdote, with its implicit literary allegory (keyed to the name of the woman, "Novella") illustrates the extension into medieval literature of the conflict between figural and rational discourse. Ekphrasis, the figure of figurative language, becomes a vehicle for the conflict by its overdetermination of the sensate. Joel Fineman recently defined epideictic discourse as:

> what happens when metaphor and mimesis meet . . . With metaphor added to it, mimesis becomes more than merely lifeless imitation, just as metaphor, grounded by mimetic reference, is more than extravagant ornamentation. Thus conjoined, in accord with a familiar ideal of poetic decorum—a decorum whose consequence receives sometimes more and sometimes less metaphysical inflection—mimesis and metaphor accomplish a discourse of special vividness. (Fineman, *Shakespeare's Perjured Eye*, 3–4)

That "special vividness" of epideictic poetry generally, and ekphrasis in particular, imparts a dramatic action to the passages so affected. It is this dramatic action that renders the image sensual by conveying the actuality of the body's presence: "I will draw this for you in words," says Himerius, "and will make your ears serve for eyes" (*Orationes* X; Baldwin, 18). The drama of the body in the word is both diegetic and extradiegetic: referring to the discursive subject's relation to the narrative and the reader/listener's involvement in it.

In the classical and medieval periods, sensual imagery often serves to dramatize a split between mind and body. Ethical or theological implications aside, the body's otherness stems precisely from its protean capacity for sensual representation. In *Confessions* I, Augustine reproaches his younger self for "sensual mimesis" by physically responding to his reading of Virgil's *Aeneid*. Bernardus Silvestris, commenting on Aeneas' crossing of the River Styx in Book 6, equates the body with Charon's boat. He anticipates Dante in signifying Hell as a corporeal space principally because of the body's identity with sensual perception.

> Charon has a stitched and leaky boat, which we interpret as the human body. It is stitched together—composed of diverse elements and humors. It has leaks, the openings of the senses . . . The sails which drive the ship by catching breezes are the two eyes which draw the body to different ends through delight of pleasures and the lechery of revellers. As you read in the *Timaeus*, this sense, when something new and therefore delightful seizes it, causes the body to be moved with hasty and inordinate force. (*Commentary*, 75)

But the success of the ekphrastic trope does not only imply an ability to implicate the body. Ekphrasis also problematizes the image itself. It calls attention to the vulnerability of the referential claims made by the image. Visual representations were held to be natural rather than conventional signs: "imitations of natural objects, the handiwork of God," as Leonardo da Vinci put it, in contrast to poetry, which "contains only lying fictions about human actions" (Mitchell, 78).

Ekphrasis calls such polar dichotomies into question by showing the power of language to represent natural objects, while at the same time exposing the narrative content of visual discourse. For painting was just as likely as poetry to represent "lying fictions about human actions." Indeed, many of the famous examples of ekphrasis from classical times depicted historical scenes in the midst of epic history. Homer's ekphrasis of the paintings on the shield of Achilles and Virgil's description of the scenes on Aeneas' shield are *mises en abyme* of the epic histories each tells. They also suggest the conventional (and cultural) relativity of both image and text.

In sum, ekphrasis reveals the drama of the image, its elusive relationship to the reality it purports to convey in terms not unlike those Picasso has used to describe painting:

> You see, for me a painting is a dramatic action in which reality finds itself split apart. For me the dramatic action takes precedence over all other considerations. The pure plastic art is only secondary as far as I'm concerned. *What counts is the drama of that plastic act.* (Gilot and Lake, 51)

Although Picasso is talking about modernist art, his conception describes accurately what happens when ekphrasis is deployed in historical texts. The drama of the image splitting reality apart may be followed in two works whose relationship has not previously been discussed.

Near the beginning of each of their stories, Aeneas and the Lover in Guillaume de Lorris's *Roman de la Rose* encounter a set of ekphrastic portraits painted on walls of spaces in which each will undergo a formative lesson in love. The ekphrastic passages constitute important reading lessons for the two heroes, while forcing us, as readers, to recognize a complex reality in which speaking subject (hero) and text dramatically oppose one another across and though the ekphrastic tropes that reveal themselves as images of difference.

Virgil and the Ekphrasis of History

Three ekphrastic moments in the *Aeneid* model a drama of history as the discovery of identity for Aeneas. Each moment offers a different version of historical perspective and narrative authority. We will look briefly at all three, then in more detail at the first, since that is the one that serves as subtext to Guillaume de Lorris.

In Book 1, Aeneas confronts his own past as mythological history when he gazes at the story of the Trojan War painted on the walls of the Temple of Juno in Carthage. The past here is the *Trojan* story that stands both as prelude and warning to the *Roman* story that the *Aeneid* recounts. The ekphrasis dramatizes the sundering of past from future, while simultaneously splitting Aeneas's subject into a present dominated by sensual subjectivity and a future defined by a *cogito*.

At the beginning of Book 6, Aeneas looks at the bronze doors of the temple of Apollo on which Daedalus has sculpted his biography omitting, significantly, the story of his son, Icarus, which his grief would not permit him to record. Daedalus, for Virgil, is the persona of the visual artist as antitype.[1] In this book, and with Daedalus's example as warning, Virgil develops a new typology of the hero as ethical artist. Book 6, the midpoint of the epic, recounts Aeneas's journey to the underworld in search of his father from whose lips he will learn his destiny and that of his descendants.

Book 8 of the *Aeneid* contains an ekphrastic description of the shield Aeneas will use in the combat that brings the work to a close. Fashioned Daedalus-like by Vulcan, at Venus's request, the shield inscribes history as prophecy on its face where Aeneas sees portrayed the future triumphs of Republican and imperial Rome. This passage, often cited as a locus classicus of ekphrasis, can best be understood not as an isolated example but, on the contrary, as the culmination of the sequence of ekphrases we are discussing. The sequence forms an iconoclastic program intent on making image subservient to word, as passion—whether Juno's, Dido's, Turnus' or Aeneas'—is made subservient to reason in the progress of the *Aeneid*.

To achieve his narrative of history as logos, Virgil seeks to create a rhetoric based on logic rather than emotion, on mind rather than body. To do so, he must subordinate the senses to the *cogito*, beginning with vision, the principal sense giving access to the inner life in classical theories. In his three main ekphrases of history, Virgil articulates a shift from vision as somatic, producing its effects through bodily sensation, to vision as conceptual. The shift is more than a simple question of aesthetics; it involves opposing theories of history: the personalized history of the Trojan War, symbolized by Homer's *Iliad* and its hero, Achilles, to an impersonal theory of transcendent history signified by *pietas* as exemplified by a line of heroes, each one forging a link in a logos of history.

The ekphrasis in Book 1 thus must be read in contrast to that of Book 8 within the economy of the *Aeneid*. In the first passage, Virgil deploys what we may call a "politics of the gaze," to which he gradually opposes "a politics of vision or prophecy" that culminates in the scene of Aeneas' shield in Book 8.[2] Since many medieval commentaries, like that of Bernardus Silvestris, stopped after Book 6, taken as a prefiguration of

Christ's harrowing of Hell, we will concern ourselves with the ekphrasis in Book 1, recognizing that for Virgil this was but the first step in a schema in a rhetoric of logos.

Aeneas and the Politics of the Gaze

In Virgil's first ekphrasis, Aeneas, at the lowest ebb of his fortunes since fleeing from Troy, enters Dido's new city of Carthage only to confront a magnificent mural painting of his past. Invisible beneath a protective cloud provided by his mother, Venus, Aeneas gazes at the Trojan story depicted on the walls of Juno's temple. At this stage, the painted Aeneas of Trojan history has more reality than the allegorically shrouded pre-hero of Virgil's text. The passage stresses this duality by cutting back and forth from the drama of history to the drama of the present as seen through Aeneas' emotions.

> He *sees* the wars of Troy set out in order:
> the battles famous now through all the world, the sons of Atreus
>   and of Priam, and
> Achilles, savage enemy to both.
> . . .
> He *watched* the warriors circling Pergamus:
> here routed Greeks were chased by Trojan fighters
> and here the Phyrgian troops pursued by plumed
> Achilles in his chariot. Nearby,
> sobbing, he recognized the snow-white canvas
> tents of King Rhesus—with his men betrayed,
> while still in their first sleep, and then laid waste,
> with many dead, by bloody Diomedes
> . . .
> Elsewhere young Troilus, the unhappy boy—
> he is matched unequally against Achilles—
> runs off, his weapons lost. He is fallen flat;
> his horses drag him on as he still clings
> fast to his empty chariot, clasping
> the reins. His neck, his hair trail on the ground,
> and his inverted spear inscribes the dust.
>   (Mandelbaum, trans., 1, 647–77; *Aen.* 1.456–78)

This last image of Troilus' spearhead writing his story in the dust of the Trojan plain might tempt us to argue Virgil's partiality for the superiority of the ekphrastic image over its visual counterpart, the putative model for the poetic scene. Or, we might be tempted to make the same claims for the pathetic evocation of the bereaved Trojan women at the moment when the goddess Pallas Athena rejects their pleas for help, thereby condemning them to collective rape by the victorious Greeks—a scene evoked, but elided in the averted gaze of the angry goddess:

> Meanwhile the Trojan women near the temple
> of hostile Pallas; hair disheveled,
> sad beating at their breasts, as suppliants,
> they bear the robes of offering. The goddess
> averts her face, her eyes fast to the ground.
>
> (Mandelbaum, trans., 1, 678–82; *Aen.* 1.479–82)

The superiority of ekphrasis over visual image might be seen in the climactic scene of the passage:

> Three times Achilles had dragged Hector round
> the walls of Troy, selling his lifeless body
> for gold. And then, indeed, Aeneas groans
> within the great pit of his chest, deeply;
> for he can see the spoils, the chariot,
> the very body of his friend, and Priam
> pleading for Hector with defenceless hands.
>
> (Mandelbaum, trans., 1, 683–89; *Aen.* 1.483–87)

While we cannot help acknowledging Virgil's mastery of the ekphrastic mode, artistic talent, be it the painter's skill or the poet's rhetorical prowess, is not really at issue here. We need to look beyond details, beyond technique, to the figures of difference in their cultural and social implications. We can accept as a given that Virgil uses ekphrasis to achieve that actuality or special vividness we associate with poetic theatricality. He does so not for any effect of "decorative dilation," as traditional handbooks of rhetoric assert, but to remind us that Aeneas' presence as hero of a new epic cancels the closure of Trojan history assumed by the painting.

Intended as a celebration of Juno's triumph over the Trojans, the mural projects assumptions as premature and incomplete as Carthage itself. Aeneas is thus a spectator to more than a painting: he sees, and we see through him, the drama of the past confronting a series of possible futures. These hypotheses play out in terms of Aeneas's subjective and emotional reaction to the painting. In the last analysis, the painting turns out not only to portray the wrong answers, but to solicit Aeneas to make the wrong assumptions.

Ekphrasis thus plays a metacritical role by introjecting a didactic moment of artistic self-examination. And this liminal critique tells us how we need to read and understand the text as a complex figuration of history or perhaps it would be more accurate to say as a figuration of a complex cultural web of signification in which historical past and prophetic future link Rome and Aeneas in their difference from other cities, other heroes, and other rulers.

We must remember that at the moment Aeneas views the painted history of Troy's destruction, he does so from a doubly liminal position: on the threshold of the epic that bears his name, he has not yet emerged as more than a passive agent of fate. Indeed, in contrast to the painted self he perceives on the walls—"He also recognized himself in combat / with the Achaean chiefs"—Aeneas the spectator is invisible, shrouded from sight by a protective mist: *neque cernitur ulli* (*Aen.* 1, 440). The Carthaginian crowd with whom he invisibly mixes—*per medios miscetque viris*—can see his historically determinate *image*, but *not* his presently indeterminate *being*. This tableau itself evokes compellingly Plato's distinction, in the *Timaeus*, between eternal being and temporal becoming, a contrast he felt humans all too prone to confuse through their habit of mistaking false forms—temporal and insubstantial—for eternal ones.

The second liminal element in Aeneas's situation at the moment he views the painted wall also concerns temporally bounded versus eternal forms within the ideological perspective of the *Aeneid*. The painted wall of Trojan history becomes a synecdoche for the walls of Carthage as a figure of likeness to the walls of Troy and both are images of difference from the future walls of Rome. The text makes this point in an exclamation uttered by Aeneas immediately prior to the ekphrastic passage, "O fortunati, quorum jam moenia surgunt!" (*Aen.* 1, 437):

> . . . "How fortunate are those
> whose walls already rise!" Aeneas cries
> while gazing at the rooftops of the city.
>   (Mandelbaum, trans., 1, 619–21)

Virgil's preface to the *Aeneid* valorizes *moenia* as a synecdoche for Rome in its difference from other cities, a difference that plays on the Platonic differentiation of temporal versus eternal forms:

> . . . dum conderet urbem
> inferretque deos Latio—genus unde Latinum
> Albanique patres atque altae moenia Romae.
> (*Aen.* 1, 5–7)

[. . . until he brought a city into being / and carried in his gods to Latium; / from this have come the Latin race, the lords / of Alba, and the ramparts of high Rome. (Mandelbaum, trans., 1, 9–12)]

One might well argue that Virgil privileges poetry over painting in these passages by showing that painting represents the past, while poetry can embrace past, present, and future. It is true that the painted image cannot represent, as the poetic passage does, Aeneas in his doubly liminal state, poised between eternal being and temporal becoming: his situation as the invisible spectator of his own history.

Still, I am not persuaded that these are the real issues at stake here. For one thing, they detract from the recurrent images of emotionalism the text associates with Aeneas' response to this confrontation with his past.

> He sees the wars of Troy set out in order
> . . .
> Achilles, savage enemy to both.
> He halted. As he wept, he cried: Achates.
> Where on this earth is there a land, a place
> that does not know our sorrows? There is Priam!
> Here, too, the honorable finds its due
> and there are tears for passing things; here, too,
> things mortal touch the mind . . .
> (Mandelbaum, trans., 1, 647, 650–56; *Aen.* 1.456, 458–62)

The emotional coefficients create a force field of positive and negative attitudes toward figural art, particularly art which theatricalizes the body. Virgil will ultimately prefer a drama of the mind. Consequently, emotion becomes an important marker of difference among rhetorical models, and ekphrasis, a main vehicle for sensorial language.

In this scene, ekphrasis initiates an indictment of rhetorical images aimed at demonstrating concretely the ideological incompatibility of art and history. The dialectic marks the whole Carthaginian interlude culminating in the immolation of Dido, at the end of Book 4. There, her death becomes a paradoxical sign (*omina*) of the death of that figural art which dramatizes body. Dido chooses a death that will transform her body—that the epideictic rhetoric had earlier evoked as a symbol of beauty—into a rational sign and a sign of belated rationality:

> . . ."Moriemur inultae,
> sed moriamur" ait. "Sic, sic juvat ire sub umbras.
> Hauriat hunc oculis ignem crudelis ab alto
> Dardanus, et nostrae secum ferat omina mortis."
>
> > (*Aen.* 4, 659−63)

[. . ."I shall die unavenged, but I shall die," / she says. "Thus, thus, I gladly go below to shadows. May the savage Dardan drink / with his own eyes this shadow from the deep / and take with him this omen of my death." (Mandelbaum, trans., 6, 909−13)]

We need not speculate on the causes for the hostility to imagistic discourse: the text itself makes its opposition clear enough in an authorial intervention midway through the ekphrastic passage of Book 1.

> Sic ait atque animum pictura pascit inani
> multa gemens largoque umectat flumine vultum.
>
> > (*Aen.* 1, 464−65)

[He speaks. With many tears and sighs he feeds / his soul on what is nothing but a picture. (Mandelbaum, trans., 1, 658−69)]

Aeneas feeds his soul on empty pictures, and very soon, at the end of the passage in fact, he will turn from contemplating still images to a moving picture:

> Haec dum Dardanio Aeneae miranda videntur
> dum stupet obtutuque haeret defixus in uno
> regina ad templum, forma pulcherrima Dido,
> incessit . . .
>
> > (*Aen.* 1, 494−97)

[But while Aeneas, the Darden, looked in wonder at these scenes, / rapt and bedazed, fixed on this one thing, / the queen, Dido of most beautiful form, enters the temple . . .]

The seduction of the senses by artistic images could hardly be more clearly portrayed, or more deceptive. From the standpoint of classical rhetoric, the description of Dido represents the same epideictic/ekphrastic mode used for the painted murals. But if there is no difference of rhetorical mode, there is a definite difference in the psychosomatic impact of the Didonian ekphrasis that renders the seductive power of images still more explicit. Virgil allows us to judge that difference by delivering the image directly to the reader, unmediated by Aeneas.

> But while the Darden watched these scenes in wonder,
> while he was fastened in a stare, astonished,
> the lovely-bodied Dido neared the temple,
> a crowded company of youths around her.
> And just as, on the banks of the Eurotas
> or through the heights of Cynthus, when Diana
> incites her dancers and her followers,
> a thousand mountain-nymphs press in behind her,
> she wears a quiver slung across her shoulder;
> and as she makes her way, she towers over
> all other goddesses; gladness excites
> Latona's silent breast: even so, Dido;
> so, in her joy, she moved among the throng
> as she urged on the work of her coming kingdom.
>   (Mandelbaum, trans., 1, 698–711; *Aen.* 1.494–504)

Venus and the "Politics of the Gaze"

The power of the image to seduce, forcefully rendered at the literal level of event, should not blind the reader, as it does Aeneas, to the politics of presentation Virgil sets in motion. With Dido's goddesslike appearance, Virgil makes fully manifest the dialectic of visual art as an allegory of desire. The last two lines, "talis erat Dido, talem se laeta ferbat / per medios instans operi regnisque futuris" (*Aen.* 1, 503–04), particularly the final three words, lay bare the underlying philosophical, political, and aesthetic dialectic. Politically: Troy and Carthage versus Rome; philosophically, art as an allegory of desire and becoming versus history as the representation of being (i.e., reality in the Platonic sense); aesthetically: the desire to experience the visible versus the prophetic duty to discover the hidden meaning of history. Such are the marks of difference activated by Dido's deceptively majestic appearance.

She is an icon (and an agent) of the visible world. Through her over-determined status as sensate image—"regina . . . forma pulcherrima Dido" (*Aen.* 1.496)—Virgil introjects a recognizable Platonic dialectic between rational discourse, the language of being, and corporeal discourse, the sensorial language of becoming. Intelligence and reason, the attributes of unchanging being, look beyond worldly forms to contemplate the invisible world seeking the secrets of Nature. Intelligence and reason seek not to imitate, to reiterate what already exists, but to generate new discourse, new forms by interrogating Nature as *potentia*, that is, as hitherto unrevealed power.[3]

Corporeal discourse, rooted in the contemplation and imitation of created objects, apprehends by opinion rooted in sensation without reason. As the language of the visible world, corporeal discourse deals in images, portraying "what is always in the process of becoming and perishing and never really is" (*Timaeus* 28a). This opposition between rational and sensorial discourse grounds Plato's distinction between poetry and philosophical dialogue.

Socrates' initial purpose for making these distinctions in the *Timaeus* directly addresses the issues of political power and statecraft so central to the *Aeneid*. Poets, Socrates observes, caught up with imitating the visible world, and history as event, have failed to find a discourse capable of demonstrating how the city-state may attain to true greatness: in short to realize its potential for being as opposed to becoming.

Socrates was speaking of Greek poets present and past. As part of his general agenda of political and cultural appropriation, Virgil undertakes to show that the Roman *poeta* differs from "the tribe of imitators" disparaged by Socrates precisely as Rome differed from Troy, or Athens. The difference lay in the ability of its poets and "pious" culture hero, Aeneas, to recognize and deploy philosophical agendas. The *Aeneid* accepts Socrates' challenge and casts the matrix of its Platonic schema in ideologically hierarchical terms of power in which reason and history ally with the prophetic, invisible world in which resides being, the eternal paradigm, and thus truth. The combined messages of Books 6 and 8 will make this clear.

Ekphrasis plays a crucial role in this schema by serving as a deictic, a dramatic discourse marker that splits apart the apparent reality of the immediate image from its underlying philosophical implications. The dramatic fracturing of reality takes the form of the contending claims of mind and body: desire and rational reflection, gratification of the self over against the realization of civic goals.

Virgil situates these contending forces in the mythic origins of Aeneas's being: Venus and Anchises, the divine mother and human father. The maternal and paternal models appear in the context of the ekphrastic system that provides a structuring progression to the epic, and they belong to the opposition between mind and body, rationality and sensuality that defines the concept of licit and illicit image within the Virgilian poetics.

Venus and Anchises stand behind the three key ekphrastic moments in the *Aeneid* in Books 1, 6, and 8. The negative connotation of "lying images" so powerfully evoked in the midst of the first ekphrasis and implied in the sensual description of Dido, *Regina . . . forma pulcherrima Dido*, has a counterpart immediately preceding the description of the murals on the Temple of Juno. There, one finds a highly imaged and sensuous description of Venus disguised as a beautiful noblewoman whom Aeneas only belatedly recognizes as his goddess mother. As she disappears, he exclaims:

"Quid natum totiens, crudelis tu quoque, falsis
ludis imaginibus? Cur dextrae jungere dextram
non datur ac veras audire et reddere voces?"
                    (*Aen.* 1, 407–09)

[And when Aeneas recognized his mother, / he followed her with these words as she fled: / "Why do you mock your son—so often and / so cruelly—with these lying apparitions? / Why can't I ever join you, hand to hand, / to hear, to answer you with honest words?" (Mandelbaum, trans., 1, 579–84)

The powerful ejaculation of longing for the present/absent mother—a tour de force of poetic theatricality in the context—suggests Virgil's awareness of the power of unconscious desire on poetic language. Aeneas voices a yearning and an anxiety to see the mother and her secrets. This is the real moment of alterity—Venus, the true mythic other motivating the ekphrasis of history in the sequence that follows: the murals and the entry of Dido. For Virgil's didactic purposes, Venus motivates those scenes while Aeneas' exclamation conveys the ideological issues at stake.

Aeneas' longing backward look and expressed desire to see and hold his mother predicates a politics of seeing that we may distinguish as gaze versus vision. Aeneas' passionate yearning to see his mother physically illustrates an intransitive and reflexive mode of seeing that betrays the presence and participation of the body, the viewer's body, as subject. What Aeneas' exclamation does, in fact, is to reveal himself, his own desire. Venus's alterity, as woman, mother, and goddess, stands between her and her son in this scene. More importantly, as the ensuing instances—the mural and Dido's entry—make clear, the gaze is a form of perception very different from the prophetic vision Virgil presents in Books 6 and 8.

Within the economy of Books 1–4, the gaze fixes itself on bodily images, false images that inflame the senses and pervert rational judgment. Venus represents another way of seeing, a perception grounded in subjectivity and desire; attributes that are philosophically at odds with the allegory of history that Aeneas ultimately personifies. Dido's spectacular entry in Book 1 theatricalizes the implications of the lubricious gaze initiated by Aeneas' glimpse of Venus. The rhetorical glitter of this scene distracts attention from what is in fact a dramatic substitution of Dido for Venus as the object of the longing gaze.

Venus poses the question of alterity or identity: where alterity and body, what Aeneas longs to see of Venus, fuse in the sensuous image that is withheld. Otherness is a fact of language that cannot be denied, however inconvenient. Yet the *Aeneid* does not seek to explore the feminine other, but rather to constrain it within an allegory of history as identity or sameness, which Virgil locates in the rational discourse of prophecy in Books 6 and 8 and links to the spectral image of the father, Anchises. Dido must then be doubly sacrificial: first, as the illegitimate consort marking Aeneas' transition between two licit spouses; and second, as the rhetorical substitute for Venus as the object of Aeneas' lubricious gaze. The *Aeneid* does not attempt to deny the power of the mythical other, but it does seek to deflect the force of its interrogatory gaze through the exemplary story of Dido and the ultimate subordination of the venereal gaze for the prophetic vision.

Prophetic vision identifies the rhetoric of rationality with the Virgilian artistic project recast as what the classicist, Michael Putnam, has recently termed, "the ethical artistry practised by Aeneas from standards set him by his father towards the end of [Book 6]."[4] Putnam sees this ethical artistry as set forth in the famous ekphrasis of the story of Daedalus inscribed on the doors of the Temple of Apollo at the beginning of Book 6. We will not now follow the path of that deflection from the mythical other of the mother, Venus, to the ethical identiy of the father, Anchises. Instead, let us turn instead to the medieval period where the mythical other resurfaces as a prime element in romance. It was less the concept of prophetic vision and the logos of history that interested the medieval allegorizers of romance, than the suppressed story of the venereal gaze.

The *Roman de la Rose* pursues the rhetoric of the somatic gaze and its counterpart, corporeal discourse, as adumbrated by Virgil with Aeneas' ekphrastic gaze at Venus, or the Ovidian stories of Actaeon and Diana and Narcissus and Echo (*Metamorphoses* III, 138–252; and 339–510). The *Rose* could pursue these topics due to the "liberation" of the ekphrastic program from its subordination to history that Virgil had worked so hard to achieve. Paradoxically, this liberation turns out to have been a consequence of medieval commentary on the *Aeneid*.

Medieval Commentary and Virgilian Ekphrasis

As we have seen, the order of history represents Virgil's attempt to subordinate image, the unsettling and uncontrollable tropes of alterity embedded in mythological language, to the rational, Platonic model elected as dominant by mainstream classical and medieval culture. In making the leap from the classical epic to medieval romance, from ekphrasis and allegory in Virgil to Guillaume de Lorris's versions of these tropes in the *Roman de la Rose*, we might recall the real sense of Horace's dictum from his "Epistle to the Pisones, 'On the Art of Poetry,'" *ut pictura poesis* that has played a perennial role in discussions of word and image.[5]

Horace was not arguing in favor of interartistic expression, but rather of the need for a variable critical perspective: sometimes close up, sometimes looking from a distance, sometimes in full light, at other times in half-light. If we back away from the *Aeneid*, we must ask how successfully the discourse of history disentangles itself from the language of desire so powerfully evoked as a dramatic challenge to be overcome. In short, how successfully does Virgil subordinate sensate image to rational idea?

He succeeds in deflecting the politics of the gaze toward an allegory of historical vision. He does not succeed in fully suppressing the questions raised about the nature of the image. Medieval commentators as adept as ourselves at viewing from a critical distance recognized the ability of image to destabilize verbal meaning. They understood the *Aeneid* as allegory, and even as an allegory of the deflected gaze—what we have been looking at. And they also understood the role of ekphrasis as an instrument for mediating the gaze.

In his twelfth-century *Commentary on the First Six Books of the Aeneid*, Bernardus Silvestris singles out the ekphrasis in Book I to propose strategic modes of perception for resisting the threat of the image. Images can never be understood safely without the mediation of an interposed ethical theory. By way of illustrating the danger, Bernardus glosses Aeneas as a naive reader of the painted images bemused by an inability to discern the difference between referential and figurative representation. In a kind of wild prefiguring of right hemisphere versus left hemisphere perception, Bernardus suggests a dual theory of apprehension implicitly linked to right- versus left-eyed dominance. For us, the interest lies in the connection he makes between skewed viewing and the implicit sexuality of the gaze. Since Dido, for Bernardus, signifies Passion that rules Carthage "because in this world such is the confusion that desire rules and virtues are oppressed," the painted images signify objects of desire, temporal goods.

> Aeneas "feasts his eyes on empty pictures." Because the world is new to him and he is wrapped in a cloud (that is, in ignorance), he does not understand the nature of the world; therefore these please him, and he admires them. We understand his eyes as the senses, some of which are true and some false; just as there is a right eye and a left one, so too we know certain senses are true and others false. We understand the pictures to be temporal goods, which are called pictures because they are not good but seem so, and therefore Boethius calls them "images of true good." And thus he fills his eyes (his senses) with pictures (that is, with worldly goods). (*Commentary*, Book I:13)

Taking his cue from Boethius, Bernardus directly invokes the Platonic schema from the *Timaeus* by way of urging the superiority of the spiritual allegorical vision of the mind's eye over that of the senses, the physical eyes. In so doing, his gloss translates the historical content of the ekphrasis into a direct figuration of the desire it was meant to conceal in Virgil's text. Bernardus does so to acknowledge the material power of the image to subvert, a force he seeks to combat by denying the reality of its referential status, which is what he means when he says that images don't portray what they seem to.

Images do not portray what they seem to because they portray instead the desire, the psychology of perception of the painter or viewer, something he also tells us. Bernardus himself does not have to come to grips with the implications of his gloss; he remains within the space of the verbal text, confronting the visual image only hypothetically. Still, the implications of his work are far-reaching. By liberating the image from the constraints of material referentiality, he leaves it free to double back on its own origins, or to interrogate the intentionality of its perceivers.

This movement in turn opens the space of the medieval manuscript to explore the rhetoric of perception as sensual event, perhaps even the principal event in the literature of love that developed around the romance in the twelfth and thirteenth centuries. It is a commonplace to see Ovid as a subtext for romance and lyric passages that explore the sexuality of the gaze, but the allegorization of Virgil, particularly the ekphrastic passages in *Aeneid* I, offer equally strong, though largely ignored, dialectical matrices.

The *Roman de la Rose* and the Ekphrasis of the Gaze

Take the series of ekphrastic portraits at the beginning of Guillaume de Lorris's *Roman de la Rose*, for example. The ekphrases occur after several prologues that remove the Lover in space and time from the "real" world to the inner world of a dream vision, which the author says he experienced some five years earlier. Within the context of medieval oneiric taxonomy, as codified by Macrobius, the dream affords a free play of the subjective imagination; an enigmatic experience of visual stimuli that "conceals with strange shapes and veils with ambiguity" (Macrobius, 90).

The *Roman de la Rose* takes the dream as visual allegory very seriously. Almost all illuminated manuscripts of the *Rose* (and a number of its manuscripts are illuminated) portray the beginning of the dream on the incipit folio, as we may see in incipits like that of Morgan MS 185 (Figure 1). The author tells us that some five years prior to writing, his younger self dreamt he had awakened on a fine spring morning, dressed, and gone into a countryside with flowers, birds, and a stream, along whose bank he walked. Soon, he encountered an orchard garden—which we later learn to be the "Garden of Delight," and a kind of natural temple of Amour. High walls surround the garden, and on the walls, the Lover finds portraits of personifications of the physical and psychic states inimical to love and youth: Envy, Covetousness, Poverty, Old Age, and so forth.

Both in the text and in the illuminations, Guillaume's Lover confronts his ekphrastic experience shrouded in a dream that matches Bernard's gloss on Aeneas's mist: the cloud of unknowing. Both dream and mist serve Venus's ends, as the Lover, like Aeneas, intially, will serve Venus and her other (medieval) son, Amor. The ekphrastic encounter is the first "event" that befalls the Lover, in his dream state, when he reaches the wall surrounding the *Jardin de Déduit*, a privileged hunting ground of Amor, the God of Love. The ten ekphrastic portraits establish a representational system by which personification and a redeployment of classical subtexts inaugurate the allegorical matrix that generates the work. But like the ekphrastic images in Virgil that prepare Dido's entry, Guillaume's ekphrastic portraits give way to living personifications once we and the Lover have understood the system and entered the garden.

Like the scenes of Trojan history Aeneas observes on the walls of the Temple of Juno in Carthage, the ekphrastic personifications Guillaume's Lover confronts constitute "false images," that is, negative examples, inimical to the "politics" of the narrative to come. But the ekphrastic rhetoric of these false images plays a strategic role in combating the neo-Platonic, antisensorial spirituality underlying Bernardus Silvestris's critique of precisely the kind of sensual imagery the *Roman de la Rose* seeks to explore: the "strange shapes and ambiguities" of the venereal gaze. Guillaume de Lorris's first task must be to displace Boethian iconoclasm.

He does so by a psychology of perception that separates the image from the subjective act of viewing. In terms of medieval philosophy, he moves from a realist to a conceptualist theory of the sign. For Guillaume as for Virgil, the ekphrasis serves as a metacommentary showing the reader-viewer how to enter the allegorical world of the narrative. All the ekphrastic personifications represent psychological states that affect ways of viewing the world, even the physical personifications like Vieillesse and Povreté. They show that it is not the image itself that represents "worldly goods" or "lying images," as Bernardus would have it, but the intentionality of the viewer that invests them with ethical value. In aggregate, the ekphrastic portraits open the text to a free play of image production and image reception at two levels: in the verbal text itself and in the manuscript illuminations.

Often dismissed as "mere" illustrations, the miniatures do much more than simply repeat visually the textual elements. In the illuminated manuscripts of the *Roman de la Rose*, one discovers that the presence of the illuminations in the textual space creates two contrasting narrative systems. This may be seen, unexpectedly, in those manuscripts in which the program of illumination was laid out and the rubrication completed, but where the actual drawings were never executed, so that one confronts a page with verbal text and vacant pictorial space forming, literally, an aporia (Figure 2). The double narrative schema appears even more striking, of course, where the program has actually been executed, with attention given to page layout (Figure 3). Here we enter the world of the book where visual perception combines with aural experience to generate meaning.

The illuminations, incorporated in the midst of the textual space, dramatize the *paragone* of text and image, reminding us that ekphrasis was one of the early manifestations of the contest. The confrontation in the same manuscript folio of visual and verbal representations of the same material argues, at least ostensibly, a level of self-consciousness that bears looking into. For the fact that all of the ekphrastic portraits are illuminated, coupled with the fact that they tend to be the first textual passages to receive visual treatment—following the incipit miniatures—suggest that the ekphrastic program played a crucial role in the *Rose*'s unbinding of the rhetorical image. Parenthetically, we need to bear in mind that illustration was a form of highlighting; only passages seen as key in the economy of the work *were* illustrated, and the ekphrastic portraits are the only sequence of illustrations in the entire work.

Illuminations, especially these, have been treated as though they were figures of identity with the text, a visual representation of the narrative. It seems closer to the mark to view the illuminations of the ekphrastic portraits as one part of a dual system in which the illumination stands in relation to the text as its symbolic other. The illumination profits from its status outside of language less to illustrate the text to which it is dialectically linked than to demetaphorize it. That is, it confronts the rhetorical image of the text with a literal image, thereby graphically showing the difference between them. As the text's other, it enacts literally the meeting of metaphor and mimesis contained, and constrained, within the verbal epideixis. By translating the descriptions of gazing into the act of gazing, the illuminations oblige the reader to perform the actions of the Lover, described by the text as looking at the portraits, and of the narrator who actually describes and comments them. By this gesture, the reader's own performative experience imitates, and confirms, the *Rose*'s bipartite narrative economy.

The illuminations expose another aspect of narrative reality: the fact that, as Michael Riffaterre has recently pointed out, description generates narrative (Riffaterre, 282). The portraits point up what Riffaterre calls the diegetic function of the descriptive in the text. They do so by singling out the nuclear element of description around which the rest of the narrative builds. In this case, the nucleus of description—the portraits of social, physical, and psychic states inimical to love—introduces into the narrative the social and philosophical agenda on which the work depends.

Love, as the value-laden marker of social caste portrayed by Guillaume de Lorris, grounds itself in description, particularly physical description. The *Rose* authorizes intense gazing at the body, in all its manifestations, for it is the body's appearance, at least in the first instance, that determines exclusion and inclusion in the garden of love. Physical description, in the ekphrastic portraits, incorporates inner qualities; that is, in fact, one definition the text implies for allegory: the corporeal representation (= visual description) of a system of ethical values. The miniatures, then, must be seen as pictures of description, where description is an authoritative representation of the body, exposed to our and the Lover's gaze. The portraits show that allegorical description literally reverses inner and outer reality by giving bodily shape to moral and ethical abstractions associated with the inner being.

In short, the miniatures turn back upon the text in part to show what it is doing. At the simplest level, the miniature portraits do combine with their rubrics to show concretely how personification allegory works. But they also constitute a real enigma in the space of the text—a language of the other and an ironic allegory of the verbal text's desire to be image. At the same time, since they vary more than their poetic counterpart from one manuscript to another, the miniatures demonstrate how the ekphrasis turns the viewer's gaze back onto itself to discover more than meets the eye. In short, as the text's unconscious, the illuminations reveal the psychodrama inherent in the poetic allegory. The subject is, as Lacan argued, an effect of the signifier (see Fineman, "Structure of Allegorical Desire," 46).

Envy and the Diegetic Gaze: Morgan Library MS 132

Let us conclude by following these ideas through two illustrations of Envy. One of the interesting things about the representation of Envy is the specular character of her portrayal. Perhaps for obvious reasons, she tends not to appear by herself, in contrast to the other portraits; less obvious may be the fact that she may stand for or evoke the persona of the artist. Figure 4, for example, shows Envy in the company of the *Rose* poet himself, Guillaume de Lorris. Portrayed as a tonsured clerc holding a book, Guillaume points to Envy.

Like Virgil's ekphrasis in *Aeneid* 1, the poetic narrative consists of two parts: a description of the portrait of Envy that begins, "Apres fu pourtraite Envie," and continues by describing her faults. Then, the poetic text recounts the Lover's reaction to the portrait, his judgment, beginning, "Lors vi qu'Envie en la painture/avoit trop laide regardeure" (see Appendix for text and translation of this section). But whereas Virgil continually interwove description and reception, Guillaume separates them, a division reproduced in the manuscript layout.

The folio serves as a deictic highlighting the bipartite narrative by its use of decorated initials. The beginning of the ekphrasis, "Apres," is signaled by an illuminated capital "A" that serves as a bracketing frame for text column and the illumination at the top. The shift within the ekphrasis from description of the portrait to description of Envy's qualities evokes a second illuminated initial, the "E" of "Envie est de tel cruaute." Then the final shift from impersonal ekphrasis to subjective reception by the Lover appears in the lower third of the second column with the only illuminated initial of that column, the "L" of "Lors vi qu'Envie en la painture." Visually, the folio marks the ekphrastic movement and its reception. The illuminated initials and rubrication of the miniature both link the visual system to the poetic text and indicate the dual narrative systems (and separate stages of manuscript production) at issue.

Looking rapidly at the miniature from a purely material standpoint, we find that it both illustrates and distances itself from the poetry in simultaneous gestures. On the one hand, it illustrates the ekphrasis by using colors and "escriture" described in the poetic text (although the colors here are not the same as those specified—in contrast to Morgan 185).[6] It reproduces the double movement of ekphrasis and reception in the text in which Guillaume gazes at the portrait and then analyzes it. The miniature presumably incorporates the ekphrasis by showing Guillaume holding the book (a kind of visual ekphrasis) and pointing to the literal portrait; and by suggesting something unusual about this particular portrait since none of the others is privileged by the presence of the author.

On the other hand, the miniature distances itself from the poetry in at least three ways: by not showing the content of ekphrasis, that is, details of verbal texts; by "translating" the textual given into the textual intention (i.e., the text describes Envy as a portrait, but "narrates" her as personification allegory; the portrait shows the latter); and finally, by representing Guillaume, the author-narrator, rather than his younger self as the specular partner to Envy.

At a more conceptual level, we find in the miniature a series of gestures that constitute the image as the allegorical other to the text:

- The deictic figure and finger of the illustrated author indicates something to be seen in the portrait of Envy. The characters facing one another and the seeming walleye of Envy, coupled with the author's pointing finger, infuse a ludic quality of voyeurism.
- The adumbration of narrative by the presence of two persons, a departure from the practice of the other miniatures (where we find only the single figure), coupled with the descriptors just noted reminds us of our own status as viewers, and solicits the question "What?" Our own voyeurism is evoked as a desire to see and know more than the image conveys.

These observations suggest an asymmetry between illustration and text in which the miniature calls attention to the continued presence of unanswered questions that the text had promised to explain: "si vos conterai et dirai de ces ymages la semblance"; "Ces ymages . . . si come j'ai devisé" (vv. 136–37, 461–62). The illustration thus inhabits the space of the text as a deictic of an enigma. As such, it cannot be seen as a nonverbal representation completing the sense of the poetic text. It must be seen as a representative space in its own right predicating new meaning on the ekphrasis. Instead, the illustration serves as a negative space of interrogation, a second "language" that glosses the first at one level by saying, "this is what is in the text"; then, in a second movement, it solicits the question, "What is to be seen?" "What really is in the text?"; and in a third movement, the rhetoric of the image raises the question, Which subject? Whose signifier?

Finally, the miniature constitutes a reading of the ekphrasis different from that made by the Lover. This divergent reading makes us conscious of the plural discourses of desire and the way that allegory constantly enacts the split between the subject and its language. This consciousness will finally doom the pretensions of Guillaume's project, suggesting that its incompletion was not accidental but foreordained:

Ceci est li *Romanz de la Rose*
ou l'art d'amor est tot enclose
(vv. 37–38)

[This is the *Roman de la Rose* Where the art of love is entirely encompassed (where we must understand "art" in the sense of a treatise that "explains it all")]

Envy and the Diegetic Gaze: Morgan Library MS 185

Let us look quickly at the second portrait of Envy from Morgan 185 (Figure 5). This is the same manuscript whose incipit we looked at earlier. We need not analyze this miniature as thoroughly as we did Morgan 132, although if we did we would discover an even greater asymmetry between text and illumination. The miniature is almost independent of literal reference to the text except for showing Envy and having a gold and azure color motif as specified by the text (vv. 461–46 already cited).

Note how the manuscript stresses the independence of the miniature by signaling the specular confrontation between l'Amant and Envie—which the Morgan 132 miniature took as its subject matter—only by means of the illuminated initials (the same system we saw in Morgan 132) and by rubricating "L'Amant" in red (at the end of the penultimate line in the second column) just before the "Lors vi qu'Envie en la painture" on the final line of column 2. Envy and l'Amant are both color coded at the beginning and end of the ekphrasis.

The miniature departs from the literal text altogether to provide an allegorical gloss in the manner of Bernardus Silvestris. It corresponds to only four lines of the text from the beginning of the Lover's reception of the ekphrasis:

Lors vi qu'Envie en la painture
avoit trop laide esgardeüre;
ele ne regardast neant
fors en travers, em borneant.
(vv. 279–82)

[Then I saw that Envy in the painting had an extremely nasty way of looking: she never gazed at anything except obliquely, out of one eye, (sense of ambiguously)]

In fact, Envy is not looking at nothing here; she is looking at a scene that the text may solicit but does not describe. A couple making love—in the Victorian sense of the term. Where does the couple come from?

The couple issues from the venereal matrix of the allegory, of course, confirming our own sense of the sexuality of the gaze that permeates the *Rose* in general and this manuscript in particular, where the incipit page (Figure 1), in addition to the narrative scenes already mentioned, contains six medallions of heads of the key male and female characters in the right and bottom margin. The heads turn partially toward the page and one another, partially toward us as we look at them, emphasizing the reciprocity of the gaze.

The image of Envy suggests a complex genesis. The couple at whom Envy gazes does not come from the ekphrasis of the immediate context. The image anticipates the narrative to come, portraying the Lover and the reembodied Rose. At one level, the miniature may be read as a *figura* anticipating what is to come as the already said. The miniature achieves this by glossing the term "borneant" as would a good philologist. Parenthetically, we should recall that Morgan 132 also shows Envy as "borgne," although it takes the descriptive detail no further. Morgan 185, however, realizes the narrative inherent in the descriptor: "em borneant" (v. 282).

Jacqueline Cerquiglini has shown the carnavalesque implications of the lexical group: "louche," "borgne," "borgneer," "loucher," and other terms indicating the obliquity of the regard. We have here an authentically medieval instance of the voyeur. But the one-eyed voyeur, Cerquiglini tells us, is none other than the clerkly author:

> The furtive gaze defines the *clerc* in all the ambiguity of his position. It defines his social status . . . and his esthetics. His shifty look even signifies his stratagem. This strait is unanimously attributed to the *clerc* probably because of his connection with dialectics . . . (Cerquiglini, 485)

This suggests another prolepsis in our image. Following Cerquiglini, we may take the walleyed Envy in a double sense: by its ambiguity and desire, it also signifies the clerkly author, Guillaume. Guillaume/Envy gazing at the Lover and the Rose enacts the ambivalent subjectivity of the older author recounting and watching his younger self that the Prologue establishes as the narrative strategy.

Both the miniatures we have looked at deconstruct the poetic text that generates them by showing what the text *does* rather than what it says.

This specular referentiality is not neutral. As Linda Hutcheon has shown in *A Theory of Parody*, autoreflexivity is often a sign of parody. The *Rose* offers ample signs of self-parody: Guillaume introduces a nascent parodic system in which the poet consciously portrays his younger persona, the Lover, as a buffoon at key moments; Jean de Meun subsequently systematizes and exploits to the hilt this parodic element in his asymmetrical "conclusion."

When we recall that the image production was posterior to the text by over a hundred years in each of our manuscripts, we may well be authorized to see in the portrait of Envy a proleptic figuration of the other clerkly author, Jean de Meun, portrayed later in this same manuscript (Figure 6), looking (*borneant?*) at or declaiming from the *Rose* that he appropriates so devastatingly. Let us not forget that it is this same Jean de Meun who renames his predecessor's work the *Miroër aus amoreus* ["Mirror of (or for) Lovers"] and who evokes the role of mirrors in a manner strongly reminiscent of Bernardus Silvestris's concept of right- and left-eyed ambiguous perception:

si font bien oeill anferm et trouble
de chose sangle sambler double
et parair ou ciel double lune
et .ii. chandeles sambler d'une.
    (*Rose*, ed. Lecoy, vv. 18209–12)

[weak and troubled eyes make a single thing seem double; they put a double moon in the sky, and make two candles appear from one.]

These miniatures, finally, reveal how unstable and vulnerable a rhetorical trope ekphrasis really is: ever on the verge of being parodied by the allegory of its own mimetic desire to be image.

Notes

    1. As Michael Putnam has recently pointed out in an article to which I am indebted for this section: "Daedalus, Virgil and the End of Art."
    2. I use the terms "gaze" and "vision" in the sense proposed by Norman Bryson, *Vision and Painting: The Logic of the Gaze*. Bryson analyzes the difference in viewing introduced by Alberti's concept of vanishing perspective in painting as

opposed to the nonperspectival system of Byzantine painting espoused by the medieval West. The nonperspectival system, he argues, "had been physical, had been somatic, yet the body was never individually interpellated and never saw itself . . ." (106). The Albertian system "introduced a viewpoint which is not that of a separate creature or personality, but an impersonal arrangement, a *logic* of representation which changes the viewer himself into a representation, an object or spectacle before his own vision . . . Albertian space returns the body to itself in its own image, as a measurable, visible, objectified unit" (106).

I differ from Bryson in believing that the representational viewpoints he locates in painting techniques were already implicated in Western rhetoric.

3. Plato, *Timaeus*. First then . . . we must make a distinction and ask, What is that which always is and has no becoming, and what is that which is always becoming and never is? That which is apprehended by intelligence and reason is always in the same state, but that which is conceived by opinion with the help of sensation and without reason is always in a process of becoming and perishing and never really is . . . (28a. Hamilton & Cairns, 1161).

4. Putnam, "Daedalus, Virgil and the End of Art," page 1 of a typescript of the article to appear in the *American Journal of Philology*.

5. Ut pictura poeisis: erit quae, si propius stes,
    Te capiat magis, et quaedam si longius abstes.
    Haec amat obscurum; volet haec sub luce videri,
    Iudicis argutum quae non formidat acumen;
    Haec placuit semel, haec deciens repetita placebit.
        (Horace, *Epistularum*, *Liber* II, iii,
            De Arte Poetica Liber, 361–65.)

[A poem is like a picture; one will seem more pleasing viewed nearer, another if seen from further away; one prefers half-light; another wishes to be seen in full light, without fearing the shrewdness of the critic; one pleases once, another will please repeatedly.]

6. The two descriptions of the paintings come at the beginning and the end of the section. Manuscripts respect the prescription for "blue and gold" coloring, while the "escritures" take the form of the rubrication, often in red. The poetic text leaves little doubt that the process is consciously ekphrastic, if anything the references to process are overdetermined.

Si vi un vergier grant et lé,
Tot clos de haut mur bataillié,
Portret dehors et entaillié
A maintes riches escritures.
Les ymages et les pointures
Dou mur volentiers remirai;
Si vos conterai et dirai
De ces ymages la semblance
Si com moi vient a remembrance.
            (vv. 130–38)

. . .
Ces ymages bien avisé,
Que, si come j'ai devisé,
Furent en or et en azur
De totes pairs pointes ou mur.
(vv. 461–64)

References

Baldwin, Charles S. *Medieval Rhetoric and Poetic to 1400*. Gloucester, MA: Peter Smith, 1959.

Bernardus Silvestris. *Commentary on the First Six Books of Virgil's* Aeneid. Translated with introduction and notes by Earl G. Schreiber and Thomas Maresca. Lincoln: University of Nebraska Press, 1979.

Bernardus Silvestris. *The Commentary on the First Six Books of the* Aeneid *of Vergil Commonly Attributed to Bernardus Silvestris*. Edited by Julian Ward Jones and Elizabeth Frances Jones. Lincoln: University of Nebraska Press, 1977.

Cerquiglini, Jacqueline. "'Le Clerc et le louche': Sociology of an Esthetic." In *Medieval and Renaissance Representation: New Reflections*. Edited by Stephen G. Nichols and Nancy J. Vickers. Special Issue of *Poetics Today* 5(1984): 479–91.

Christine de Pizan. *The Book of the City of Ladies*. Translated by Earl Jeffrey Richards. New York: Persea Books, 1982.

Clay, Diskin. "The Archeology of the Temple to Juno in Carthage (*Aeneid* 1.446–493)." *American Journal of Philology* (1987).

Curnow, Maureen Cheney. *The* Livre de la Cité des Dames *of Christine de Pisan: A Critical Edition*, pp. 76–96. Ph.D. dissertation, Vanderbilt University, 1975. Ann Arbor, MI: University Microfilms, 1976. 2 volumes.

Curtius, E. R. *European Literature and the Latin Middle Ages*. Translated by Willard R. Trask. New York: Pantheon, 1953.

Da Vinci, Leonardo. "Paragone: Of Poetry and Painting." *Treatise on Painting*. Edited by A. Philip McMahon. Princeton, NJ: Princeton University Press, 1956.

Fineman, Joel. *Shakespeare's Perjured Eye: The Invention of Poetic Subjectivity in the Sonnets*. Berkeley: University of California Press, 1986.

———. "The Structure of Allegorical Desire." In *Allegory and Representation*, pp. 26–60. Edited by Stephen J. Greenblatt. Baltimore: Johns Hopkins University Press, 1981.

Gilot, F. and C. Lake. *Life with Picasso*. London: Neolson, 1964.

Guillaume de Lorris and Jean de Meun. *Le Roman de la Rose*. Edited by Félix Lecoy. 3 vols. Classiques Français du Moyen Âge 92, 95, 98. Paris: Champion, 1965–70.

Guillaume de Lorris and Jean de Meun. *The Romance of the Rose*. Translated by Charles Dahlberg. Princeton, NJ: Princeton University Press; Hanover, NH: University Press of New England, 1983.

Hutcheon, Linda. *A Theory of Parody: The Teachings of Twentieth-Century Art Forms*. New York: Methuen, 1985.

Macrobius. *Commentary on the Dream of Scipio*. Trans. William Harris Stahl. New York: Columbia University Press, 1952.

Mitchell, W. J. T. *Iconology: Image, Text, Ideology*. Chicago: University of Chicago Press, 1986.

Plato. *The Collected Dialogues*. Edited by Edith Hamilton and Huntington Cairns. Bollingen Series LXXI. Princeton, NJ: Princeton University Press, 1961.

Putnam, Michael. "Daedalus, Virgil and the End of Art." *American Journal of Philology* (forthcoming).

Riffaterre, Michael. "On the Diegetic Functions of the Descriptive." *Style* 20 (Fall 1986): 281–94.

Virgil. *Aeneid* in P. Vergili Maronis *Opera*. Recognovit brevique adnotatione critica instruxit Fredericus Arturus Hirtzel. Oxford: Clarendon Press, 1942.

Virgil. *The Aeneid of Virgil*. Trans. Allen Mandelbaum. New York: Bantam: 1981.

Figure 1. The Pierpont Morgan Library. New York. Ms. 185, Folio 1. Incipit/*Romance of the Rose*. Paris, second half of fourteenth century.

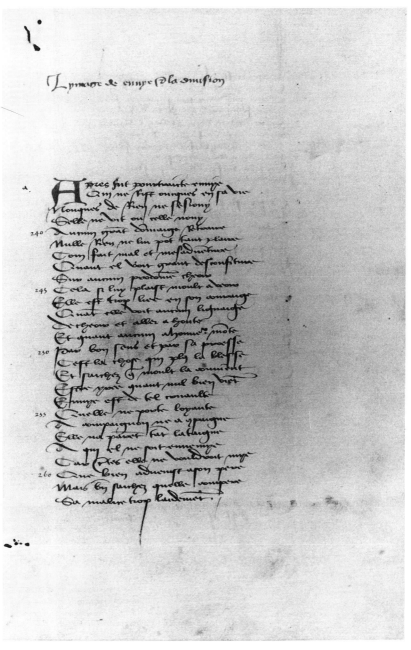

Figure 2. University of Pennsylvania, Philadelphia. Ms. Penn Fr. 1, Folio 5. *Romance of the Rose*: Rubric and layout for illumination never completed. France, mid-fifteenth century.

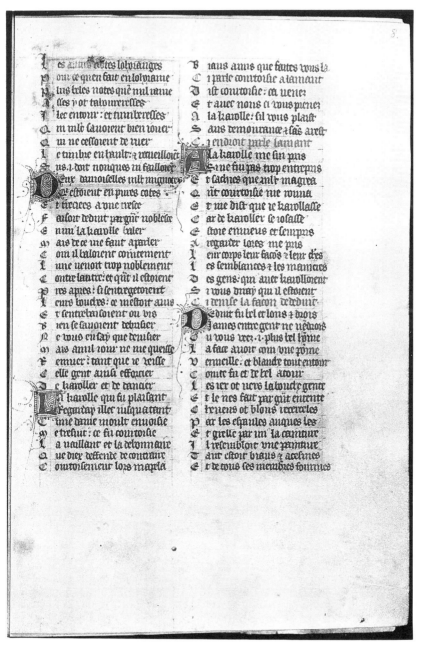

Figure 3. The Pierpont Morgan Library. New York. Ms. 132, Folio 8. *Romance of the Rose*: Page layout with discourse annotation. Paris, late fourteenth century.

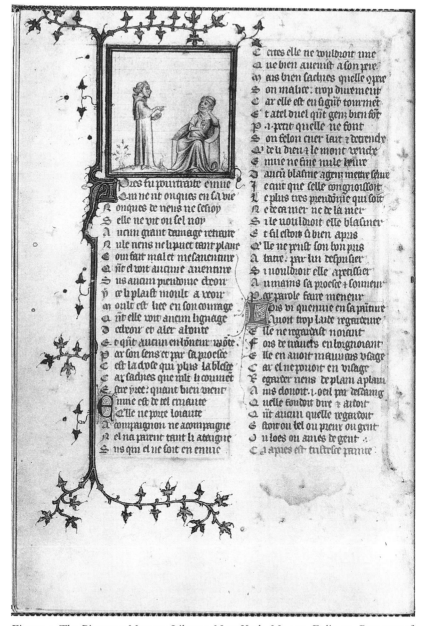

Figure 4. The Pierpont Morgan Library. New York. Ms. 132, Folio 3v. *Romance of the Rose*: Portrait of poet/narrator with Envy (illumination) and Ekphrasis of Envy (text).

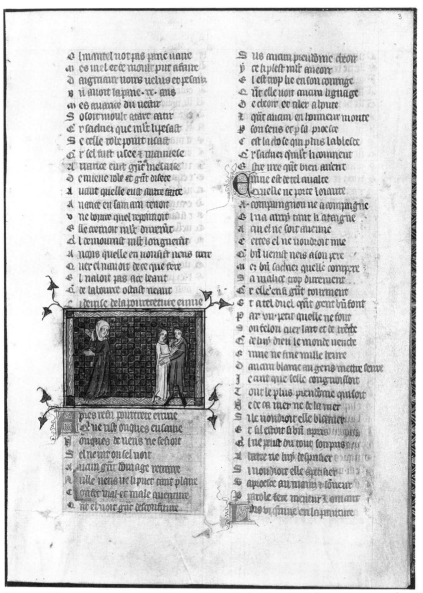

Figure 5. The Pierpont Morgan Library. New York. Ms. 185, Folio 3. *Romance of the Rose*: Portrait of Lovers with Envy looking obliquely (illumination) and Ekphrasis of Envy (text).

Figure 6. The Pierpont Morgan Library.New York. Ms. 185, Folio 30. *Romance of the Rose*: Portrait of Jean de Meun as Continuator of the *Rose* reciting while looking obliquely at the manuscript.

Lori Walters

7. Illuminating the *Rose*: Gui de Mori and the Illustrations of MS 101 of the Municipal Library, Tournai

MS 101 of the Municipal Library of Tournai is one of the most distinctive fourteenth-century manuscripts of the *Roman de la Rose*. Bearing the date of 1330, it is devoted to Gui de Mori's rewriting of the allegorical romance [1] and includes emendations by an anonymous editor. The program of illumination presents variations on well-known iconography of the *Rose* besides introducing elements not found elsewhere.[2] In general, the illustrations refer directly to the text and follow the logical sequence of events in the work. It is evident that the person responsible for masterminding the production of the manuscript was responding to Gui's version of the *Rose*.[3] Although different critics have dealt with Gui's reworking of the original text of the *Rose* and the illustration of the Tournai manuscript, no one has yet treated the relationship between the two. I intend to indicate several ways in which the planner provides a commentary both on Gui's text and on the modifications made by the anonymous editor. My conclusions must necessarily remain tentative, since I have not yet completed a survey of all of Gui's modifications of Jean de Meun's text.

The planner integrates Gui's preoccupation with the theme of the humbling of the *orgueilleux d'amour* into the program of illuminations. Gui adds Orgueil to the original list of ten anticourtly vices and makes it the focus of his entire system. Consequently, the planner places Orgueil at the center of the frieze of personification characters that decorates the walls of the Vergier de Deduiz on the initial page of the text. The planner takes pains to indicate that both the male suitor and the female object of desire are not prideful in love. The respective capitulations of these figures receive greater iconographic elaboration than is usual in manuscripts of the time.

Whereas on one level Gui's reworking of the *Rose* is a clerkly and didactic art of erotic love, on another level it represents a quest for an understanding of the divine mysteries associated with God's love for his creation. Gui himself first suggests this second level of meaning by making reference to Hugh of St.-Victor's mystical treatise *De arra animae* (also written *De arrha animae*) in the prefatory passage he added to the Prologue of Guillaume de Lorris. The miniature of the Virgin Mary heading the table of contents and the scribal colophon appearing at the work's conclusion indicate a religious or mystical reading of the allegorical narrative. Miniature and colophon form a frame that points to the higher significance of the actions recounted in the poem.

The planner also reacts to the new persona presented by Gui. The authorial signature "Gui de Mori" occurring in several places in the Tersan and Tournai manuscripts points to the existence of the "real person" who composed the major reworking of the *Roman de la Rose*. At the same time, Gui inserts himself into the fabric of his narrative by becoming a character in the passages he adds to the *Rose*.

The new authorial persona created by Gui de Mori takes its place within the problematics of the manuscript. In the planner's scheme, Gui becomes a mediator between the "parfaite joie mondaine" [perfect earthly joy] and the "joie sans fin" [joy without end] the scribe alludes to in the final verses of the colophon. Gui's position is not without conflict. Gui presents himself as a cleric whose ecclesiastical vows are sometimes at odds with his role as servant of love. Several of the illustrations refer indirectly to the incongruous situation of an ecclesiastic bound to observe a vow of chastity while enjoining others to follow a love that on one level is erotic. By situating Gui's persona within the Christianizing frame of the manuscript, the conceptualizer at once actualizes Gui's real or potential conflicts and hints at their ultimate resolution. Through his poetic service as rewriter of the *Roman de la Rose*, Gui fits into God's ultimate design for the universe.

In this study I shall examine how Gui's version of the *Rose*, one of the most extensive reworkings of the text known to exist, was received by the workshop that produced what I shall henceforth refer to as the Tournai *Rose*. The manuscript represents the final stage of a long process of revision by Gui. An earlier version of his rewriting dating from 1290 was found in the Tersan manuscript, so called because it once belonged to the abbé de Tersan.[4] Although the Tersan manuscript has dropped out of sight, a few crucial passages are preserved in Méon's first modern edition of the *Rose*.[5] Besides the versions appearing in the Tournai and Tersan manuscripts, we can imagine a whole series of rewritings of which no physical trace remains.[6] In addition to Gui's changes to the original text of the *Rose*, he devised a system of diacritical marks that indicate the nature of those changes.[7] The Tournai manuscript, bearing Gui's system of diacritical marks, is the medieval equivalent of a critical edition of the *Roman de la Rose*.

Before considering the most important modifications Gui made to the text, a short description of the manuscript is in order. The Tournai *Rose* is made up of 348 pages. Besides the 331 pages of text, 4 pages are devoted to a table of contents preceding the text, and the remaining pages have been left blank. The text is transcribed in two columns of approximately 34 verses each.[8] With the exception of the illustration on the initial page of the text and the image of Deduiz's garden on folio 12v, each miniature takes up only one column of the text. Of the 31 illustrated pages, 14 pages in Guillaume de Lorris's section (including the anonymous conclusion) and 13 pages in Jean de Meun's continuation contain miniatures or historiated letters and marginalia. Two pages display only a miniature, one of which heads the table of contents. Two pages are decorated solely with marginalia; one page contains only an historiated initial. Besides these illustrations, numerous gold painted letters, accompanied and filled with blue and rose, enrich the text.[9] Of the ornamental letters, 15 are decorated with heads of characters. Several folios have been replaced by others. Eight folios were reinstated in the fourteenth century according to a text of the same family.[10] Two folios were replaced in the fifteenth century.[11] Six or seven folios are still missing from the manuscript.[12]

Gui's first important modification of the text of the *Rose* is the addition of a totally new Prologue.[13] The eighty-eight verse passage that precedes Guillaume de Lorris's original Prologue begins with a clerkly topic containing echoes of the beginning of Richard de Fournival's *Bestiaire d'amours*, a work which uses bestiary material to convey the experience of erotic love.[14] The topic of man desiring knowledge by his very nature is incorporated into a loosely constructed syllogism to justify Gui's own writing project: given that everyone desires knowledge, that the desire for knowledge of a thing is proportional to the importance of that thing, and that love is the most important thing of all, thus, he implies, his task of conferring knowledge about love is of utmost importance.

In order to strengthen his argument about the significance of love, Gui cites Hugh of St.-Victor's notion that all hearts need love. Hugh's mystical treatise, the *De arra animae* (written before 1141), takes the form of a dialogue between a person and that person's soul. Singling out a certain "Brother G," Hugh addresses the work to his fellow monks of the religious community of Hamersleben where he was educated before going to the Abbey of St.-Victor in Paris. Hugh's stated purpose is to instill in the monks a desire for the love of God and the joys of heaven. The title, translated variously as the *Soliloquy on the Ernest Money of the Soul*[15] or *Le Gage des divines fiançailles*,[16] comes from a Middle Latin term meaning "the gifts given at the time of betrothal." The work speaks of an ultimate union between God in the guise of an invisible Lover and his bride, the soul.

Gui goes on to explain how he was led to compose his reworking of the romance: other lovers asked him to console them in their sufferings. His narrative stance resembles that of Andreas Capellanus, who in undertaking his treatise *De amore* was supposedly responding to the request of his friend Walterius.[17] As in the case of Andreas, Gui can be seen, although to a lesser degree, to be mitigating the responsibility for his text. Gui's friends requested that he "retrouvaisce . . . aucun dit d'Amours" [rework . . . a love poem], and Gui mentions that he chose the *Rose* because it was the best one he knew.

In the Prologue Gui defines further his relationship toward his writing project. He implies that it would be very hard, if not impossible, for him to produce a work on love as good as the *Rose*. Thus, instead of trying to "trover noviaus dis" [compose new poems], he prefers to "ensivir le letre / Celui ou ciaus ki ont rismé" [imitate the subject matter[18] / Of that person or those persons who rhymed] the *Rose*.[19] Since Gui modifies rather than completely rewrites Guillaume's text, he conceives of his task in different terms from those of his predecessors. Guillaume de Lorris affirms in his Prologue that "la matire est et bone et nueve" [the subject matter is good and new (v. 39)]. Gui, on the other hand, is conscious of the hazards involved in undertaking "noviaus dis" [new poems]; the writer who tries to innovate often ends up producing something ugly. Gui's terminology may express the feeling, perhaps widespread, that subsequent writers had a hard time equaling the combined achievement represented by the *Rose*.

Gui sets forth the effects that he hopes to produce through his modifications of Guillaume's text: he wants to render it "plus entendables / et a oïr plus delitables" [easier to understand / And more pleasant to hear]. In many cases Gui appends passages in which he attempts to explain what Guillaume left unclear. In other instances he adds details to Guillaume's descriptions; for example, he develops the portraits of existing figures such as Haine and Envie.[20] Gui is also capable of inventing new personifications

like Plaisance[21] and Orgueil.[22] On the other hand, he often eliminates realistic details. His taste is for the abstract rather than for the particular. In
the main, Gui tries to render the work more understandable by reducing
its digressive nature.[23] With the notable exception of Narcissus, most
mythological references disappear from Gui's verses. Thus depaganized,
the work acquires a decidedly Christian cast. Accordingly, Gui lards his
additions to the *Rose* generously with references to the Church fathers and
the Bible as well as to Classical and vernacular authors.[24]

Gui's changes tend to bring closer the two parts of the *Rose*. He remains faithful to the courtly spirit of Guillaume's text[25] even though he
expresses that spirit in a different way. If, on the one hand, Gui omits
references to famous romance characters from Guillaume's section,[26] he
also deletes all allusions to castration and therefore all appearances of the
word "coilles" from Jean's continuation.[27] Less antifeminist than Jean de
Meun,[28] he is also more preceptive than either of his predecessors. From
the beginning of Guillaume's text, Gui downplays the character of the
work as the narration of an amorous encounter with a particular person.
For example, he removes the four verses (vv. 1505–8) that apply the lesson
in the Narcissus episode to ladies in general and in particular to the one
the Poet-Narrator is trying to attract. Rather than trying to seduce a
woman by means of the poem, he gives instruction to others on the subject. Gui codifies tactics for winning over a woman's heart. In Gui's hands
the *Rose* becomes a more clerkly and didactic art of love. Although it does
not completely lose its character as romance, Gui's text comes to resemble
a moralized instruction manual on amorous behavior. The author extracts
precepts from the situations portrayed in the work. Gui, however, readily
admits the limitations of his methods. Whereas at the midpoint of the *Rose*
he declares that his work consists of general rules on love he abstracted
from the texts of Guillaume de Lorris and Jean de Meun, in another passage he claims that strategies for the seduction of a woman cannot be
completely standardized because all women are different.[29]

In the second major modification of the *Rose*, Gui transforms Guillaume's Narcissus episode into a clerkly taking to task of the *orgueilleux
d'amour*.[30] An important intertext of Gui's Narcissus episode is the vernacular romance *Floris et Lyriopé* written by Robert de Blois in approximately 1250.[31] In composing his work, Robert drew on both Ovid's
original myth and the *Alda*, a ribald Latin play composed by Guillaume
de Blois, a Benedictine monk, around 1170. The *Alda* was well known in
the Middle Ages.[32]

Although the relationship between these various texts does not admit adequate treatment in the space of a chapter,[33] I shall compare briefly *Floris et Lyriopé* to Gui's Narcissus episode. In both renditions of the Narcissus myth, the author praises the role of beauty that inspires the act of falling in love and condemns pride that can prevent an amorous experience from taking place. Of the 1,758 verses that comprise *Floris et Lyriopé*, the first 1,503 are devoted to the story of Floris and Lyriopé, the parents of Narcissus. Because Lyriopé is so full of pride, Floris must resort to trickery in order to win her love. Disguising himself as his sister Florie, he enjoys her company. When Lyriopé becomes pregnant, Floris has to leave the country and can only return when Lyriopé's father has died. Although Floris and Lyriopé finally get married, the author points out that Lyriopé's original disdainful stance regarding love leads to the sullying of the family name.

In the 255 verses remaining in the poem, Narcissus goes on to repeat his mother's mistake of ignoring the demands of love. In this case the error has fatal consequences. One of the many spurned female admirers of Narcissus calls upon God to avenge her. Narcissus accordingly falls in love with his own image; it is the beauty of his reflection in the fountain that ensnares him and results in his death. In the Epilogue the narrator decries the pride that has caused so much misfortune to both the mother and her son.

Reversing the emphasis placed on the respective stories of Narcissus and Lyriopé, Gui de Mori devotes 76 verses of his tale to Narcissus, whereas Lyriopé figures in a final passage of 30 verses. Gui's retelling closely follows the version of Robert de Blois; Gui borrows and develops Robert's opposition between pride and beauty. The God of Love is avenged for the sin of the man too proud to love a woman. Gui introduces the detail of the arrow of Biautez that strikes the Lover's heart; the arrow of Biautez overcomes the power of the arrow of Orgueil. Love is born from contemplation of the beauty of the love object. The contrast between pride and beauty structures not only the Narcissus episode but also much of the rest of Gui's version of the *Rose*. Besides the inclusion of Orgueil among the anticourtly vices, Gui stresses pride in his interpolation on the five evil arrows of love.[34]

The inclusion of the short summary of the story of Lyriopé, Narcissus's mother, in the final section of the Narcissus episode in the Tournai *Rose* suggests that Lyriopé was partially responsible for the tragic outcome of her son's life. As an *orgueilleuse d'amour*, she set a bad example for Narcissus to follow. The large miniature on folio 12v that gives an icono-graphic survey of the major events in the Jardin de Déduit, including an image of the Lover at the Fountain of Narcissus, shows that the Lover's fate is different from that of Narcissus because of his ability to love the Rose, the symbol of the feminine Other. The Lover is depicted leaving the Fountain to go select his own particular blossom. The God of Love strikes the Lover with his arrows as he stands before a rosebush poised to pluck the Rose. The female figure found in the illustrations near the conclusion of the action in the manuscript can be seen as an exemplary heroine who in assenting to the Lover's demands renounces her earlier reservations to his entreaties. These illustrations reflect Gui's concern for the response of both sexes, which is seen in his treatment of the male Narcissus and the female Lyriopé in his rewritten Narcissus episode.

Gui adds more details to his self-portrait in an interpolated passage appearing near the midpoint of the entire text of the *Rose*.[35] There the God of Love announces that yet a third servant of love will come along after Guillaume de Lorris and Jean de Meun. His name will be Gui de Mori. Although he will not have the illustrious reputation of his two predeces-sors, he is nonetheless "uns hom d'onneur et de pris" [a man of honor and worth] well qualified to give advice on romantic matters.

Gui bolsters his authority as a good counselor. As opposed to both Guillaume de Lorris and Jean de Meun, Gui is "in such a prison" that he cannot follow all the rules of love he recommends to others.[36] Acknowl-edging a vow of chastity, Gui reveals that he must be either a monk or a priest.[37] Gui here expresses a feeling of constraint toward his vow of chas-tity; his conflict recalls the questioning of the vow in Genius's speech. Genius, we recall, asks himself why virginity is the true way to God for some and not for others. He then admits that this is a problem he himself will be unable to resolve and leaves it to the theologians.[38] A contradiction is apparent in Gui's persona; he is drawn to love but realizes that he should not be.

In the midpoint passage Gui also complains that people have been spreading rumors about him.[39] He casts his problem in the allegorical terms of the original fiction: "Malebouce et sa compaignie/Li feront mainte vilonnie" [Evil Mouth and his companions will do him (Gui) much harm.][40] Although the reason for the disapproval is left unspecified, since Gui mentions it after his avowal of constraint toward his vow of chastity we can surmise that criticism was raised about a monk or a priest writing about love. Gui acknowledges that his preoccupation with the

Rose took him away from his usual occupations: he was often observed reading it instead of his psalms. It is nonetheless difficult to reconcile the censure Gui received for his work on the *Rose* with the enthusiasm with which his friends asked him to compose a poem on love. The disparity might be indicative of two audiences with different expectations for a work produced by Gui. Gui seems to direct his rewriting of the *Rose* to fellow monks interested in gaining instruction on love. We can understand that this aspect of the work might be poorly received by conservative members of his monastic public. Although in his Prologue Gui does imply that his version of the *Rose* can be understood as an allegory of the search for divine love, the work nonetheless retains its character as a manual of seduction.

Gui de Mori modeled his persona not only on Guillaume de Lorris's Poet-Lover but also on Andreas Capellanus's clerkly narrator in the *De amore* (1184–1186). The latter work is divided into three parts. In the first two, Andreas advises his friend Walterius on the art of love. In several sections of the work, especially the Preface, Andreas seems himself no stranger to the emotion. He expounds on the ambiguous nature of the clerk's attitude toward love in chapter 7 of Book I. He reasons that, although clerks are not supposed to experience physical passion, all men sin in the flesh, and clerks are even more subject to temptation than other people because they have leisure time and are well fed. In Book III Andreas contradicts his previous conciliatory attitude toward love, denouncing it adamantly and advising to his friend Walterius the contemplation of higher things. The contradictions inherently present in the clerkly figure writing about love mark the texts of Andreas and Gui.

Gui's persona is a complex one. While praising the love of God, he is nonetheless attracted by earthly pleasures. His statement that unlike Guillaume de Lorris and Jean de Meun he cannot follow all the advice on love he gives to others is tinged with genuine regret. In other passages Gui evidences an inordinate amount of familiarity with and interest in erotic matters for one pledged to remain chaste. In one instance, Gui adds reflections on the seduction of nuns to the speech of la Vieille. She recommends the giving of gifts, and even advises the suitor to bring along an extra one when he goes courting, because nuns always travel in pairs.[41] Gui also has a long addition on the degrees of love pronounced by the God of Love.[42] The division into four degrees rather than five has its origins in Andreas Capellanus, but he adds an explanation of the nuances of sensual pleasure that is all his own.[43] The reader suspects that the author of these additions is either a wayward monk or one who had taken his vows comparatively late in life. Starting in the twelfth century, new monks were no longer exclusively drawn from among the oblates, but also from among adults who had lived in secular society and often knew sensual love before vowing to renounce it.[44]

Despite the impression that Gui's narrator is recounting "real life" experiences, many of these could have their source in literary common-places. Although the section on the love of nuns may have been drawn from the actual experience of a delinquent monk, it could also have been inspired by Andreas's discourse on the love of nuns in the *De amore*.[45] Whereas Andreas's narrator admits his pleasure in undertaking the se-duction of a nun, he refrains from carrying the enterprise to its conclusion because of the enormity of the sin involved. Furthermore, the passage in which Gui says that he prefers to read the *Rose* instead of concentrating on his psalms is an example of a literary topic found in line 9 of "La Mort Rutebeuf." Gui de Mori is not the first author to have his integrity at-tacked: his Classical predecessor Ovid comes immediately to mind. The Old French tradition offers the example of Marie de France, who in the Pro-logue to her *lai*, "Guigemar," complains that people jealous of her literary success impugn her reputation. Gui de Mori could have received all his knowledge of love from handbooks like the *Rose* rather than from personal experience. The mystical teacher Hugh of St.-Victor in fact believed that all arts and sciences could be acquired from books in the cloister. In Hugh's system, all natural knowledge served as an introduction to theology.[46]

Whether Gui's persona represents a total literary fabrication or con-tains some of the internal conflicts of the real person who created him, its complexities cannot be easily dismissed. There is something unseemly about a priest or monk who acts as a counselor on erotic love. The doubt remains that he may practice what he preaches or that his interest in the subject may hide a repressed desire difficult to keep under control. At the same time, Gui seems to realize that he should not participate in the amo-rous activity he counsels to those unfettered by a vow of chastity. Such reflections about Gui on the part of the reader, I believe, are in large part inspired by the insertion of his persona within the Christianizing frame of the manuscript. I shall later touch upon some of the ways in which the conceptualizer casts Gui as an actor in a drama of sin and repentance.

The Tournai manuscript proposes multiple meanings of the quest for the Rose. On the most basic level, the work prescribes correct amorous conduct. A man and a woman fall in love, and they are offered to the reader as examples of people who do not let pride impede their courtship. The planner gives frequent reminders that a man and a woman are each going to come under Love's spell. For example, the miniature on folio 9 depicts Oiseuse inviting the Lover to enter the garden. In the marginalia on the left, a couple embraces while a dog and a rabbit look on.[47] On the right, in an interesting reversal of both the usual elements composing the miniature of the Carole de Deduiz in other manuscripts and the features found in the miniature located directly above it on the same page, a man tries to lead away a woman who would seem to prefer to remain in the dance.[48] The marginalia stress the nature of the action that will occur in Déduiz's garden: a man and a woman will fall in love and consummate their relationship.

The illustrations on the initial page of the text of the Tournai *Rose* introduce the reader to the theme of the *orgueilleux d'amour*. In the miniature occupying most of the top half of the page, the protagonist views the anticourtly vices displayed on the wall of the Vergier de Déduiz. Gui has added an eleventh evil to the list—Orgueil. The personified figure of Orgueil forms the center of the group of faults. The visual representation of the vice corresponds to Gui's fourteen-verse description added to Guillaume's text. In accordance with Gui's addition of Orgueil to the usual list of ten uncourtly vices, the planner indicates that both lover and lady avoid the danger of excessive pride in love. In the first part of the *Rose*, the planner shows that the Lover falls under Love's dominion, whereas in Jean's continuation the interest switches to the woman's response.

Consider the illustration that directly follows the representation of Oiseuse welcoming the Lover to the garden. A large miniature (found on folio 12v) unaccompanied by marginalia, it gives an iconographic summary of the events that take place within the confines of the *vergier* (Figure 3 at the end of this chapter). On the left Oiseuse admits the Lover to the garden. This scene is followed by one in which seventeen personifications dance in the carol before the God of Love who holds a bow in his left hand and five arrows in his right. In the center of the miniature, the Lover stands in front of the fountain. To the right of this scene, the God of Love follows the Lover into a little thicket where he appears before a group of animals. In the bottom row of images, the God of Love watches the Lover as he goes to pluck a rose; then Love shoots an arrow that strikes the Lover in the eye. Unlike the majority of *Rose* manuscripts, the Tournai *Rose* contains no independent representation of Narcissus at the fountain. The emphasis is on the Lover rather than Narcissus, and the planner inte-

.

grates the scene at the fountain of Narcissus into the major plot line dealing with the Lover falling in love with the Rose.

The events occurring in the garden correspond closely to Gui's modifications of the original text of the *Rose*. For example, Gui, unlike Guillaume de Lorris, lists several animals that populate the garden in the text in the right column of folio 18. These are the very same animals depicted in the thicket before the Lover and the God of Love in the miniature on folio 12v. The scenes in the miniature evoke the theme of the *orgueilleux d'amour* treated in Gui's modified version of the Narcissus episode. The Lover escapes Narcissus's fate as a man crippled by pride. Unlike Narcissus, he fails to see his reflection in the fountain, and he goes on to fall in love with his particular rose. Presumably the Lover has assimilated correctly the lesson taught by Gui's negative exemplum: he learns he must obey Love's commands. The illustrations further drive the lesson home to the reader of the manuscript.

The final miniatures in the Tournai *Rose* work in conjunction with Gui's rendition of the Narcissus episode as well as with its representation in the large illustration just described to develop the theme of the humbling of the *orgueilleux d'amour*. The planner treats the Pygmalion episode as a gloss or digression relevant to the main line of the story. The principal iconographic reference to Pygmalion appears in the marginalia; it functions primarily to reflect on the seduction of the woman at the end of the romance. We should note that the coordination of the Narcissus and Pygmalion episodes finds its place in a more general tendency to integrate the sections of Guillaume de Lorris and Jean de Meun through iconographic echoes[49] and by sustained emphasis on the plot line. In the second section of the *Rose*, for instance, the planner often gives the reader a visual reminder that the primary objective is the taking of Jealousy's castle.[50]

In the last four illustrated folios of the manuscript, the planner represents the seduction of the woman as the overcoming of the pride of the *orgueilleuse d'amour*. Although the final group of illustrated folios contains some traditional elements, these are rearranged and coordinated in such a way as to create a distinctive presentation of the final taking of the Rose much different from anything encountered in other manuscripts. The rubric, "L'ymage d'entre les pileres" [The image between the pillars] introduces the first miniature located on folio 156v (Figure 4). The miniature depicts Venus aiming her arrow at a female figure who appears in the tower of Jealousy's castle. The illustration conveys visually the comparison made in the text between the tower statue and Pygmalion's lady. The rubric, "C'est li contes del ymage de pynalion" [This is the story of Pygmalion's image] precedes the telling of the myth of Pygmalion. In the marginalia on the left, Zeuxis is shown trying to sculpt an image of perfect beauty; on the right, a man, presumably Pygmalion himself, serenades a woman with a portative organ. The second miniature, which is found on fol. 167v, shows Venus and the God of Love in front of Jealousy's castle, as in the preceding miniature. In this case, however, Venus has let fly her arrow, which has gotten the lady in the stomach; she raises her hands in surprise. These themes are explored in greater detail in the marginalia at the bottom of the page. On the left, Venus, wearing a golden crown, has, as in the miniature on the same page, just let fly her flaming arrow. On the right is portrayed Jealousy's castle with the lady in the central tower. Honte, Peur, and Dangier precipitously leave the castle. Both the miniature and the marginalia represent correctly what is going on in the text on the page on which they occur. The myth of Pygmalion is framed by two miniatures that emphasize the main plot line of the allegorical romance. The planner presents the Pygmalion story as a digression or gloss grafted onto the narrative moment between the aiming of the arrow and the striking of the lady. As with the Narcissus episode, the planner closely relates the Pygmalion legend to the taking of the Rose.

In the next two illustrations, the planner focuses on Bel Acueil's final capitulation to the Lover's demands. The planner plays upon the religious imagery employed by Jean de Meun. The rubric, "Comment l'amant aora l'image" [How the Lover adored the image] (folio 169v), accompanies a miniature portraying a woman under an ornate Gothic portico. A man wearing a sac over his shoulder kneels before her, placing his cheek on her thigh. In the left-hand marginalia, the same man (dressed as a pilgrim) embraces the woman standing up under a less decorated Gothic portico. On the right, the pilgrim uses a large green stick to open a passage to arrive at a rosebush covered with red roses. The culmination of the action takes place on the last illustrated folio of the manuscript. The rubric, "Si com li amans quelle le bouton" [How the Lover picks the bud] (folio 170v), introduces a miniature in which the Lover picks a flower from a rosebush located just to the right of the portico (Figure 5). The lady to his left observes his action with a blank expression, her arms stretched out and her hands open. The figure represents Bel Acueil who is always female in this manuscript. In the marginalia on the left, the Lover embraces a female figure; in the center, a flowering rosebush stands under a portico; and on the right, the music of a flute player perched on the branches of the marginal decoration awakens the dreamer.

Whereas the woman never appears as a discrete entity in the text, the very fact of representing in the manuscript the various manifestations of the Lover's lady gives her a concreteness she does not have without the illustrations. The woman who is being seduced takes on several forms in the text: she is evoked in the tower image and in Pygmalion's statue brought to life through the combined efforts of the sculptor and Venus. The woman also keeps her metaphorical status as "the Rose." The feminine presence likewise appears in the form of Bel Acueil, whose gestures toward the Lover finally turn to total acceptance of his desires. In the ultimate scene of seduction in the text, the vision of the pilgrim penetrating the tower image with his staff alternates with that of the Lover deflowering his coveted blossom. The conceptualizer of the Tournai *Rose* renders pictorially many of these avatars of the beloved. In addition to depicting the female presence as a tower image, Galatea and a rose, the planner chooses to represent Bel Acueil as a woman. (Because of the masculine gender of the name, Bel Acueil is represented as a man in the majority of manuscripts.) The reader, I think, considers these various female figures not only as what they represent metaphorically, but also as images of the Lover's lady. When Bel Acueil regally opens her arms in a gesture of assent in the miniature on folio 170v, we see not only a personification, but a real woman who accords her favors to the Lover.[51]

In the final miniature of the manuscript, the female figure gives herself over in total submission to the Lover's demands. The planner has used references to the Pygmalion myth to reinforce Gui's clerkly and didactic retelling of the Narcissus story. Through the iconographic rendition of the final taking of the Rose, the planner teaches a lesson in love that complements Gui's original exemplum. The Lover and his beloved demonstrate to the reader that the call of the God of Love cannot be ignored: love, as Ovid and Virgil had said, conquers all.[52] Unlike Narcissus and Lyriopé, the Lover and the woman (represented variously as Bel Acueil, Galatea, the Rose, and the tower statue) set a good example for others to follow. The lady of the Tournai manuscript can be interpreted as an exemplary figure who does what the heroine of the *Roman de la Rose* should do.

The typical romance "happy ending" is that of a marriage, and it is quite possible that a prominent member of Tournaisian society commissioned the manuscript to celebrate a wedding in the family. In the marginalia gracing the initial page of the text (Figure 2), the God of Love, enthroned in a tree, shoots arrows at a young woman and a young knight (or squire) located on either side of him.[53] In a tree to the right of the kneeling male figure hangs a shield bearing a coat of arms. In an article written in 1946, Lucien Fourez identified the arms as those of the Pourrés family, well known members of the Tournaisian bourgeoisie.[54] It now seems impossible to give a more precise identification of the owner of the arms because Fourez failed to cite his sources. Although the arms in the Tournai *Rose* do not correspond exactly to any representation in the heraldic documents available at the present time, they do appear to belong to the Pourrés family.

The planner's coordination of the Narcissus and Pygmalion episodes in the program of illumination is all the more striking since Gui de Mori had originally eliminated the Pygmalion episode from the text of the *Rose*. These verses constitute an example of what Gui terms "subtractions reprises" [reinstated omissions], verses originally deleted by Gui de Mori, but reintroduced into the Tournai *Rose*. I believe that the copyist of the Tournai *Rose*, who may either be identical to the planner or a close collaborator, returned the "subtractions reprises" to the place they had occupied in a former version.[55] The restored verses include the comparison of the statue to Pygmalion's image and the scabrous opening of the way that leads to the roses, both of which also receive illustration in the manuscript. These passages restore a distinctly erotic tone to Gui's more discreet and refined version of the *Rose*.

The planner plays upon both the amorous/didactic and mystical interpretations implicit in Gui's text. The copyist of the *Tournai* Rose added a colophon which sets forth two alternate (and simultaneous) readings of the work:

> Escris fu l'an mil et .CCC.
> Et .XXX., porfitans as gens
> Est li quel se voelent tenir
> Au siecle, por eaus maintenir
> En estat de parfaite joie
> Mondaine, ou d'ensievir le voie
> De venir a joie sans fin,
> Qui voet ensievre le chemin
> Des blances brebis desus dites,
> Que li dous paistres a eslites
> Pour mener el biau parc joli,
> Ou tuit puissons jouer od li.[56]

[It was written in the year 1330. / It is profitable for those who wish to remain in secular life / In order to keep them in a state of perfect earthly joy / Or to follow the way that leads to joy without end / Whoever might want to follow the path / Of the white sheep (mentioned above) / Whom the good shepherd has chosen / To lead into the beautiful, lovely park / May we all be able to play there with him.]

The colophon contains distinct echoes of the passage concerning the Park of the Good Shepherd pronounced by Genius. Drastically reduced in size by Gui, Genius's sermon has been restored to its original state in the Tournai *Rose*. These facts convincingly support the hypothesis that it was the scribe who was responsible for putting the "subtractions reprises" back into the text. Although the copyist does undo some of Gui's changes by rendering the text more erotic, he/she remains true to the spirit of Gui's work that suggests the compatibility of two seemingly contradictory readings of the Rose quest. The copyist also brings out the similarities between Gui de Mori and Jean de Meun. In exchanging Guillaume's Vergier de Déduiz for the Park of the Good Shepherd, Jean was the first to posit an analogy between an erotic and a divine quest of the Rose.

The meaning of the passage of the Park of the Good Shepherd remains one of the most problematical questions in *Rose* criticism today.[57] It is difficult to reconcile Genius's impassioned plea to engage in sexual intercourse with his pious description of the Park. Critics tend to emphasize one part of the message to the detriment of the other. Some of those who see Jean de Meun as an advocate of a type of pagan naturalism go so far as to identify him as an adherent of Aristotelian and Averroïst views that challenge the value of continence. Other critics believe that Genius uses sexual terms as a metaphor for divine love. Whereas modern readers tend to assume that Genius's message is not compatible with orthodox Christian beliefs, medieval readers seriously debated the question. It is my contention that the Tournai *Rose* proposes Holy Matrimony as a way for the laity to resolve the apparent contradictions between Genius's call to procreate in an indiscriminate manner and Christian doctrine.

The colophon acquires several different meanings within the context of the Tournai *Rose*.[58] The "perfect earthly joy" could refer to sexual love legitimized by marriage (and ideally producing many offspring) that would lead the partners to heaven, the "joy without end." For clerics sworn to chastity, the two paths diverge. An ecclesiastic chooses to forego the pleasures of secular existence in order to dedicate himself entirely to the "joy without end." Even for someone who has taken a vow of chastity, the two paths are not necessarily entirely mutually exclusive. A monk or a nun may first know physical love before deciding to renounce it. The analogy between earthly and divine love was a frequent preoccupation of writers of romance and its generic derivatives. In developing Perceval's relationship to Blanchefleur and the Grail mysteries, authors of continuations, sequels, and wholesale rewritings wrestled with the ambiguities present in Chrétien de Troyes's unfinished *Conte du Graal*. The veneration of Chrétien's Lancelot for Guinevere approached the sacred. The combination of the erotic and the sacred seen in the Tournai *Rose* recalls Marie de France's "Eliduc." Eliduc's first wife enters a nunnery in order to allow her husband to marry the young woman with whom he has fallen in love. After the new couple has lived together happily for several years, Eliduc enters a monastery and his second wife joins his former spouse in the convent. For Marie de France, love, be it conjugal or even adulterous, can lead to sanctity. In the Tournai *Rose*, human passion and the love that connects God and the human race are viewed as manifestations of the same impulse, a desire which can, if properly directed, lead to a knowledge of heaven.

The scribal colophon works along with a miniature of the Virgin Mary and Jesus to form a religiomystical frame for the text. The miniature introducing the table of contents (Figure 1) shows the Virgin Mary crowned and seated. She holds the Infant Jesus in her left hand and a book in her right hand. Jesus raises his right hand in a sign of benediction and bears a globe of the world in his left hand. Marc-René Jung was the first to discern a Christian interpretation in the Tournai *Rose*. Jung reasons that since not only the miniatures but also the marginal decoration are related to the text they illustrate, the miniature at the head of the manuscript must certainly be an integral part of the work. Jung believes the mystical interpretation of the manuscript to be the work of either the copyist of the Tournai *Rose* or the patron of the manuscript.[59]

The lessons taught by the Tournai *Rose* point in several directions—they hold out the possibility of earthly bliss or eternal joy, or both to those lucky enough to be able to walk the two paths. Although the colophon can be applied to clerical and lay readers, it appears to be directed primarily toward a secular audience. Holy Matrimony represents a way for the laity to achieve the dual goals of earthly and otherworldly happiness. If indeed the manuscript commemorates a wedding, the initial page of the text would mark the meeting ground between the earthly and the divine. On the first folio of the text we see one male figure (represented in clerical garb) setting out on a search for love and another (depicted as a knight or squire) who celebrates the results of a completed quest that the sacrament of marriage will eventually legitimize in the eyes of the Church. Holy Matrimony is, after all, the sanctification of a sexual relationship. On the most elementary level, the miniature of Mary and Jesus decorating the table of contents is an image of the fecundity that is the desired result of the legitimate coupling of a man and a woman. On a higher level, the miniature figures the divine counterparts of the bonds of love set forth in the text of the *Rose*.[60]

The manuscript book encourages the reader to view Mary as an alternative to the heroine of the *Roman de la Rose*. The planner portrays Mary and Bel Acueil, one of the avatars of the female protagonist, in similar poses. Both have people kneeling at their feet;[61] the portico on folios 169v and 170v recalls Mary's throne. Indeed, the reference to Mary as the "heavenly rose" was widespread in the Middle Ages.[62] Mary represents the infinite *dépassement* of the fictional heroine of the *Rose*. Whereas the heroine acts in a way befitting a secular and a literary ideal, viewed from a religious perspective she is a figure of Eve, whose *félix culpa* brought about humanity's reuniting with God. Eve's sin necessitated the redemption of the human race through the coming of Christ, itself made possible only by means of Mary. Thus, although human nature was originally diminished because of one woman, it rose to even greater heights because of a second woman. The human race ultimately gained access to the kingdom of God through the mediation of woman.[63]

Ostensibly about profane love, the Tournai *Rose* incites meditation on the mysteries associated with Mary, including, for example, those of the Incarnation, the Annunciation, and the Virgin Birth.[64] The planner ingeniously exploits religious iconography to enrich the significance of the text of the *Rose*. The frame created by the portrayal of the Virgin Mary at the beginning of the manuscript and the colophon opposing secular to divine love at the end places the quest for the Rose within a wider context than that of the original text of the *Rose*. Thus the search for the red flower, originally physical in nature, takes on religious or mystical connotations. Human love becomes an emblem for the more complete affection that connects man to God. The two levels of interpretation coexist beautifully within the space provided by the illuminated manuscript.

In addition to the miniature of the Virgin Mary that heads the table of contents of the Tournai *Rose* (the only direct religious reference I have encountered at the beginning of a fourteenth-century manuscript of the *Rose*), another religious allusion appears in the marginalia accompanying the miniature, found on folio 137, that illustrates Nature's confession to Genius. The three images found in the bottom margin essentially summarize Nature's speech. In the first scene on the left, God's ordering (*ordenance*) of the world is conveyed by an image of Christ forming the animals.[65] In the center scene, God confers the guardianship of the world on Nature. Nature is shown kneeling before Christ who holds up an Isidorian diagram of the world divided into Asia, Europe, and Africa. On the far right, Nature preaches to humanity. In her speech she makes several major points; one is that the essential forms of the universe maintain and perpetuate themselves. Of all God's creatures, only man goes against this basic principle. Man should fulfill God's will by creating offspring; he is enjoined to "reproduce and multiply." Nature also acknowledges her own insufficiencies. Natural law is unable to explain the most important fact of divine revelation, the Incarnation of Christ.[66]

In including passages on the subject originally left out of Nature's speech in the Tersan manuscript or a more immediate predecessor of the Tournai *Rose*, the conceptualizer shows an evident interest in the Incarnation. The verses corresponding to lines 19033–19114 and 19118–19160 of Lecoy's edition of the text are "subtractions reprises." In these passages Jean de Meun claims that Plato, one of the wisest ancient philosophers, was incapable of understanding what was comprised by the belly of a virgin. The mystery of the Incarnation was made possible through the aegis of the Virgin Mary. Although unknown to the Jews and pagans, the Incarnation was nonetheless foretold in such works as Virgil's *Bucolics*. The idea that texts without an overt religious message can prefigure divine truths can of course apply to the *Roman de la Rose*, especially in the version supplied by the conceptualizer of the Tournai manuscript.

Besides responding to Gui's editorial work on the *Rose*, the planner provides an implicit commentary on Gui's self-portrait. I have already explored some of the complexities of Gui's authorial persona. It seems inappropriate for a monk or a priest to set himself up as an advisor on erotic matters. Forbidden to marry, he is unable to profit from the lessons on earthly love he gives to others. Gui is nonetheless not totally immune to the attractions of physical passion, which certainly must have been the case for the majority of clerics sworn to a vow of chastity.

In the miniature on the initial page of the text, the planner portrays Gui as an actor in an erotic love quest as well as a clerkly figure who serves love in bookish ways. In the interior of an historiated letter T that heads the Prologue added by Gui, we see a monk who, having taken off his scapulary to work, sits at a desk and writes in an open book. Although one critic identifies the figure in the initial as Guillaume de Lorris,[67] it seems more logical to view him as Gui de Mori. Since the letter heads the beginning of Gui's new Prologue to the *Rose*, it might well celebrate Gui's own role in the recasting of the work. If the monk in the initial letter is indeed meant to depict Gui in his role as clerkly author, then the second cleric approaching the wall of the garden in the initial miniature would appear to represent Gui in his role as lover.[68] As in most illuminated manuscripts of the *Rose*, the protagonist appears as a tonsured cleric. The contradictions inherently present in the clerkly figure writing about love are exacerbated in Gui's case because he, unlike many other clerics, had taken ecclesiastical vows that preventing him from marrying.

An implicit reference to a concupiscent cleric and artisan figure appears in the marginalia treating Zeuxis and Pygmalion found on folio 156v. The reference to Zeuxis appears in an intervention in which the Poet-Narrator, speaking in the first person, expresses his inability to describe Nature. Even writers like Plato and Aristotle could not do it, he says, nor could painters like Pygmalion or Zeuxis. The Poet-Narrator had first tried to represent Nature correctly, but then silenced himself upon recognizing his presumption. He realizes that God made Nature the origin of all beauty, which goes beyond human understanding. As for the source of the reference to Zeuxis, Cicero in his *Rhetoric* recounts the story of the five young women presented naked to the artist to extract a prototype of perfect beauty. In the marginal depiction of Zeuxis, the five models cavort in front of the artist. The genitalia of one of the women is clearly outlined in orange; several other models make gestures that could be interpreted as either covering up their sex organs or playing with them. In the Tournai *Rose*, Zeuxis is presented as an artist who cannot represent the marvels of nature in such a way as to reveal the transcendent reality that lies behind them.

The positioning of the marginal representation of Zeuxis reveals that the planner has conflated the stories of Zeuxis and Pygmalion. In the actual sequence of the poem, the episode of Zeuxis precedes that of Pygmalion by over 4,000 lines of verse. The planner of the manuscript juxtaposes the episodes dealing with Zeuxis and Pygmalion in the margins of the page in order to bring out common themes.[69] Pygmalion appears to the right of the scene of Zeuxis and the five models. The hairdo and the dress of the woman he serenades with a portative organ, although conventional, are identical to those of the statue Zeuxis is in the process of fashioning. In the Tournai *Rose*, the stories of Pygmalion and Zeuxis have been combined to form the story of one character who, rather than trying to express something that goes beyond the merely physical, falls in love with his own creation. As a monk or a priest who has difficulty remaining true to his ecclesiastical vows, Gui de Mori would fit into the category of a flawed clerical author, one who got caught up in the message he had been preaching to others. The planner implies that, when motivated by sexual desire, Gui de Mori is unable to realize his transcendent purpose as clerkly writer bound by a vow of chastity.

The correct conduct for an ecclesiastic such as Gui is to convey God's message while himself abstaining from the actions he counsels to others. The image of a cleric preaching to a group of people appears several times in the manuscript illuminations, as if to remind us of the proper uses and abuses of the word by those pledged to work for divine purposes. In the marginalia on folio 98v, Faus Semblant dressed as a Dominicain preaches to the God of Love and his barons. The marginal decoration on folio 155v shows Genius, dressed as a bishop, delivering his sermon. A burning brandon, symbolic of his sensual message, falls on his listeners. A look at the first lines of the Prologue reveals Gui's ultimate motivation for writing: "Toute discrete creature / Desire asavoir par nature" [Each individual creature / Aspires to knowledge by its very nature]. Citing Hugh of St.-Victor's *De arra animae*, Gui claims that the most important knowledge to obtain is that of love because no heart can live without it. The love extolled by Hugh was more spiritual than physical in nature.[70] A person who reads Gui's Prologue and sees him depicted on the same page in the manuscript as a participant in the erotic love quest is incited to make up a story to explain the discrepancies between the way Gui portrays himself and the way the planner represents him. We can imagine that Gui, perhaps influenced directly by Hugh's mystical treatise, turned away from the physical manifestations of love to its divine counterparts. Unless Gui's espousal of divine love is a joke or a lie, at some time in the past his personal quest for the Rose had had to shift from the desire for sensual satisfaction to a search for knowledge of divine truths. The planner also implies that Gui is a muddled thinker who has to be guided to the right path, which is that he must abstain from the actions he counsels to others who are not bound by a similar vow of chastity. By means of the frame created by the miniature of the Virgin and Child and the colophon at the conclusion of the work, the planner intimates that for an ecclesiastic like Gui, devotion to the Virgin Mary should replace love of earthly women.

Thanks to his clerkly service as writer, especially in his revised role as nonparticipant in the love quest, Gui fits into the overall design of a Christian universe. Gui's editorial work on the original text of the *Rose* included making it more logical and orderly; he divided it up into sections and chapters that by and large corresponded to the headings in the table of contents (the table in the Tournai *Rose* also contains headings corresponding to the sections reintroduced into the text by the copyist, however). Through his ordering of the parts of the book, his personal *ordenance*, he takes part in God's transcendent scheme as set forth in Nature's speech.[71] Finally, the miniature of Mary holding the Christ child in one hand and a book in the other that heads the manuscript is an image of the Incarnation. This figuration of the Word made flesh points to the ultimate compatibility of human realities and divine truth.

In addition to the religious interpretation present in the Tournai *Rose*, other indications point to the manuscript having been produced by a workshop associated with a monastery. Early fourteenth-century Tournai possessed at least six religious communities.[72] One of the two hands that executed the manuscript was that of Pierart dou Tielt, who had close ties with the Benedictine monastery of St.-Martin de Tournai.[73] Sometime after 1349, Pierart replaced Jean de Bruielles as restorer of the books in the library of Gilles li Muisis, abbot of the monastery between 1331 and 1352.[74] Pierart worked on the illuminations of all the texts composed by Gilles,[75] an admirer both of chastity and the *Rose*.[76] Gilles regarded the *Rose* as a didactic and exemplary work, a type of collection of the sayings of many authority figures.[77] Defining beautiful works as ones which "saintement font les gens vivre" [make people live a holy life], Gilles dubbed the *Rose* the most beautiful work he knew.[78] Gilles's comment raises the suspicion that he may have been familiar with the Tournai *Rose*. At the very least, it reveals that Gilles, a leading cleric of his time, believed that the *Rose* could lead people to piety.

Because the names Gui de Mori and Pierart dou Tielt do not figure in the obituary list of St.-Martin de Tournai,[79] we can assume that neither was a monk in the monastery. Writing for a primarily clerical audience, Gui was probably associated with one of the other religious communities located in Tournai. Pierart produced works for a secular as well as a religious clientele. He appears to have been the head of a very active Tournaisian workshop, which often did work for lay patrons as well as for the cathedral and the abbey.[80] Pierart began working under the Master of the Ghent Ceremonial, but his mature style shows great independence of his teacher.[81]

There is an additional reason to believe that the relationship between Gilles and Pierart was a close one: both were chroniclers of the events of their time. In 1347 Gilles, having gone blind, had his memoirs dictated. This work constitutes a history of his abbey and city in the first half of the fourteenth century. Pierart seems to have assumed the role of chronicler either right before or just after Gilles's death in 1352. On several folios left blank at the end of a manuscript of the *Queste del Saint Graal* (Paris, Bibliothèque de l'Arsenal, MS 5218, dated 15 August 1351 and produced in Tournai) that Pierart states in a colophon he transcribed, illuminated, and bound, he writes an ecclesiastical history of the world beginning with the birth of Christ, which includes mention of events occurring in Tournai in 1277.[82] Pierart states that in that year 26 people were crushed to death when they participated in a procession held annually to commemorate the intercession of the Virgin Mary on behalf of the people of Tournai during the Great Plague of 1092.[83] Pierart adds that in that same year construction was begun on a new wall that would extend from the portal of Kokriel to that of Bordiel on the banks of the Escaut. Information on the building of this wall also figures in one of the chronicles authored by Gilles li Muisis.[84]

Further hypotheses about the Tournai *Rose* suggest themselves. The manuscript may have been produced to celebrate the wedding of someone closely associated with the monastery. St.-Martin de Tournai played a focal role in the life of Tournai; its abbot Gilles li Muisis was a very powerful figure who dealt with many of the leading European political personalities of his time. One can also speculate on the identity of the planner of the Tournai *Rose*. Lucien Fourez proposed Gui de Mori himself,[85] but Gui worked on the Tersan manuscript in 1290 whereas the Tournai *Rose* bears the date of 1330, and a forty-year career would appear inordinately long for someone living in the Middle Ages. A close study of the manuscript leads me to believe that the copyist was closely allied with, if not identical to, the conceptualizer, and that Gui de Mori was not the copyist. Pierart dou Tielt also comes to mind as a likely candidate for the role of planner since he executed much of the decoration of the Tournai *Rose*. Moreover, twenty years after the completion of that manuscript, he did all the work on the Arsenal manuscript of the *Queste*. The hypothesis of Pierart as planner of the Tournai *Rose* is seemingly contradicted by the presence of partially effaced marginal notations written in black lead on several folios on which Pierart did the illustrations.[86] Although it is hard to imagine he would have written them for himself, we cannot entirely rule out the possibility.

In conclusion, the Tournai *Rose* was probably designed in a workshop in Tournai that had close ties with the Benedictine monastery of

St.-Martin. Due to the destruction by fire of the municipal archives in 1940, we will probably never be able to determine the exact role of the historical figures who seem to have contributed to the making of the Tournai *Rose*: Pierart dou Tielt, Gilles li Muisis, Gui de Mori, and the young couple portrayed in the manuscript. Although we may never be able to establish with certainty the planner's identity, what we do know about his/her role is the following: that person at once transposed Gui's double reading of the *Rose* into the program of illuminations while providing a commentary on his textual emendations and his authorial persona. In accordance with his association with a monastery, the conceptualizer also placed Gui's work within the context of God's overall design as set forth in certain verses of Jean de Meun's section of the *Rose*.

Notes

1. The prior studies of Gui's work are the following: Ernest Langlois, "Gui de Mori et le *Roman de la Rose*," *Bibliothèque de l'École des Chartes* 68 (1907): 1–23; Marc-René Jung, "Gui de Mori et Guillaume de Lorris," *Vox Romanica* 27 (1968): 106–37; David Hult, "Gui de Mori, lecteur médiéval," *Incidences* 5 (January–April 1981): 53–70. In making reference to the original text of Guillaume de Lorris and Jean de Meun, I shall refer to Félix Lecoy's three volume edition (Classiques Français du Moyen Âge 92, 95, 98 [Paris: Champion, 1965–70]). I thank the National Endowment for the Humanities for awarding me a travel grant during the summer of 1989 that enabled me to examine the manuscript firsthand.

2. For a study of the illuminations of the manuscript, consult Lucien Fourez, "Le *Roman de la Rose* de la Bibliothèque de la Ville de Tournai," *Scriptorium* 1 (1946–47): 213–39.

3. I shall henceforth refer to the person who oversees the work on the manuscript as the "planner" or the "conceptualizer." This person may exercise other functions besides that of planner. For example, he/she may be a rubricator or an illuminator. Consult Beat Brent, "Le texte et l'image dans la *Vie des saints* au Moyen Âge: rôle du concepteur et rôle du peintre," *Texte et image: Actes du Colloque International de Chantilly* (October 13–15, 1982) (Paris: Les Belles Lettres, 1984), 31–40.

4. For a description of the Tersan manuscript, see: Langlois, "Gui de Mori," 1–3; E. Langlois, *Les Manuscrits du "Roman de la Rose"* (1910; Geneva: Slatkine Reprints, 1974), 163–66; Jung, "Gui de Mori," 106–08; Hult, "Gui de Mori," 57–61.

5. According to Jung ("Gui de Mori," 106), the manuscript belonged in the Öttingen-Wallerstein collection before being sold in 1934. Its current owner has not been identified. For further information on the Tersan manuscript, see Hult, "Gui de Mori," 57–58.

6. Hult, "Gui de Mori," 69–70.

7. The diacritical marks are enumerated by Langlois, "Gui de Mori," 11; Fourez, "Le *Roman de la Rose*," 213–14; Jung, "Gui de Mori," 110–11.

8. Fourez, "Le *Roman de la Rose*," 218.

9. Ibid., 218–19.

10. Folios 32, 37, 114, 115, 116, 132, 162, 168. Paul Faider et l'Abbé Pierre Van Sint Jan, *Catalogue général des manuscrits des Bibliothèques de Belgique*, vol. 6: Catalogue des manuscrits conservés à Tournai (Gembloux: Duculot, 1950), 108–09. The folios indicated do not correspond exactly to those given by Langlois, "Gui de Mori," 5.

11. Folios 118 and 119. Ibid.

12. Fourez, "Le *Roman*," 219.

13. Consult Langlois, "Gui de Mori," 11–14 for the complete text of Gui's Prologue.

14. Ibid. 11 n.1.

15. Hugh of St.-Victor, *Soliloquy on the Ernest Money of the Soul*, trans. Kevin Herbert, Mediaeval Philosophical Texts in Translation 9 (Milwaukee, WI: Marquette University Press, 1956).

16. Ledrus, M. "Hugues de St. Victor: Le gage des divines fiançailles (*De arrha animae*), *Museum Lessianum, Compagnie de Jesus, Section ascétique et mystique*, 12 (Louvain, 1923).

17. André le Chapelain, *Traité de l'amour courtois*, trans., intro., and notes by Claude Buridant (Paris: Klincksieck, 1974).

18. Refer to Armand Strubel's analysis of the use of the related terms "lettre/senefiance" in allegorical literature on p. 242 of his section of the *Précis de littérature française*, ed. Daniel Poirion (Paris: Presses Universitaires de France, 1983). It is logical that Gui de Mori would borrow Guillaume de Lorris's definition of the term "lettre," which according to Strubel means "matire" (i.e., "subject matter").

19. Langlois ("Gui de Mori," 14) believes that in using the term "those persons" ("ciaus") Gui is referring to Guillaume de Lorris and the author of the anonymous continuation included in the manuscript rather than to Guillaume de Lorris and Jean de Meun. Langlois reasons that if Gui had believed the two parts of the romance to be by two different authors (Guillaume de Lorris and Jean de Meun), he would not have hesitated between "that person" ("celui") and "those persons" ("ciaus"). Although the rubrics in the Tournai *Rose* attribute the anonymous continuation to Guillaume, Gui, having seen several manuscripts that lacked the continuation, could have doubted its authenticity.

20. Jung, "Gui de Mori," 112–13.

21. The portrait of Plaisance appears on pp. 181–85 of F. W. Bourdillon, *The Early Editions of the "Roman de la Rose"* (London: The Bibliographical Society at the Chiswick Press, 1906).

22. Langlois published the fourteen-verse description of Orgueil on pp. 16–17 of his article on Gui de Mori.

23. See Jung, "Gui de Mori," 117 for a list of the important omissions in Guillaume's section of the *Rose*.

24. Pierre-Yves Badel, *Le "Roman de la Rose" au XIVe siècle: Etude de la réception de l'œuvre*, Publications Romanes et Françaises 153 (Geneva: Droz, 1980), 145.

25. Badel, *Le "Roman,"* 145: "Au total, ce remaniement reste fidèle à l'esprit courtois."

26. Jung, "Gui de Mori," 115, 117.

27. I thank Sylvia Huot for bringing this point to my attention.

28. Colette Mazure, "Gui de Mori: Remanieur du *Roman de la Rose*," thèse de licence, Université Catholique de Louvain, June 1961, 58 claims that Gui attenuates the antifeminism of Jean de Meun. See also Jung's comments in "Gui de Mori," 126.

29. Ibid., 145–46. Consult Jung, "Gui de Mori," 124–26 for additional information on the rules of love.

30. Jung, "Gui de Mori," 120–22 gives the text of the Narcissus episode.

31. Paul Barrette, *Robert de Blois's "Floris et Lyriopé,"* University of California Publications in Modern Philology vol. 92 (Berkeley and Los Angeles: University of California Press, 1968).

32. Ibid., 60–66.

33. I am preparing a book-length study of the Tournai *Rose*. It bears the provisional title, *Gui de Mori and the "Book of the Rose": The Literary, Artistic, and Historical Context of MS 101 of the Municipal Library of Tournai*.

34. Bourdillon, *The Early Editions*, 176–77.

35. The text of this passage appears in Langlois, "Gui de Mori," 7–9.

36. According to Langlois ("Gui de Mori," 8 n. 2), "cette prison ne peut être que l'état ecclésiastique de Gui."

37. Langlois, "Gui de Mori," 14 states his view that Gui de Mori was in all probability a priest.

38. Consult Lecoy, ed. *Roman*, vv. 19569–98 and his notes on these verses. The value of continence was a question debated by such thinkers as Thomas Aquinas around the time Jean de Meun was composing his continuation of the *Rose*. St. Thomas himself was unable to conclusively resolve the issue.

39. For the text of this passage see Langlois, "Gui de Mori," 8–9.

40. Hult, "Gui de Mori," 65.

41. See Langlois, "Gui de Mori," 21–22.

42. Jung, "Gui de Mori," 133.

43. Jung, "Gui de Mori," 134.

44. Jean Leclercq, *Monks and Love in Twelfth-Century France* (Oxford: The Clarendon Press, 1979), 8–16.

45. André le Chapelain, *Traité de l'amour courtois*, 142–43.

46. David Knowles, *The Evolution of Medieval Thought* (New York: Vintage Books, 1962), 142.

47. See John V. Fleming, *The "Roman de la Rose": A Study in Allegory and Iconography* (Princeton, NJ: Princeton University Press, 1969), 186–87 for a study of the hunt motif seen in the marginalia.

48. Fourez, "Le *Roman*," 221.

49. For instance, the miniature of the God of Love and the Lover on fol. 22

closely resembles the second representation of the same two characters on fol. 95. To cite another example, the motif of Jealousy's castle, the subject of the miniature on fol. 41v (the last miniature located in the section authored by Guillaume de Lorris), is picked up again in the miniature on fol. 111 (Faus Semblant kills Male Bouche), in both the miniature and marginalia on fol. 113 (Cortoisie, Largece, Faus Semblant, and Atenance Contrainte speak to la Vieille) and fol. 131 (la Vieille leaves Bel Acueil and goes to see the Lover), and in the marginalia on fol. 167v (described in detail in this study). For complete descriptions of all illustrations, consult Fourez, "Le *Roman*."

50. The precise references appear in the following paragraph of this study.

51. Another example of the planner's tendency to have us envision a real woman behind the figure of Bel Acueil occurs in the depiction found in the marginalia on fol. 36 of the Lover kissing the rosebud. Bel Acueil stands to the right of the Lover with her hands open in a gesture of assent. The Lover, on his knees, embraces a rosebud on a bush. To the left of the bush appears a disembodied woman's head. (This marginal image accompanies a miniature which shows Venus holding a flaming torch flanked by Bel Acueil and the Lover.)

52. Cortoisie quotes Virgil's *Bucolics* on this point in v. 21302 of the *Rose*.

53. François Avril, Curator of Manuscripts at the Bibliothèque Nationale, believes that the kneeling figures may be the donors of the manuscript. Fourez, "Le *Roman*," 215 also thinks the knight on fol. 5 is the person who commissioned the manuscript. Furthermore, Avril claims they may be the same figures as those seen kneeling on either side of the Virgin and Child in the miniature on fol. 1 (figure 1). (The two sets of figures were done by different artists. Refer to n. 62 of this study.) The motif of the God of Love enthroned in a tree is a typical one that probably had its origins in Apuleius. See Edwin Panofsky, *Studies in Iconology: Humanistic Themes in the Art of the Renaissance* (1939; New York: Icon Editions, 1967), p. 101 and figure 75.

54. Fourez, "Le *Roman*," 215–16. I asked Michel Pastoureau of the École des Hautes Études to investigate the identification of the heraldry that was questioned by Alison Stones. I quote from Pastoureau's letter to me dated October 14, 1988: "Malgré toutes mes recherches, je n'ai trouvé qu'un seul document sur les armoiries de la famille Pourrès (ou Pourret) de Tournai. Il s'agit d'un sceau appendu à un document daté de 1285 et à un autre daté de 1286; il appartient à Henri Pourrès, juré puis prévôt de la ville. On y voit un écu chargé d'un burelé et brisé d'un lambel; pas de trace du franc-quartier à l'arbalète. Ce sceau est décrit par De Raadt (J.-T.), *Sceaux armories des Pays-Bas et des pays avoisinants*, tome III, Bruxelles, 1901, p. 152 (notice *Porret*). Fourez ne me semble pas s'être trompé et je crois qu'on peut lui faire confiance pour le franc-quartier à l'arbalète évoquant une appartenance à la confrérie des arbalétriers de Saint Georges." The arms do not correspond exactly those of Henri Pourrés (variants Pourrès, Fourrés, Pouret, Pouré, etc.). Fourez, "Le Roman," 215–16 n. 5 mentions three other male members of the Pourrès family, Gilles and Diérin, "clercs," and Jehan, "bourgeois." One of them was perhaps a member of the society of the crossbowmen of Saint George.

François Avril stated that the hypothesis that the manuscript was produced to commemorate a wedding, although not conclusively demonstrable, was not contradicted by anything in the illuminations. A possible objection to the hypothesis is the absence of a shield bearing the arms of the bride in the tree next to the kneeling female figure located in the marginalia on fol. 5. Avril claims that since the wedding would have taken place in middle class rather than in aristocratic circles, there would not have been as great a need to indicate the woman's lineage. Michel Pastoureau found the hypothesis especially intriguing in light of the subject matter of the work.

55. This opinion is shared by Mazure, "Gui de Mori," 71.

56. The text of the explicit is reprinted by Jung, "Gui de Mori," 113 n. 20.

57. For a more detailed treatment of the topic, consult pp. 62–63 of Heather Arden's *The Romance of the Rose* (Boston: Twayne Publishers, 1987).

58. The ambiguity is compounded by the contorted syntax of the passage.

59. Jung, "Gui de Mori," 113 n. 20.

60. This point would be reinforced if the two kneeling figures in the miniature were seen as the same as the pair on their knees on either side of the God of Love in the marginalia on fol. 5 (figure 2). The resemblance between the two couples was brought to my attention by François Avril. Their similarity is even more impressive when one takes into account that the miniatures were executed by two different artists, Pierart dou Tielt (figure 1) and the Master of the Ghent Ceremonial (figure 2).

61. For a study of another *Rose* manuscript that combines the erotic and the sacred in a related way, see Sylvia Huot's article, "Vignettes marginales comme glose marginale dans un manuscrit du *Roman de la Rose* au quatorzième siècle," in *La Présentation du livre*: Actes du colloque de Paris X-Nanterre (Dec. 4–6, 1985), ed. E. Baumgartner and N. Boulestreau (Littérales: Cahiers du Département de Français, 2; Nanterre: Centre de Recherche du Département de Français de Paris X), 173–86. In a similar vein, Per Nykrog in *L'Amour et la rose: le grand dessein de Jean de Meun*, Harvard Studies in Romance Languages 41 (Lexington, KY: French Forum Publishers, 1986), 61 proposes that the image of the "Fontaine de Vie" in the *Rose* can be read concurrently as a symbol of the Trinity and of the female genitalia.

62. Mary and the fictional heroine are similar in their lack of pride, which in the Augustinian tradition was seen as the motive behind the Fall. See John Bugge, *Virginitas: An Essay in the History of a Medieval Ideal* (The Hague: Martinus Nijhoff, 1975), 20–26.

63. In the medieval mentality, Eve was seen as a prefiguration of Mary just as Adam was a prefiguration of Christ.

64. Leclercq, *Monks and Love*, 66 cites the example of a Franciscan monk who dedicated the *Remedies of Love* to the Virgin Mary. Leclercq, 115 also discusses the *Eructavit*, a work in which the vocabulary of secular love is applied to the mystery of the Incarnation.

65. This is a typical image of the creation found, for example, on fol. 24 of London, British Library, MS Stowe 17; see Lillian M. C. Randall, *Images in the Margins of Gothic Manuscripts* (Berkeley and Los Angeles: University of California Press, 1966), Image 139.

66. Fleming, *The "Roman,"* 201.

67. Fourey, "Le *Roman*," 220 n. 17.

68. François Avril believes the two figures represent the same character: the cleric approaching the wall of the garden is the same as the monk transcribing the manuscript. Avril points out that unlike the copyist, the standing cleric is wearing a traveling cloak and gloves. The cloak indicates that he is engaged on a journey.

69. John Vincent Fleming, "The *Roman de la Rose* and its Manuscript Illustrations," 2 vols., dissertation, Princeton University, 1963, p. 181. According to Fleming, both these episodes treat the theme of idolatrous images.

70. Jung, "Gui de Mori," 113.

71. In the rubrics of the Tersan manuscript, it is specified that Gui divided Jean's section of the *Rose* into five parts (he had already apportioned the first section into three parts; see Jung, "Gui de Mori," 2). Each part is further subdivided into chapters. The chapter headings in the text correspond by and large to those found in the table of contents. Fourez, "Le *Roman*," 218 states his belief that the table of contents is the work of Gui de Mori. Since the Tersan manuscript did not seem to contain a table of contents (see Jung, "Gui de Mori," 112 n. 17 and Langlois, *Les Manuscrits*, 165) and the table in the Tournai *Rose* includes chapter headings of passages reintroduced into that manuscript, I believe that the table is more likely to have been created by the copyist of the Tournai *Rose* than by Gui de Mori himself. However, since the Tersan manuscript did not contain Gui's system of diacritical marks, Gui may have directly supervised the production of one or several manuscripts executed between the Tersan and Tournai manuscripts. He may have added a table to these manuscripts, a table later augmented by the copyist of the Tournai *Rose*.

72. A. F. J. Bozière, *Tournai, ancien et moderne* (Tournai: Delmée, 1864).

73. In his description of the manuscript found on pp. 301–02 of the section on manuscripts in the catalog, *Les Fastes du Gothique: le siècle de Charles V*, Galéries nationales du Grand Palais (October 9, 1981–February 1, 1982), François Avril states that the manuscript represents the work of at least three artists. In a private consultation held during July 1988 in the Manuscript Room of the Bibliothèque Nationale, Avril, after examining my copy of the microfilm, said he discerned two hands in the manuscript, that of the Master of the Ghent Ceremonial (also known as the Cérémonial de Saint-Pierre au Mont Blandin) who did all the work on fol. 5, and that of Pierart dou Tielt. In the case of the decoration he attributes to Pierart, some may have been produced by one or several illuminators working directly under Pierart's supervision. Avril cited in particular the decoration on fol. 6 and fol. 9.

74. Avril, "Manuscrits," *Les Fastes*, 348.

75. Albert D'Haenens, "Pierart dou Tielt: Enlumineur des oeuvres de Gilles li Muisis," *Scriptorium* 23 (1969): 83–93.

76. Badel, "*Le Roman de la Rose*," 75–82.

77. Ibid., 81.

78. Here are the verses that follow Gilles's previously quoted statement: "J'ay pau trouvet plus bielle chose, Que c'est dou romanc de le Rose; Bénit soit qui le trouvèrent" [I have not found a more beautiful thing than the *Romance of the Rose*;

Blessed be those who wrote it]. Kerwyn de Lettenhove, ed. *Poésies de Gilles li Muisis*, 2 vols. (Louvain: Lefever, 1882) I: 86.

79. Dom Ursmer Berlière, *Monasticon Belge*, Vol. I: Provinces de Namur et de Hainaut (Liège: Centre National d'Histoire Religieuse, 1973).

80. Avril, "Manuscrits," 348. Alison Stones, Professor of Art History at the University of Pittsburgh, shares this view.

81. Ibid.

82. Ibid.

83. Here is an account of the event written by Bozière, *Tournai*, 387: "En 1277 . . . la procession se rendait, comme d'usage, à la maison des lépreux du Val d'Orcq et pour éviter l'encombrement au sortir de la ville, le clergé prenait par une porte et les fidèles par une autre. Cette mesure n'empêche point que 26 personnes trouvèrent la mort étouffées dans la foule."

84. *Bulletin de la Société Historique et Littéraire de Tournai*, vol. 1 (Tournai: J. Casterman, October 1849), 120: "Gilles li Muisis, chroniqueur contemporain, nous apprend qu'en 1277 on commença à faire les tours et les murs de la ville au dessus de l'Escaut jusqu'à la porte Kokriel."

85. Fourez, "*Le Roman*," 239. The reasons Fourez gives for believing that Gui was the planner of the Tournai *Rose* are the following: the manuscript is very carefully executed; the manuscript is the only one containing the rewriting by Gui in which all the diacritical marks are scrupulously indicated; the decoration of the manuscript is totally different from the classical program of illuminations; much of the decoration is directly connected to passages of the romance reworked by Gui.

86. During a private consultation, François Avril pointed out the marginal notations in black lead on fol. 40v to me. There appear to be others, still fainter, on fol. 42v.

Figure 1. Folio 1. The table of contents is headed by a miniature of the Virgin Mary crowned and seated. She holds the Infant Jesus on her lap; a male and a female figure kneel on either side of them.

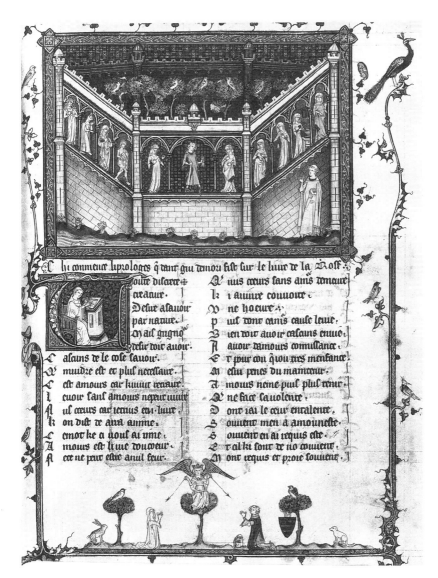

Figure 2. Folio 5. A large miniature precedes the new Prologue to the *Rose* composed by Gui de Mori. It depicts a tonsured cleric who approaches the enclosure surrounding the Vergier de Deduiz. Eleven anticourtly vices are depicted on the wall of the garden. The historiated initial shows a tonsured cleric who is writing at his desk. In the marginalia at the bottom of the page, the God of Love seated in a tree shoots an arrow at a knight and a lady who are kneeling on either side of him.

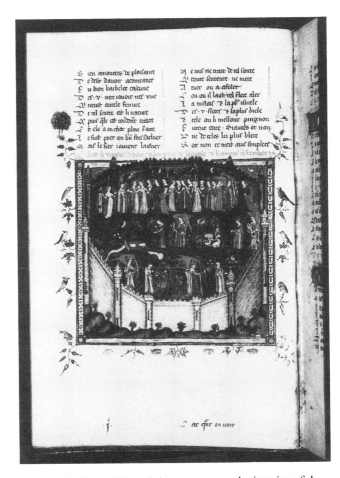

Figure 3. Folio 12v. The miniature portrays the interior of the Vergier de Deduiz. At the top of the illustration, the participants in the Carole de Deduiz join hands. In the remaining scenes, the Lover makes his way through the garden followed by the God of Love.

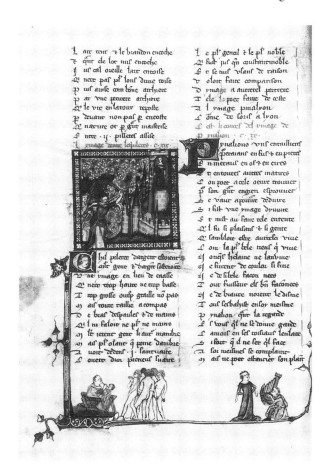

Figure 4. Folio 156v. In the miniature Venus aims an arrow at the image between the pillars. In the bottom left margin, Zeuxis tries to fashion an image of perfect beauty based on his observation of 5 naked female models. In the bottom right margin, a man (probably Pygmalion) serenades a woman with a portative organ.

Figure 5. Folio 170v. The miniature shows the Lover picking a
flower from a rosebush under a Gothic portico. A woman with
her arms extended stands to his side. In the bottom left margin, a
man embraces a woman; a rosebush stands under a Gothic portico to their right. In the bottom right margin, the dreamer is
awakened from his slumber by the music of a flute player seated
on the branches of the marginal decoration.

Part IV

The Reception of the *Rose* in France

Sylvia Huot

8. Authors, Scribes, Remanieurs: A Note on the Textual History of the *Romance of the Rose*

The [*Romance of the Rose*] was no sooner written than it was rewritten; and the process of revision and *remaniement* continued throughout the fourteenth and fifteenth centuries.[1] The poem was abridged, expanded through the addition of interpolations, and altered through a combination of deletions and additions. A study of the manuscript tradition reveals that scribes sometimes worked from two or more sources at once; in this way the interpolations of a given remaniement found their way into the manuscript tradition, in some cases showing up in manuscripts of several different families. Scribes also introduced more modest changes in the text, correcting lines that to them seemed corrupt or inappropriate and adding the occasional comment. Although only Guillaume de Lorris and Jean de Meun are remembered as authors of the *Rose*, they are by no means the only writers who worked on the poem.

The study of multiple versions and variant readings of the *Rose* allows us to see how this important poem was understood by its medieval readers, how it was reinterpreted and adapted for different audiences. In addition, the manuscript tradition of the *Rose* offers valuable evidence for medieval notions of authorship and textuality, while the modern reception of the *Rose* and its textual history shows how our own ideas of authorship and textuality have affected both the editing of the poem and our understanding of it. Here, by way of example, I will examine the work of two participants in the textual history of the *Rose*: the cleric Gui de Mori, late thirteenth-century author of what is probably the most extensive rework-

This essay draws on a larger study I have prepared on the reception and manuscript tradition of the *Rose*, forthcoming with Cambridge University Press under the title *The "Romance of the Rose" and Its Medieval Readers: Reception, Interpretation, Manuscript Transmission*. The project has been supported by Faculty Summer Stipends from Northern Illinois University and by a Fellowship from the John Simon Guggenheim Memorial Foundation.

ing of the *Rose*, and Gui's contemporary, the anonymous redactor of what is now known as the *B* text. These two versions, though contemporary, reflect different attitudes toward the poem itself and toward its status as a text with multiple authors. These differences in the treatment of the poem's inscribed author(s) are partly responsible for the very different critical reception afforded each version in the modern period.

In 1290 Gui de Mori completed his reworking of the *Roman de la Rose* as he then knew it: Guillaume de Lorris's romance, completed by what is now referred to as the anonymous continuation, but which Gui perceived as an integral part of the text.[2] Gui added several passages to the romance, including an eleventh portrait on the wall of the Garden, that of Orgueil; a lengthy exposition of the ten arrows of Love; interpolated passages in the descriptions of the various allegorical personifications; a revision of the story of Narcissus to include reference to his mother, Lyriopé, whose story is borrowed from the romance *Floris et Lyriopé*; and a long addition to the God of Love's teachings, enumerating the first four degrees of love (sight, speech, touch, and kiss).[3] In addition to these long interpolations, Gui also added a number of short interpolations and minor modifications. Gui's work on Guillaume de Lorris has been studied in some detail. It has also been noted that not long after he completed his work, Gui discovered Jean de Meun's continuation of the *Rose* and incorporated it into his project, effecting even more considerable changes in this portion of the poem than he had in the part by Guillaume de Lorris. The chronology of Gui's work is explained in a rubric in the now lost manuscript known as *Ter*, portions of which were fortunately transcribed by Méon and Langlois before it disappeared. Here Gui hypothesizes that Jean de Meun, provoked by Guillaume's boasts of having captured the Rose so easily, removed the original ending and added his own material in order to prolong the quest.[4] A somewhat similar statement also appears in the MS Tournai, Bibl. Mun. 101 (MS *Tou*).

The presentation of Gui's work in MS *Tou* is truly extraordinary in the context of fourteenth-century vernacular manuscripts. The manuscript, which was made in 1330, does not necessarily date from within Gui's lifetime; and it contains a somewhat modified version of his remaniement. What makes it of such value in studying Gui's work is its system of marginal annotations, explained in the Prologue (fol. 5v): a horizontal bar ("une petite vergiele") indicates "k'ele aura bouté / Tout hors le superfluité" [that it has done away with superfluous material]; a star ("une estoilete petite") marks "ce que g'i ajousterai" [what I will interpolate], with marginal flourishes indicating the length of the interpolation. Gui also notes that bar and star together indicate "risme noviele" [new rhyme]: the use of new words to express the original idea. He informs us that the technical terms ("propres nons") for these signs are "subtraction," "addition," and "mutation." Finally, he explains that a rose marks a "subtraction reprise," lines that were originally omitted but are now restored, again with marginal flourishes running the full length of the restored passage and a second rose appearing at its end.

As a result of this system, the manuscript not only transmits a particular version of the *Rose* but also provides a map of the ongoing processes of interpolation, abridgment, and restoration that characterize both the activity of remaniement and the *Rose* manuscript tradition in general. The marginal signs allow each reader or copyist to construct a personalized version of the *Rose*: interpolations can be kept or omitted, deletions can be left out or taken back. David Hult stated the case succinctly, pointing out that Gui "leaves himself open to an infinite number of future textual variants, all of which will depend on the viewpoint of each new reader."[5] This point is fully borne out in the manuscript tradition.

Gui's contributions to Guillaume de Lorris have survived, in whole or in part, in ten manuscripts known today, and some of his interpolations even appear in Molinet's prose version of the *Rose*.[6] His reworking of Jean de Meun, however, had much less impact on the *Rose* manuscript tradition. Aside from the ill-fated MS *Ter*, only four manuscripts transmit to us Gui's work on Jean de Meun, each in a different version. MS *Tou* has departed from the original by restoring thousands of lines that Gui had omitted; it also lacks a number of significant interpolations that appear in another manuscript of Gui's work, the fifteenth-century MS B.N. fr. 797, which I will designate MS *Mor*. The latter lacks the prologue of MS *Tou*, but otherwise contains a complete text of Gui's remaniement. For the most part it reflects the deletions recorded in MS *Tou*; but it does contain certain passages deleted from MS *Tou* or marked there as *subtractions reprises*. The MS Copenhagen, Royal Library G.K.S. 2061-4° (*He*), contemporary with MS *Tou*, contains a number of Gui's modifications. As will be explained below, however, the text in MS *He* cannot be identified as that of Gui de Mori; rather, it is an independent version of the *Rose* into which some of Gui's interpolations have been inserted and from which some of his deletions—including many that have been restored in MS *Tou*—have been made. MS *He* follows Gui's text most closely in the final passages of the poem, from around v. 19000 to the end. Finally, a few of Gui's interpolations in the discourses of Reason and Ami have been added—after the fact, but still within the fourteenth century—to MS Bibl. Nat. fr. 24390 (*Ke*).[7] It may have been an annotated manuscript such as this that provided the model from which MS *He* was copied.

MS *Tou* and MS *Mor*, the two most complete versions of Gui's remaniement, can be respectively distinguished by their treatment of the relationship between human and divine love, and between the natural and the sacred. In MS *Mor*, all references to sacred mysteries have been deleted from the discourse of Nature; her concerns remain strictly sublunary. Similarly, Gui omitted all traces of Genius's claims that procreation is the means to salvation, as well as his comparison of the Garden of Delight to the park of Heaven. Genius has, in effect, been turned back into the figure that appears in Alain de Lille's *De Planctu Naturae*, while Nature is a fairly straightforward conflation of Alain's Natura and Boethius's Philosophia. Gone from Nature's discourse are not only her discussions of the Incarnation, but also her lengthy digressions on such topics as optics and dreams. The single largest deletion, whereby 594 lines were reduced to a mere 38, was that of vv. 17891–18484, of which only vv. 17951–54, 17983–18012, and 18243–46 remained; but many other shorter passages were removed as well, including the reference to the castration of Origen; allusions to pagan mythology; and Nature's acceptance of the role of Faux Samblant and Contrainte Attenance, based on the acknowledgment that such "barat" is necessary for the cause of Love (vv. 19315–38). What is left of the discourse of Nature is the description of the cosmos; the reconciliation of free will and divine foreknowledge; the account of rainbows and other heavenly signs; the discussion of nobility, contrasting the nobility of lineage with that of the heart; and the enumeration of human vices. The discourse of Nature is thus rendered clearer, much more focused, and less frivolous. Nature does not get distracted from serious philosophical issues by a rambling exposition of optical illusions, and from there by the story of Venus's adultery with Mars. Appropriately, Gui omits Nature's self-deprecating comment on her own loquaciousness, "Fame sui, si ne me puis tere . . ." [I am a woman, so I cannot keep quiet . . . (vv. 19188–90)]. Gui's Nature has had her dignity restored; she is less human, less a fictional character than a device for introducing certain philosophical points. She contributes to the moral framework of the poem, setting forth human vices and virtues and establishing the individual's responsibility for his or her actions.

Genius is similarly reduced to his much more limited role as conceived by Alain: in a much abridged version of his sermon—reduced from 1163 to 123 lines—he acknowledges the authority of Nature as conferred by God and condemns sodomites and those who fail to adhere to Nature's laws. The deleted passages include the discussions of homosexuality and castration and most of the exhortations to sexual intercourse; the myths of the fall of the Golden Age and the founding of Thebes; the description of the pagan Hell; the review of Guillaume's Garden of Delight; and the entire exposition of the *biaus parc*. Genius does advise Love's troops to follow the works of Nature, to beget offspring, and to avoid sin. As the link between the natural and the divine, he presides over the miraculous transmission of life through procreation. He is a spokesman for the possibility of sexual activity within a moral framework. But that is all that he is. He offers no cosmology, no story of civilization, no attempt to explain the meeting of the erotic and the sacred in the moment of conception.

The issue of divine love is not lacking from MS *Mor*, however: Gui simply relocated it, inserting a long interpolation into the discourse of Reason that addresses the divine origins of all love.[8] Here Reason speaks of the Incarnation and stresses that all human love and friendship is rooted in the love of God. She cites Augustine, stating that "amours si est confourmable / Del amant a la chose amable" [love is conformance of the lover to the thing loved (fol. 37v)] and that the most ennobling object of love is clearly God himself. Reason further explicates love through the metaphor of a fountain that flows from God in two streams: one, *charité*, circulates through the world and returns to God, while the other, *convoitise*, dissipates itself in the world. Reason makes it clear that the superior form of love is charity. However, even though sexual love is identified with *convoitise*, Reason does acknowledge that such love can assume a noble form when it is based on affection and friendship rather than erotic desire; she goes on to stress, as in Jean de Meun, that those who engage in sexual activity—presumably envisioned in the context of marriage—ought to do so for the purpose of procreation.

These interpolations concerning the union of God and humanity and the fountain of love that flows from God through His creation are Gui's corrected version of the corresponding passages in Jean's discourses of Nature and Genius. Gui recognized the importance of grounding any discussion of love in an exposition of divine love; but he felt that Reason, not Nature or Genius, was the appropriate figure to offer such teachings. Humanity approaches divinity through the rational intellect, not through the natural sex drive. In this respect Gui reveals concerns similar to those that would later be voiced by Jean Gerson, who complained that Jean de Meun frequently "atribue a la persone qui parle ce qui ne le doit appartenir" [attributes to the person speaking that which is inappropriate], citing the example of "Nature parlant de paradis et des misteres de nostre foy" [Nature speaking of paradise and of the mysteries of our faith (ed. Hicks, 85)].[9] Moreover, Gui may have felt that Reason herself was not fairly represented if her words to the Lover did not include an exhortation to look beyond the world of the senses. Insofar as Reason is illuminated by faith, she is a guide not only to the moral issues of this life but also to spiritual awakening.

This particular aspect of Gui's remaniement, however, is no longer present in MS *Tou*. Perhaps because this manuscript was prepared for a different kind of audience, MS *Tou* restores the discussions of the Incarnation, Heaven, and Hell to the discourses of Nature and Genius; while the corresponding interpolations in the discourse of Reason are absent. The redactor of MS *Tou*, whether Gui or a later scribal editor, favored a view of the *Rose* as a poem that directly confronts the place of sexuality in the cosmic order. From this perspective, Genius, a figure of mediation between the natural and the divine, is the appropriate persona for the exposition of proper and improper sexuality, defined in terms of an orientation toward the fruit or the pleasure of sexual intercourse, respectively.

The more worldly tenor of MS *Tou* is further reflected in its inclusion of numerous other passages that are omitted from MS *Mor*, and which MS *Tou* itself marks as *subtractions reprises*. One important restoration effected in MS *Tou* is that of the numerous pagan fables included by Jean. Gui had nothing against pagan writers: indeed his interpolations in the discourse of Reason are replete with allusions to Aristotle, Cicero, and Seneca. Mythology, however, was another matter. In MS *Mor*, the allusion to Dedalus and the stories of Mars and Venus, Pygmalion, and Deucalion and Pyrrha are absent; while in MS *Tou*, all but the latter are restored. Equally important is the differing treatment of the poem's protracted ending. Following the discourse of Genius, Gui's original plan, preserved in MSS *Mor* and *He*, brought the poem to a rapid close. He deleted the entire story of Pygmalion and removed the lengthy digressions surrounding the plucking of the Rose. The single longest deletion in the poem's conclusion is that of vv. 21317–667, which include the Lover's praise of his own genitals, the metaphors of pilgrimage, relic, and sanctuary, and the graphic account of the penetration to the Rose. The transition from v. 21316 to v. 21668 is handled like this:

21316	Je, qui l'en rench mercy .c. mile,
xxx	Con cilz qui pas n'iere courciez
xxx	Me sui lues mout bien escouriez,
xxx	Et passe avant pour la main tendre
21668	Au rainssel pour le bouton prendre.
	(MS *Mor*, fol. 133v)

[I, who gave a hundred thousand thanks, like one who is not at all unhappy, betook myself and stepped forward in order to reach out my hand and take the bud.]

Gui does allow the Lover to reach the Rose, to impregnate it, and to express his pleasure; he evidently held no objection to the consummation of the erotic quest, but only to an overly lascivious treatment of the climactic moments. His previous work on the poem had established the groundwork for a morally acceptable erotic relationship, one based on mutual love and trust and pursued within the bounds set by Reason and Nature. The removal of the more blatantly pornographic passages and pagan fables, along with the inappropriate theological references, made the *Rose* acceptable for circulation within Gui's clerical community. MS *Tou*, perhaps because it was destined for lay patronage, is governed by less strict standards.[10]

In many respects, however, MSS *Tou* and *Mor* agree in their presentation of Gui's work, containing much text in common. In spite of the different versions of Reason, for example, both manuscripts identify her with Scriptural authority. In an interpolation on friendship, Reason cites not only Cicero, Seneca, and Aristotle, but also Sirach, adding the wisdom of the Old Testament to that of the philosophers; in an interpolation on justice, she cites Gregory the Great and the Book of Wisdom; her discussion of Fortune is amplified by the story of the imprisonment and subsequent release of the Old Testament Joseph. The doubling of pagan and Biblical authority is especially striking in the discussion of injustice, where the tragic story of Virginia, victim of a corrupt judgment, is followed by the miraculous tale of Susannah, saved from false judgment by divine intervention (Daniel 13). Virginia and Susannah are similar characters: both are faced with a choice between sexual violation and death, and both—like that other pagan woman, Lucretia, whose story is subsequently told by the Jaloux—prefer death. For the two pagan women, death is the only possible solution, the only means by which they can dramatize their plight in the eyes of the populace, thus achieving posthumous redress through the imprisonment and suicide of Appius and the exile of Tarquin respectively. The Biblical heroine, however, has a higher authority to whom she can appeal her case and through whom she can be vindicated without having to die. The importance of divine authority is reiterated as Gui's interpolation continues, citing the example of the pagan King Avenir, a ruthless persecutor of Christians, and the ex-courtier, now a Christian convert, who upbraids him.[11] It is the convert's Christian faith that gives him the courage and moral authority to confront the evil king and the power to deliver his sermon without losing his life in the process. And Joseph, of course, is saved from prison by his God-given ability to read dreams. By the addition of Christian exempla, Reason's authority is expanded, and her teachings acquire a greater degree of optimism: powerful though Fortune may be, she can always be overturned by the greater power of divine Providence.

The strengthening of Reason's moral authority is paralleled by the deletion not only of mythological references but also of bawdy or sexually provocative passages. In Jean de Meun, for example, Reason's discussion of Nero's assorted crimes includes both homosexuality and incest. The story of Nero is retained by Gui, but the allusions to his sexual escapades are gone; instead, Gui states simply that "Moult fist d'autres maus grant plenté / Plains de malvaise volenté" [he committed many other evil deeds, full of ill will (MS *Tou*, fol. 63r)]. Similarly, Reason's allusion to Genius's excommunication of the sodomites (vv. 4313–14) is deleted. In MS *Tou*—which may, in this case, reflect Gui's original plan—the process of bowdlerization is extended to the debate regarding the word 'coilles'. The story of the castration of Saturn is deleted entirely; since the offending word is thus absent, there can be no accusations of bawdiness and hence no debate about language. The removal of the debate about language posed a bit of a problem, since it does contain a certain amount of orthodox material about the nature of language and the importance of discretion. Gui solved this dilemma by inserting portions of the deleted text into the discourse of the God of Love in Guillaume de Lorris: in an expansion on Love's "clean speech" commandment following v. 2102, we find vv. 7005–12 and 7023–30. In the area of language, at least, Gui wanted no conflict between Love and Reason. The patron deity of love poetry, served by Guillaume de Lorris, Jean de Meun, and Gui de Mori alike, could not be perceived as instilling irrational linguistic values. Similarly, Reason, whose wisdom is clearly needed if poetry is to retain its edifying function, cannot be allowed to violate the principles of poetic decorum; and as Jean Gerson was later to point out, something is very wrong when Cupid appears more reasonable than Reason herself.[12]

Gui wanted the character of Reason to be morally unambiguous, just as he wanted the didactic structure of the poem to be clear: as he states in his prologue, his goal was to render the *Rose* "plus entendables / Et a oïr plus delitables" [easier to understand and more pleasant to listen to (fol. 5v)]. Reason argues for friendship over erotic desire; in Gui de Mori's *Rose*, Ami in turn suggests the possibility of integrating friendship and erotic love. Ami is, after all, in some sense the personification of friendship, and it is no accident that after hearing Reason discourse about *amitié*, the Lover should comment, "Adonc d'Ami me resovint" [then I remembered Friend (v. 7201)]. Jean de Meun's Ami devotes a hundred lines to the description of true friendship (vv. 8025–8124). Gui's Ami expands the discussion of friendship and love, reminding the Lover that the God of Love himself had recommended confiding in a friend; indeed Gui inserts into Ami's speech vv. 2672–74 and 2677–80 from the God of Love's commandments (MS *Tou*, fol. 82v). Gui's Ami points out that in love, five people are united in a network of mutual trust: the two lovers, each lover's friend and confidant, and the go-between to whom messages are entrusted, and who necessarily knows the lovers' secrets unless they are literate enough to manage a written correspondence. Erotic love, in other words, need not be seen as being in opposition to the form of love recommended by Reason.

Gui's Ami does warn about the existence of women who deceive men for the sake of material gain, claiming to love when they do not. He tells the Lover to beware, for the power of love is such that even wise men have been known to fall in love with these temptresses. Ami cites Reason on this point, quoting lines (a version of vv. 4306–10) that Gui had deleted from the discourse of Reason itself. But while such women do pose a threat, this does not mean that love itself must be avoided; one simply has to find a woman "plaine de francise . . . vaillans et courtoise" [full of frankness . . . valiant and courteous (MS *Tou*, fol. 79v)]. Such a relationship, marked by mutual generosity, will not necessarily include full sexual consummation:

> Et par amors vous habandonne
> Et son avoir et sa personne;
> Ou sans se personne, l'avoir
> Poés a vo voloir avoir;
> Qu'elle crient, espoir, l'avant garde
> Qui les roses desfent et garde.
> . . . . . .
> Mais congiét avés dou closier
> D'aler auques priés dou rosier.
>
> (Ibid.)

[And out of love she abandons to you her belongings and her person; or without her person, you still have access to her belongings; for perhaps she fears the guard that defends and watches over the roses . . . But you have permission to go into the enclosure and closely approach the rosebush.]

Gui's Ami then proceeds to explain that the complexities of the feminine character are such that no general rules can be given for courting women: "Lor acointance est arbitraire" [their acquaintance is arbitrary (MS *Tou*, fol. 80r)]. In an obvious allusion to Andreas Capellanus's *De amore*, he states that he will not attempt to describe the manner of address appropriate for men of each social class to use with women of the various classes; one must simply learn to judge the particular situation at hand.

Gui does devote considerable space to the issues of jealousy and marital harmony. Gui's Ami distinguishes between "jalousie" and "langheur," explaining that while a certain languorous yearning is appropriate to love, jealousy is not.[13] Once again he cites Reason, drawing on her celebrated litany of the paradoxes of love (vv. 4263–4300) in order to establish the distinction between these two states of mind. There Reason refers to amorous languor: "C'est langueur toute santeïve, / c'est santé toute maladive" [it is a healthy languor, it is a sickly health (vv. 4275–76)]. Ami reinterprets this statement, explaining that "langheur" is a form of lovesickness from which one can quickly recover:

Et pour cou Raisons la soutive
Dist que c'est santés maladive,
Car il n'est nus si langereus,
Quant li jours vient bons eüreus,
Que il poet la joie saisir,
Dont il a eü tel desir.
                    (MS *Tou*, fol. 84v)

[And therefore subtle Reason said that it is a sickly health, for there is no one so languorous, that he cannot achieve joy when the happy day arrives that he has so desired.]

Whereas the languorous lover is sustained by hope, jealousy is a form of despair:

Mais jalousie la sauvage,
Qui ne poet de son cuer la rage
Oster, est par Raison clamee
Esperance desesperee.
                    (Ibid.)

[But savage jealousy, which cannot remove the rage from its heart, is what Reason calls despairing hope.]

Jealousy causes love to turn to hatred, producing those violent emotions so contrary to Reason: "Pour ce ensi Raisons le define / Que c'est amoureuse haïne" [Therefore Reason defines it as amorous hatred (ibid.)].

Gui de Mori's Ami emerges as a figure strangely in agreement with Reason in his assessment of love. True, he does advise the Lover to use force and deception in outwitting the guardians of the Rose; and in an interpolation, he even recommends enlisting the help of a valiant man known as Faux Samblant (MS *Tou*, fol. 70v). Gui does, however, delete Ami's justification of adultery (vv. 7375–84). And as Ami's account progresses, and he distinguishes the different possible kinds of love affairs, the ideal that emerges is one based on friendship, generosity, and trust; the dark passions condemned by Reason are associated with jealousy and greed, neither of which, in Ami's opinion, can coexist with real love. Just as, on the issue of linguistic decorum, Gui smoothed out the differences between Reason and Love, so he seems here to be aiming at a reconciliation of sorts between Reason and Ami, Love's advocate.

Gui also modifies Jean's negative portrayal of marriage. The long discourse on jealousy makes it amply clear that the Jaloux, when he finally takes the stage, is being held up as a wholly negative example: it is neither marriage nor the feminine character, but rather male jealousy that is the object of satire. Not that women are always blameless. In a move characteristic of his ongoing effort to impose a linear thematic order on Jean's poem, Gui transplants Genius's account of the wife who demands to know her husband's secrets (most of vv. 16317–666) into the discourse of Ami. This scenario directly follows that of the Jaloux and is introduced in MS *Tou* by the rubric, "C'on ne se fie trop en feme" [that one should not trust a woman too much (fol. 91r)]: the evils of too little trust and of male domination are paired with an illustration of the dangers involved in trusting one's wife too much and hence of female domination. But here too, Gui makes sure that the episode is seen as warning not against love or marriage, but only against indiscretion and imbalance. Gui's Ami explains that women should assume household responsibilities and should have freedom to come and go and to converse with their neighbors, as long as the husband remains the head of the household. Friendship and love, not tyrannical domination, are the substance of the marriage bond; Ami advises husbands "que vos femes amés, / Et vos amies les clamés" [that you love your wives, and consider them your friends (ibid.)]. In this way, married couples can achieve "Loiauté, pais, et concordance" [loyalty, peace, and harmony (ibid.)].

Gui's treatment of marriage anticipates criticisms that would be leveled against Jean de Meun during the famous *querelle*. Both Christine de Pizan and Jean Gerson attacked Jean's negative portrayal of marriage; Christine insinuated, in her epistle "Reverence, honneur avec recommendacion," that a man deceived by a woman has only himself to blame: "Et se tu dis que tu en es assotéz, si ne t'en assote mie" [and if you say that you're bedazzled by her, well then, don't get bedazzled (ed. Hicks, 18)]. Christine also found it particularly incongruous that the priest of Nature, who presides over procreation and urges sexual activity, should be the one who warns men to flee women. Gui clearly was troubled by similar concerns. His revisions result in a single, unified treatment of marriage, appropriately located entirely within Ami's discourse about relations between the sexes. Gui thereby erases an important link that Jean de Meun had established between Ami and Genius; the latter is accordingly freed of his antifeminist and antimarital associations, so that it becomes easier to interpret his sermon, with its strong statements in favor of procreation, as referring to conjugal sex.[14] Marriage itself is portrayed more favorably overall: martial discord is indeed a danger, but it can be avoided if both parties are reasonable and adhere to the rules of friendship.

Finally, Gui's revisions of Ami reflect the same bowdlerizing spirit manifest throughout his work. He deleted certain pagan references, such as the elaboration of Zephyrus and Flora (vv. 8383−92) and Juvenal's comment that if a man can find a chaste woman, he should make a sacrifice to Juno (vv. 8677−84). And according to the marginal signs of MS *Tou*, Gui originally deleted the story of Abelard and Heloise, which may have offended him on several counts: it is the story of a fallen cleric, it involves castration, and it cites various authoritative arguments against marriage. Again, Gui seems almost to anticipate the criticisms that his fellow churchman Gerson will make over a century later.[15] Gui's approach to the *Rose*, while more worldly than that of Gerson, is marked by a certain unmistakable clericalism.

In addition to the foregoing substantive changes, Gui also introduced structural changes into the *Rose*. His reorganization of the first part of Reason's discourse, for example, clarifies the logical progression of her teachings. Gui placed the discussions of natural love for one's offspring (vv. 5734−64), erotic desire (itself somewhat rearranged: vv. 4347−98, 4517−58, 4567−98, 4399−4514), and avarice (most of vv. 4739−5334, also somewhat rearranged) together in one section, creating a hierarchy of depravity: natural love is neither good nor bad, erotic desire is bad, and avarice is the worst. This section includes interpolations on the follies of youth and the evils of wealth. Following the Lover's initial accusation that Reason must be counseling him to hate, Gui placed all of the arguments concerning friendship, adding lengthy passages on the qualities to look for in choosing a friend and the differences between true and false friends. He also inserted an explicit statement clarifying that the young hero's desire for the Rose, focused entirely on pleasure, is not the right kind of love. The discourse of Ami, in turn, is even more drastically rearranged: here Gui replaced Jean's digressive ring structure with a linear order, moving all of the discussions of the Golden Age—used by Jean de Meun to frame the discourse of the Jaloux—into one place and relocating some of Ami's advice, placed by Jean at the end of his discourse, into the first half of his speech, along with the other recommendations for managing a love affair.[16] A similar imposition of linear progression is apparent in Gui's treatment of the poem's other major discourses.[17] At his hands, Jean's brilliantly kaleidoscopic poem becomes much more like a treatise, a sequentially ordered treatment of the many facets of love.

I turn now to the *B* version of the *Rose* that, like Gui's remaniement, exists in multiple recensions exhibiting greater and lesser degress of variance from the standard text and often showing signs of having been combined with material from other manuscript families. Since the anonymous *B* redactor chose to work almost exclusively on Jean de Meun, my examination of this rewritten *Rose* will focus once again on that portion of the poem.

The *B* remaniement, like that of Gui, includes both deletions and interpolations; and the *B* manuscripts vary considerably in the extent to which the deleted material has been restored, in the extent to which interpolations are present, and even in the ways in which material proper to the *B* text has been blended with material from the standard text. Because of the mutability of the vernacular text and the unceasing editorial activities of medieval scribes, illustrated so vividly in the annotation and multiple versions of Gui de Mori's remaniement, it is impossible to reconstruct exactly what the original *B* text or texts may have been: here we lack the "master" edition, with the careful notation of additions, subtractions, restorations, and mutations, that we are so lucky to have in the case of Gui de Mori. Nonetheless, from the judicious comparison of manuscripts we can derive a good understanding of the nature of the *B* remaniement and the ways in which it evolved in the manuscript tradition. The two best sources for the original *B* text are the early fourteenth-century MS Bibl. Nat. fr. 25524 (*Bi*) and the late thirteenth-century MS Turin, Bibl. Univ. L.III.22 (*Be*). Some of the changes effected in *B* resemble those made by Gui. We find evidence for discomfort with Reason's use of the word 'coilles' and, in different *B* recensions, various ways of adapting or suppressing entirely her defense of plain speech. The discourse of Faux Samblant has been reworked and, as in MSS *Tou* and *Mor*, it now contains explicit allusions to Saint Augustine's treatise on monastic life; but compared to the hundreds of lines added to Faux Samblant by Gui, the *B* interpolations, totaling a few dozen lines, are quite modest. Deletion of troublesome or digressive material in the discourses of Nature and Genius can also be associated with the *B* text, since these portions of the poem are omitted entirely in MS *Bi*. On the other hand, whereas Gui tended to delete mythological material, the *B* text not only retains such passages but also inserts new ones. Overall, then, the *B* text represents a related, but not identical, approach to the *Rose*, a somewhat different set of priorities regarding the text and the identification of shocking, difficult, or irrelevant passages.

Of all the *B* manuscripts, the one that departs most from Jean de Meun's text is MS *Bi*. This manuscript appears to be itself an abridged version of the *B* remaniement, for it lacks certain interpolations present in all other *B* manuscripts. Jean de Meun's continuation here has been re-duced to some three thousand lines, or approximately one sixth its usual length. In fact, due to the extreme abridgment of Jean's portion, the mid-point of MS *Bi* is Guillaume's description of the kiss. There results a bipartite narrative structure: the first half moves through the Lover's en-counters with a series of allegorical figures, building to a climax with the intervention of Venus and the kiss; the second half finds him once more on the outside of an enclosed space, moves through a second series of encounters, and reaches the final climax with the second intervention of Venus and the plucking of the Rose.

In effect, Jean de Meun's continuation has become exactly that: a con-tinuation and resolution of the narrative begun by Guillaume de Lorris. Most of the material that has no precedent in Guillaume's delicate poem—the Jaloux, la Vieille, Nature and Genius—is omitted entirely, leaving no trace. In the mind of this medieval editor, evidently, such material had no place in a poem devoted to a young man's initiation into the art of love. The major exception to this pattern is that most of the discourse of Faux Samblant is left intact in its *B* version; a rather odd exception, considering that virtually any other portion of Jean's poem has more bearing on love, seduction, or the quest for the Rose than do the words of Faux Samblant. It must be noted, however, that Faux Samblant could not be removed entirely since he is instrumental to the plot: it is he who vanquishes Male Bouche and paves the way for the Lover's reunion with Bel Acueil. One can only assume that, given Faux Samblant's important role in the erotic quest, the redactor of MS *Bi* or its source found it appropriate to include the passage outlining his identity.

The discourses of Reason, Ami, Richesse, and the God of Love do remain, but all are significantly abridged. Reason's discourse, for example, is reduced from 3000 to a mere 300 lines. Reason becomes an authority on the nature of love and a rival for the Lover's affections; she offers her arguments against the follies of love and begs him to love her instead, which he refuses. The debate as to whether or not she is counseling the Lover to hate and the discussion of the types of love remain for the most part. Gone, however, are the philosophical passages relating to youth and old age, wealth, Fortune, and justice; the various classical exempla, such as Nero, Seneca, and Cressus; and, since the word 'coilles' has disappeared along with the reference to Saturn, there is no debate about language either. Instead of rejecting Reason for her uncourtly language, the Lover bases his rejection of her on the argument that "Il n'est hons a bourc ne a vile" [there isn't a man in city or town (MS *Bi*, fol. 70r)] that Reason does not want as her lover. If he accepted her as his *amie*, says the Lover, she would have more than a hundred thousand other lovers as well: "Trestout le monde averiés; / Trop vous abondoneroiés" [you would have the whole world; you would abandon yourself utterly (ibid.)]. The Lover complains that he does not approve of "communal" love. Although Reason taunts him for being "jalous" and insists that she would never cuckold him, the Lover remains unmoved, resting his case with the words, "Ne je ne vous en croirai pas: / Or avez gastés tous vos pas" [I will never believe you; you have wasted your efforts (MS *Bi*, fol. 70v)]. This version of Reason and the Lover is clearly much more focused on the nature of love than was Jean's original text. Love is opposed to hate; private erotic love is opposed to universal charity. Such issues as the ravages of Fortune, the behavior of judges and monarchs, the interpretation of dreams, and the nature of language simply are not relevant to this much more narrowly conceived confrontation of eros and reason.

The Lover's attack on Reason for her thousands of lovers is not unique to this manuscript; within the fourteenth century alone, it figures in several other *B* manuscripts and in nearly a dozen manuscripts of other families. It typically appears as an interpolation in the Lover's rejection of Reason, immediately preceding his accusations of bawdy language. It is most likely that the passage began as a replacement for the language debate—such is its role in MS *Bi*—and was retained in later manuscripts when the deleted material was restored, and added as an interpolation to still others. The *B* remanieur has simply come up with an equally humorous and less problematic climax to the conflict of love and reason.

The debate about communality and privacy illustrates the same clash of perspectives as that about plain speech and euphemism: in both cases, the Lover sees Reason as a bawd, while she sees him as small-minded, uncomprehending, and obsessed with sex. In the discourse of erotic love, it is love itself, and sexual functions, that must be "glossed," that is, veiled in linguistic euphemism, metaphors, and allegorical images.[18] This thematic is developed at considerable length by Jean de Meun. As the Lover comes to learn, and as is vividly illustrated by the intervention of Faux Samblant, the discourse of love must never acknowledge the real object of desire; Reason's assertion that a primary purpose of language is "por fere noz volairs entendre" [to make our wishes known (v. 7071)] is directly contradicted by the Lover's other advisers. In the Lover's eyes, Reason's casual use of explicitly sexual language rends the carefully constructed mask of amorous discourse. From Reason's perspective, of course, the situation is reversed: the purpose of language (and of glossing) is not to disguise but to reveal meaning, and the reader or listener is intended not to be distracted or lulled by the words and surface images, but rather to look beyond these to the higher truths that they imply. The linguistic debate not only reveals the Lover's sexual anxieties, but also casts in high relief the problematics of erotic allegory and lays the groundwork for the poem's controversial conclusion, where the act of sexual intercourse is described in considerable detail without ever using the words 'coilles' or 'viz'.

Such poetic gamesmanship was evidently too much for the redactor of MS *Bi*. As I have said, the discourse of Genius, with its disturbing demonstration of the power of allegorical language to conflate the sacred and the erotic, is deleted entirely; the conclusion of the poem is greatly reduced and, while traces remain of the imagery of sanctuary, the overall erotic tenor of the concluding lines is considerably attenuated. Following Bel Acueil's agreement to grant the Lover the Rose, the poem ends like this:

21316	Je, qui l'en rent merci .c. mile,	
21561	A genous vois sans demourer,	
21562	Ausinc comme pour aourer	
21563	Le bel saintuare honorable.	
xxx	Puis m'en entrai sans nule fable,	
xxx	Pour baisier la bele chassete	
xxx	Dedans l'archiere petite[te].	
21565	Mais toute iert ja tombé par terre:	[MS: guerre]
21566	Au feu ne puis riens tenir guerre.	
21611	Entre les piliers me mis,	
21612	Mais je n'i entrai pas demis.	
21613	Moi pesoit que plus n'i entroie,	
21614	Mais outre pooïr ne poaie.	
21745	Ains que d'ilec me remuasse,	
xxx	En brisant la tres bele chasse,	
21747	Par grant joliveté coilli	
21748	La flour dou bel rosier foilli.	
21749	Ainsinc oï la rose vermeille.	
21750	Atant fu jours et je m'esveille.	

(MS *Bi*, fol. 108r)

[And I, who gave a hundred thousand thanks, went down on my
knees as if to worship the beautiful honorable sanctuary. Then I went
in, it is no lie, to kiss the beautiful casket inside the little archway. But
everything was in ruins from the war: nothing can stand up to fire. I
placed myself between the pillars, but I didn't even get halfway in. I
was sorry not to go in farther, but I couldn't do any better. Before
moving from there, breaking the beautiful case, in great joy I plucked
the blossom of the leafy rosebush. Thus I had the red rose. Then it
was daybreak, and I awoke.]

While in this version it is still clear what the Lover is doing, and the sexual
act is still expressed in terms of religious worship, many details have been
omitted: the imagery of pouch and staff, and the Lover's delight in having
been endowed with such marvelous equipment; the repeated assaults on
the entryway and the insistence on its narrowness; the Lover's comments
that he was the first to pass that way, his observation that the young lady
in question had not yet begun to charge an entrance fee, and his casual
speculation as to whether or not other men had been there since; and the
spilling of the seed and the allusion to the Rose's ensuing pregnancy. The
redactor made the best of a difficult situation, allowing the Lover to possess the Rose—Guillaume de Lorris himself, after all, had already strongly
hinted that such was to be the outcome of the quest—while preserving
decorum as much as possible.[19]

The debate about plain speech and the final plucking of the Rose
stand in an interesting sort of opposition: in one passage, explicitly sexual
terminology is used in a fable about justice and in a discourse about language and interpretation; in the other, a series of metaphors are used to
describe sexual activity. An ongoing exploration and exposition of the relationship between language and eros, and of the power of words to hide
or to reveal, to arouse or to subdue, runs throughout Jean's *Rose*. It is
hardly surprising that a medieval reader disconcerted by Reason's plain
speech would object to the poem's conclusion as well. Such was certainly
the case with Gui de Mori, Christine de Pizan, and Jean Gerson. MS *Bi*
thus fits into a recognizable pattern in medieval *Rose* reception.

Just as the remanieur chose to modify the erotic allegory, keeping
eros to a minimum, so he sought to redefine the terms of the debate between Reason and the Lover. The question of private ownership is briefly
raised by Jean's Reason when she tells the Lover that his only real belongings are spiritual in nature, since all else is transitory. The phenomenon of
private property is evoked by Ami as one of the consequences of the fall

of the Golden Age (vv. 9607–34). These passages are deleted from MS *Bi*, but they may nonetheless have provided the inspiration for the Lover's rejection of Reason; one can assume that the remanieur was working from a complete text of the *Rose*. Just as erotic love in a fallen world entails a discourse of mystification and masked desire, so it also problematizes the ideal of communality; and the Lover's courtly ethos commits him to a view of love as strictly private and nontransferable, focused upon a single object at the exclusion of all others. He desires to possess the Rose, not to share it with all mankind. Reason's concept of "bone volenté commune" [communal good will (v. 4656)], of a community of philosophers joined by their common love of wisdom, is as foreign to the Lover as is her practice of plain speech about sexual matters for the purpose of conveying philosophical truths. Communality of love violates the Lover's most cherished principles; as he says, "J'en voil une avoir moie quite" [I want to have one (girl friend) all my own (MS *Bi*, fol. 70r)].

In short, the *Bi* redactor, while discreetly omitting objectionable words and sidestepping the problematics, so central for Jean de Meun, of an erotic poetic language, manages to preserve what for him must have been the essence of the confrontation between Reason and the Lover: the Lover is unable to grasp rational love, or to recognize it as a viable alternative to his current state. He sees it first as the absence of love, hence as hate; and then, in a comic reversal, as an alarming proliferation of love, a promiscuity that knows no bounds. Erotic love, as prescribed by the God of Love in the fateful encounter beside the fountain, remains for him the defining context for all discourse and the moral standard against which all loves are measured.

The discourse of Ami in MS *Bi* is similarly abridged to include only those parts that are directly relevant to the Lover's education, which in this case revolves around the art of seduction; the entire second half of Ami' discourse (vv. 8207–9972) is deleted. Not only is the Jaloux gone—after all, he is not meant as a model for the Lover to imitate—but also the discussions of the Golden Age and of the origins of private property, government, and law. The page that contained whatever there was of the text between vv. 7880 and 8189 is now missing; but since a page of this manuscript holds only sixty lines (a single thirty-line column on each side), it is clear that most of the intervening material, the discourse on poverty and true friendship, must have been deleted as well. This, of course, is in keeping with the treatment of the discourse of Reason, from which philosophical digressions are absent.

The suppression of the second half of Ami's discourse results in the removal of much of the poem's antifeminist diatribe. It would seem that the *Bi* redactor found this material unsuited to a poem ostensibly about love, dedicated to a lady, and containing the commandment to honor and serve women:

> Toutes fames ser et honore,
> en aus servir poine et labeure;
> et se tu oz nul mesdisanz
> que aille fame despisant,
> blasme le et di qu'il se taise.
>
> (vv. 2103–07)

[Serve and honor all women, strive and labor to serve them; and if you hear any slanderer who goes around defaming women, confront him and tell him to be quiet.]

The remanieur seems to have taken this piece of advice to heart, using his scribal powers to silence the detractors of women within the *Rose* itself. In MS *Bi*, the Jaloux is excised; so, at a later point in the poem, is Genius's warning about disclosing secrets to one's wife (omitted in the deletion of vv. 15774–20680), as well as the entire discourse of la Vieille (omitted in the deletion of vv. 12511–14722); and so even are Ami's antifeminist comments. Included in the omitted second half of his discourse are such topics as the insatiable greed of most women (vv. 8252–72, 8317–22) and the inability of women to accept advice or chastisement, however sound (vv. 9933–56). Some antifeminist material is deleted from the first half of Ami's discourse as well, not only in MS *Bi* but also, though to a lesser degree, in other *B* manuscripts. Gone are vv. 7579–7688, in which Ami complains that women, while naturally eager to give themselves over to prospective lovers, have come to expect gifts in exchange for such favors; warns against the likelihood of losing one's beloved to other suitors; and urges the use of force, explaining that women often prefer it that way. Thus, while Ami does still counsel the Lover to placate the Rose's guardians through the use of gifts and feigned innocence—in effect, to win his lady by masking the sexual nature of his intentions and softening her heart with little love-tokens—he at least does so with a minimum of antifeminist commentary. And he concentrates on allaying fears, wearing down resistance, and capturing the allegiance of Bel Acueil, without suggesting that the Lover seek to create a good opportunity for rape. In effect, Jean de

Meun's Ami has been recast in the image of Guillaume's Ami, and his advice brought into line with the commandments of the God of Love, much as Reason's discourse was brought back into the parameters of her advice in Guillaume de Lorris, and her words censored to conform to the God of Love's preference for courtly discourse.[20]

The discourse of Richesse is retained, but shortened, principally through the deletion of vv. 10059–80 and 10110–200; her stark warnings about poverty and hunger were perhaps seen as an unpleasant touch, and certainly irrelevant to the elaboration of an art of love. We recall that the discussions of poverty were omitted from Reason and Ami as well; the remanieur apparently took to heart Guillaume de Lorris's exclusion of poverty from the courtly garden, the space of the erotic quest. And interestingly, the reference to Richesse's refusal to help the Lover is omitted from the God of Love's encounter with his barons through the deletion of vv. 10659–88. The God of Love's discourse about wealth and poverty in the context of love service is similarly removed, through the deletion of vv. 10753–86, 10791–856, and 10859–88. Clearly, the *B* remanieur did not appreciate the emphasis on the enmity between Wealth and Love. Significantly, this enmity is an invention of Jean de Meun; Guillaume de Lorris had placed Richesse among the participants in the carol, identifying her as a follower of the God of Love. Again remaining as true as possible to Guillaume, the *B* remanieur downplayed the negative role that Jean devised for Richesse, showing only that the Lover is not going to buy his way to the Rose—a rather uncourtly way of winning one's beloved in any case.

As I have said, the one major anomaly in MS *Bi* is the presence, virtually intact, of the discourse of Faux Samblant. Certain digressive passages are deleted. For example vv. 11567–610 (the exposition of Matthew 23) interrupts Faux Samblant's explanation of his practice of acquiring power by spreading about the secrets he learns during Confession; these lines are replaced by a four-line passage elaborating on the disclosures. Other major omissions are vv. 11687–756 (a digression within the discussion of the Antichrist, in which Faux Samblant reiterates his power); 11819–65 (the conflict between Jehan and Pierre); and 11873–96 (Faux Samblant does not worry about God's judgment). Interestingly, most of the allusions to Guillaume de Saint-Amour and to the disputes between the mendicants and the University of Paris are also deleted (vv. 11269–72, 11395–466, 11761–64). Instead, the authority cited against mendicancy is Saint Augustine's "livre de l'uevre des moines" [*De opere monachorum* (fol. 80r)]. The discourse has thus been somewhat streamlined. And while the polemic against mendicancy and ecclesiastical corruption remains, it is no longer cast in terms of the particular events taking place in Paris in the 1250s; the passage is generalized and dehistoricized. This move may have been intended to render the passage less controversial; or perhaps only to adapt the argument to the concerns of an audience unfamiliar with Guillaume de Saint-Amour. In the main, however, Faux Samblant's argument stands as the only significant digression from the story of the erotic quest.

Two other seeming digressions that remain are the stories of Adonis and Pygmalion. At first glance this too might seem inconsistent with the otherwise evident desire to "stick to the story"; however, we must see this as evidence that these two mythological exempla were perceived, at least by our redactor, as making an important contribution to the romance. First of all, there is a clear precedent in Guillaume de Lorris for the use of mythological figures with the strategic retelling of the story of Narcissus. As others have pointed out before me, the stories of Adonis and Pygmalion constitute an important response to that of Narcissus.[21] These three exempla form a mythographic program within the conjoined *Rose* that reflects the dilemma of unrealizable love set up by Guillaume de Lorris and the resolution offered by Jean de Meun. Within MS *Bi*, so much shorter than the original poem, the three tales are in much closer proximity, and the mythological material takes up a greater proportion of the whole; it is thus of even more prominent importance.

By deleting much of the material in Jean de Meun that had no precedent in Guillaume de Lorris, the *B* remanieur created a more unified, less digressive poem. While MS *Bi* is an extreme example, it reflects the overall tone of the original *B* text.[22] The *B* remaniement is more like a romance than the *Rose* that we know: the narrative frame is less obscured and the courtly spirit of Guillaume's poem is preserved for the most part. Interestingly, the *B* remanieur also deleted that portion of the God of Love's discourse devoted to the identities of the poem's authors and the fact of Jean de Meun's continuation. If one had only the *B* text to go on, the *Rose* would appear to be the work of a single anonymous poet. MSS *Bi* and *Be*, along with MS Bibl. Nat. fr. 12587, which almost certainly lacked the authorship passage in its original state,[23] are among the few *Rose* manuscripts that have no rubric or other indication of the change of authorship between Guillaume and Jean. The poem is seamless: an allegorical account of falling in love and eventually winning the lady's consent, cast as a dream, including an exposition of love, friendship, and seduction, and narrated by the young man who had the dream.

It is not that the *B* remanieur had no interest at all in the figure of the poet or in poetic tradition. All such allusions are deleted from MS *Bi*; but MS *Be*, while deleting the references to Guillaume and Jean, does retain the God of Love's allusion to Tibullus (ed. Lecoy, vv. 10478–91) and even inserts a brief allusion to Adonis at this point: Venus's grief for Tibullus exceeds even that which she felt for Adonis. This interpolation appears in most *B* manuscripts. The reference to Adonis comes from Ovid's *Amores* 3, 9, the elegy on the death of Tibullus, in which the same comparison with Adonis exists (v. 16). The *B* remanieur thus recognized the Ovidian source for the passage and chose to strengthen its presence in the *Rose*, adding lines that both anticipate the subsequent story of Adonis in the *Rose* itself and stress the importance of the poet as a beloved disciple of Cupid and Venus. At a slightly later point in the God of Love's discourse, in an interpolation following v. 10800, the *B* remanieur inserted the story of the contest between Apollo and Marsyas; again, while this passage is missing from MS *Bi*, it does appear in the other *B* manuscripts.[24] The God of Love identifies himself with Apollo, condemning Marsyas and comparing him to Juno, enemy of Venus. Thus two models for the poet do appear in the standard *B* text: Tibullus, faithful servant of Love, and Apollo, the musician god. The specific identities of the *Rose* poets are effaced, as is the fact that there were two of them. But the poetic discourse fostered by the God of Love and exemplified in the *Rose* is nonetheless presented as heir to the classical tradition, and associated with the high-style, inspired verse of Apollo.

Gui de Mori and the *B* remanieur are parallel examples of late thirteenth-century readers and rewriters of the *Rose*. Yet their reception by modern critics has not been parallel, most likely due, at least in part, to the different degrees of authorial presence manifested by each. Gui de Mori's presence in his version of the *Rose* is quite strong. Not only did he compose the long prologue preserved in MS *Tou*, outlining his desire to rewrite the *Rose* and explaining his system of marginal annotations, Gui even inserted himself into the God of Love's famous discourse at the midpoint of the *Rose*: after foretelling Guillaume de Lorris's death and Jean de Meun's subsequent birth and continuation of the poem, the God of Love goes on to explain that at a still later time, a third person will come along who, although less talented than Guillaume or Jean, will also serve Love and love the *Rose*, and will contribute to the ongoing writing of the poem.

It is probably because of his strong presence in the text that Gui de Mori has been accepted as something akin to an author by modern critics. Ernest Langlois, whose overriding concern was with establishing the text of the *Rose*, deplored Gui's intrusions, which bothered him all the more because Gui was working from an early and probably very good copy of the poem. Nonetheless Langlois considered it worthwhile to publish an article in the *Bibliothèque de l'École des Chartes* containing extracts from Gui's work, a description of some of the changes he made, and a list of manuscripts containing some of his interpolations.[25] In more recent years, Marc-René Jung and David Hult have published work on Gui de Mori, Jung concentrating on Gui's reworking of Guillaume de Lorris and, in particular, his attitudes toward love, and Hult addressing the question of whether or not Gui is to be considered an author.[26] Gui's reworking of the poem is so extensive and his presence so powerful that one is strongly encouraged to conclude that the remanieur is something very close to an author, and that, in the Middle Ages, the rewriting of previously existing text takes its place, along with other forms of adaptation, translation, continuation and *conjointure*, as a type of literary creation.

In contrast, the *B* remaniement does not come equipped with a self-proclaimed "author," and the tradition of *Rose* studies has treated it as a manuscript family endowed with significant variants rather than as a new text. Langlois does not give Gui de Mori's alterations among his variant readings, nor does he describe them in his book-length study of the *Rose* manuscript tradition. These are not part of the *Rose* textual tradition; they are the work of an independent writer, addressed in a separate article. On the other hand, his study of *Rose* manuscripts does include a detailed account of the *B* family (*Manuscrits*, 359–405), and he gives many *B* variants in his edition of the *Rose*. But there have been no articles devoted to the analysis of the *B* interpolations and deletions, to the remanieur's ideas about love and poetry, or to his status as an authorial figure. Gui's self-conscious and explicit stance as remanieur at once denies him a central place in *Rose* textual history while granting him a certain status as a medieval writer; the anonymity, the self-effacement of the *B* remanieur has the opposite effect, enshrining his work as the basis of an important *Rose* manuscript family while at the same time reducing his status from literary creator to that of producer of variants and "common errors."

The work of Gui and the *B* remanieur respectively represents two degrees of poetic appropriation and alteration of the *Rose*: a radical transformation effected by a poet who saw himself as its third (if least distinguished) author, and a less far-reaching, though still quite significant, reworking by an anonymous remanieur. Both Gui de Mori and the *B* remanieur encountered the *Rose* at a time when Guillaume's poem still circulated independently of Jean's continuation and determined people's understanding of what the *Rose* was.[27] Like the *B* remanieur, Gui suppressed passages that violated the spirit of the *Rose* as he understood it, such as all those involving the word 'coilles', and sought to reduce the digressiveness of the poem; he felt a certain need to justify Jean's continuation. But while our two remanieurs may have shared a common distaste for overly plain speech and the theme of castration and a desire to temper antifeminist passages and to reduce digressiveness, their interest in the *Rose* was ultimately quite different. Paradoxically, it is Gui, the almost-author, whose version of the *Rose* retains the most information about the poem's "real" authors and about its textual history; whereas the *B* remanieur, remembered only as an agent of mouvance, suppresses information about the poem's authorship and textual history by deleting vv. 10491–644. Gui's system of marginal annotations enables the reader or future copyist to distinguish at a glance between "original" text and remaniement and to reconstruct the original, in part or in whole, if he or she so desires. Thus Gui's work, in spite of his role in the God of Love's discourse as the third *Rose* poet, is not fully integrated into the *Rose* text: it remains self-consciously, explicitly, a version, bearing within itself the instructions whereby the changes wrought can be undone and the original restored. And Gui takes care to proclaim the preeminence of the two original *Rose* poets and to clarify their relationship, not only by retaining the God of Love's explanatory discourse, but also through his own assertion that Jean suppressed Guillaume's original ending in order to extend the erotic quest. Thus Jean de Meun himself becomes, for Gui, something of a remanieur: like Gui, he deleted certain lines and added (a great many) others. The distinction between author and remanieur is indeed interestingly blurred in Gui's understanding of literary history. And just as Gui indicated all of the changes he made in the text, so he also left what he considered to be Guillaume's original ending, allowing the reader to choose between the different versions of the poem. In his hands, the *Rose* becomes a complex palimpsest of versions and rewritings, the collaborative effort of three different poets working during the course of the thirteenth century.

The *B* remanieur, on the other hand, seems to have been most interested in preserving the integrity of Guillaume's *Rose*. He did not introduce changes into this portion of the text. Jean's continuation, however, was considerably rewritten and abridged, apparently with an eye to making it a more suitable continuation of Guillaume's courtly allegory. Gui altered Jean's continuation, but did not seek to shorten it; he seems rather to have

liked the idea of extending the erotic quest, making it the vehicle for philosophical teachings and social commentary. He delighted in the play of
versions and poetic voices, emphasizing the identities of the poem's authors, now three in number, and the contribution each had made. The *B*
remanieur, on the other hand, was interested in preserving the *Rose*'s character as a dream narrative teaching of love, punctuated by exemplary
mythological figures who variously resisted or served love and art: Narcissus, Marsyas, Adonis, Pygmalion. He aimed for unity, not plurality, of
both theme and voice.

The *B* remaniement circulated more widely, both texts fared
somewhat similarly in the subsequent *Rose* manuscript tradition, giving
rise to multiple versions and producing interpolations that migrated into
other textual families. But it was Gui's attitude of admiration for the *Rose*
poets and his understanding of the poem as an expanding compendium
that was to dominate medieval *Rose* reception. The tendency in the *Rose*
manuscript tradition was toward the accumulation of text, in spite of the
occasional abridgment. The poem easily absorbed interpolations, while
deletions tended to be restored, often through the addition of text in the
margins, on flyleaves, or on extra pages added for that purpose. Such a
process is implied in Gui's marginal annotations, which identify interpolations for easy borrowing and mark deletions so that these can, if desired,
be restored from another manuscript. But the names of the remanieurs did
not accompany their added verses; it was Gui's interpolations about such
topics as *orgueil* or friendship that entered the manuscript tradition and
not those in which he names himself.

The names of the two original authors, on the other hand, did survive. The *Rose* was known throughout the Middle Ages as a poem by
Guillaume de Lorris and Jean de Meun, even when it contained material
that did not derive from either of these two poets. If it accumulated text,
it did not accumulate authors; but neither were the names of the two
primary authors effaced, the *B* remanieur's efforts notwithstanding. Jean
de Meun in particular acquired an authority, a place in the vernacular
canon, from which he could not be dislodged and which was not achieved
by later poets who worked on the *Rose*; the poem was soon unimaginable
without his continuation.[28] Moreover, the relative stability of the *Rose*
manuscript tradition from about the middle of the fourteenth century on
contrasts markedly with the proliferation of interpolations and reworkings
during the first few decades of the poem's circulation. Interpolations that

already existed were copied frequently, some showing up in as many as one fourth of the surviving manuscripts; but new ones were rarely produced. This, too, reflects the great authority of Jean's text: rather than feeling free to alter it as they wished, late medieval scribes were more likely to preserve the integrity of the text and even to compare manuscripts, seeking the most complete text possible.

Above all, the manuscripts preserving the work of Gui de Mori and the *B* remanieur illustrate the remarkable richness and diversity of medieval responses to the *Rose*. The versions that survive reflect a wide range of perspectives on such crucial issues as the conflict of Eros and Reason; the respective roles of Reason and Nature; and the place of erotic love in the cosmic order. The early history of the *Rose* is one of editorial redaction and textual criticism, of poetic imitation and creative adaptation, and of intertextual reworking, as again and again this great and elusive poem was reread and rethought.

Notes

1. I have examined the importance of one fairly widespread interpolation in my "The Medusa Interpolation in the *Romance of the Rose*: Mythographic Program and Ovidian Intertext," *Speculum* 62 (1987): 865–77. For background concerning the use of rubrics as a commentary on the *Rose*, see my "The Scribe as Editor: Rubrication as Critical Apparatus in Two Manuscripts of the *Roman de la Rose*," *L'Esprit Créateur* 27 (1987): 67–78; and "'Ci parle l'aucteur': Rubrication of Voice and Authorship in *Roman de la Rose* Manuscripts," *SubStance* 56 (1988): 42–48. On the *Rose* manuscript tradition, see Ernest Langlois, *Les Manuscrits du "Roman de la Rose": Description et classement* (Lille: Tallendier / Paris: Champion, 1910); I cite manuscripts according to his sigla. For a general study of the medieval reception of the *Rose*, see Pierre-Yves Badel, *Le "Roman de la Rose" au XIVe siècle: Étude de la réception de l'œuvre*, Publications Romanes et Françaises 153 (Geneva: Droz, 1980). Unless otherwise indicated, I cite the *Rose* in the edition by Félix Lecoy, *Le Roman de la Rose*, 3 vols. Classiques Français du Moyen Âge 92, 95, 98 (Paris: Champion, 1965–70). I will also refer at times to the edition by Ernest Langlois, *Le Roman de la Rose*, Société des Anciens Textes Français, 5 vols. (Paris: Firmin-Didot, 1914–24).

2. The anonymous continuation is published by Langlois as a variant reading under his v. 4058.

3. The major studies of Gui de Mori are those by Ernest Langlois, "Gui de Mori et le *Roman de la Rose*," *Bibliothèque de l'École des Chartes* 68 (1907): 249–71; Lucien Fourez, "Le *Roman de la Rose* de la Bibliothèque de la ville de Tournai," *Scriptorium* 1 (1946–47): 213–39, pl. 21–24; Marc-René Jung, "Gui de Mori et

Guillaume de Lorris," *Vox Romanica* 27 (1968): 106–37; David F. Hult, "Gui de Mori, lecteur médiéval," *Incidences* n.s. 5 (1981): 53–70. Hult's study essentially reappears in his book, *Self-Fulfilling Prophecies: Readership and Authority in the First "Roman de la Rose"* (Cambridge: Cambridge University Press, 1986), pp. 34–64. See also the study by Lori Walters, "Illuminating the *Rose*: Gui de Mori and the Illustrations of MS 101 of the Municipal Library, Tournai," in the present volume. Both Langlois and Jung publish important excerpts from Gui's work. Langlois gives Gui's Prologue (pp. 259–62) and the passage that he inserted at the midpoint, announcing himself as the third *Rose* poet (pp. 255–57). Jung, in addition to providing a detailed description of Gui's overall reworking of Guillaume de Lorris, publishes Gui's version of the Narcissus story (pp. 120–22), the interpolation on the degrees of love (pp. 127–33), and the interpolation in the discourse of Ami in Jean de Meun on the impossibility of giving general rules in love (pp. 124–26).

4. Hult gives the full text of Gui's statement about his work on the two parts of the *Rose*, based on the transcriptions by Méon and Langlois, in *Self-Fulfilling Prophecies*, pp. 36–39.

5. Hult, *Self-Fulfilling Prophecies*, p. 42. The phenomenon of certain sections of the poem being viewed as "detachable" is not limited to Gui de Mori. Dieuwke van der Poel has shown that marginal signs in an early fourteenth-century manuscript of a Middle Dutch translation of the *Rose* probably indicate passages marked for deletion; see her "Over gebruikersnotities in het *Rose*-handschrift K. A. XXIV," *De Nieuwe Taalgids* 79 (1986): 505–16.

6. On the presence of Gui de Mori in the *Rose* manuscript tradition, see Langlois, "Gui de Mori," pp. 270–71. Langlois lists five manuscripts, in addition to MSS *Tou* and *Ter*, that contain passages from Gui de Mori; he does not mention MSS *He* or *Ke*. An additional manuscript containing Gui's version of Guillaume de Lorris together with the standard version of Jean de Meun was sold in 1988 by the firm of Ader, Picard, Tajan; see the sale catalog, *Manuscrits et livres anciens* (Paris, Hôtel George V, 16 September 1988), no. 152. I am indebted to Heidrun Ost of the University of Kiel for information regarding this manuscript.

7. The excerpts from Gui transcribed on the last page of MS *Ke* were printed by Joseph Morawski, who did not recognize them as the work of Gui de Mori, as "Fragment d'un *Art d'aimer* perdu du XIIIe siècle," *Romania* 48 (1922): 431–36. See also my "Notice sur les fragments poétiques dans un manuscrit du *Roman de la Rose*," *Romania* 109 (1988): 119–21.

8. Although MS *Mor* dates from the fifteenth century, I am convinced that the unique passages that it contains do derive from Gui de Mori and are not late additions. The language of these passages is no different from that found throughout MS *Mor* and exhibits traits consistent with a late thirteenth-century date, such as careful observance of the subject case and pretonic vowels in hiatus before a tonic vowel (e.g., *meïsmes*). Since MS *Tou* is much earlier and more fully preserves Gui's dialect, however, I will cite from its text for passages appearing in both manuscripts.

9. All texts pertaining to the *querelle* are cited in the edition by Eric Hicks, *Le Débat sur le "Roman de la Rose,"* Bibliothèque du XVe siècle 43 (Paris: Champion, 1977), p. 85.

10. MS *Tou* was made for a member of the Pourrès family of Tournai, possibly on the occasion of a marriage. See Fourez, *"Roman de la Rose* de la Bibliothèque de la Ville de Tournai" (see n. 3).

11. The story of King Avenir appears in the legend of Barlaam and Josaphat, which circulated in various Latin and vernacular versions; see Jean Sonet, S. J., *Le Roman de Barlaam et Josaphat,* vol. 1: *Recherches sur la tradition manuscrite latine et française,* Bibliothèque de la Faculté de Philologie et Lettres de Namur 6 (Namur: B.F.P.L. / Paris: Vrin, 1949). Gui's treatment of the episode is fairly close to that in the version by Gui de Cambrai, edited by Hermann Zotenberg and Paul Meyer as *Barlaam und Josaphat,* Bibliothek des Literarischen Vereins 75 (Stuttgart: Literarisches Verein, 1864); the episode in question is pp. 7–10.

12. Gerson says, "Je me deuil trop pour dame Raison et pour Chasteté de ce que il a fait dire par Raison la sage a ung fol amoureux teles gouliardies; auquel par avant Cupido, qui se dit Dieux d'amours, avoit deffandus tous villains parlers et ors et tous blasmes de fames,—come se Cupido fust plus chaste et raisonnables que dame Raison et Chasteté" [I grieve for Lady Reason and for Chastity, insofar as he has had wise Reason say such obscenities to a foolish lover; whereas earlier Cupid, who calls himself the God of Love, had forbidden all evil and dirty speech and all attacks on women—as if Cupid was more chaste and more reasonable than Lady Reason and Chastity], in "Traictié d'une vision faite contre le *Roman de la Rose,*" ed. Hicks, *Débat,* p. 85.

13. Alluding to *De amore,* Gui cites the doctrine that jealousy is necessary for love. The Lover, taken aback by Ami's condemnation of jealousy, says: "J'oÿ dire, n'a pas granment, / Que cis pas amors n'amoit mie / Qui n'estoit jalous de s'amie; / Et vous issi le deffendés: [I recently heard it said that he who is not jealous of his girl friend does not really love her; and here you forbid it (MS *Tou,* fol. 84r)]. This provides the excuse for Ami's discourse on jealousy and languor, leading into the discourse of the Jaloux. The necessity of jealousy in love is the second of the rules of love given at the end of Book 2 of *De amore.*

14. Christine asserts that Genius, in exhorting procreation, "ne pansa oncques a mariage, le bon homme" [never thought of marriage, that fine gentleman ("Pour ce que entendement humain," ed. Hicks, *Débat,* p. 143)].

15. Gerson complains about Jean de Meun's use of Ovid, Abelard and Heloise, Juvenal, and various pagan myths in his "Traité contre le *Roman de la Rose,*" ed. Hicks, *Débat,* pp. 76–77.

16. Poirion pointed out the use of "emboîtement" in the discourse of Ami in his *Le "Roman de la Rose"* (Paris: Hatier, 1973), p. 125. Jean's use of digression is purposeful and brilliant; the *Rose* is in fact a tightly knit poem, in which a myriad of themes and motifs kaleidoscopically appear, disappear, and reappear, in ever-changing combinations. Gui, however, preferred a different sort of order. His changes in the discourse of Ami include the insertion of vv. 8997–9008, along with much interpolated material, before v. 8252; the insertion after v. 8424 of most of vv. 9463–9634, itself followed by the discussion of friendship and love; after which follow vv. 9823–38, somewhat rearranged and combined with interpolated material; vv. 9703–12 and 9696–9702, along with the interpolations on jealousy and languor; and finally the discourse of the Jaloux, beginning with v. 8425. While

these are not the only changes Gui made in the structure of the discourse of Ami, the above examples are sufficient to demonstrate his efforts to transform Jean's concentric ring structure into a linear progression.

17. For example, the deletion of digressive material gives Gui's version of nature's discourse an orderly linear progression, contrasting sharply with the concentric structure of the original; see Lee Patterson's chapter in this volume.

18. On the use of the terms "glose" and "gloser" in the *Rose*, see Gaston Paré, *Le Roman de la Rose et la scolastique courtoise*, Publications de l'Institut d'Études Médiévales d'Ottawa, 10 (Paris: Vrin; Ottawa: Institut d'Etudes Médiévales, 1941), pp. 26–30. Reason's linguistic arguments have been much commented upon. See, for example, Daniel Poirion, "Les Mots et les choses selon Jean de Meun," *L'Information Littéraire* 26 (1974): 7–11; Maureen Quilligan, "Words and Sex: The Language of Allegory in the 'De planctu naturae,' the 'Roman de la Rose,' and Book III of 'The Faerie Queen,'" *Allegorica* 1, 1 (1977): 195–216; John V. Fleming, *Reason and the Lover* (Princeton, NJ: Princeton University Press, 1984), pp. 97–135.

19. Guillaume looks forward to an eventual capture of the Rose in his allusion to "li chastiaus riches et forz / qu'Amors prist puis par ses esforz" [the rich and strong castle that Love later took through his efforts (vv. 3485–86)]. See Douglas Kelly, "'Li chastiaus . . . Qu'Amors prist puis par ses esforz': The Conclusion of Guillaume de Lorris's *Rose*," in Norris J. Lacy, ed. *A Medieval French Miscellany*, Papers of the 1970 Kansas Conference on Medieval French Literature, University of Kansas Publications: Humanistic Studies 42 (Lawrence: University of Kansas, 1972), pp. 61–78; David Hult, *Self-Fulfilling Prophecies*, pp. 171–74.

20. MS *Bi* appropriately omits most of Jean de Meun's Apology, deleting vv. 15123–272. The modification of the poem is such that the disclaimers addressed to lovers and to women are no longer needed.

21. For example, see Daniel Poirion, "Narcisse et Pygmalion dans le *Roman de la Rose*," in *Essays in Honor of Louis Francis Solano*, ed. Raymond J. Cormier and Urban T. Holmes, Studies in the Romance Languages and Literatures 92 (Chapel Hill: University of North Carolina Press, 1970): 153–65; Kevin Brownlee, "Orpheus's Song Resung: Jean de Meun's Reworking of *Metamorphoses* X," *Romance Philology* 36 (1982): 201–09; my *From Song to Book* (Ithaca, NY: Cornell University Press, 1987), pp. 96–99.

22. MS *Bi* also was not an isolated case. Langlois reports the existence of a single bifolio leaf, which he designates MS *Bï*. Since this leaf was the outer leaf of a gathering and is numbered (as gathering 20), it is possible to calculate the number of lines contained in the first nineteen gatherings as well as the number contained in the twentieth. The calculations show that the first nineteen gatherings would have been missing 6406 lines, and that gathering 20 reduced vv. 12507–15466 to 240 lines. These figures correspond exactly to the text of MS *Bi*. See Langlois, *Manuscrits*, pp. 166–67.

23. MS Bibl. Nat. fr. 12587 is missing the page that would have had the God of Love's discourse on authorship. However, it is quite unlikely that this passage was ever in the manuscript. Although Langlois places MS fr. 12587 in his *L* family, he acknowledges that the manuscript follows the *B* text in many places, including the midpoint passage. Since only one page is missing, the manuscript was lacking

at least 152 lines between vv. 10352 and 10672; approximately the same as MSS *Be* and *Bi*.

24. Langlois give the Adonis and Marsyas interpolations among his variants under v. 10518 and vv. 10830–31, respectively.

25. Langlois, "Gui de Mori" (see n. 3).

26. Jung, "Gui de Mori et Guillaume de Lorris"; Hult, "Gui de Mori, lecteur médiéval" and *Self-Fulfilling Prophecies* (see n. 3).

27. Gui tells us himself that he first read the *Rose* without Jean's continuation. Other evidence for the early independent circulation of Guillaume's poem is provided by the thirteenth-century MS Bibl. Nat. fr. 1573, to which Jean's continuation was clearly added after the fact, and the late thirteenth- or early fourteenth-century MS Bibl. Nat. fr. 12786, the only surviving *Rose* manuscript that does not contain Jean's continuation. See Hult, *Self-Fulfilling Prophecies*, pp. 21–24, 89–92.

28. Jean de Meun came virtually to eclipse Guillaume de Lorris as author of the *Rose*. See Badel, pp. 62–68, 331; Hult, *Self-Fulfilling Prophecies*, pp. 56–59.

9. Discourses of the Self: Christine de Pizan and the *Romance of the Rose*

In the decade between 1395 and 1405, Christine de Pizan successfully established herself as a major figure in French literary history. This process necessarily involved a complex coming to terms with the dominant discursive practices of the late-medieval literary tradition: the creation of a new and distinctive voice within the context of this tradition. For Christine, this posed a special set of problems. It was not simply a question of attaining and demonstrating her formal mastery of various established literary genres. Her identity as a woman inevitably problematized her status as an "official" speaking subject in all of these generic contexts. This explicitly female status, it should be stressed, was from the outset an essential component of Christine's complex authorial persona: Indeed, she was the first French literary figure who explicitly incorporated her identity as a woman into her identity as an author.[1]

Christine's self-figuration as first-person female voice required that the two principal vernacular literary discourses of the late fourteenth century be radically modified in order for her to speak through them. The first of these—which I shall refer to as "courtly," in the broadest sense of the term—involved a limited set of linguistic registers characterized by elegance and propriety. Its privileged subject matter was the lyric ego's poetic articulation of a first-person love experience. Authority came from within the courtly system itself, which was thus self-enclosed and self-sufficient. Within this system, the basic speech situation involved a male desiring subject who addressed a silent female object both of desire and of discourse. The privileged model courtly text was the *Roman de la Rose*, and in particular the part written by Guillaume de Lorris.

The second dominant system of literary discourse in late fourteenth-century France was what I shall refer to, again in the broadest sense of the term, as the "clerkly." Both the subject matter and the linguistic substance of clerkly discourse were, by definition, learnèd. A wide variety of moral, philosophical, theological, political, and historical topics were addressed by means of the writings of the classical and Christian *auctores*. The authority of the *clerc* derived from his mastery of the books of his illustrious predecessors and his ability to redeploy these books in contemporary contexts. The clerkly voice was by definition male, linked to Latin as father-language and to the dominant association of Latin learning with exclusively male social institutions (cathedral schools, monastic orders, urban universities, governmental bureaucracies). In addition, clerkly discourse was often characterized by a deep misogynistic strain, which in part served to define it. In this context, woman as object of discourse was a kind of negative object of desire. The privileged model clerkly text was also the *Roman de la Rose*, most especially the part written by Jean de Meun.

In the present chapter I propose to examine how Christine used her responses to the *Rose* in order to create a new kind of discourse of the self; how her powerful strategies of reading and misreading of the *Rose* function both to establish and to authorize her new identity as woman writer, poet and clerk, within precisely those traditional literary discourses that had seemed to exclude this possibility. A twofold process is at issue here: On the one hand, Christine utilizes courtly diction to critique and to expand the courtly system. On the other hand, she uses the learned discourse of *clergie* to critique and expand the clerkly system.

I will be focusing on three of Christine's early works: the *Epistre au Dieu d'Amours* (1399), the *Dit de la Rose* (1402), and the *Epistres sur le Débat du "Roman de la Rose"* (1401–1402). In each case, I am primarily interested in the implications of her treatment of the *Rose* as subtext, and I will be engaging therefore in a kind of Foucauldian deductive reading. The form and the content of her critique of the *Rose* are important not simply for their own sake but also for what they imply about Christine as originary voice. What kind of identity and authority *must be assumed* in order for these three works to be viewed as the products of a coherent discursive ego? For the act of reading in early fifteenth-century France presupposed this kind of causal relationship between writer and text; and Christine strategically exploited this presupposition for her own polemical ends.[2]

In terms of the focus of the present volume, I will be examining Christine's early engagement with the *Roman de la Rose* as an extended act of self-legitimation. For the purposes of my argument, I would like to suggest the following progression: In the *Epistre au Dieu d'Amours*, Christine represents the inadequacies of both the courtly and the clerkly registers of the *Rose*, on that poem's own terms. She thus speaks "through" the mouth of a corrected version of the *Rose*'s structurally central authoritative character, Cupid; there is no explicit self-figuration at the diegetic level. In the *Dit de la Rose*, Christine employs an exclusively courtly discourse simultaneously to critique and to renew the courtly register of the *Roman*, by recontextualizing it. Here, it is the central metaphor of the earlier poem that is transformed, that is, the rose itself. The *Dit* is recounted directly in the first-person by Christine's courtly persona; Christine as character, figured as a courtly writer, plays a key role on the level of the plot. In the *Débat* dossier, Christine adopts an exclusively clerkly discourse to confront the clerkly arguments and authority of the *Rose*. Here, she speaks entirely in her own voice, dispensing with fictional frames and constructs altogether. She presents herself as a learnèd female *clerc* directly engaged in interpretive activity in a contemporary sociohistorical context. Here, it is the central author figure of the *Roman* that is at issue, as Jean de Meun is both undermined and exploited.

To summarize: In the *Epistre au Dieu d'Amours*, Christine confronts and displaces the *Rose*'s Ovidian Cupid with a corrected Cupid of her own. In the *Dit de la Rose*, she confronts and displaces Guillaume de Lorris both as poet and as protagonist with a fictionalized version of herself as poet-protagonist. In the dossier of the *Epistres sur le "Roman de la Rose,"* she confronts and displaces Jean de Meun as authoritative vernacular clerk with a historically "real" self-representation as learnèd woman author.

The *Epistre au Dieu d'Amours* is the first of Christine's longer works and is presented as a letter written by Cupid from his celestial court to all loyal lovers. This construct allows Christine to present herself indirectly as Cupid's secretary, who writes down and then, presumably, reads out her royal master's missive.[3] At the same time, as Charity Cannon Willard has pointed out, Christine's "concept of the God of Love comes directly from the *Roman de la Rose*."[4] This, I think, is the necessary starting point for an understanding of the kinds of intertextual strategies at work in Christine's poem.

The letter itself is a response by the God of Love to a series of complaints he has received from women, and a careful rhetorical structure is in evidence throughout. After a brief prologue (vv. 1–16) establishes the fictional epistolary frame, Cupid announces the first category of offenders whom he must reprimand:

> Si se plaingnent les dessusdittes dames
> Des grans extors, des blasmes, des diffames,
> Des traïsons, des oultrages trés griefs,
> Des faussetez et de mains autres griefs,
> Que chascun jour des desloiaulx reçoivent,
> Qui les blasment, diffament et deçoivent.
>
> (vv. 17–22)[5]

[Thus the above-mentioned ladies complain of the great crimes, the accusations, the slanders, the betrayals, the great outrages, the deceptions, and the many other pains that they receive every day from disloyal men, who blame, defame, and deceive them.]

It is a question then of deceptive courtly lovers, those who manipulate the linguistic and behavioral codes of *fin'amors* in order to disguise their true identity and purpose. In socioliterary terms, they are "chevaliers / et escuiers" [knights and squires] whose custom it is to "traÿr" [betray] ladies "par beaulx blandissemens, / Si se faignent estre loyauls amans / Et se cueuvrent de diverse faintise" [with sweet words, and they pretend to be loyal lovers and disguise themselves in various false ways (vv. 33–37)]. In the terms of the *Roman de la Rose*, these deceptive lovers are following the Ovidian advice of the character Ami. Or, to say the same thing in a different way, they are utilizing the character Faux Semblant as a behavioral and linguistic model in an amorous context, acting, in the words of Christine's Cupid, "par faulx semblans" (v. 50) [by false seeming]. At the same time, their comportment involves a breakdown of the key opposition between the categories of *mesdisant* and *courtois*, which, in the courtly system, must, by definition, exist in complementary distribution. These unworthy lovers repeatedly alternate between the role of *amant* and the role of *losengier*. And Cupid's treatment of them in these terms exploits courtly discursive conventions simultaneously to characterize and to condemn this first category of offenders, who are in addition juxtaposed by positive counterexamples taken from contemporary French history (vv. 17–259).

The second category of offenders reprimanded by Cupid are not lovers but writers, more particularly, bookish, misogynistic clerks, who are cited in pseudolegal terms parallel to those used earlier:

Si se plaingnent les dessusdittes dames
De pluseurs clers qui sus leur mettent blasmes,
Dittiez en font, rimes, proses et vers,
En diffamant leurs meurs par moz divers;
Si les baillent en matiere aux premiers
A leurs nouveaulx et jeunes escolliers,
En maniere d'exemple et de dottrine,
Pour retenir en age tel dottrine.

(vv. 259–66)

[Thus the above-mentioned ladies complain of the many clerks who accuse them in prose and verse books, defaming their morals in varied words; and they give these books as school texts to their young, beginning students, by way of example and doctrine, to be retained into adulthood.]

Cupid responds to these misogynistic clerks by deftly manipulating clerkly discourse for his own purposes. First, he summarizes the standard antifeminist charges. They characterize women as "decevables, / Cautilleuses, faulses et pou valable / . . . mençongieres, / Variables, inconstans et legiers" [deceitful, crafty, false, and worthless . . . untruthful, changeable, inconstant, and flighty (vv. 271–74)]. Next, Cupid critiques the bookish authority upon which clerkly discourse rests:

Et ainsi font clers et soir e matin,
Puis en françois, leurs vers, puis en latin,
En se fondent dessus ne sçay quelz livres
Qui plus dient de mençonges qu'uns yvres . . .
Et s'aucun dit qu'on doit les livres croire . . .
Qui des femmes les malices proverent,
Je leurs respons que ceulz qui ce escriprent
En leurs livres, je trouve qu'ils ne quistrent
En leurs vies fors femmes decepvoir.

(vv. 277–80, 309, 311–15)

[Thus the clerks write their verses both morning and evening, now in French, now in Latin, basing themselves on books that repeat more lies than a drunkard . . . And if anyone says that we should believe these books . . . which demonstrate women's evil nature, I answer that those who wrote these things in their books, in my opinion, only sought to deceive women in their lives.]

Three specific clerkly texts are singled out for special treatment: Ovid's *Remedia amoris* and *Ars amatoria*, and the *Roman de la Rose* of Jean de Meun. Furthermore, the two Ovidian texts are treated largely in terms of their function in Jean's vernacular poem. Thus both the *Ars amatoria* and the *Rose* are viewed as practical manuals on how to deceive women, with the French poet being authorized by the Latin one, whose work he continues. Several important points are at issue here. First, we have a negative rewriting of the positive utilization of the *translatio studii* topos at the midpoint of the conjoined *Rose* text, where it had functioned to authorize Jean de Meun's poem as a worthy continuation of the poetic service to the God of Love exemplified by the Latin elegiac poets in general and Ovid in particular.[6] In Christine's *Epistre*, Cupid himself denounces not just the authorial stances of Ovid and Jean (whose poetic service he emphatically refuses) but also the clerkly construct of bookish authority that links the two poets together.[7] For Christine's Cupid this link has a purely negative resonance:

> Et meismement pouëte si soutil
> Comme Ovide, qui puis fu en exil,
> Et Jehan de Meun ou Romant de la Rose,
> Quel long procès! quel difficile chose!
> Et sciences et cleres et obscures
> Y met il la et de grans aventures!
> Et que de gent soupploiez et rovez
> Et de peines et de baraz trouvez
> Pour decepvoir sanz plus une pucelle,
> S'en est la fin, par fraude et par cautelle!
> (vv. 387–95)

[And even a poet as subtle as Ovid, who was later exiled, and Jean de Meun in the *Roman de la Rose*: What great exertion! What an elaborate enterprise! And what great adventures he described there! And how many people are entreated and begged, and how much effort and trickery is there in order to accomplish nothing more than the deception of a maid through fraud and cunning, for that is the ultimate goal!]

At this point, Cupid levels his potentially most serious charge against clerkly authority as such. First of all, this involves a critique of the misogynistic content of clerkly books on the grounds of insufficient experience on the part of their authors: the *auctores* (both Latin and vernacular) simply did not have enough knowledge about women to speak authoritatively on the subject. The authority of the written word is thus subjected to an experiential standard that is grounded in empirical (i.e., nonbookish) reality. At the same time, the *auctores* are, as it were, detached from their texts and judged as human beings in specific historical circumstances.[8] A perspective is thus created from which bookish authority can be criticized from the outside. In the context of this kind of newly "personalized" authorial intentionality, the clerkly misogynist's identity as such renders his position suspect: he is an interested party:

> Et s'on me dit li livre en sont tuit plein . . .
> Je leur respons que les livres ne firent
> Pas les femmes, ne les choses n'i mirent
> Que l'en y list contre elles et leurs meurs.
> (vv. 407, 409–11)[9]

[And if anyone says to me that books are full of them (i.e., misogynistic doctrines) . . . I answer that women did not write the books, nor did they put into them the things one reads there against women and their behavior.]

Indeed, what occurs at almost the precise midpoint of the *Epistre* (immediately following Cupid's negative treatment of the male, misogynistic poetic geneology linking Ovid and Jean de Meun) is the explicit articulation of an *absence* of any corresponding geneology of female authors. This absence is represented as a potential presence:

> Mais se femmes eussent les livres fait
> Je sçay de vray qu'autrement fust du fait,
> Car bien scevent qu'a tort sont encoulpées . . .
> (vv. 417–19)

[But if women had written the books, I know for a fact that they would have been written differently (otherwise), for they well know that they are wrongly condemned . . .]

Furthermore, the witty author/character configuration of the *Epistre* enables this declaration of absence on the level of plot (and with regard to the past) to function simultaneously as an affirmation of presence on the level of composition (and with regard to the present). The statement concerning the lack of female clerks in the past is made by—indeed, is the very mark of—Christine de Pizan as female clerk writing in the present. She is in the very process of writing a "livre" that is both by a woman and about women and therefore very different ("autrement . . . fait," otherwise made) from the existing misogynistic (male-authored) clerkly tradition. Christine as author thus responds to the clerkly inadequacies that her character Cupid criticizes—by means of articulating, of *writing* these very criticisms, that is, as *clerc*.

Christine qua poet-author is thus implicitly established as female clerk by Cupid, the same mythographic figure who had explicitly authorized Jean de Meun as clerkly poet-author in the *Rose*. And it is thus only at this point in the *Epistre* that Cupid (and Christine) embark on a recuperation of clerkly discourse, which is utilized to disprove the misogynistic position, as it were, on its own terms. Cupid first employs the classical tradition (vv. 437–558), citing a series of clerkly counterexamples to demonstrate that women are "loiales" (v. 433) rather than "fausses" (v. 425); more often deceived than deceiving: Medea (vv. 436–44), Dido (vv. 445–60), and Penelope (vv. 461–70). Next, Cupid turns to the Christian tradition (vv. 559–714), where he focuses on woman's role in the two key moments of human history: the Redemption and the Fall. Beginning with the New Testament, Cupid first praises the exemplary fidelity of Christ's female followers, then invokes St. Mary as the ultimate demonstration of God's valorization of woman (vv. 581–83, 589–92), and finally cites the example of Jesus's positive treatment of women (vv. 593–94). Cupid then moves to the Old Testament, to rehabilitate Eve. Not only are the circumstances of Eve's creation interpreted as marks of divine favor, but she is definitively declared "innocent" of original sin with regard to intentionality:

> Si ne fu donc fraude ne decepvance,
> Car simplece sanz malice celée,
> Ne doit estre decepvance appellée.
> (vv. 616–18)

[It was thus not fraud or deception, for simplicity that conceals no malice should not be called deception.]

This is of course a significant correction of the key clerkly justification for misogyny, and it leads to an extended discussion of the inherently positive aspects of woman's nature (emphasizing woman's disinclination, even incapacity, for a variety of particularly grievous sins).

Cupid concludes his *Epistre* by summarizing the two categories of offenders he has been reprimanding and correcting, and he reiterates their definitive punishment, banishment from his court:

> Pour ce conclus en diffinicion
> Que des mauvais soit fait punicion
> Qui les blasment, diffament et accusent
> Et qui de faulz desloiaulz semblans usent
> Pour decepvoir elles; si soient tuit
> De nostre Court chacié, bani, destruit,
> Et entrediz et escommenié,
> Et tous noz biens si leur soient nyé,
> C'est bien raison qu'on les escomenie.
> (vv. 775–83)

[Therefore I definitively conclude that punishment be meted out to the wicked, those who slander, defame, and accuse (women), and those who use false, disloyal appearances to deceive them: May they all be driven out of our Court, banished, dismissed, condemned, and excommunicated; and may all our goods be denied to them, for it is quite just that I excommunicate them.]

Thus on the one hand, we have bad courtly lovers, those who misuse courtly discourse in order to deceive women. On the other hand, we have bad clerkly writers, those who misuse clerkly discourse in order to defame women.

In this context, I suggest, Christine de Pizan's entire *Epistre au Dieu d'Amours* functions as a corrective rewriting of the famous speech of Jean de Meun's Dieu d'Amours at the structural center of the conjoined *Rose* text. Jean's Cupid, we remember, asked his assembled troops for two different kinds of help: he asked that Guillaume de Lorris (qua protagonist) be helped as courtly lover and that Jean de Meun (qua narrator) be helped as clerkly writer. Within the context of the *Rose*, both Guillaume's courtly loving and Jean's clerkly writing are authorized as poetic service to the God of Love—by the God of Love himself. This intricate and witty construct is both derived from the Ovidian tradition and used to authorize Guillaume and Jean within the context of the Ovidian tradition. The figure of Cupid in the *Rose* thus functions to present the poem's discursive practice as successful on its own terms. Christine's Cupid, on the contrary, calls into question precisely this success. In order to expose and correct the discursive inadequacies of the *Rose*, he strategically employs a superior, more authentic *courtoisie* and *clergie* that allow for, indeed require, a female authorial voice. The *Epistre au Dieu d'Amours* thus involves Christine's transformation of Cupid, the authoritative character at the *Roman*'s structural center.

In the *Dit de la Rose*, it is the central metaphor of the earlier poem—the rose itself—that Christine submits to a corrective transformation. In this way the courtly register of the *Rose* is, as it were, detached from the clerkly and treated in isolation, on its own terms: Christine employs an exclusively courtly discourse to effect her critical rewriting.

The narrative structure of the *Dit de la Rose* involves two clearly differentiated episodes. The first is a miniaturized courtly pageant ostensibly narrated in the third person. The second episode is a courtly dream vision, narrated in the first person. The *Dit*'s first episode (vv. 25–263)[10] takes place during a courtly festival, set at the elegant Parisian residence of the Duc d'Orléans in January 1401. The Duke's "hostel" (v. 43) is depicted as a kind of idealized courtly space, closed off from the outside world in an indoor, urban version of the Vergier de Déduit in the *Rose*. *Courtoisie* (v. 48) has assembled all the guests and presides over their activities, which constitute an exemplary embodiment of courtly behavior and speech, including the discussion and performance of literary works. In the midst of this refined and sumptuous setting, the goddess Loyauté arrives, a personification character sent by the Dieu d'Amours (vv. 83ff.). Loyauté announces the purpose of her visit to the assembled company in a set of three *balades*. (Indeed, in the first part of the *Dit*, all of the goddess's direct speech is in the form of intercalated lyrics.) She has been sent by Cupid to found the Order of the Rose, and for that purpose has brought a quantity of freshly cut, beautiful roses, both white and red. These flowers are to be distributed to each male guest in exchange for, and as a sign of, his joining the Order by means of swearing an oath (a *veu*), which is coterminous with the third *balade*. It is thus "par convenant" (v. 158) that these "chevaliers bons et tous de noble sente, / et tous amans" [fine knights, all of noble birth and all lovers (vv. 169–70)] are to receive the gift of the rose. The oath itself promises a perfect correspondence between language, behavior, and intentionality in matters of love:

> A bonne amour je fais veu et promesse
> Et a la fleur qui est rose clamée,
> A la vaillant de Loyauté deesse . . .
> Qu'a tousjours mais la bonne renommée
> Je garderay de dame en toute chose
> Ne par moy ja femme n'yert diffamée:
> Et pour ce prens je l'Ordre de la Rose.
> Et si promet a toute gentillesse
> Qu'en trestous lieux et prisée et amée
> Dame sera de moy comme maistresse.
> Et celle qui j'ay ma dame nommée
> Souveraine, loyauté confermée
> Je lui tendray jusques a la parclose,
> Et de ce ay voulenté affermée:
> Et pour ce prens je l'Ordre de la Rose.
>   (vv. 197−99, 201−12)

[To good Love, to the flower called the rose, to the valiant goddess Loyalty, I vow and promise . . . that I will always protect ladies' good reputation in all things, and that woman will never be slandered by me: and therefore I take the Order of the Rose. And I also make the noble promise that I will esteem and love ladies everywhere as if they were my lady. And I will give to her whom I have named my sovereign lady tested loyalty for my whole life, and I freely affirm this: and therefore I take the Order of the Rose.]

After each of the male guests has taken this oath, he receives his rose from Loyauté, who then departs (vv. 240−50). The company proceeds to celebrate its adherence to the new Order, before finally dispersing, each in possession of his rose: "partis s'en sont, congié ont pris, / emportant la rose de pris" [they left; they took their leave, carrying off the valuable rose (vv. 262−63)].

In this first episode of the *Dit*, a double process of transformation takes place for the rose in the *Roman*. First of all, there is a concretization, a literalization. At the diegetic level, Christine's rose is just a flower. It is no longer a metaphor for the courtly beloved, figuring woman as the silent object of (erotic) desire and discourse. There is thus a defusing of the basic courtly metaphoric construct that had functioned at the level of plot in the *Roman* to represent the unfolding relationship between the lover and the beloved. The act of plucking and taking possession of the flower is both literalized and deprivileged: it no longer signifies sexual conquest as it had in the *Roman*, where it thus functioned as the ultimate sign of closure.[11] In Christine's *Dit*, on the contrary, the cutting of the literal roses functions as a kind of opening signal (see vv. 153–56, 180–82). Temporally speaking, it precedes the central events of the *Dit*'s first episode; narratively speaking, it initiates these events. Furthermore, it is, in an important sense, the cutting of the roses that enables Loyauté—the key female personification character—both to speak and to found the Order. Finally, Loyauté's act of cutting the flowers is carefully differentiated from the act by which the *Dit*'s male lovers take possession of them.

In addition to transforming the significance of the *Roman*'s rose by literalizing it, Christine (in the first episode of her *Dit*) simultaneously remotivates the rose in a figurative context. On the one hand, the rose functions as the emblem of the Order. On the other hand, it signifies the successful completion of the individual speech act that establishes membership in the Order, that is, the oath (the *veu*, the *promesse* that must be *jurer*, *advouer*). It is thus both the sign and the guarantee of authentic courtly speech, which cannot by definition be used duplicitously. For Loyauté's oath has presented the index of true courtliness not as mere verbal competence but rather as the proper relation between speech practice and intentionality. It is thus the relationship between the male courtly lover and the female courtly beloved that is redefined by means of Christine's transformation of the figurative significance of the rose. And in this new context, a woman author's voice is possible within the courtly discursive system, speaking neither as beloved nor as lover. It is this new kind of courtly female voice that is at the center of the second and final episode of the *Dit de la Rose*.

This episode opens with a transition section (vv. 264–83) in which Christine as first-person protagonist is explicitly introduced into the story line for the first time. The entire first episode, which seemed to have been recounted from a third-person perspective, is thus placed, retrospectively, into the first person as we learn that Christine the character has been present at the courtly festival from the outset. The reader's awareness of her earlier status as witness is effected by the first instance of her self-presentation as participant. Interestingly, this presentation stresses her separation from the other characters and her solitude:

Et je qui n'oz pas le cuer noir
Demouray en cellui manoir
Ou ot esté celle assemblée,
Ou je ne fus de riens troublée.
(vv. 264–67)

[And I whose heart was not sad remained in the manor where that festival had taken place, and I was not troubled in the slightest.]

In addition, the introduction of Christine as character marks her as the favored protégée of the goddess of Chastity, Diana. This special status is figured at the level of plot by the snowy whiteness of both her bed and her bedroom, for no sooner has Christine appeared on the scene at the close of the soirée than it is time for her to go to sleep. Several points are worth mentioning with regard to this initial association with Diana. First, in terms of the story line of the *Roman*, Chasteté was the "head" of the hierarchy of characters whose task it was to guard the rosebushes (see *Rose*, vv. 2807–49). She was thus, in a sense, the chief enemy of the courtly male lover/protagonist and her function was to short-circuit the courtly system as set forth in the *Rose*. Christine remotivates the figure of Chasteté as operative in the *Roman* in order to write herself *into* a new kind of courtly discourse as speaking subject. Second, the explicitly chaste whiteness of Christine's nocturnal decor establishes a witty but important contrast between the dream vision of the Lover in the *Rose* and that which is about to take place in the *Dit*. For as soon as Christine falls asleep, Loyauté comes to her in a dream.

This dream (vv. 283–552) is almost entirely composed of the long speech that Loyauté makes to the sleeping Christine (vv. 294–551). This speech (in narrative verse) explicitly and exclusively addressed to Christine the character in private (see v. 293) complements the goddess's earlier speech (in lyric verse) to a male courtly audience in public, where Christine the character had functioned as silent and invisible witness. Amours has sent his "messagiere" (v. 311) to Christine to accomplish two things on his behalf. First (vv. 314–496), Loyauté explains that Amours had her found the Order of the Rose to combat the widespread abusive practice of *mesdire* [anticourtly calumny, slander] among the nobility, most particularly as it pertains to women. For:

> sur toutes autres diffames
> Het Amours qu'on parle des femmes
> Laidement en les diffamant.
>   (vv. 484–86)

[what Love hates above all other slanders is speaking villainously of women by slandering them.]

Second (vv. 497–547), Loyauté explains that the God of Love has "commissioned" Christine herself to publicize and to spread the Order. It is by means of the elaborate deployment of this conceit that Christine's identity as courtly poet and professional writer is explicitly incorporated into the story line of the *Dit*. Through Loyauté, Cupid empowers Christine to designate those worthy women everywhere who can confer membership in the Order:

> Amours . . .
> . . . veult qu'ayes legacion
> De faire en toute nacion
> Procureresses qui pouoir
> Ayent, s'elles veulent avoir,
> De donner l'Ordre delictable
> De la belle rose agreable
> Avec le veu qui appartient.
>   (vv. 498, 504–10)

[Love . . . wants you to have the authority to appoint procureresses in every country, who will have the power (if they so choose) to bestow the delightful Order of the lovely, pleasing Rose, as well as the oath that goes with it.]

It is at this point in the *Dit* that a final transformation is effected upon the figure of the rose: the sign of adherence to the Order among the future members who will respond to Christine's message will no longer be the literal roses distributed by Loyauté at the moment of the Order's founding. Rather, these will be replaced by artful representations:

Car quiconques d'orfaverie
D'or, d'argent ou de brouderie
De soye ou d'aucune autre chose,
Mais que soit en façon de rose,
Portera l'ordre qui donnée
Sera de la dame, ordonnée
De par toy pour l'Ordre establir,
Il suffist.

(vv. 536–43)

[For it will be sufficient that whomever is granted membership in the Order by a lady designated by you wear an insignia of worked gold or silver, or of embroidered silk, provided that it be in the form of a rose.]

Finally, Loyauté presents Christine with a written document (*bulles*, v. 544) which guarantees her "*commission*" (v. 546) from the God of Love. At the level of plot, this document also guarantees the truth of the dream in which Loyauté appeared, for when she awakens Christine finds it at her bedside:

Si me pensay que c'estoit songe,
Mais ne le tins pas a mençonge
Quant coste moy trouvay la lettre.

(vv. 556–58)

[And I thought that it was a dream, but I did not consider it to be a lie when I found the letter beside me]

Once again, Christine simultaneously recalls and transforms a key construct from the *Roman de la Rose* in order to establish the difference between that courtly discourse and her own and to establish her new kind of poetic self in terms of and by means of this difference. Here, Christine cites the famous rhyme-word pair that opens Guillaume de Lorris's *Roman* (*songe/mensonge*) in order to contrast her dream (and her poetics) with his. At the same time, Christine's construct stresses the primacy of the written artifact.

In the final section of the *Dit de la Rose*, Christine's service to "Bonne Amour" (v. 525) is explicitly presented in terms of her identity as a writer:

the plot of this courtly fiction thus serves to motivate and to authorize its composition. It is to fulfill her *"commission"* (v. 595) from Cupid that she has written the *Dit*, which explains what the commission is and how she received it (vv. 602–06). The last stage of this process involves Christine speaking directly to her extratextual audience as an authoritative courtly voice. First, she addresses the men in her extratextual audience, encouraging them to be worthy of joining the Order. Second, she addresses the virtuous "dames amoureuses" (v. 612), empowering them to admit worthy men into the Order:

> De par la deesse je donne
> Le plain pouoir et habandonne
> De donner l'Ordre gracieux
> A tous nobles . . .
> (vv. 622–25)

[On behalf of the goddess I give and grant full power to bestow the gracious Order on all noble men . . .]

This final speech act is essential to the successful functioning of the *Dit* as courtly discourse. It involves, also, a speaking female subject who is neither the beloved nor the lover. Rather, the courtly system has been expanded to include a new kind of female voice, outside the economy of desire but empowered to comment authoritatively upon that economy by means of courtly discourse.

In Part I of the *Dit*, to summarize, the Order of the Rose is founded for the intratextual public.[12] Cupid authorizes Loyauté to act for him. No role is played by Christine as character, except that of witness. The fact that her direct intervention as character is not required for the intratextual founding of the Order highlights her role as author in this regard. In this context, Christine's transformation of the *Roman*'s central metaphor is of great importance. The metaphoric equivalency of rose and woman as object of desire in the earlier poem is strategically undone in the first part of the *Dit*, where literal roses emblematize (in a nonmetaphoric way) the Order and its oath, that is, a corrected courtly code that precludes both the speech practice and the mode of signifying of the *Roman*.

In Part II of the *Dit*, the Order of the Rose is redefined and expanded so as to include the extratextual public. Here the role played by Christine as character is crucial and overlaps with her status as author. For she is the "means" by which this expansion of the Order outside the boundaries of the text is to be accomplished. Again, within the fictional hierarchy of courtly literary activity, it is Cupid who authorizes Christine through the mediation of Loyauté. In addition, a corresponding "expansion" is effected with regard to the rose as signifier. For the extratextual members of the extratextual Order, an extratextual representation of the rose is posited, involving visual icons of the flower, composed of luxurious cloth, to be displayed on clothing or flags. Christine thus attributes a new kind of significance—a new kind of signifying—to the figure of the rose, once she has divested it of the metaphoric function it had in the courtly system of the *Roman*. For the iconographic representations of the rose to be worn by the extratextual members of Christine's Order function as indexes of a full or proper reading of the *Dit*.[13] For the ultimate effect of Christine's "corrected" courtly discourse on the properly disposed reader is "corrected" courtly speech and behavior in the real world, in history. This conception of the dynamics of reading necessarily involves an extraordinary claim for Christine's authority as speaking, and writing, subject, as author figure. It also has important implications for her notion of the nature of literary discourse and of the author-text-reader relationship. All of this is elaborately and dramatically illustrated in the dossier of the *Débat sur le "Roman de la Rose."*

The *Débat* represented a new phase of Christine's long engagement with the *Roman*, one which was crucial to her development of a new kind of authorial self. For the purposes of my argument, it is important to stress that there were two different "debates," two different contexts for the documents that collectively constituted the *Débat*. On the one hand, there were the series of letters, treatises, sermons, and poems written to attack or to support the *Roman de la Rose* between the spring of 1401 and the winter of 1403. Christine de Pizan, later joined by Jean Gerson (the Chancellor of the University of Paris), attacked the *Roman* while Jean de Montreuil (Provost of Lille and sometime royal secretary), Gontier Col (first secretary and notary to the King), and Pierre Col (Canon of Paris and Tourney) defended it. This set of documents in chronological order constitutes what I shall call the "first level" of the debate's historical existence and lies outside my immediate concerns. What I will be focusing on is the "second level" represented by the dossier that Christine created by rearranging and recontextualizing a strategically chosen selection of the original documents—by in effect transforming the debate into a "book" of which she was the author. The act of making this book was itself a polemical, public gesture of appropriation and control on Christine's part, with important implications for the authority of her public voice.

The dossier is dated February 1, 1402, and contains seven component parts. The first three define the dossier as such: There are two dedicatory epistles and a brief introductory statement of the genesis and the chronology of the *Débat*. Four letters follow that had been written earlier and are here re-presented in a new context, a new kind of speech situation: they are directed simultaneously to their original, particular addressees; to the two privileged addressees of the dossier considered as a unit; and to a more generalized reading public. It is in these four letters that Christine's public position as reader of the *Rose* is explicitly stated in detail. Before offering an analysis of this position, I will consider the first three components of the dossier that establish, elaborate, and reinforce the authorial identity that is implicit in Christine's reading of the *Roman*.

The two dedicatory epistles are complementary. Together they open the frame that creates a "book" out of letters that have already been exchanged. The first dedicatory epistle is to a woman, a kind of ultimate courtly audience, Isabeau de Bavière, Queen of France. The second dedicatory epistle is to a man, a kind of ultimate clerkly audience, Guillaume de Tignonville, the Provost of Paris, who is also, significantly, a *chevalier*. In both cases the power politics of literary patronage is very clearly at issue.

When she addresses the Queen, Christine stresses the subject matter of the *Débat*, treating her opponents in a cursory manner. This subject matter is presented in terms of an implicit solidarity between speaker and addressee:

> moy simple et ignorant entre les femmes . . . sui meue a vous envoyer les presens epistres, esquelles, ma tres redoubtee dame—S'il vous plaist moy tant honnourer que oïr les daigniéz—pourréz entendre la diligence, desir et voulenté ou ma petite puissance s'estent a soustenir par deffenses veritables contre aucunes oppinions a honnesté contraires, et aussi l'onneur et louenge des femmes (laquelle pluseurs clercs et autres se sont efforciéz par leurs dittiéz d'amenuisier, qui n'est chose loisible ne a souffrir ne soustenir). (pp. 5–6)[14]

> [although I am very simple and ignorant among women . . . I am moved to send you the present letters. In these letters, my most awesome Lady, if you deign to honor me by listening to them, you can understand my diligence, desire, and wish to resist by true defenses, as far as my small power extends, some false opinions denigrating the honor and fair name of women, which many men—clerks and others—have striven to diminish by their writings. This is a thing not to be permitted, suffered, or supported. (pp. 65–66)]

When she addresses the Provost of Paris, Christine presents the debate by stressing her relationship with her opponents, downplaying the subject matter as such and asking Guillaume de Tignonville both to help her argument and to judge in her favor:

> Pour ce requier vous, tres sçavant, que par compassion de ma femmenine ignorance, vostre humblece s'encline a joindre a mes dictes vraies oppinions par si que vostre saigesce me soit force, ayde, deffense et appuyal contre si notable et esleuz maistres . . . Et avec ce suppli la bonne discrete consideracion de vostre savoir que vueille discuter et proprement eslire le bon droit de mon oppinion. . . ." (pp. 7–8)

> [Therefore, I ask, most wise man, that, out of compassion for my feminine ignorance, you see fit to add your sound views to my writing, so that your wisdom may be strength, aid, defense, and support for me against such notable and elevated masters . . . And in this letter I request the favorable and discreet exercise of your wisdom so that you consider and rightly choose the cause which I favor. . . . (pp. 68, 67)]

The chronological "explanation" of the quarrel that follows sets up an ongoing narrative temporality and context for the exchange of letters. At the same time, Christine's identity as correspondent is carefully established. First, there is a progression from the spoken to the written word: the initial disagreement between Christine and Jean de Montreuil ("mon seigneur le prevost de Lisle, maistre Jehan Johannes," p. 8)[15] is presented as having taken place in a recent conversation. Second, Christine herself is carefully presented not as the aggressor but as the respondent in the debate. Not only does Jean de Montreuil initiate the dispute as such by provocatively praising the *Roman de la Rose*, but he also initiates the correspondence by sending to Christine a copy of his own letter to an unnamed "sien amy notable clerc" (pp. 8–9) whom he attempts to persuade to accept his position. Christine responds with a letter of her own, of which a copy is subsequently requested by Gontier Col, who wants to argue against Christine's position. Christine's self-presentation as "character" in the *Débat* thus involves several important features worth noting. First, she functions from the outset as a publicly accepted female *clerc*. This identity is implicit in her role as disputant, for her clerkly opinion is presented as sufficiently important to be solicited by major contemporary male clerkly voices within the Parisian intellectual establishment. Second, Christine significantly expands the role of the "lady" as correspondent, in terms of preexistent vernacular literary models. The figure of Toute-Belle in Guillaume de Machaut's epistolary *Voir-Dit*—the most famous literary male/ female exchange of letters in the fourteenth century—is particularly important in this regard. Toute-Belle was both love object and love poet, and though it was she who initiated the epistolary relationship (at once amorous and literary) with Machaut, it was, at her request, the male poet who served as teacher and guide in literary matters. Furthermore, Machaut was the "author"—again at Toute-Belle's request—of the literary work that collected, arranged, and contextualized the letters between poet and lady.[16] Unlike Toute-Belle, Christine as correspondent functions exclusively as reader and writer; she is not at all a love object. In addition, *she* is the author figure in terms of the letter collection considered as a whole.

It is thus important to note that Christine suppresses Jean de Montreuil's original letter (which, interestingly, has never been recovered) and begins her selective re-presentation of the epistolary exchange with Gontier Col's letter (dated September 13, 1401) requesting a copy of Christine's reply to Jean de Montreuil. It is in response to Gontier Col's request, therefore, that Christine's long letter to Jean de Montreuil appears as part of the débat exchange. Christine's reading of the *Roman de la Rose* thus appears as doubly solicited, and the débat itself as a public event already underway. Both of these impressions of course are created by Christine as "author" of the dossier, and both function in important ways in the public establishment and valorization of her new authorial self.

Christine's letter to Jean de Montreuil contains the most explicit and elaborate critical response to the *Roman de la Rose* in her career up to this point. Her arguments involve a series of attacks on several of the major characters and episodes in Jean de Meun's poem. Jean's Raison is reproached both for her use of obscene language and for her statement that it is better to deceive than to be deceived. La Vieille is attacked for giving pernicious advice to young women. Genius is denigrated because his words serve to excite lust. Le Jaloux is condemned in tandem with Genius for defaming women and undermining the institution of marriage. Finally, the Taking of the Rose, the concluding episode in Jean de Meun's poem, is criticized as obscene and provocative.

Christine's overall critical strategy thus involves a systematic insistence on authorial responsibility and on reader response, both in a moral context. She attributes to literary discourse an inescapably exemplary character: literary texts by definition present themselves as models to be imitated, in behavior and in speech. It is because of this perspective that she refuses to accept the distinction between author and character with regard to the moral valence of a particular passage. What she foregrounds relentlessly are the extratextual consequences of literary mimesis, the links between literature and history. What is important about this concept from my point of view is not at all its relevance or validity for an "accurate" or "correct" reading of the *Roman de la Rose*. I am concerned, rather, with how Christine's notion of the moral dimension of literary discourse is part of her own self-definition as a writer. For this is how she conceives of her own literary vocation, her new kind of female authorial identity.

At the same time, the key question of clerkly authority is at issue. Christine's self-empowering claim to speak as a female *clerc* necessitates a redefinition of clerkliness so as to make possible this kind of speaking subject.[17] In her letter to Jean de Montreuil, this is how she speaks: She deploys a battery of learnèd arguments, appositely citing the texts of various *auctores*. On the one hand, this involves a confrontation with her fifteenth-century clerkly opponents, where the question is her authority as a reader. On the other hand, this involves a confrontation with Jean de Meun himself, perceived as the embodiment of the kind of clerkliness that precludes Christine's own clerkly identity. Here, the question is her authority as a writer.

Both kinds of authority are at issue when, toward the end of her letter, Christine engages in a strategic act of autocitation. Arguing against the misogynistic position of Le Jaloux, Christine maintains that women simply do not engage in a variety of particularly grievous sins that are, as it were, reserved for men:

> Et comme autrefoys ay dit sur ceste matiere en un mien dictié appellé *L'Epistre au Dieu d'Amours*: ou sont les contrees ou les royaumes qui par [les] grans iniquitéz [des femmes] sont exilliéz? . . . je pry tous ceulx qui tant . . . font [Genius] auctentique et tant y adjostent foy qu'ilz me sachent a dire quans ont veuz accuséz, mors, pendus ou reprouchiéz en rue par l'encusement de leurs femmes: si croy que cler les trouveront seméz. (pp. 17–18)

> [As I have said previously on this subject in my work called *Epistre au Dieu d'Amours*, where are those countries and kingdoms which have been ruined by the great evils of women? . . . I pray all who hold [Genius's] teaching authentic and put so much faith in it, that they kindly tell me how many men they have seen accused, killed, hanged, and publicly rebuked by the accusations of their women? I think they will find them few and far between. (pp. 52, 51)]

First of all, Christine is here treating herself as a bookish authority who can be cited in good clerkly fashion to buttress an argument. Second, she is illustrating her own point with regard to authorial responsibility and rhetorical distancing between author and character: she claims as her own words those that were spoken in the *Epistre* by the character Cupid. Third, Christine emphasizes the difference between the fictional *Epistre* and this real one, which is also a function of the increased authority, independence, and definition of her evolving public persona, her new authorial self. She no longer needs to speak through the authoritative fictional construct that is the God of Love but has reached a point where she can—having created it—speak in her own voice, clearly situated in history. Thus she recontextualizes the earlier charge brought by her character Cupid against misogynistic clerks in general, by directing it (in yet another autocitation, vv. 313–18) against Jean de Meun in particular:

> Mais vrayement puis que en general ainsi toutes blasma, de croire par ceste raison suis contrainte que onques n'ot accoinctance ne hantise de femme honnourable ne vertueuse, mais par pluseurs femmes dissolues et de male vie hanter—comme font communement les luxurieux—, cuida ou faingny savoir que toutes telles feussent, car d'autres n'avoit congnoissance. (p. 18)

> [But truly since he blamed all women in general, I am constrained to believe that he never had acquaintance of, or regular contact with, any honorable or virtuous woman. But by having resort to many dissolute women of evil life (as lechers commonly do), he thought, or feigned to know, that all women were of that kind; for he had known no others. (p. 52)]

In this context she fulfills, in a real *epistre* written in her own name, the prediction made by her character Cupid, in a fictional *epistre* written in his (fictional) name, concerning the necessity of female experience for an authentic depiction of woman's nature. Cupid, we remember, had added that if women had written the books, a very different picture would have emerged (vv. 408–22). This is now what Christine claims quite explicitly to be doing:

> ... veritablement mon motif n'est simplement fors soustenir pure verité, si comme je la sçay de certaine science estre au contraire des dictes choses de moy nyees; et de tant comme voirement suis femme, plus puis tesmoingnier en ceste partie que cellui qui n'en a l'experience, ains parle par devinailles et d'aventure. (p. 19)

> [... my motive is simply to uphold the pure truth, since I know by experience that the truth is completely contrary to those things I am denying. And it is precisely because I am a woman that I can speak better in this matter than

one who has not had the experience, since he speaks only by conjecture and by chance. (p. 53)]

At the same time, she appropriates an alternative clerkly tradition, in the context of which she chooses to situate her new, learnèd female voice:

> . . . et quant a parler de tout le bien qui ou dit livre puet estre noté, certes trop plus de vertueuses choses, mieulx dictes, plus auttentiques et plus prouf-fitables—mesmes en politiquement vivre et morallement—, sont trouvees en mains autres volumes fais de philosophes et docteurs de nostre foy, comme Aristote, Seneque, saint Pol, saint Augustin et d'autres—ce savéz vous—, qui plus vallablement et plainement tesmongnent et enseignent vertus et fuir vices que maistre Jehan de Meun n'eust sceu faire. (p. 22)

> [. . . do you wish to speak of all the good which can be found in this book? Certainly, far more virtuous things, eloquently expressed, closer to the truth, and more profitable to the decorous and moral life can be found in many other books—books written by certain philosophers and by teachers of our faith, like Aristotle, Seneca, St. Paul, St. Augustine, and others, as you well know. For these testify and teach how to pursue virtue and flee vice more clearly and plainly than Master Jean de Meun has ever been able to do. (p. 55)]

Christine's self-portrayal in the dossier of the *Débat* thus involves a kind of superior clerkliness, which allows her to confront and to displace Jean de Meun as authoritative vernacular clerk. The ultimate "proof" of her identity as historically "real" learnèd woman author lies in the status of the debate itself, as speech situation. Simply by participating in this kind of public discursive interchange, Christine establishes her own clerkly, au-thorial credentials; hence the importance of the dossier as format in terms of her new kind of public self.

This is, I think, what is ultimately at issue in the final two letters of the dossier. Gontier Col questions Christine's status as reader and disputant because she is a woman in letter number three. Christine responds in letter number four by reaffirming her identity as female clerk as the source of her authority. The *fact* of the epistolary exchange is the most powerful confirmation of Christine's position, and her opponents are thus made to bear witness to her public identity as a new kind of clerkly speaking subject.

It is interesting, in this context, to consider the key difference be-tween Christine's letters and those of the Rhodophiles when viewed as illocutionary acts.[18] Her opponents write directives: their goal is to con-vince Christine to change her mind and to recant her opinions. Her letters, on the other hand, are representatives: her goal is not to convince or to convert her opponents but to represent her own position, her own reading of the *Roman de la Rose*—which means nothing less than the represen-tation of her new authorial self. Even at the level of the inscribed dedicatees of the dossier as a whole, Christine is primarily concerned with creating prestigious and authoritative public witnesses to her aggressive act of self-representation. The appropriate conditions that allow the débat to take place imply and thus establish the key features of Christine's identity as clerkly speaking subject. It is therefore highly significant that Christine acted to take final and complete control of the *Débat* as written artifact by means of an additional letter, which both expanded the original dossier and definitively effected closure. Dated October 2, 1402, this letter is a long and detailed response to the epistolary attack made by Pierre Col on Chris-tine's position as contained in the initial dossier. Pierre's letter itself is strategically excluded from Christine's second collection.

Christine's final letter is the longest in the dossier and constitutes a kind of definitive statement of her reading of the *Roman de la Rose* and of Jean de Meun. On the one hand, previous points are recapitulated and significantly expanded. On the other hand, a variety of new approaches are employed that involve increasingly sophisticated and self-assured use of her "personal" identity as woman author. The culmination of Chris-tine's argument, of her interpretation of the *Roman*, is in fact a clear ar-ticulation of this identity in contradistinction to the limited possibilities for female identity contained in Jean de Meun's poem. A particularly rev-elatory moment comes as she answers Pierre's charge that she attacks Jean de Meun only because she envies him and his status as author:

> . . . je te promet n'y ay aucune envie. Et pour quoy aroie? Il ne me fait froit ne chaut, ne mal ne bien ne oste ne donne; ne il ne parle d'estat dont je soie par quoy aye cause de indignacion, car je ne suis mariee ne espoir estre, ne religieuse aussy, ne chose qu'il die ne me touche: je ne suis Bel Aqueil, ne je n'ay paour de la Vielle, ne boutons n'ay a garder. Et si te promés que je aimme biaux livres et subtilz, et biaux traités, et les quiers et les cerche et les lis voulantiers si rudement comme les sache entendre. Et si n'aimme point celluy de la *Rose*, la cause si est simplement et absolument pour ce que il est de tres mauvaise exortacion et deshonneste lecture, et qui plus penetre en couraige mal que bien. (p. 147)

[. . . I assure you I feel no envy. And why should I? He makes me neither hot nor cold, does me neither good nor ill; he neither gives nor takes away; he does not speak of my particular situation—why then should I feel indignant? For I am not married, nor hope to be, nor am I a nun, so that nothing he says pertains to me. I am not Fair Welcome: I do not fear the Old Woman; I do not have any rosebuds to guard. Yet I assure you that I love beautiful, wise, and well-written books. I seek them out and read them eagerly (within the limits of my understanding), and if I do not love that book of the *Rose*, it is simply because the work teaches an evil and dishonorable lesson, and sows far more evil than good. (p. 142)]

By this point, Christine's reading of the *Rose* has quite literally become a discourse of the self. Over the course of the *Débat*, she has confronted Jean de Meun qua author by means of a powerful deployment of the clerkly discourse he himself had used. Now at the end of the *Débat*, having established her own authoritative clerkly identity, she displaces Jean as author figure. For her final letter ends with a self-portrait, a miniature literary autobiography in which the different stages of her career as a professional writer are presented in sequence (Hicks, ed., pp. 148–50; trans., pp. 143–44). The concluding stage is her involvement in the *Débat* itself, which she presents as one of her literary works, as coterminous with the dossiers she has made. Her final gesture of control in this regard is thus to effect closure:

Et quant a moy, plus n'en pense faire escripture, qui que m'en escripse, car je n'ay pas empris toute Sainne a boire: ce que j'ay escript est escript . . . mieulx me plaist excerciter en autre matiere mieulx a ma plaisance . . . Si feray fin a mon dittié du débat non hayneux commencié, continué et finé par maniere de soulas sans indignacion a personne. (pp. 149–50)

[For my part, I do not intend to write any more about the matter, whoever may write to me, for I have not undertaken to drink the entire Seine. What I have written is written . . . I prefer [now] to devote myself to another subject more to my taste . . . I will now bring to an end my book of the debate, which has never been spiteful, but was begun, continued, and ended pleasantly, without personal enmity. (p. 144)]

Christine's dossier of the *Epistres sur le Débat du "Roman de la Rose"* constitutes an extended act of self-presentation in and through history. At the same time, it is the culmination of her long critical engagement with the *Rose* both as reader and as writer. Throughout the dossier she expertly employs clerkly discourse to confront the single most authoritative clerkly figure in the medieval French literary canon: Jean de Meun. In doing so she expands the very terms of the clerkly discursive system in such a way as to authorize her own identity as clerkly speaking subject. In this context her dossier, her book, her *dittié* of the *Débat* is at once the product and the proof of her legitimacy as female clerkly author.[19]

Notes

1. For Christine's identity as medieval woman author, and the implications of her "feminism" in this context, see Sylvia Huot, "Seduction and Sublimation: Christine de Pizan, Jean de Meun and Dante," *Romance Notes* 25 (1985): 361–73; E. Jeffrey Richards, "Christine de Pizan and the Question of Feminist Rhetoric," *Teaching Language Through Literature* 22, 2 (1983): 15–24; and Christine Reno, "Christine de Pizan: Feminism and Irony" in *Seconda miscellanea di studi e ricerche sul Quattrocento francese*, ed. Franco Simone, Jonathan Beck, Gianni Mombello (Chambéry/Torino: Centre d'Études Franco Italien, 1981), 129–32. For further discussion of Christine's feminism see Joan Kelly-Gadol, "Early Feminist Theory and the Querelle des Femmes, 1400–1789," *Signs* 8 (1982): 4–28; Mary Ann Ignatius, "A New Look at the Feminism of Christine de Pizan," *Proceedings of the Pacific Northwest Conference on Foreign Languages* 29 (1978): 18–21; Douglas Kelly, "Reflections on Christine de Pisan as a Feminist Writer," *SubStance* 2 (1972): 63–71.

2. See Michel Foucault, "What is an Author?" in *Textual Strategies*, ed. Josué Harari (Ithaca, NY: Cornell University Press, 1979), 141–60.

3. Charity Cannon Willard, *Christine de Pizan: Her Life and Works* (New York: Persea, 1984), 47, 62.

4. Charity Cannon Willard, "A New Look at Christine de Pizan's *Epistre au Dieu d'Amours*," in *Seconda miscellanea di studi e ricerche sul Quattrocento francese*, ed. Franco Simone, Jonathan Beck, Gianni Mombello (Chambéry/Torino: Centre d'Études Franco-Italien, 1981), pp. 82–83.

5. All citations from the *Epistre au Dieu d'Amours* are from Maurice Roy, ed., *Œuvres poétiques de Christine de Pisan*, vol. 2 (Paris: Firmin Didot, 1891). Translations are mine.

6. See Karl D. Uitti, "From *Clerc* to *Poète*: the Relevance of the *Romance of the Rose* to Machaut's World" in *Machaut's World: Science and Art in the Fourteenth Century*, ed. M. Cosman and B. Chandler (New York: New York Academy of Sciences, 1978), 209–16.

7. This is also, it seems to me, a response to Jean's clerkly self-defense against charges of misogyny in his so-called *apologia* in vv. 15165–212 of the *Rose*. See Kevin Brownlee, "Reflections in the *Miroër aus Amoreus*: The Inscribed Reader in Jean de Meun's *Roman de la Rose*" in *Mimesis: From Mirror to Method*, ed. John D. Lyons and Stephen G. Nichols (Hanover/London: University Press of New England, 1982), 60–70.

8. This has already begun in vv. 313–15, where the limitations of clerkly treatments of women "en leurs livres" were explained as a consequence of the limited clerkly experience of women "en leurs vies."

9. See Christine Reno, "Feminism," pp. 128–29.

10. All citations from the *Dit de la Rose* are from Maurice Roy, ed., *Œuvres poétiques de Christine de Pisan*, vol. 2 (Paris: Fimin Didot, 1891). Translations are mine.

11. Guillaume de Machaut's brief (106 vv.) *Dit de la Rose* is also relevant in this context. The plucking of the Rose by Machaut's narrator-protagonist does not effect narrative closure, and its precise metaphoric significance remains suggestively ambiguous. The degree to which Christine's response to the *Rose* was mediated in this instance by Machaut's remains to be investigated.

12. It is important to note Charity Cannon Willard's conclusion that "aside from the poem there is no evidence that an Order of the Rose was ever established" ("Christine de Pizan and the Order of the Rose" in *Ideals for Women in the Works of Christine de Pizan*, ed. D. Bornstein [Detroit: Michigan Consortium for Medieval and Early Modern Studies, 1981], 51). Willard reaffirms and elaborates this view in *Christine de Pizan*, pp. 168–69. But cf. Eric Hicks's nuanced discussion of the relation between public ceremony and poetic composition in the case of the *Dit de la Rose*, which presupposes the historical existence of Christine's Order (in the "Introduction" to his edition of *Le Débat sur le "Roman de la Rose"* (Paris: Champion, 1977), xlii–xlvi. Both scholars stress the importance of contemporary historical models for the Order of the Rose, in particular the Marshal Boucicaut's "Ordre de l'écu verd a la dame blanche" founded on Easter day, 1399, and praised by Christine in *Autres Ballades* XII, and the "Cour amoureuse, dite de Charles VI" (see A. Piaget, *Romania* 20 [1891]: 416–54 and *Romania* 31 [1902]: 597–603; and especially C. Bozzolo and H. Loyau, *La Cour amoureuse, dite de Charles VI: Étude et edition critique des sources manuscrites* [Paris: Léopard, 1982]).

13. In Peircian terms, it is as if an icon of smoke functioned as an index of real fire. For the distinction between index and icon see Charles S. Peirce, *Collected Papers II: Elements of Logic*, ed. Charles Hartshorne and Paul Weiss (Cambridge MA: Harvard University Press, 1932), 156–73.

14. All citations are from the excellent edition of Eric Hicks. Translations are from Joseph L. Baird and John R. Kane, *La Querelle de la Rose: Letters and Documents*, North Carolina Studies in the Romance Languages and Literatures 199 (Chapel Hill: University of North Carolina Press, 1978).

15. See Hicks (p. 197): "le surnom Johannes paraît avoir été choisi comme 'une sorte de constatation permanente de sa qualité de clerc' . . . (A. Thomas, "Le Nom et la famille de Jehan de Monstereul," *Romania* 37 [1908]: 594–602)."

16. For the importance of epistolarity in the *Voir-Dit* and its relation to the lover/beloved configuration see Kevin Brownlee, *Poetic Identity in Guillaume de Machaut* (Madison: University of Wisconsin Press, 1984), 94–156. See also Jacqueline Cerquiglini, *"Un engin si soutil." Guillaume de Machaut et l'écriture au XIVe siècle* (Paris: Champion, 1985) and William Calin, *A Poet at the Fountain: Essays on the Narrative Verse of Guillaume de Machaut* (Lexington: University Press of Kentucky, 1974).

17. In this general context see Susan Groag Bell, "Christine de Pizan (1364–1430): Humanism and the Problems of a Studious Woman," *Feminist Studies* 3 (1976): 173–84.

18. See Mary Louise Pratt, *Toward a Speech Act Theory of Literary Discourse* (Bloomington: Indiana University Press, 1977), pp. 80–99 and John R. Searle, "Classification of Illocutionary Acts," *Language in Society* 5 (1976): 1–23.

19. This essay originally appeared in the *Romanic Review* 79 (1988): 199–221.

Pierre-Yves Badel

10. Alchemical Readings of the *Romance of the Rose*

In 1735, when Abbot Lenglet-Dufresnoy edited the *Roman de la Rose*, he appended a body of prose and verse texts relating to alchemy; of these texts, the most important are the *Fontaine des Amoureux de Science* by Jean de la Fontaine (otherwise known as Jean de Valenciennes), the *Remontrances de Nature à l'alchimiste errant avec la Réponse du dit alchimiste* by Jean de Meun, and Nicolas Flamel's *Sommaire philosophique*. Lenglet-Dufresnoy regarded alchemy with a possibly feigned skepticism; at any rate, his curiosity about alchemy is shown by his publication of an *Histoire de la philosophie hermétique* in 1742, a work that he supplemented with a revision of an earlier bibliography, the *Bibliotheca chimica* of Pierre Borel.[1]

This collection of alchemical texts has not attracted the interest of literary historians, although D. M. Méon reproduced it, with an improved text, in volume 4 of his edition of the *Roman de la Rose*, appearing in 1814.[2] André Vernet's authoritative article did, however, reinstate the authentic title of the *Remontrances de Nature*, namely the *Complainte de Nature*; more importantly, Vernet's study restored this *Complainte* to its author, the painter, sculptor, and architect Jean Perréal.[3] Aside from this study, which examines Jean de Meun's reputation as an alchemist in order to refute it, the only other work that merits our attention is a very brief article by Lodovico Frati, who found some short texts attributed to Jean de Meun in alchemical manuscripts preserved in the library of the University of Bologna.[4]

Vernet's article should provide stimulus for a renewal of research on the extent to which alchemical circles may have been familiar with Jean de Meun. Frati's article permits us to think that other unedited texts may still surface. The present study, however, is concerned with a somewhat different topic, for two recent articles have posed a new question, less about Jean de Meun than about Guillaume de Lorris: could he have had recourse

Translated by Benjamin Semple

to an alchemical code in writing the first *Roman de la Rose*? Charles Méla and Daniel Poirion are inclined to think so, and this idea is worth closer examination.[5]

Historians of medieval literature are almost completely ignorant about alchemy, even if they are attracted by the occult; students of alchemy have very little knowledge of medieval literature. Worse yet, many of those who have a strong interest in alchemy write as if they themselves wish to be adepts. Their writings, lacking historical perspective, do not contribute to the production and exchange of verifiable information. In their writings, it is as if alchemy transcended history, as if the secrets of transmutation had been transmitted through the centuries for the greater profit of their souls. The conception of alchemy as not only an experiment on matter but also a sort of ascetic regimen and spiritual exercise may well predate the twentieth century—may even have already been established in the classical age. Nonetheless, in texts of the Western Middle Ages, there is no evidence of this conception, at least not before the fourteenth century, when one begins to find writings that require delicate interpretation. The Middle Ages defined alchemy in numerous ways, but in essence the definitions state that it is a technique that allows imperfect metals (lead, tin, iron, and copper) to be changed into perfect metals (gold or silver). As for the qualifications required of an alchemist, they are no more demanding than those required for any technician, be it a hunter or poet.

It is difficult to begin a study of these documents. The Latin and French texts are often unedited; collections compiled in the seventeenth and eighteenth centuries simply reproduced printed books of the sixteenth century. Most of these editions are not critical editions, for the boundaries of alchemical works are so ill-defined that editing them is an arduous task. It is an urgent necessity that these works, as well as their versions and glosses, be dated if the history of alchemy is to be retraced. From the very outset, the authenticity of the authorship claimed for these works is suspect: dozens of alchemical texts have been attributed to Albertus Magnus, Roger Bacon, Raymond Lulle, Arnold of Villanova. Are there not many people who even today stubbornly refuse to admit that Nicolas Flamel was in no way an alchemist and that he did not write the *Sommaire philosophique*?[6]

The texts are not easy to understand. Their language is sometimes allegorical. Furthermore, the texts name and describe the substances used and the procedures employed in imprecise and ill-defined terms. The first consequence of this was that copyists, ignorant of the meaning of the text, lacked a clear understanding of what they were transcribing and altered the text as they pleased. The result for us today is that one must be both a philologist and a chemist in order to reconstruct from the words in the text the reality to which these words once referred.

Nevertheless, the extant alchemical texts have been enumerated or described in good catalogs.[7] The literary historian finds a trustworthy guide to the study of alchemy in introductory texts such as those that we owe to Robert Halleux.[8] These introductory readings show that most alchemical texts in French are translations. Many of the texts leave something to be desired, inasmuch as they are lacking in imagination and incapable of inspiring the slightest emotion in the reader. The most accomplished text is the *Fontaine des Amoureux de Science* by Jean de Valenciennes.[9] Given this situation, one can well understand why alchemical literature might consider the *Rose* a valuable acquisition—worth at least as much as the Grail![10]

Jean de Meun owes his reputation as an alchemist to an eighty-four-line passage.[11] By citing parallel passages in Vincent of Beauvais and Albertus Magnus, the editors of the *Rose* have shown that Jean was echoing the theories of his day. He does not concern himself with the specific operations that result in the elixir, the white tincture (for silver), and the red tincture (for gold). Sublimation, calcination, coagulation, fixation, solution, distillation, ceration—these terms and several others are absent from Jean's passage. He indicates with great clarity, however, the principle behind the enterprise. First, the metals are reduced to their primary matter, a combination of sulfur and mercury, according to a procedure that, if successful, will render a black substance, although this color is not mentioned by Jean de Meun, who, moreover, does not use the words "putrefaction" and "mortification." He alludes more vaguely to the second phase of the Work, that leading to the elixir; but one can see that this phase consists of combining the spirits (sulfur, mercury, arsenic, ammonia) and the bodies (the metals), which have been separated and purified beforehand. It is clear overall that, whatever the complexity of the operations undertaken, the initial substances must disappear if the elixir is to appear.

These lines from the *Rose* were occasionally copied as a separate text.[12] A Latin adaptation was composed by Egidius de Vadis, or Gilles Dewès, who was tutor to the children of Henry VII and then to Mary Tudor, as well as royal librarian and author, in 1532, of one of the first French-English manuals for learning French.[13] This man's interest in alchemy was great enough for him to copy numerous texts and for him to write, in 1521, a *Dialogus inter Naturam et Filium Philosophiae.*[14]

It occasionally happens that these lines taken from the *Rose* precede one of the poetic works attributed to Jean de Meun. Here is a list of such works:

1. A *Balade maistre Jehan de Mung*: this is not really a ballad, but a formula, set into verse in the sixteenth century, for the production of "moon," that is, silver.[15]
2. A *Calcination* that must date from the fifteenth or sixteenth centuries.[16]
3. A *Clef de Sapience de l'art de l'alkymie* attributed to Jean de Meun in a manuscript of 1516;[17] six other manuscripts refer to this text, which is also called the *Ballade Sapientie* or *Trinité*. It consists of fifty-four octosyllables that, in essence, reproduce a passage near the beginning of the *Fontaine des Amoureux* written in 1413 by Jean de Valenciennes.[18] In the *Fontaine*, these verses constitute the first of two passages that describe transmutation in wholly allegorical terms; the second, to be found at the end of the *Fontaine*, translates a famous and entirely allegorical text, the *Tabula Smaragdina* of Hermes.[19] It is difficult to know whether Jean de Valenciennes appropriated two enigmatic poems that already existed or if, on the contrary, copyists extracted these two enigmas from his work.
4. A manuscript in Bologna seeks to make Jean de Meun author of the poem of Jean de Valenciennes or, if not of the entire work, at least of the translation of the *Tabula Smaragdina*.[20]
5. A collection of alchemical and scientific texts from the fourteenth century, preserved in the Bibliothèque de l'Arsenal, closes with a *Récapitulacion d'iceste art par maniere de verificacion et de probacion selon maistre Jehan de Meun mise et descripte en son Rommant de la Rose*: in this work, the extract from the *Rose* has been extended without a break by a piece of alchemical verse, preserved in nine manuscripts and variously bearing the title *Fleur d'Alkimie*, *Ballade*, or, very equivocally, *Testament* or *Codicille*.[21] The oldest version has 252 lines and is attributed to the mathematician Jean de Murs. In one manuscript dating from 1524, this version, a somewhat expanded alchemical formula, is supplemented by a prose commentary; other versions insert reflections on the necessity of combining theory with practice, or interpolate lines from the *Rose* concerning such topics as the influence of the stars or the forge of Nature. With these additions, the *Fleur d'Alkimie* swelled to 352 lines.

The sixteenth century attributed a prose treatise to Jean de Meun. In 1557, a collection was printed in Lyon; it opens with the *Miroir d'Alquimie de Rogier Bacon* and contains, in addition, the *Miroir de Maistre Jehan de Mehun*.[22] The collection was printed again in Paris in 1612 and 1613. The *Miroir d'Alchimie* of Jean de Meun was even translated into German and published in 1771. Upon investigation, the *Miroir* of Jean de Meun turns out to be nothing other than a slightly revised version of the *Miroir* of Roger Bacon![23] It would appear that the editor, excited as he was by the idea of publishing works attributed to two renowned authors, did not read the treatises that he was having printed. The *Miroir d'Alchimie* translates a widely available *Speculum Alkimiae* that Latin manuscripts of the fifteenth century do attribute to Bacon, although today it is no longer considered his.[24] Manuscripts of the sixteenth and seventeenth centuries contain another translation of the *Speculum*, which goes by the title *Livre de maistre Juppiter* and is very different from the one published in 1557.[25]

Jean de Meun's reputation also made its way into Latin treatises. Catalogs of alchemical manuscripts furnish several instances of this phenomenon:

1. The *Libellus de Alkimia* or *Semita recta* is an important treatise whose attribution to Albertus Magnus is still being debated. The editions of this work, including Borgnet's, reproduce a text that features numerous additions, one of which is Jean de Meun's opinion "in suo magno opere" [in his great work] on bleaching mercury.[26]

2. A fifteenth-century Latin manuscript at Oxford reproduces formulas of Jean de Meun and affirms that in one year, a great master of the Roman curia sold fifty marks of silver made from these formulas.[27]

3. Ideas from the second half of the fourteenth century are fairly well set forth in a frequently glossed treatise, the *Liber de magni lapidis compositione*, also called *Textus Alkimie* or designated by the incipit of its preface, *Studio namque florenti*. This book is often anonymous, but it is also attributed to different authors;[28] among them we find Jean de Meun, for several manuscripts attribute at least part of the treatise to him.[29] In a manuscript copied in 1512, the text as a whole is called *Textus de Maduno*.[30] In the sixteenth century, this treatise is attributed to *Johannes de Muris Parisiensis*.[31]

4. A manuscript of 1516 contains a *Tractatus sive Dicteria alkymie ma-*

gistri Johannis Meheum; this brief defense of alchemy is based on the authority of philosophers and, especially, on Jean de Meun; it quotes some lines from both the *Rose* and the *Fleur d'Alkimie*, which it calls *Codicille*.[32]

In its arid way, the list of treatises and formulas attributed to Jean de Meun confirms that alchemical texts are perpetually changing. They are often glossed, and several texts may be combined into one. It is difficult to identify and date the successive layers of text. The author is often unknown; an attribution is generally no more than a way of associating a theory or formula with the authority of an eminent name. The author's scientific, moral, and social reputation counts for much more than the plausibility of attributing a given work to him. The collections in manuscript and printed form were often written by amateurs who simply compiled everything they came upon and for whom knowledge was to be amassed, not sorted.

As for Jean de Meun, there is scant information. The texts in French are not old, dating from the end of the fourteenth century at the earliest. They are short and few in number. Their content has a single merit, which is to strip alchemy of the mystery and sentiment sometimes attached to it. It also appears that confusion between Jean de Meun and Jean de Murs might have favored an increase in the poet's reputation as a scientist. At the end of the fourteenth century, Jean de Meun was the author of the *Rose*, but what else was really known about him? Could he be situated in time? Jean de Murs, who was within more recent memory, might unwittingly have provided some substance for the figure of Jean de Meun.[33] It becomes apparent, especially from the manuscript tradition, that there is almost complete separation between the *Rose* and the corpus of the pseudo-Jean de Meun. The poems in French and the *Miroir* are read in alchemical compilations from which the *Rose* is absent except for the passage on alchemy, which is sometimes included. And Jean de Meun the scientist is unknown to readers of his poetic works: the *Rose*, the *Testament*, the *Codicille*, and sometimes the *Trésor*.

*   *   *

The Lenglet-Dufresnoy edition documents an evolution that dates from the sixteenth century. One great fifteenth-century writer claims to have devoted himself to alchemy: Pierre Chastellain, a poet who deserves to be better appreciated. His poetry is unusually difficult, and not just when he is describing his attempts to produce gold. In the *Temps recouvré* (ca. 1454), he refers to Jean de Meun twice. The first reference, in which the poet speaks of his protector, remains an enigma:

> Adonc le fis chevalier par le
> Point dont maistre Jehan de Meung parle.

[Thereupon I made him a knight by the point that Master Jean de Meun speaks of.]

The second reference is a four-line quotation on alchemy extracted from the *Rose*.[34] Nothing allows us to infer that Chastellain interpreted the *Rose* in its entirety as pertaining to alchemy.

In 1498, Simon de Phares composed a *Recueil des plus célèbres astrologues* in which he states that according to some people, Jean de Meun amassed a treasure of eighteen million gold pieces for Charles V, this feat being accomplished "par la puissance et vertu de la pierre des philosophes" [by the strength and virtue of the philosopher's stone].[35] This anecdote, however, does not pertain to literature.

The *Complainte de Nature* that André Vernet restored to Perréal and dated as 1516 expressly refers the reader to a passage of the *Rose* that condemns those "qui euvrent de sophisterie" [who accomplish a task through sophistry]. Jean de Meun is mentioned along with and even before the eminent authorities. In fact, as Vernet and Méon before him showed, the *Rose* is the "principal source" of Perréal, who owes to it his framework and his conception of Nature.[36] But one does not find the slightest trace of an alchemical reading of the *Rose* in Perréal.

The *Giroflier aux dames*, a short text dating from 1526 at the very latest, brings new evidence to bear on the issue of misogyny. In defense of the *Rose*, a certain Princesse des Fayes claims in the *Giroflier* that the *Rose* is misunderstood, for he who wrote it did not have time to "rymoier la glose" [put the commentary into verse], whereby, "suyvant Philosophie" [according to Philosophy] he would have explained that "son amye . . . ce fut la pierre qu'on dit philosophale" [his beloved . . . was what one calls the philosophers' stone].[37] The princess says no more about this; but the *Giroflier* shows that an alchemical reading of the *Rose* has become a possibility. This task will be realized by Jacques Gohory.

Gohory deserves to be better known.[38] A lawyer by education, he took up the study of nature. The list of his works is extensive: he translated

Titus-Livy, Machiavelli, and also *Amadis*. He published original works in Latin and French that reveal a fascination for the inventions of abbot Trithème, creator of a secret language of numbers called steganography. He also admired Paracelsus. In the faubourg Saint-Marceau-lez-Paris, he created a botanical garden in which he cultivated plants unknown to Europeans, including *petum*, or tobacco. In his laboratory, with admiring friends and visitors looking on, he mixed pharmaceutical concoctions. As an alchemist, he is important to us for two reasons: first because of his work as an editor, and second because of his reading of the *Rose*.

In 1561, he edited a collection entitled *De la Transformation metallique: Trois anciens tractés en rithme françoise*. This collection is hardly unfamiliar to us, for it includes the *Fontaine des Amoureux de Science* by Jean de Valenciennes; the *Remontrances de Nature*, which Gohory attributes to Jean de Meun; the passage from the *Rose* "auquel ledict Meung tracte manifestement de l'art susdict, et a cause duquel seul, plusieurs achaptent ledict *Romant*" [in which the said Meun treats openly of the aforementioned art, and for the sake of this passage alone many people buy the said *Romance*]; the *Sommaire philosophique*; and other minor works.[39] This collection, reprinted in 1590 and 1618, made its way into the Lenglet-Dufresnoy edition. It is therefore due to Gohory that the poem of Perréal is attributed to Jean de Meun. The collection enjoyed astonishing success; this success was studied by André Vernet, who emphasized in particular the German translation of the *Remontrances*, executed in 1612 by the Rosicrucians. But Vernet also showed that Jean de Meun was so little known that his name could be misconstrued as "Mesung."

In 1572, Gohory published a new book, an edition of the *Livre de la Fontaine perilleuse, avec la Chartre d'Amours: autrement intitulé le Songe du verger*.[40] This *Fontaine perilleuse* is not the *Fontaine des Amoureux* by Jean de Valenciennes. We have no manuscripts of this poetic text, but it undoubtedly dates from the fifteenth century. In it, the narrator reports a dream. A ship without oars takes him to a fountain. He is then witness to a brief event. A child drinks water from the fountain and immediately a burning arm holding a dart pierces his heart; the child thinks he will die from the blow. An old man arrives on the scene and undertakes to heal him. He leads him through the garden of Doux Amer [Bittersweet] and through a Gaste Forest [Wasteland] to an infernal vale where lovers are tormented. This is the Chartre d'Amours [Prison of Love]. After instruction, the child returns to the perilous fountain and vows not to drink of its waters again.

Gohory comments on the text he edits in less than forty short pages.

He believes this "oeuvre tres excellent de poësie antique" [most excellent piece of ancient poetry] to be a work of steganography, that is, an allegory that treats of "science naturelle occulte" [occult natural science], of the art of alchemy. He has searched in vain for its author, but he is sure that the poem is of great antiquity and that it was imitated by the authors of the *Rose*! To establish these points, Gohory uses a method that consists of comparing passages of the *Fontaine perilleuse* to passages of texts believed to be alchemical. This method of "exposition par conference seulement des autres auteurs semblables" [demonstration by collation only with other similar authors (p. 29v)] is imposed by the need not to divulge the secrets of alchemy. Gohory thus compares words, lines of text, and elements of the narrative and its setting with quotations from texts of which some are undoubtedly alchemical and others are considered to be so by Gohory: for example, the *Songe de Poliphile*, Apuleius's *Golden Ass*, Ovid's *Metamorphoses*, chivalric romances, and the *Roman de la Rose*, which "n'est qu'une vraye paraphrase du nostre: comme apparoistra cy apres par la collation des deux ensemble" [is no more than a paraphrase of our text: as will be apparent hereafter when the two works are collated (p. 31)].[41] The method produces a confused, allusive, and repetitive commentary. Gohory often writes "d'abondance du coeur" [from the fullness of his heart (p. 31v)], with the result that it is not always clear which text he is discussing. The commentary is interrupted by digressions; Gohory criticizes bad translators of Italian works, relates personal anecdotes, refers the reader to his own writings. Out of this disorder emerges an idea: the *Fontaine perilleuse* describes, allegorically, the two major phases of transmutation: reduction to primary matter and regeneration. The phases are indicated by the double title—*The Perilous Fountain with the Prison of Love*—and by the duality of the dream characters, the child and the old man. When the poem he is glossing neglects an element in the alchemical scenario, Gohory is astonished. For example, alchemy establishes a correspondence between its operations and the movement of the stars. The work should be begun in spring, in the sign of Aries. The *Fontaine* does not say a word about this, an omission that astounds Gohory (p. 34v).

Gohory does not comment directly on the *Rose*, which he uses to explicate the *Fontaine* and which furnishes him with many passages for his comparisons.[42] But, although his remarks on the *Rose* are scattered, they lead to an interpretation. For Gohory, the *Rose* is "le plus docte livre que nous ayons aujourd'huy en nostre langue françoise" [the most erudite book we have today in our French language (p. 2v)], except for the *Fon-*

taine. Mario Equicola, Gerson, and Le Franc have interpreted the *Rose* clumsily (p. 30). The error of commentators has been to ascribe to "la morale ce qui estoit de la physique" [to the moral that which belongs to the physical (p. 40v)]. In fact, the *Rose* treats "la science minerale couvertement" [mineral science in a covert manner (p. 32v)]. Some books speak openly about alchemy, others speak:

> par paraboles, enygmes, et allegories continuees . . . soubs voile et couleur de fable ou histoire plaisante . . . Quant à Jean de Meun il se peut dire avoir usé des deux moyens ensemble, c'est à scavoir du parler figuré en sa description de la fontaine pardurable decoulant soubz l'olive, et en l'enigme de la Lune, aussi de s'estre declaré apertement en la clef:

> > Nonobstant c'est chose notable
> > La Chemie est art veritable etc.
> > [vv. 16053–54]

> Dont il conclud à la fin de son oeuvre que

> > Richesse n'estoit pas si riche
> > [v. 21722]

> que luy: ce qui monstre bien que l'art d'amour il y traite par chiffre. (p. 3)

> [Through parables, enigmas, and sustained allegories . . . under the veil and in the appearance of a fable or amusing story . . . As for Jean de Meun, he can be said to have used both methods, for he uses figurative speech in his description of the eternal fountain flowing under the olive tree, and in the enigma of the Moon, and he also expresses himself openly in the key, "Nonetheless, it is to be noted that Alchemy is a true art, etc." (vv. 16053–54). From which he concludes at the end of his work that "Wealth was not as rich" (v. 21722) as he, which clearly shows that he is treating of the art of love in code.]

Gohory is especially interested in the beginning of the *Rose* and in the discourse of Genius, where the setting imagined by Guillaume de Lorris is taken up again. According to Gohory, Jean de Meun is not really criticizing Guillaume; rather, he

> samble blasmer et reprendre du tout la *Fontaine* de Lorris: ce que toutes fois il ne fait pas, estant eaue necessaire en la premiere partie de l'oeuvre . . . Mais il veult faire entendre que le Parc qu'il décrit, c'est à scavoir de la seconde oeuvre, et la fontaine pareillement sont beaucoup plus beaux et nets, et plus parfaits, que ceux de la premiere n'estant que préparatif à la seconde. (p. 37)

[seems to criticize and entirely censure the *Fountain* of Lorris, a thing that he does not do at all, for water is necessary to the first part of the Work . . . But he wants to show that the Park he is describing, that is to say, the second part of the Work, and its fountain, are much more beautiful and pure, and much more perfect, than those of the first part, which are only preparatory to the second part.]

For Gohory distinguishes two phases within the framework of the alchemical scenario. The first is corruption, reducing the metals to undifferentiated primary matter. The second is generation and the rendering of the tincture that makes transmutation possible. Guillaume speaks of the first phase when he describes the springtime, the river "poi maindre de Saine" [a bit smaller than the Seine (v. 112)], and the Fountain of Narcissus, that

> *perilleux mirail* [v. 1569] celle ou il fait Narcissus soy mirer et mourir. Et est ditte perilleuse celle fontaine pour l'eau de la premiere oeuvre qui tend a corruption du suget (combien que sous conservation de l'espece) à différence de celle qui est en la deuxieme partie. (p. 32v)

> [*perilous mirror* (v. 1569) in which he makes Narcissus look at his reflection and die. And that fountain is said to be perilous because of the water in the first part of the Work, which aims at the corruption of the subject (although the essence is preserved) as opposed to the water in the second part.]

The peril of "l'eau premiere venant d'estrange veine" [the first water, which comes from a foreign vein (p. 39)]—a citation of v. 20452—proceeds "de feu épriz" [from an ignited fire] that in the *Rose* is "le brandon de Venus (v. 3406), et le feu des Philosophes contre nature . . . sans lequel l'eau n'a puissance de dissoudre" [the torch of Venus (v. 3406), and the fire of the Philosophers who work against nature, without which the water lacks the power to dissolve (p. 39v)]. It is

> le premier fleuve preparant ou extrayant la Fontaine Perilleuse, et icelle tue le coeur de l'enfant, duquel sourd la fontaine de vie . . . En la premiere decoction, apparoit une noirceur qui est la mort de la matiere par separacion de son humidité sur laquelle le feu lors agit. Ainsi cette mort n'est pas vraye estant une corruption soubz conservation de l'espece. (pp. 40–40v)

> [the first river that prepares or feeds the Perilous Fountain; the latter kills the heart of the child, from which the fountain of life surges . . . In the first application of heat there appears a black substance that is the death of matter, through separation from its moisture, upon which the fire then acts. Thus

this death is not a true death, but a corruption with the essence being preserved.]

This death that is not a death is a necessary stage that prepares the second part of the Work, in which the subject is revivified. A second water replaces the first water; the second water is "eau de vie qui se peut accomoder à la fontaine savoureuse: à la description de laquelle et du parc de l'aignelet Ian de Meun a esté si excellent" [life-giving water, which can be equated with the delectable fountain: Jean de Meun excelled in describing this fountain and the park of the lamb (p. 39v)]. Hence the wealth of excerpts from the discourse of Genius.

Gohory also allows for a third phase in the alchemical enterprise: once the elixir has been concocted, it is projected onto inferior metals, thus changing them into silver or gold. This third stage is abstracted from Jean de Meun's account of the final approach to the Rose: "Ainsi nous avons veu deux saisons de la Rose, reste a deduire la troisieme qui fait la conclusion de l'oeuvre de I. de Meun" [thus we have seen two stages of the Rose; it remains to deduce the third stage, which forms the conclusion of Jean de Meun's work (p. 43v)]. After citing vv. 21675–700 and 21711–12, Gohory adds:

Icy finablement se montre le but où tend l'art, c'est à scavoir, de parfaite santé du corps humain . . . *la grande medecine*, qui est blasonnee, *pierre rouge*, qui est l'escarboucle dessus nommé par I. de Meun [v. 20498], et par les Arabes elixir. A cette cause . . . acheve . . . le Rommant de la Rose par la richesse.

> Quant en si hault degré me vey
> Que j'eu si noblement chevy
> [vv. 21713–14]

. . . j'estoye devenu (dit. I. de Meun):

> Si riche que pour veoir affiche
> Richesse n'estoit pas si riche.
> [vv. 21721–22]

Là où fault entendre en vieil langage voir affiche pour vraye affirmation. (p. 44v)

[Herein is finally seen the end to which the art is directed, that is, for the perfect health of the human body, *the great cure*, which is highly praised, and the *red stone*, which is called a carbuncle above by Jean de Meun (v. 20498)

and which the Arabs call elixir. For this reason the *Roman de la Rose* ends
with a reference to Wealth: "When I saw myself in such a high state, which I
had reached in such noble fashion" (vv. 21713–14) . . . I had become (says
Jean de Meun) "so rich that—it is a true affirmation—Wealth herself was not
so rich" (vv. 21721–22). Here "voir affiche" in the old language must be understood as "true affirmation."]

Gohory's alchemical reading thus turns on the two gardens of the
Rose. When appropriate, Gohory uses other details: the ugly images on
the wall of the garden could be "empeschemens en la personne de l'Artiste,
ou d'autres exterieurs" [inner obstacles, within the artist himself, or exterior ones] such as, for example, the envy that profane and greedy people
direct at alchemists. "Oysiveté . . . est ce loisir qui est requis à l'entrepre-
neur de tel oeuvre" [Idleness . . . is the leisure necessary to the one undertaking such a task (p. 37v)]. Gohory notes that Franchise [Openness,
Sincerity] is "blanche comme neige" (v. 1191) [white as snow (p. 38)] and
that the water of the fountain is "plus claire que d'argent fin" (v. 1525)
[clearer than refined silver (p. 38v)]. The crimson bud (v. 1658) with its
"odeur souveraine" (v. 1667) [sovereign fragrance] is the quintessence of I.
de Rupescissa (p. 43). The second and third parts of the work, taken collectively, seem to be symbolized by Bel Accueil [Fair Welcome]. Finally,
"Le serpent qui contient la principale difficulté de la science est celuy que
traitte I. de Meun au Rommant de la Rose [vv. 19851–64], que je mets icy
volontiers pour les annotations que j'en ay trouvees par conference de divers exemplaires" [the serpent that contains the principal difficulty of this
science is discussed by Jean de Meun in the *Rose* (vv. 19851–64); I put it
here without any reservation because of the annotations that I found concerning it in collating diverse copies (p. 48)]. If this affirmation is correct,
it shows that Gohory was not definitively the first person to read this
passage of the *Rose* alchemically. Gohory promises, furthermore, to "de-
viser une autre difficulté aussi grande que la quadrature du cercle, c'est
a scavoir du cercle triangulier, et triangle cerculier de Ian de Meun"
(vv. 19107–8) [to analyze another problem as great as the squaring of the
circle, namely that of the triangular circle, or circular triangle of Jean du
Meun (p. 34)]. He does not keep this promise, but one can guess that for
him these paradoxical expressions symbolized the alchemical work itself,
or the mercury of mercuries.

Gohory does not make us feel that he considers alchemy as other than
a material undertaking. There is no trace of spiritual alchemy in his writings. He insists, like many others, on the necessity of secrecy; he de-

nounces the envious and the greedy; he alludes to the obstacles that the alchemist himself can create for his work; and he makes clear that the alchemist must possess a morality and a piety beyond reproach. But one cannot deduce from the overall tenor of his commentary that Gohory considers alchemy to be a discipline of the soul, a death and resurrection of being. His reading of the *Rose* is made possible by an energetic reduction of the detail of alchemical operations to two or three major parts; but this reading contains no hint of spiritual tension. It is the reading of a curious and even enthusiastic technician, but the salvation of the workman is not at stake in the Work.

Gohory's two books had a considerable effect. After them, it was taken for granted that the *Remontrances de Nature* was by Jean de Meun. When Jean de Meun the alchemist was cited, it was almost always the *Remontrances* that was quoted. Furthermore, the *Rose* was considered a book of alchemy in the same way that the *Metamorphoses*, the *Songe de Poliphile*, *Amadis*, and *Perceforest* were considered to be books of alchemy. From the sixteenth century on, even the texts and dogma of Christianity became the object of alchemical interpretation!

The Breton storyteller Noël Du Fail does not seem to have believed too strongly in the miracles promised by the alchemists. Nevertheless, out of friendship for his compatriot, the doctor Roch Le Baillif, he wrote the preface to the *Demosterion*, a treatise that Le Baillif, an admirer of Paracelsus, published in Rennes in 1578. Du Fail refers to Jacques Gohory the Parisian; he alludes to the curiosities of Brittany and to the chivalric romances that are "figures philosophiques" [figures of philosophy]; and he writes as follows:

> Jean de Meun ce grave Theologien en l'accomplissement de son romant de la rose ressemble avoir apporté les vieilles pieces du voyage de Colchis pour la conqueste de la Toison d'Or.

> [That grave theologian Jean de Meun, in composing his *Roman de la Rose*, has as it were brought back the old pieces of the voyage to Colchis in quest of the Golden Fleece.]

Bernard Palissy battled vigorously against alchemy in the name of practicality in his *Discours admirables*, published in Paris in 1580. Twice, he mentions the *Rose* among books of alchemy and in the company of Gébert and Arnold of Villanova.[43] This does not prove that he had read the *Rose*, but does at least show that he had wind of Gohory's ideas. In 1590, an anonymous author wrote a *Bref Discours sur la pierre des philosophes*, in which he cites two verses by "Jehan de Mehung"; upon investigation, these verses prove to be taken from the *Remontrances*.[44] Doctor Pierre Borel de Castres, author of a precious bibliography, the *Bibliotheca Chimica*, published in Paris in 1654, did not forget to include the works of Guillaume de Lorris and Jean de Meun: *Remontrances*, *Miroir d'Alchimie*, *Roman de la Rose*, *Testament*, and *Operis Calcinatio* (p. 155).[45]

Since then, little has changed. When C. G. Jung cites Jean de Meun, he is thinking of the *Remontrances*.[46] Contemporary alchemists still exploit Gohory's ideas. In 1978, Bernard Husson wrote, "The place of hermeticism in its alchemical form, at the heart of medieval romance, is far more important than one might imagine, and greatly exceeds the scope of verse works, of which the *Roman de la Rose* is the best known, not to mention the *Golden Legend*."[47] In books for the general public, Serge Hutin presents Jean de Meun as an adept, author of the *Remontrances*. He quotes at length from the Mary translation of the *Rose*, including the passage on the fountain of life. The olive tree covered with fruits and flowers symbolizes the Great Work; the carbuncle symbolizes the Philosopher's Stone: "The carbuncle placed at the summit of the fountain of youth in the *Roman de la Rose*—chapter 18 [sic]—symbolizes the marvelous enlightenment gained by the adept in the accomplishment of the Great Work."[48] Thus the same passages as ever remain the object of alchemical interpretation.

✳   ✳   ✳

Are things any different in the articles by Daniel Poirion and Charles Méla?[49] The more recent of these articles, "Guillaume de Lorris, alchimiste et géomètre," is due to Poirion. The body of the article does not entirely keep the promise made by the title, for only the "geometrician" is discussed. But the introduction notes the earlier study by Méla. Poirion hesitates to accept Méla's conclusions. Could the Art of Love be a metaphor for another art, for alchemy? According to Poirion, this question cannot be answered without historical data that Fulcanelli and Jung fail to provide. But curiously, this initial prudence falls by the wayside in the conclusion, where the topic of alchemy resurfaces. This time, it is in a slightly confused fashion, first because "alchemy" is used metaphorically—what is at issue is literary alchemy, or the alchemy of the word—but also because it is linked to the idea of a "parenté" [kinship] between Guillaume's *Rose* and "l'emblématique alchimique" [alchemical emblems], and then to the rather different idea of the use of a "code alchimique" [alchemical code] in the *Rose*.

The vacillation in this article can be better understood when one realizes that Poirion has already attempted, in his book on the *Rose*, to establish a connection between alchemy and the thought of Guillaume de Lorris.[50] Poirion endows the *Rose* with a metaphysical and mystical dimension: the narrative signifies passage to adulthood and integration into courtly society, but that integration does not fully exhaust the meaning of the *Rose*. This art of love hardly resembles Ovid's; it is not a manual for seduction. It focuses on the Lover himself, who learns the price of suffering and discovers that to love is to die to oneself. At this juncture, Poirion could have alluded to religion as a model and to the words of Christ and Saint Paul. He could have contented himself with the observation that love has a spiritual, though non-Christian, value. Yet it is at this point that the question of alchemy is raised. The presentation of alchemy may be influenced by Jung, or at any rate by René Alleau, whose article "Alchimie" in the *Encyclopedia Universalis* is cited. For Alleau, alchemy is both spiritual and material: its principal function is

> *to use matter to release the spirit by using the spirit to release matter*. This mutual deliverance can only be effected by the supreme art, the traditional "Art of Love" of timeless chivalry. Far from refuting or denying the Incarnation, alchemy not only affirms the incarnation, by contemplating it, but glorifies it. Deliverance is not an escape but rather a new birth, a second genesis, that of the reign of man who achieves through art that which is the work of nature.[51]

The relationship established by Alleau between alchemy, the art of love, and chivalry is a new embodiment of Gohory's thought, and this conception of alchemy is implied by the analogy—although this word is inadequate—that Poirion sees between Guillaume's romance and the art of alchemy. Of course, one cannot read the romance "as a treatise on alchemical practice. . . . It is unlikely that the allegory would reveal to us the operations of the Great Work" (p. 90).[52] Nevertheless, the modern conception of alchemy permits Poirion to consider the speculations of alchemists and the symbolism of alchemy (rose, metals, colors, putrefaction, sublimation) as vital sources for the *Rose*.

The situation is similar in Méla's article, except that his study remains sufficiently ambiguous that one cannot completely discard the idea that for him, the *Rose* is an allusive description of an actual practice. Méla's article, which appeared in the journal *Europe*, is not addressed solely to medievalists. Nevertheless, the author in no way dispenses with a rhetoric that is characterized in part by an attempt to rival that of the text that he is discussing. The critic—how can we blame him?—rejoices in being able to equal the work he is examining. He experiments with being a writer. While performing an alchemical reading of the *Rose*, he plays with the very codes that are found in the writings of the alchemists. Emphasizing the theme of corruption and regeneration in the *Rose*, he unmakes and remakes words. This has some very striking results, such as a paraphrase in which the words of the commentator are mingled with those of the author on whom he is commenting; a constant use of puns (for example, in *genest* [broom flower] he finds *je nais* [I am born] in *paintures* [paintings], *pointures* [punctures, piercings]); allusions that presuppose considerable intellectual culture on the part of the reader, not to mention some knowledge of alchemical themes; a strong sense of concise phrasing; a taste for pathos; and, curiously, a taste for the type of sentence that resolves a specialized problem in a few words: the article ends by solving the problem of the etymology of the Provençal word *joi*. Ellipsis as a compositional technique makes this critic difficult to read. But one cannot fail to be fascinated, as well as irritated, by a procedure that, in sum, seeks to eliminate the distance that a beautiful text puts between itself and us—a text, moreover, that uses a language, and is rooted in a culture, that are foreign to us. It is as if the commentator were exploiting every possible rhetorical ornament solely so that the reader will be moved and aroused by the medieval text.

The problem lies in knowing whether bringing the text to life in this way does not sometimes lead to false conclusions. What is a sermon worth if its exegesis of Scripture lacks substance? In examining Jean de Meun's lines on art as the ape of nature and his lines on alchemy, Méla begins by turning Nature into an alchemist and alchemy into a procedure that is as much spiritual as material. The phoenix sets the tone for a concert in which four voices sing in unison, those of Aristotle's philosophy, of religion, of Eros, and of alchemy: for the phoenix, symbol of corruption and regeneration, of the dead and resurrected Saviour, and of the beloved woman, is also one of the names given to the Philosopher's Stone. All these voices harmonize to proclaim that life is death and death is life, that one must die in order to be resurrected, be lost in order to be saved.

This is the theme that Méla discerns in Guillaume de Lorris through a close examination of the fountain of Narcissus, also the Fountain of Love. The commentary draws the text in three directions. First, eroticism:

the troubadours, Chrétien de Troyes, and Ovid furnish classic references. Second, religion: the water (*eve* in Old French, *aqua* in Latin) is Eve (*Eva*), the *crystal* is *Christ*. And third, alchemical techniques: these are evident in the repetition of the signifier *roz* or *ros* (*rose, rosée, rossignol* [rose, dew, nightingale]) and the signifier *or* (Latin *aurum* [gold]),[53] as well as in the presence of colors such as the vermilion of the rose and the pomegranate, the black and white of the flowers: "Colors that undoubtedly symbolize the three phases of the Work, nor should we forget the particular rainbow effect emblematized by the peacock's tail" (p. 78).[54] These three elements, then, do not have the same importance; for, whereas in Poirion's article alchemy is a possible connotation for the Art of Love, in Méla's article eroticism and religion are accompanying melodies that are dominated by alchemy. This is what makes Méla's article original.

What permits this reading is not alchemy but the language of alchemy, which is often "veiled." Some texts are simply enigmas. Thus, as we saw, the *Fontaine des Amoureux de Science* begins and ends with purely allegorical texts. Formulas and treatises speak not of gold and silver but of sun and moon. Alchemy does not have any vocabulary of its own. The preferred metaphors of alchemy come from the areas of fantastical zoology (dragon, phoenix, unicorn), of biology (germ, infant, milk, blood, corruption, seed, grain, flower), and of religion (paradise, miracle, salvation, trinity). This last category becomes more important in the fourteenth century.[55] It is easy to imagine how far astray one can be led by technical terms such as those we found in Jean de Meun, terms like *esprits* [spirits] and *corps* [bodies]. From the fourteenth century on, a relationship that requires careful study is established between the secrets of alchemy and the mysteries of faith. Passion and resurrection, transfiguration and transubstantiation, are appropriated by certain treatises. Is this in order that alchemical operations be better understood, or so that we may have greater knowledge of the mysteries of faith? Whatever the answer, this connection is certainly preparatory to the syncretism of the classical period, which gave birth to the notion of esoteric alchemy.

Alchemy does not appear to have reached this point by the end of the thirteenth century, but a fortiori, by the beginning of that century. In the thirteenth century, the alchemy whose great texts are just beginning to be translated is not a theory of love or a religion. It is a technique whose language has no sense except insofar as it refers to the exercise of a specific skill. It suffices to read the *Fontaine des Amoureux de Science* to gauge the distance separating an authentic alchemical text from the *Rose*, in which it is impossible to uncover the least reference to the concerns of a practitioner. Medieval alchemy is a technique without any particular spiritual value; it is not the death and resurrection of matter or of the alchemist. Given this state of affairs, Guillaume's romance would not seem to gain any supplementary meaning by allusions to alchemy. Should we say then that the *Rose* at least uses the elements of the alchemical code? This would be to ignore the fact that alchemy has no code of its own, aside from a scenario that is linked to a specific practice. The fountain, the tree, love, birds, and waters do indeed belong to alchemy; but do they not first belong to literature? It may well be that the myth of Narcissus teaches that one must "die to oneself in order to live again through love" (Méla, 81–82),[56] but it is unlikely that initiation into the secrets of alchemy is one of the things at stake in the *Rose*.

*   *   *

The alchemical reading of the *Roman de la Rose* poses cogently the problem of valid interpretation. As for the alchemical reading in and of itself, it has a long prehistory. It was formulated by Jacques Gohory, whose testimony is of capital importance because he was at the intersection of French, Spanish, and Italian culture, of the Middle Ages and the Renaissance, and of alchemy and literature. Would an alchemical reading of Guillaume de Lorris have been proposed today if its promoters had not been caught up—unwittingly?—in this tradition that, since the sixteenth century, has caused the Art and the *Roman de la Rose* to be associated?

One question remains: the *raison d'être* of the lines that Jean de Meun wrote on alchemy. The rare answers given are far from satisfactory.[57] But are these the only lines whose presence in the *Roman de la Rose* continues to furnish scholars with a delightful conundrum?

Notes

1. Nicolas Lenglet-Dufresnoy, *Le Roman de la Rose*, 3 vols. (Paris, 1735): see volume 3, pp. 171–296; *Histoire de la philosophie hermétique: accompagnée d'un catalogue raisonné des écrivains de cette science*, 3 vols. (Paris: Constelier, 1742).

2. D. M. Méon, *Le Roman de la Rose*, 4 vols. (Paris: P. Didot l'aîné, 1813–14); see volume 4, pp. 123–290.

3. André Vernet, "Jean Perréal, poète et alchimiste," *Bibliothèque d'Human-*

isme et Renaissance 3 (1943): 214–52. The splendid miniature that adorned the dedicatory copy of the *Complainte* was found after 1943; the miniature is reproduced in Jacques Van Lennep, *Alchimie: Contribution à l'histoire de l'art alchimique* (Brussels: Crédit Communal de Belgique, 1984), p. 96.

4. Lodovico Frati, "Poesie alchimistiche attribuite a Jean de Meun," *Archivum Romanicum* 3 (1919): 321–26. Cf. Serena Della Vidova and Daniela Gallingani, *Regesto dei manoscritti in lingua francese existenti presso la Bibliotheca Universitaria di Bologna* (Bologna: Pátron, 1983): the information of these two authors does not always agree with Frati's information, and they display an ignorance of Old French that is almost as great as Frati's! These publications do not permit us to form a clear idea of the collection of alchemical works gathered by the counts of Caprara and preserved in Bologna.

5. Charles Méla, "Le Miroir périlleux ou l'alchimie de la rose," *Europe*, no. 654, *Le Moyen Âge maintenant* (October 1983): 72–83; Daniel Poirion, "Guillaume de Lorris, alchimiste et géomètre," *L'Information littéraire* 36 (1984): 6–11.

6. Cf. Robert Halleux, "Le Mythe de Nicolas Flamel ou les mécanismes de la pseudépigraphie alchimique," *Archives Internationales d'Histoire des Sciences* 33 (1983): 234–55.

7. Dorothea Waley Singer, *Catalogue of Latin and Vernacular Alchemical Manuscripts in Great Britain and Ireland*, 3 vols. (Brussels: Lamertin, 1928–31) (= DWS); William Jerome Wilson, "Catalogue of Latin and Vernacular Alchemical Manuscripts in the United States and Canada," *Osiris* 6 (1939): 1–22; James Corbett, *Catalogue des manuscrits alchimiques latins antérieurs au XVIIe s.*, 2 vols. (Brussels: Secrétariat administratif de l'U.A.I., 1939–51) (= Corbett).

8. Robert Halleux, *Les Textes alchimiques*, Typologie des Sources du Moyen Âge occidental (Turnhout: Brepols, 1979); "Alchemy," in *Dictionary of the Middle Ages*, ed. Joseph R. Strayer (New York: Scribner, 1982), vol. 1, pp. 134–40; "L'Alchimie," in *Grundriß der Romanischen Literaturen des Mittelalters*, 8: *La Littérature française aux XIVe et XVe siècles*, ed. Daniel Poirion (Heidelberg: C. Winter, 1988).

9. This text has often been printed but does not exist in a critical edition. Citations are from Méon, *Le Roman de la Rose*, vol. 4, pp. 245–88 (see # 2)

10. See the curious book by Paulette Duval, *Recherches sur les structures de la pensée alchimique (Gestalten) et leurs correspondances dans le Conte du Graal* (Paris: Champion, 1975).

11. *Roman de la Rose*, ed. Félix Lecoy (Classiques Français du Moyen Âge 92, 95, 98 [Paris: Champion, 1965–70]), vv. 16035–118; ed. Ernest Langlois (Classiques Français du Moyen Âge 92, 95, 98 [Paris: Champion, 1965–70]), vv. 16065–148. Subsequent citations of the *Rose* follow the line numbers of Lecoy's edition.

12. MS Paris, Bibl. Nat. lat. 11202, fol. 26v–27 (attributed to Jean de Meun); Cambrai, Bibl. Mun. 920, fol. 137v–137bis (anonymous).

13. See "Dewès," in *Dictionary of National Biography*, ed. L. Stephen (London, 1888). *An Introductorie for to lerne to rede, to pronounce and to speke French trewly* was reedited, along with *L'Esclarcissement de la langue francoyse* by Jean Palsgrave and F. Genin (Paris, 1852). The incipit of the translation of the lines from the *Rose* is: "Ars volens naturam Suam imitare dominam" [Art wishing to imitate nature,

her mistress]; MSS Cambridge, Trinity College 1400, fol. 149v–150; Leiden, Bibl. Univ. Voss. Chym. F. 35, fol. 99. The latter manuscript appears to have been copied from the Cambridge manuscript, which is in Dewès's hand.

14. *Theatrum Chimicum*, ed. Lazarus Zetzner (Strasbourg, 1659), 2: 85–123. Published by the heirs of L. Zetzner.

15. Incipit: "Qui veult estre enfant," a text edited by L. Frati, "Poesie alchimistiche," pp. 325–26.

16. Incipit: "La calcination que je devise": MSS Bologna, Bibl. Univ. 457, box VII-2, p. 89 and 1445, fol. 71v (Frati, p. 323).

17. Incipit: "Une chose est qui la scauroit": MS Orléans, Bibl. Mun. 291, fol. 13, copied by P. Bureteau; on Bureteau, see Max Quantin, "Notice sur Pierre Bureteau, religieux célestin, chroniqueur et poète," *Bulletin de la Société des Sciences Historiques et Naturelles de l'Yonne* 29 (1875): 409–41. This piece of poetry is attributed to Jean de Meun in three other manuscripts: Bologna, Bibl. Univ. 457, box VII-2, p. 89; and 1445, fol. 73v (Frati, p. 323); London, Wellcome Library 497, fol. 431–33. It is anonymous in three manuscripts: Cambrai, Bibl. Mun. 920, fol. 137 (fifteenth century); Montpellier, Faculté de Médecine 448, fol. 39–39v (title: *Ballade Sapientie*, according to Corbett, 2: 94); Paris, Bibl. Nat. fr. 2017, fol. 20–20v (title: *Trinité*).

18. See Méon, 4: 249–52. The text is longer than in the *Clef de Sapience*. Furthermore, the last four lines of the *Clef* are to be found on page 285, just before the translation of the *Tabula Smaragdina*. It is noteworthy that, according to Frati (pp. 323–24), there are two manuscripts (Bologna, Bibl. Univ. 457 and 1445) in which the *Clef* is followed immediately by the *Tabula*, and the entire work attributed to Jean de Meun.

19. Méon, 4: 285–87. The lines that translate the *Tabula* can apparently be found in the MS Bologna Bibl. Univ., box XXVIII-1 as well; in this manuscript they are attributed to Hermes (Frati, p. 325).

20. MS Bologna, Bibl. Univ. 457, box XXXIV-3 (Frati, p. 325).

21. Incipit: "Qui en son cuer vouldra penser": MS Cambrai, Bibl. Mun. 920, fol. 167–168v (title: *Practica de Jean de Muris*). Attributed to Jean de Meun in MSS Paris, Bibl. de l'Arsenal 2872, fol. 475v–477v; Bibl. Nat. fr. 2017, fol. 37–43v (title: *La Fleur d'Alkimie*); Bibl. Nat. fr. 19068, fol. 101–106 (title: *Testament*, date: 1524); London, Wellcome Library 497, fol. 3–12v; Bologna, Bibl. Univ. 179, fol. 144v (title: *Testament*); Bibl. Univ. 457, box XXI-7, fol. 203; Bibl. Univ. 457, box XXXI-4, p. 252 (title: *Ballade*). A ninth manuscript was indicated by Ernest Langlois, *Les Manuscrits du "Roman de la Rose": Description et classement* (Lille: Tallendier/Paris: Champion, 1910), p. 154; this manuscript was put up for sale on July 13, 1977; see *Catalogue of Western Manuscripts and Miniatures* (London: Sotheby Parke Bernet, 1977), p. 37. Finally, some passages from the poem are cited in the *Tractatus sive Dicteria Alkymie* of the MS Orléans, Bibl. Mun. 291: in that manuscript, the poem is entitled *Codicilium*.

22. Described in Baudrier, *Bibliographie Lyonnaise* 10: 254–56. The *Miroir de Bacon* is on pp. 5–33, the *Miroir de Maistre Jehan de Mehun* on pp. 109–34. Both belong to the first part of a four-part volume.

23. Incipit of the pseudo-Bacon: "Les philosophes anciennement en plusieurs sortes et diverses manieres parloyent" (translation by Guillaume Rabot,

1550); incipit of the pseudo-Meun: "Les philosophes anciennement en plusieurs sortes et diversement parloyent."

24. Incipit: "Multifarie multisque modis loquebantur olim philosophi" (DWS, 194). Ed. in *Theatrum Chimicum* 2: 377–85. See D. W. Singer, "Alchemical Writings attributed to Roger Bacon," *Speculum* 7 (1932): 80–86; Lynn Thorndike, *A History of Magic and Experimental Science* (New York: Columbia, 1934), vol. 3, pp. 174–75.

25. Incipit: "En plusieurs et diverses manieres le temps passé parlerent les philosophes": MSS Paris, Bibl. Nat. fr. 2012, fol. 73–82 and Bibl. Nat. fr. 2011, fol. 32–41. This translation in manuscript was not done from the same Latin text as the translation of 1550–57: its prologue is longer. Furthermore, there is another *Miroer d'Alquemye*, anonymous and different from the so-called *Speculum Baconis*, cited in this manuscript: incipit: "Le miroer d'alquimie est vrayement ainsi appelé" (MSS Bibl. Nat. fr. 2012, fol. 34–47 and Bibl. Nat. fr. 2011, fol. 42v–51); the manuscripts of this version are from the sixteenth century.

26. The reader is referred to the English translation by Sister Virginia Heines, *Libellus de Alchimia ascribed to Albertus Magnus* (Berkeley: University of California Press, 1958), p. 50.

27. DWS, 302; MS Oxford, Bodleian Library, Ashmole 1451, part 2, fol. 38v–39.

28. DWS, 301; Thorndike, *History*, vol. 3, pp. 182–90.

29. Lynn Thorndike and Pearl Kibre, *A Catalogue of Incipits of Mediaeval Scientific Writings in Latin* (London: Medieval Academy of America, 1963), c. 809; see also MSS Leiden, Bibl. Univ. Voss. Chym. F. 35, fol. 152–74; Bologna, Bibl. Univ. 109–11 (according to Frati, p. 322, no. 1).

30. MS Paris, Bibl. Nat. lat. 14010, fol. 2–116. This manuscript was copied by Pierre Rogier, professor of medicine, philosopher, astrologer.

31. MS Orléans, Bibl. Mun. 290 (according to Corbett, 2, p. 143).

32. MS Orléans, Bibl. Mun. 291, fol. 11–13; on this manuscript, see above, notes 17 and 21.

33. Another example of this confusion is in the *Traité d'Arismetique* by Jehan Adam (1475): he cites illustrious mathematicians from Aristotle to "Jehan de Ligneriis, Jehan de Mehung et Jehan Loquemeren"; Lynn Thorndike, who cites this text in *Science and Thought in the Fifteenth Century* (New York: Hafner, 1929), notes that one would expect the name Jean de Murs instead of Jean de Meun (see p. 157, n. 27).

34. Ed. Robert Deschaux, vv. 1245–46 and 1880–83.

35. Ed. Ernest Wickersheimer, p. 233.

36. Vernet, pp. 235–37.

37. Ed. in Anatole de Montaiglon and James de Rothschild, *Recueil de poésies françoises des XVe et XVIe s.* (Paris: Daffis, 1878), 13: 240–80; see vv. 251–60. The date comes from the fact that a copy of the *Giroflier* was bought in Avignon, where it was printed, in 1526; see H. Harrisse, *Excerpta Colombiniana* (Paris: H. Welter, 1887), no. 105.

38. See E. T. Hamy, "Jacques Gohory et le Lycium philosophal de Saint-Marceau-lez-Paris," *Nouvelles Archives du Museum*, ser. 4, 1 (1899): 1–26; Daniel

Pickering Walker, *Spiritual and Demonic Magic from Ficino to Campanella* (London: Warburg Institute, 1958), pp. 96–106; Enea Balmas, *Saggi e Studi sul Rinascimento francese* (Padua: Liviana, 1982), pp. 23–73.

39. We can add to what Vernet (see n. 3 above) says about this collection that it is a reply to an epistle that is hostile to alchemy; this epistle was addressed by Jacques Girard to the poet Charles Fontaine, and it figures in the third part of the Lyons collection of 1557 (see above, n. 22).

40. The text is quoted according to the copy of Paris, Bibl. Nat. Rés. Ye 1813. Another copy: Bibl. de l'Arsenal, no. 8 B 10877 rés.

41. The alchemical interpretation of the myth of the Golden Fleece is very old; see Halleux, *Les Textes alchimiques*, p. 144, and, for the *Metamorphoses*, Paul Kuntze, *Le Grand Olympe, eine alchimistische Deutung von Ovids Metamorphosen* (Halle: Hohmann, 1912). On Gohory's idea of the Round Table, see the texts cited by Balmas, *Saggi*, p. 39 and by Wallace Kirsop, "L'Exégèse alchimique des textes littéraires à la fin du XVIe s.," *Dix-Septième Siècle* 30 (1978): 145–56.

42. It seems that Gohory is using the so-called Marot edition, but this point needs to be verified. Line numbers refer to Lecoy's edition.

43. Palissy, *Oeuvres Complètes*, ed. Anatole France (Paris: Charavay Frères, 1880), pp. 234–35.

44. Bernard Husson, "Un texte alchimique inédit du seizième siècle: le Discours d'auteur incertain sur la pierre des philosophes (1590)," in *Alchimie*, ed. A. Savoret, B. Husson, A. Foriani, A. Faivre, etc. (Paris: A. Michel, 1978): 33–72. The citation of Jean de Meun appears on p. 53 and in Méon, *Le Roman de la Rose*, vol. 4, p. 155.

45. In *Le Roman de la Rose au XIVe siècle* (Geneva: Droz, 1980), p. 492, I also mention the testimony on Alain Bouchart and Jean d'Espagnet. This is incorrect. Bouchart, whom I cite on p. 136, praises the "science philozophale" [philosophical science, knowledge] of Jean de Meun, but this does not necessarily mean his knowledge of alchemy. Jean d'Espagnet was an alchemist; all the same, in his edition of the *Rosier des Guerres* (1616), his allusion to the *Roman de la Rose* is there only to explain the title of the *Rosier*.

46. C. G. Jung, *Psychology and Alchemy*, trans. R. F. C. Hull (*The Collected Works of C. G. Jung*, vol. 12) (London: Routledge and Kegan, Paul, 1953), p. 258.

47. Husson, p. 38: "La part de l'hermétisme, dans sa branche alchimique, au sein de la littérature romanesque du Moyen Age, est bien plus importante qu'on ne l'imaginerait, et déborde largement le cadre d'ouvrages en vers dont le *Roman de la Rose* est le plus connu, sans parler de la *Légende dorée*."

48. Serge Hutin, *La Vie quotidienne des alchimistes au Moyen Âge* (Paris: Hachette, 1977), p. 104: "C'est l'illumination émerveillée prourée à l'adepte par sa réussite du Grand Œuvre que, dans le *Roman de la Rose*—chapitre XVIII [sic]—symbolise l'escarboucle placée au sommet de la fontaine de jouvence." See also M. Caron and S. Hutin, *Les Alchimistes* (Paris: Éditions du Seuil, 1959), pp. 58 and 147–49.

49. See above, n. 5.

50. Poirion, *Le "Roman de la Rose"* (Paris: Hatier, 1973), pp. 86–93.

51. *Encyclopaedia Universalis* (Paris: Encyclopaedia Universalis France, 1968),

1: 598: "*délivrer l'esprit par la matière en délivrant la matière elle-même par l'esprit.* Cette mutuelle délivrance ne peut être accompli que par l'art suprême, le traditionnel "Art d'Amour" de la chevalerie de tous les temps. Loin de refuser ou de nier l'incarnation, non seulement l'alchimie l'affirme car elle la contemple, mais encore elle la glorifie. La délivrance n'est pas une évasion, c'est une nouvelle naissance, une seconde genèse; celle du règne de l'homme qui achève par l'art l'oeuvre de la nature." The underlined sentence is cited by Poirion, *Roman*, p. 89.

52. One cannot read the romance "comme un traité de pratique alchimique . . . il est improbable que l'allégorie nous découvre ici les opérations du Grand Oeuvre."

53. "Le miroir peut être un instrument de perdition, mais le *mireor* (1553) promet l'or à qui le mire" [the mirror can be an instrument of perdition, but the *mireor* promises gold (*or*) to him who looks at (*mire*) it (p. 82)].

54. "Couleurs symboliques à n'en pas douter, pour les trois temps de l'Œuvre, sans oublier l'irisation particulière pour laquelle la queu du paon fait emblème." [Editor's note: the "peacock's tail" is a term used in alchemical writings to refer to a particular phase of the Great Work, characterized by the appearance of many colors.]

55. See Barbara Obrist, *Les Débuts de l'imagerie alchimique (XIV–XVe siècles)* (Paris: Le Sycomore, 1982).

56. One must "mourir à soi-même pour revivre par l'amour."

57. Besides the opening pages of Méla's article, see Alan M. F. Gunn, *The Mirror of Love: A Reinterpretation of "The Romance of the Rose"* (Lubbock: Texas Tech Press, 1952), pp. 260–65; Roger Dragonetti, "Le 'Singe de Nature' dans le *Roman de la Rose*," in *Mélanges d'études romanes du moyen âge et de la Renaissance offerts à M. Jean Rychner* (1978): 149–60.

Part V

The Reception of the *Rose* Outside France

11. The Bare Essential: The Landscape of *Il Fiore*

The following chapter on *Il Fiore* requires a rather protracted prologue about its intention. While scholars have for the most part speculated about the work's author, my intention was to approach the *Fiore* as an autonomous and anonymous artifact. This soon proved an impossible prospect, however, for the poem is denied both autonomy and anonymity by its literary parentage as well as its circumstantial history. Behind it lies the *Roman de la Rose*: the master text, the determining precedent, the French "original" transcribed into Italian. So much for autonomy, then. The problem of anonymity is more difficult to ponder, for although its authorship remains uncertain, the work cannot, should not, and must not remain without a specific author. Why has the *Fiore* provoked relentless attempts to determine exactly who wrote it, and when, and where? Something about the very fact of the work's existence, if not its literary features, seems to motivate the philological quest for an author. Its uncertain authorship constitutes an enigma as well as an objection, a misfortune as well as a challenge, for literary history. In short, anonymity is the abyss into which the work precipitates in order to lose itself altogether in the question of its provenance. But why, given the free circulation of so many anonymous medieval works, does the scholar demand of this particular text an author?[1]

We are dealing of course with a work that may, or may not, belong to Dante. Dante: the name here refers to a synthetic category, to a principle of coherence for a variegated corpus of works, to a presumed generic unity of so many stylistic, phonetic, semantic, thematic, and ideological variations found in that corpus. The name by now refers also to a massive international institution, or proliferation of institutions, founded upon the authorship of an individual who, like the rest of us, lived, worked, and died as a mortal human being. In short, the name Dante refers essentially to a *function*—the function of author. Michel Foucault has helped us to understand the nature of that function and to monitor the ways in which writers will often assume or internalize it when they sit down to write. It is hardly an exaggeration to say that no writer in literary history has more internalized the function of author, or imposed it upon his readers more mercilessly, than Dante Alighieri who wrote at the end of the thirteenth and beginning of the fourteenth centuries. Given the gradual rise of his authorial empire, and given also the prospect of adding a new work to its domain, it is not surprising that the sustained debates about whether or not the *Fiore* belongs to Dante provide a flagrant allegory of what Foucault has identified as the author's function in schemes of literary history.[2]

But there is more to the enigma of the *Fiore*'s authorship than that. The question of its provenance pervades the work for reasons that go beyond the accidental circumstances that deprive us of the convenience of knowing exactly who composed it. The fact, for example, that we can identify two historical individuals as the authors of the *Roman de la Rose* has not allayed scholarly anxieties about that poem's authorship; on the contrary, the fact of two authors, each with his monarchic function of guaranteeing coherence, linearity, and resolution, has served only to exasperate the literary status of the work as a whole. Based as it is on the principle of identity, the authorial function falls into crisis by its *dédoublement*, forcing the literary historian to insist on the schizoid and irreducibly differentiated character of the *Rose*'s two parts. One wonders whether Roger Dragonetti's bold claim that the dual authorship constitutes the *literary fiction* of the work actually subverts or only radicalizes the category of author. Where Dragonetti perceives a deliberate continuity and design linking the two parts of the romance, he infers almost by syllogism that the work must have a single author. The syllogism goes roughly as follows: if the thematic and discursive unfolding of the second part of the poem depends upon the inhibited closure of the first, and if the poem—because of this dynamic of unfolding—reenacts poetically the blossoming of a rose, then a latent but supreme design governs the poem as a whole. If such a singular and overarching design can be demonstrated, then the existence of a single author must be conceded. What is an author? A principle of hermeneutic coherence.[3]

The problem of authorship, then, already haunts the French romance that the *Fiore* transcribes into its own foreign idiom. The fact of this transcription, rather than the literary originality of the work, is what becomes most valuable about the *Fiore* for literary history. No one, as far as I know, has claimed that the *Fiore* is a great poem in its own right; but its secondary status with regard to the *Rose* nevertheless makes it a precious testimony of stylistic, phonetic, semantic, and thematic options in the history of Italian literature. Given its greater importance as a linguistic and cultural testimony than as a work of autonomous literary value, its anonymous authorship becomes a stumbling block or impediment. Scholars require an author in order to bring together into a persuasive framework the various conclusions to be drawn from the testimony. The work, in other words, *must* have an author identifiable in space and time, for only on the basis of such knowledge can philology fully appropriate the testimony and redeem its significance in the operative schemes that govern its discipline. Until such an author is found, the search itself keeps alive the promise of the testimony's importance.

These are considerations that cannot be ignored in favor of some isolationist reading of the *Fiore*. On the other hand, it seems feckless to perpetuate the quest for an author who will merely fulfill a determinate function within a particular philological paradigm. The *Fiore*, although it is not a monumental work, goes beyond linguistic or historical testimony; in the final analysis it remains a poem, hence it belongs to a redeemable transcendence. Somewhere in its compromised status as a transcription or approximation of the French *Rose* it preserves the marks of its own literary origin, marks of its own particular provenance, as it were, which is not that of the *Rose*. In certain rare moments of poetic independence, the poem reappropriates its own secondary and differentiated status in order to reveal the native landscape to which it belongs. In what follows I am concerned only with the discrete poetic gestures by which the poem reappropriates its own minimalist originality. While I do not presume to offer an extended analysis of the numerous minor features that distinguish the Italian version from its French precedent, my aim is to discover the peculiar provenance from which the *Fiore* speaks to us. In essence, then, I propose to radicalize the question of provenance in order to leave behind the question of authorship. The *Fiore* deserves such a reading, for the preoccupation with authorship seems only to perpetuate a silence about the truly essential questions raised by the poem. Where does it speak from? Where does it leave traces of its own discrete origin? How does it reappropriate poetically its own uprootedness as a linguistic and cultural artifact? These are not questions that could be answered by establishing exactly who wrote the *Fiore*. For all too long the ghostly and presumptuous face of the author has functioned as the locus and origin of the artwork's transcendence, but behind every such face lies a more vital and original ecology. Viewing it from this perspective, we will see how little the *Fiore* shares of the luxurious ecology that promotes the growth and cultural independence of the French *Rose*.

∗ ∗ ∗

France was destined to become a nation. To the west was the Atlantic; to the southwest the prohibitive frontier of the Pyrenees, where Roland came to grief; the Mediterranean to the south; to the southeast the great Alpine chain; and to the east the Jura Mountains running from Lake Geneva as far north as Basel. To his eternal credit, the king who launched the great expansion and consolidation of the royal domain, Philip Augustus, refused to join the Albigensian crusade, restrained by scruples peculiar to his feudal ethic. But his son Louis VIII, who might have shared those scruples, was married to the ambitious Blanche de Castile, and she saw in the crusade a singular opportunity to annex the southern provinces to the crown. By the mid-thirteenth century the annexation of Languedoc was final, and the national sovereignty of *la France* had become indubitable.

Who can say to what extent the second part of the *Roman de la Rose*, exploding as it does the provincial, courtly confines of the first, incorporates the national self-assurance of the land in which it flowered? Who can say whether literary "realism" is not, in Jean de Meun's case, an emblem of cultural ascendency—of a triumphant vitality that loves itself and finds the will to celebrate rather than supplement reality? Anticlericism in this respect could reflect a logic of national appropriation or reappropriation that was to become geopolitically incarnate in the figure of Philippe le Bel. What seems clear from this distance is that the *Roman de la Rose* belongs to a world that wants to belong to itself; in any case it is rooted in a national language, and perhaps the Lover's final appropriation of the rose obliquely allegorizes the success of a culture coming into possession of its natural boundaries, its monarchic sovereignty, and its own proper linguistic, cultural, and even institutional determinations. Indeed, the great thematic obsession of the *Rose* revolves around the question of property, be it in the form of wealth or wife; of what belongs and does not belong; and of appropriation and expropriation: the question, in short, of the proper, as in the *propre non* which no lover should use in an illicit letter.[4] Again: the *Roman de la Rose* belongs to a world that wants to belong to itself, and somewhere in its manifold dimensions it allegorizes the will that sustains it.

Il Fiore is an anonymous medieval translation of the *Rose* into Italian.

As a work in its own right, the *Fiore* is timid and reticent, even impoverished, and for those of us who cannot muster enough curiosity to speculate about its authorship, the poem becomes provocative primarily in those features that set it off from the *Rose* and reveal the landscape to which this peculiar flower belongs. Let us look at them.

To begin with, the *Fiore* comprises some 3250 verses in the form of a sonnet sequence as opposed to the *Rose*'s 22,000 verses in undulating couplets. The sheer discrepancy in volume suggests that the *Fiore* offers a highly abridged version of the romance. This is only partly the case: various sections of the *Rose* are omitted, to be sure; notably the opening 1700 verses describing the garden, the fountain of Narcissus, and the persecution of Amant by the God of Love. Also omitted are the digression of the jealous husband, the figure of Genius, and the Pygmalion story. But what accounts by far for the discrepancy in volume is the Italian author's reduction or condensation of the French text to its essential narrative content. This is achieved through a systematic elision of the *Rose*'s digressions and descriptive flourishes. I would call such elision the narrative essentialism of the *Fiore*'s sonnet sequence. The sonnet form, which typically represents lyric synchronicity, here promotes and even rescues the narrative dynamism of the French text.[5] In this spirit of promotion, the anonymous author chooses to modify the *démarche* of the romance. Where Jean de Meun, for example, has Reason deliver an unrestrained speech nearly three thousand verses long, our author introduces a dynamic elenctic exchange of sonnets between Reason and the Lover, thus preserving a narrative tension where the *Rose* gives it up altogether. The one conspicuous place in the *Fiore* where the narrative rhythm breaks down is in the long speech of Falsembiante, which continues over some forty sonnets, but as John Took has shown, this extended speech remains indispensable to the thematic consistency of the work.[6]

The *Fiore*'s opening sonnet, given below, offers a typical example of what I am calling the essentialism of the Italian work. Its fourteen verses summarize the long passage in the *Rose* that describes the God of Love's pursuit of Amant through the garden and his wounding him with five arrows.

> Lo Dio d'Amor con su' arco mi trasse
> Perch'i' guardava un fior che m'abellia,
> Lo quale avea piantato Cortesia
> Nel giardin di Piacere: e que' vi trasse

Sì tosto, c[h]'a me parve ch'e' volasse,
E disse: "I' sì ti tengo in mia balìa."
Alló gli pia[c]que, non per voglia mia,
Che di cinque saette mi piagasse.
    La prima à non' Bieltà: per li oc[c]hi il core
Mi passò; la seconda, Angelicanza:
Quella mi mise sopra gran freddore;
    La terza, Cortesia fu, san' dottanza;
La quarta, Compagnia, che fe' dolore;
La quinta apella l'uon Buona Speranza.

[The God of love struck me with his bow because it pleased me to
gaze upon a flower that Courtesy had planted in the garden of Pleasure: and he struck me so swiftly that it seemed to me that he flew
and said: "Now I hold you in my power." And then it pleased him,
not for my sake, to wound me with five arrows. The first is called
Beauty: it passed through my eyes into my heart; the second, Angelicalness: that one brought a great chill over me; the third was Courtesy, without doubt; the fourth, Companionship, which caused me
pain; the fifth is called by man Good Hope.]

It is in many ways a bold gesture on our author's part to drop the
entire first half of Guillaume's narrative and then to condense over two
hundred verses of the French text into a single sonnet. This accelerated
opening dramatizes poetically the action of the God of Love, who strikes
so swiftly that he seems to the Lover to fly. Its radical elision of the descriptive dimension of the *Rose*'s corresponding passage contains a number
of opening signals that we may consider paradigmatic. For example, it
utterly delocalizes or defamiliarizes the scene of action. The elaborate allegorical machinery of the *Rose,* which gives the French romance its dimension of verisimilitude, here gives way to a ghostly scene of psychic
internalization. Personification loses its persuasive realism in ways reminiscent of Guido Cavalcanti's exasperated, uncanny figures of speech. The
God of Love, the flower, and the arrows become rarefied abstractions, and
the scene evokes a twilight interiority that belies the verisimilitude created
by Guillaume's pictorial narrative.
    I will return to some of the other opening signals contained in the
sonnet, but first let us look briefly at another example of the *Fiore*'s elision

of descriptive flourishes. Sonnet 142 resumes some sixty verses of la Vieille's speech to Bel Acueil.[7] The entire passage in which la Vieille enlarges upon the virtuous qualities of Amant is reduced, in the Italian text, to a single verse: "Unquanche uon più cortese non vedesti." ["Never have you seen a more courteous man."] Stripped thus to its bare essential, to be sure, the narrative nonetheless carries on; but it loses or forfeits the vitality and textual plenitude of the *Rose*. Through the recurrent omissions, elisions, and ellipses the *Fiore*'s inhibitions are put all the more conspicuously into relief. These inhibitions are difficult to characterize, for they belong to the very tenor of the work. They have to do with the strictures of the sonnet form, the failure of the foreign idiom to approximate the discursive generosity of the French text, and the melancholic modesty that pervades the general enterprise of transcription. Having refused the option of outright translation, the *Fiore* opts for an impossible originality, condemning it to remain only a pale and denatured imitation of the *Rose*. Throughout the poem its flower confronts us with the ultimate poverty of its resources.

In this poverty lies the irrevocable literary originality of the *Fiore*. By originality I mean in this case the discrete manner in which the poem poetically incorporates the barrenness of its own landscape. Let us return to the opening sonnet, which tells how the God of Love strikes the Lover with five arrows. These arrows are called Beauty, Angelicalness, Courtesy, Companionship, and Good Hope. In the *Rose*, they are called *Beaulté, Simplesse, Franchise, Compagnie*, and *Beau-Semblant*. Commentaries tell us that the *Fiore*'s substitution of *Cortesia* for *Franchise* is due to interpolations in the manuscripts of the *Rose*. As both Castets and Gorra point out, the third arrow, *Franchise*, was originally *Courtoysie*, as the Italian version has it.[8] However, commentators have not been able to account for the Italian author's substitution of *Simplesse* with *Angelicanza*: "La seconda Angelicanza: / quella mi mise sopra gran freddore." ["The second, Angelicalness: / that one brought a great chill over me."] Guillaume de Lorris also speaks of a great chill that comes over Amant but it is produced by the effect of the first arrow, *Beaulté*.[9] But the subtle decision on the part of the Italian author to substitute *Angelicanza* for *Simplesse* and to link the former with *freddore* reveals an instance of the *Fiore*'s poetic incorporation of its own barren ecology with regard to the French text. It would seem that he exploits the resonance of the word *gelo*, or chill, in the word *Angelicanza*. A subtle wordplay indeed, but if this were merely an instance of poetic subtlety, or an occasion for a literary critic to notice an elegant pun, it would not be overly consequential. What makes the word-play significant is that here, in the opening sonnet, our author prefigures the landscape that claims the flower as its own. In the third sonnet of the sequence we are offered the first glimpse of this landscape.

> Del mese di gennaio, e non di mag[g]io,
> Fu quand' i' presi Amor a signoria,
> E ch'i' mi misi in sua balìa
> E saramento gli feci e omaggio;
>   E per più sicurtà gli diedi in gaggio
> Il cor, ch'e' non avesse gelosia. . . .

[In the month of January, and not May, was when I took Love as my lord, and put myself wholly in his power, making my pledges and paying him homage; and for greater security I gave my heart as pawn, so that he would feel no jealousy. . . .]

The *Fiore* departs here not only from the *Rose* but also from the recurrent *topos* of medieval love literature, in which spring, and particularly the month of May, figure as the season of love. Here the season is winter. We may remark in passing what once again has escaped commentators, namely that the author's choice of the gelid season gives an original intratextual resonance to the word *gelosia*. Jealousy, after all, figures as the great chill of love in the *Rose*. But here too it is a question of more than merely a felicitous wordplay, for the *Fiore*'s poverty of resource begins to attain figuration, and hence originality, in the choice of its unlikely season. This wintry flower, stripped to a January bareness, stands as a figure for the bleak essentialism of the *Fiore*, which, as I have briefly indicated, reduces, condenses, elides, and, in a word, strips the *Rose* of its luxurious fecundity.

Where does this flower grow? Does it have a specific topography or does it grow as a wintry chimera in a rarefied, unearthly space? The anonymity of the work's author and its inexplicable fate as an artifact long unknown until its recent discovery in a provincial library attest to the fact that the *Fiore* never belonged to an author as such or even to a historical tradition that could redeem the fact of its existence.[10] It existed for centuries in a remote shelter beyond access, and what is remarkable is the way it figures in its poetry this indeterminate and inhospitable exile. Exile becomes an element of poetic reappropriation as the poem figures its own isolationism. Let us look at the section where the poem turns uncanny in this way. I am referring to sonnet 33, which has not heretofore attracted any particular attention but which discloses for one brief moment the full landscape of the *Fiore*.

Quand' i' vidi i marosi sì 'nforzare
Per lo vento a Provenza che ventava,
C[h]' alberi e vele e ancole fiac[c]ava
E nulla mi valea il ben governare,
   Fra me medesimo comincià' a pensare
Ch'era follia se più navicava,
Se quel maltempo prima non passava
Che dal buon porto mi facea lungiare.
   Sì ch'i' allor m'ancolai a una piag[g]ia,
Veg[g]endo ch'i' non potea entrar in porto:
La terra mi parea molto salvaggia.
   I' vi vernai con molto disconforto.
Non sa che mal si sia chi non asaggia
Di quel d'Amor, ond' i' fu' quasi morto.

[When I saw the waves grow high from the wind that blew from Provence, breaking masts and sails and anchors, rendering useless my attempts to steer, within myself I began to think that it was madness to navigate any further until that foul weather was over which flung me wide from safe port. So I anchored myself on a beach, seeing that I could not enter port; the land seemed very wild to me. Here I weathered the winter with much discomfort. No one knows its hardship who has not experienced that love by which I nearly died.]

Castets, who undertook the first publication of the *Fiore*, declares that the sonnet is almost a translation of "le long monologue de l'Amant à la fin du poeme de Guillaume de Lorris."[11] Commentaries refer us to verses 3962–4070 of the *Rose* and note that the sonnet deploys a traditional *topos* in its comparison of the adversity of the Lover's fortune to a tempest at sea. But surely the sonnet is more radical and unsettling than that: Nothing in the narrative sequence up until this point prepares the reader for a sudden shift of scene to a boat on high seas buffeted by winds from Provence taking refuge in a deserted bay. Even more remarkable is that, while the *Fiore* moves to sea and to a desolate shore, the corresponding passage in the *Rose* draws close to the earth and its domestic cultivation. In the *Rose* passage, Amant compares himself to a farmer sowing his seeds:

> Je ressemble bien le paisant
> Qui gette en terre sa semence
> Et a joye quant il commence
> Qu'elle profitte moult en herbe,
> Mais devant qu'il en cueille gerbe
> La nyele tres fort la greve
> Qui a travers le blé se leve
> Et fait les grains dedans mourir
> Quant les espitz doivent florir
> L'espérance lui est tollue
> Laquelle trop tost avoit eut.
>   (vv. 3974–85)

[I'm like the husbandman who sows the seed and joys when it grows fair and thick in stalk, but ere he cuts the sheaves worse weather comes—the season's bad—and evil clouds appear, just when the crop should ear, and kill the grain, with all the hope the farmer had too soon.][12]

In this intersection between domestic fields and a wild cove, we have the primordial element of differentiation that sets the *Rose* off from the *Fiore* and gives the latter its own mark of origin. The *Rose* evokes the earth's fecundity, its cultivation and colonization by the husbandman; and although it also evokes the disruptions brought on by bad weather, the eventual triumph of Amant in his quest for the rose would seem to neutralize these disruptions with an implicit promise of abundant harvests to come. The *Fiore*, on the other hand, reveals its denatured landscape in the image of a desolate beach in the dead of winter. There are no cultivated fields of belonging here, no precious property threatened by the fortunes of weather. There is, properly speaking, only dislocation. The *Fiore*'s protagonist will also win his flower at the end of narrative, to be sure, but that flower belongs to a season that appears as inhospitable to its growth as the deserted wilderness along the seashore does to the protagonist who takes shelter there.[13]

Where its poverty of resource announces itself poetically, as it does in this sonnet and elsewhere, there the *Fiore* redeems its strange and minimalist originality. The author's choice of a sonnet sequence, his choice of the month of January instead of May, and his staging of the protagonist's deviation into a lost cove during a storm at sea strike me as the most essentialistic gestures of the Italian text. In these gestures we find discrete figures for the poem's anonymous or exilic genesis. The deserted beach stands in effect as an antifigure to the *Rose*'s domestic fields of belonging, and thus as a figure for the *Fiore*'s own cultural uprootedness. This Italian version of the *Rose* has no place to take root, no world to which it can belong, no earthly harvest to reap. It has instead the bleak shelter of an anonymous cove, and until the discovery of a single manuscript in the nineteenth century—as single and solitary as a flower in January—the *Fiore* had remained in that prohibitive refuge.

Roger Dragonetti has claimed that medieval love literature is above all the poet's love affair with his or her native language—its resources and riches, its hidden potentials and intimate secrets, its genetic possibilities. He has shown how the figure of the rose, in its semantic, phonetic, and visual configurations, wholly determines the manifold unfolding of the *Roman de la Rose*. He has also argued that the figure of the *fiore* likewise holds sway over the Italian version, whose author for some reason never calls his flower a rose.[14] Dragonetti finds in the name *fiore* a significant semantic and phonetic resonance with *Fiorenza*, the name by which Dante refers to Florence in *De vulgari eloquentiae*.[15] The author of the *Fiore* is Tuscan, we are told, but it is more difficult to speak of a love affair with the native language in this case, if only because the text is notoriously contaminated by Frenchisms—"an orgy of Frenchisms," Contini calls it.[16] The overwhelming presence of such Frenchisms has intrigued and also perturbed scholars searching for the peninsular provenance of the work.[17] We must finally admit that we are not in a position to determine where or to what the *Fiore* belongs. Even if its Tuscan origin were not rendered problematic by the presence of Frenchisms, this "native" language remains an altogether nonnative language, for the Tuscan dialect as such differs significantly from the stylized idiom of the poem. Like the rest of Italian poetry in its generic beginnings, the *Fiore* is composed in a supraregional, literary, and hence rarefied language. In short, it does not spring from the ground up, nor from the resources of a national language, and to that extent its flower does not share the cultural rootedness of the French rose. Italy was not, in any case, destined to become a nation until many centuries later.

I find in this ecological difference—and by ecological I mean the cultural, historical, and geopolitical life system in which literature thrives or fails to thrive—a plausible reason for the *Fiore*'s formal divergence from the *Rose*. The sonnet is an inhibited, somewhat insecure genre. Perhaps it is no accident that it was invented by an Italian rhymester in the court of Fredrick II, at the dawn of Italian literature, when intimidated bureaucrats in the administration were encouraged by the German emperor to imitate the Provençal lyric manner.[18] In the case of the *Fiore*, the essentialism to which the sonnet's formal and narrative constraints commit the Italian author strikes me as a barrenness, or as an inability to flourish. The vitality of the *Rose*, with its unhindered couplets, speaks of a more secure ecology, in the geopolitical and historic sense alluded to earlier. The nature of this ecology is of supreme importance in any assessment of the emblematic literary status of the *Fiore*, for Italian literature began essentially as a supraregional, hence in some sense decultured experimentation with the language. More precisely, it began with gestures of *transcription*, as various poets followed the Provençal lyric precedent in order to create a literary Italian idiom. It did not begin with roots in the earth, so to speak, but rather in the rarefied minds of a learned elite. Perhaps for this reason medieval Italian love poetry was destined to become the most abstract, speculative, erudite, and theological poetry in the history of literature. The abstract essentialism of the *Fiore*'s sonnet sequence, as opposed to the discursive generosity of the *Rose*'s couplets, is in this sense markedly peninsular.

A poet like Dante eventually discovered the great resources of his peninsular language in *terza rima*, but this involved another kind of love affair altogether. The *Commedia* did not bring a national language into bloom but invented a hyperlanguage rooted in another sphere; an unearthly, utopian sphere which perforce had to transfigure its flower into a celestial rose. Unlike the French rose, Dante's was condemned to be celestial, for the peninsular world below remained under the siege of social and political storms. Perhaps the *Fiore*, regardless of whether or not it "belongs" to Dante, helps us to understand part of this story of Italian literature's genetic alienation from its local province. If the *Fiore* has some essential link to Dante, one must perhaps look for it in nature of its utopian provenance, in its withdrawal to a desolate shore far from port in the month of January, and in the poet's decision to weather the winter with the poverty of his resources, waiting, attending upon, perhaps even hoping for the advent of a more clement season.

Notes

1. For an exhaustive bibliography of the debate about the *Fiore*'s authorship up until 1982, see the recent critical edition of the Società Dantesca Italiana, *Il Fiore e Il Detto D'Amore*, ed. Gianfranco Contini (Milan: Mondadori, 1984), pp. xxvii–xxxix. Over fifty of the fifty-six scholarly books and essays documented by Contini consist primarily of speculations about possible authors. This new critical edition also offers an extensive summary of the "external" and "internal" arguments supporting Dante's candidacy (pp. lxxi–xcv). Not included in Contini's bibliography are the recent essay by Aldo Vallone, "Il 'Fiore' come opera di Dante," *Studi Danteschi* 56 (1984): 141–67 and Roger Dragonetti's "Specchi d'amore: Il romanzo della rosa e Il Fiore," *Paragone* 374 (1981): 3–22. The *Fiore* is cited throughout in Contini's edition. Translations are mine.

2. Michel Foucault, "What is an Author?" in *Language, Counter-Memory, Practice*, ed. Donald F. Bouchard (Ithaca, NY: Cornell University Press, 1977), pp. 113–38; also "The Discourse on Language," in *The Archaeology of Knowledge*, trans. A. M. Sheridan Smith (New York: Pantheon, 1972), esp. pp. 221–23.

3. Roger Dragonetti, "Pygmalion ou les pièges de la fiction dans le *Roman de la Rose*," in *Orbis Mediavalis: Mélanges de langue et de littérature médiévales offerts à R. R. Bezzola* (Berne: Francke, 1978), pp. 89ff. See also "Specchi d'amore," pp. 5–8.

4. "Mes ja n'i metez propre non, / ja cil n'i soit se cele non, / cele resoit cil apelee / la chose en iert trop mieuz celee" (vv. 7461–64).

5. The most systematic treatment of the sonnet form in *Il Fiore* is undertaken by Luigi Vanossi, *Dante e il "Roman de la Rose": Saggio sul "Fiore"* (Firenze: Olschki, 1979), pp. 151–221. Although Vanossi is clearly preoccupied with the *Fiore*'s authorship (he assumes it was composed by Dante), his book undertakes the most thorough analysis to date of the *Fiore* in its manifold literary characteristics.

6. John Took, "Toward an Interpretation of the *Fiore*," *Speculum* 54 (1979): 500–27. Took applies the Robertsonian moralistic reading of the *Rose* to the *Fiore*, finding in the long speech of Falsembiante evidence of how the *Fiore*, too, like its master text, offers an implicit critique of the Lover's deviant behavior and disposition. This rigorous essay represents one of the few attempts to bracket the question of authorship and to read the *Fiore* on its own literary terms, but while Took's approach vindicates to some extent the literary integrity of the *Fiore*, it also ends up minimizing the already minimal originality of the work by insisting upon its thematically derivative approximation of the *Rose*.

7. One of the felicitous features of the Italian version over the *Rose* is the grammatical feminization of *Bel Acueil* into *Bellaccoglienza*. This gives a certain psycho-erotic coherence to the relationship with *La Vecchia*.

8. The reference comes from Claudio Marchiori's edition, *Il Fiore* e *Il Detto d'Amore* (Genova: Tilgher, 1983), pp. 4–5. This edition is based on Parodi's first critical edition, but for each sonnet of the *Fiore* it offers the corresponding passages of the *Rose* as well as a meticulous commentary. It appeared a year before Contini's new critical edition, and this perhaps explains, but does not excuse, the prejudicial mean-spiritedness with which Contini dismissed this valuable edition in his bibliography as "the work of an incompetent beginner" ("Opera di un principiante sprovveduto," p. xxvi).

9. "Et lors me print une froideur / Dont j'ay dessoubz chault pelisson / Senti au cueur mainte frisson" (vv. 1708–10).

10. The *Fiore* lay buried in nonexistence for centuries. Its codex listing in the library of the Medical School at Montpellier was discovered in the late nineteenth century by the philologist D'Ancona. The first public announcement of the work's existence comes from Ernesto Monaci in 1878, in an article published in the *Giornale di filologia romanza* (1 [1878]: 238–43). Neither D'Ancona or Monaci had seen the codex—the only one to have survived apparently—but shortly after they had planned to publish the work, the task was taken over by Ferdinand Castets, professor at Montpellier and member of the Societé pour l'Étude des Langues Romanes, which sponsored the publication.

11. Il Fiore, *poème italien du XIIIe siècle, en CCXXXII sonnets, imité du Roman de la Rose, par Durante*, texte inédit publié avec facsimile: Introduction et Notes par Ferdinand Castets (Montpellier-Paris: Maisonneuve et cie, 1881), 133.

12. The translation is from *The Romance of the Rose*, trans. by Harry W. Robbins, ed. Charles W. Dunn (New York: E. P. Dutton, 1962), 86.

13. I cannot understand why meticulous critics and commentators have failed to highlight the dramatic deviation from the *Rose* at this point in the Italian text. John Took actually cites the sonnet along with the first six verses of the following sonnet only in order to focus on the appearance of the word "ninferno." "The reference to 'inferno' in XXXIV, 3 is significant," he writes, "not because it anticipates materially the future 'cantica' of that name . . . but because it looks forward conceptually to the more sustained analysis of spiritual disorder in the 'sacro poema'" (Took, 512). Perhaps it is something in the nature of the *Fiore* itself which causes readers to pass over in silence the singlemost important revelation of the poem's facticity.

14. The title *Il Fiore* was given to the sonnet sequence by Castets. In his preface he writes: "L'ouvrage n'a pas de titre; j'ai proposé celui de *Il Fiore*, parce que dans le texte il est toujours question d'une *fleur* et jamais d'une *rose*" (Castets, 5).

15. Dragonetti, "Specchi d'amore," pp. 19ff.

16. Gianfranco Contini, "La questione del Fiore," *Cultura e Scuola* 13–14 (1965): 769.

17. For an extended discussion of how the presence of Frenchisms trouble

the thesis about Dante's authorship of the poem, see Luigi Peirone, *Tra Dante e 'Il Fiore': Lingua e parola* (Genova: Tilgher, 1982), pp. 31–55.

18. The modern sonnet-form was invented by Giacomo da Lentini (ca. 1200–50), the imperial notary of Fredrick II in Sicily (hence his nickname "the Notary"). He is generally considered the most accomplished of the Sicilian poets.

Dieuwke E. van der Poel

12. A Romance of a Rose and Florentine: The Flemish Adaptation of the Romance of the Rose

The *Roman de la Rose* of Guillaume de Lorris and Jean de Meun has been a very popular and influential work. Critics have noted the exceptionally great number of complete and fragmentary manuscripts that have come down to us, their profound influence on French and English literature, and the adaptations that were made in various languages: English, Italian, Dutch. These adaptations have not yet received the attention they deserve in international research. If the adaptations are considered as mere derivatives of the French text, one neglects the wealth of information they can provide about the reception of the *Roman de la Rose*. The attitude of the translating or adapting poet toward the original can be deduced from a comparison between original and adaptation. What he transmitted faithfully reflects what he appreciated and considered important; what he changed and the way that he changed it reflect what he felt had to be adjusted, either because he thought he could improve the text, or because he felt the text had to be transformed to suit the tastes of his own audience.[1] The adaptation thus allows us to discern the poet's ideas about literature.

The above holds true for the two Middle Dutch adaptations of the *Roman de la Rose*. Both came into being at about the same time and the translators worked independently, though it is possible that one was acquainted with the work of the other. Both were made not long after the completion of the French text and can be regarded as contemporary reactions.[2] These Middle Dutch adaptations are all the more interesting because of the differences between them. One, a fairly faithful translation, is called *Die Rose*. Only the first name of the author is known: Heinric.[3] He executed his translation by approximately 1325, shortening the text consid-

I would like to thank Dr. Josephie Brefeld, who assisted in the translation of this article. It is obvious that all remaining faults are my own.

erably: it consists of only 14412 lines (as opposed to 21780 lines in Langlois's edition of the French text). Most of the abridgments occur in the part by Jean de Meun. For example, the discourses of Nature and Genius are omitted entirely,[4] as is the story of Pygmalion. Judging from the manuscript tradition, it is likely that this translation was rather widely known: the text survives in three complete manuscripts and in seven fragments, probably derived from five codices—a considerable number for a Middle Dutch text.

The other translation is preserved in nine extant fragments only, originating from two codices and forming a total of nearly 3000 lines. This text, dating from about 1290, was called the *Tweede Rose* (Second Rose) by its editor, but I prefer to use a more neutral designation: the Flemish *Rose*.[5] The author's name is not known. Some portions of the text he translated faithfully, others he rewrote. He was a poet of exceptional stature, and he had a comprehensive overview of the entire *Roman de la Rose*, as is evident from the fact that he sometimes changed the sequence of episodes without, however, disturbing the logical coherence of the narrative. The most sensational change this adapter made concerns the allegorical framework. A complete survey of these two adaptations is far beyond the scope of this chapter.[6] Here, I will concentrate on the Flemish *Rose*, and in particular on the modifications introduced in the allegorical structure of the poem.

Due to the fragmentary transmission of the text, the adaptation technique cannot be viewed in full: for most of the text, there is no way of telling how the adapter rendered the text in Middle Dutch.[7] Another complicating factor is that the adapter used a copy of the *Rose* related to Langlois's *B* family, a group that includes some considerably shortened versions of the text.[8] This means that in some cases it is not certain whether a given episode was omitted by the adapter or was already absent in the French text from which he worked. Nevertheless, it is possible to formulate a likely hypothesis about the adapter's treatment of those portions of the text now lost. The adapter of the Flemish *Rose* went about his work very systematically and deliberately. His interventions in the allegorical structure establish a certain pattern. On the basis of the transmitted fragments it seems likely that the allegory is changed only in those episodes that recount the Lover's adventures in the garden.

One of the most important changes is made right at the beginning of the text. In the Flemish *Rose*, the story has a totally new framework. The *Roman de la Rose* is introduced as the account of a dream the narrator had five years earlier. The very beginning of the Flemish adaptation has not survived; from codicological data it can be inferred that the loss of text probably amounts to 300 lines at the most. Because of this loss, it is not absolutely certain that the format of the dream was dropped; but this seems likely to me. The introductory section of the Flemish *Rose* must have been far more extensive than that of its French source, consisting probably of 518 lines. The content of the story is as follows. A first-person narrator recounts his experience in a beautiful spot in the forest, with singing birds and flowers: a *locus amoenus*. There he sees a loving couple come riding up from the distance. They are a harmonious pair, both bedecked with chaplets of red roses, wearing the same splendid red clothing and together singing a song that expresses the perfect reciprocity of their love: "Lief ic bem dijn ende du best mijn / Nu doe met mi al dijn geuoech" [Love, I am yours and you are mine, now do with me as you wish (Ab 1: 22–23)]. In his heart the narrator is jealous when he hears their song: how he wishes he could sing such a song with the lady he loves!

They exchange greetings. The narrator invites the lovers to join him for a short rest. He is struck by the resemblance in looks and manner between the lady he has just met and his own lady, who has refused him: "Checkmate!" she said. A conversation ensues and after a while names are asked. The narrator introduces himself as "Minre met groter Quale," which literally means "Lover with a serious illness." The young man is named Jolijs, his lady Florentine. The Middle Dutch adjective *jolijs* indicates several qualities that characterize a successful lover: "cheerful," "good-humored," "chivalrous," "liable to love," "of amorous nature."[9] The name of each man epitomizes his position in the story: one is completely happy in love, the other disappointed; one is accompanied by his mistress, the other longs for his own lady-love, who is not well disposed toward him and who resembles the first lady closely.

Jolijs also explains that he and Florentine come from the realm of Cupid and Venus, the mighty divinities of Love. He served Cupid for seven years and suffered considerably before receiving Florentine as a reward. He adds that he does not want to bewail his suffering: from now on he will forever be happy with his beloved. He expresses the wish that every faithful lover would be rewarded as he was, for no one could wish for anything better. The narrator wants to know more about it: if Jolijs has served Cupid for so long, he must know the nature of love. He asks Jolijs whether he is willing to tell his story, as he hopes to learn what love is and what its characteristics are, and how he must behave in order to become happy with his own beloved, whom he loves faithfully. Jolijs grants the request, having realized the extent of the narrator's lovesickness. He expresses the hope that his story will be beneficial, and begins his narrative: When he was twenty years old, he rose early one May morning and started walking until he arrived at a garden surrounded by a wall. Jolijs begins to describe the first of the ten personifications he saw depicted on the wall, namely Hatred. Here the first fragment of the Flemish *Rose* ends.

It is only when Jolijs begins to tell his story that there is an evident resemblance with the Old French *Roman de la Rose*. The account of the author's dream in the French *Rose* has become the story of Jolijs in the Flemish *Rose*; it is he, and not the narrator, who has all the adventures in the walled garden. Furthermore, the character of Florentine reappears in the story. In other manuscript fragments two important episodes of the love story of Jolijs and Florentine are transmitted.

The first of these episodes comes from the beginning of the story, where the "I" falls in love with the Rose.[10] In the Old French text, the protagonist saw rosebushes covered with roses reflected in the Fountain of Love, where Narcissus died. He drew near to the roses and singled out one particular bud, but was not able to approach it because of the hedge of thornbushes that surrounded it. Then Cupid shot five arrows through his eye and into his heart: the "I" became the Lover.

In the adaptation, this story is rendered rather faithfully. Here the protagonist also falls in love with the Rose as in the French source. The lady from the frame narrative, Florentine, is mentioned but does not yet play an important part. There is a connection between her and the Rose, but it is quite vague. The first time the rosebushes appear, the adapter adds that Florentine and her friends look after the roses.[11] The "I" would like to pick a rose but does not. In the French text this is because he is afraid that he might provoke the wrath of the lord of the garden (Déduit); in the Flemish *Rose*, it is because he is afraid to disturb Florentine and her friends.[12] The narrator also mentions that the lady is looking at the roses while standing behind the hedge and close to the Rose.[13] In this manner, he suggests that there is a certain relation between Florentine and the Rose. He is, however, primarily interested in the Rose and not the woman. The Rose is presented unmistakably as a flower, as in the source.

Another fragment transmits an equally important episode of the love story: the section of the *Roman de la Rose* that follows the discourse of la

Vieille.[14] The Lover entered the castle by a rear door and was finally able to meet with Bel Acueil, who made him welcome. Then the Lover spoiled it by stretching his hands toward the Rose. Dangier, Peor, and Honte ran out, pushed the hands of the Lover back, reproached him, and locked Bel Acueil up again.

This episode is reworked in the Flemish *Rose*: here, the Lover is welcomed by his lady, Florentine. Beginning with the initial exchange of greetings, the adapter added several details. In the original, Bel Acueil greeted the Lover and thanked him for the chaplet, received through the agency of la Vieille (vv. 14767–73). In the adaptation, Florentine and Scone Ontfange (the Middle Dutch Bel Acueil) greet the Lover together. The lady then takes him by the hand and leads him to her room, which is very beautiful. They sit down in front of her splendid bed and she thanks him for the chaplet (Bl 3: 59–76). In the *Roman de la Rose*, then, a friendly conversation between Bel Acueil and the Lover follows the greetings, while in the Flemish *Rose* the lady plays the part of Bel Acueil: she talks with her lover. The content of the conversation, however, is scarcely different.[15]

As the episode develops, the adapter introduces some interesting changes. When the Lover in the *Roman de la Rose* reached for the Rose, Dangier jumped up to grasp and abuse the Lover, assisted by Peor and Honte. In the adaptation, Florentine calls for the three guardians when the Lover takes her in his arms in order to seize the Rose. It is important to note that in this version the guardians go into action at her request: in this text, at any rate, they are apparently not enemies of the lady, but rather her helpers. In the French *Rose* the guardians explained to the Lover in great detail that he misunderstood Bel Acueil's kind words. This tirade occurs in the Flemish *Rose* as well, but a major part is delivered not by the guardians but by Florentine herself. The point where she begins to speak is not arbitrary: it is precisely where, in the source, the guardians begin to explain that the Lover misunderstood Bel Acueil.[16] It is only when Bel Acueil is mentioned that Florentine explains that she did not mean anything dishonorable. In this manner the Middle Dutch adapter achieves a dramatic effect, which is supported by the lively language. Finally Florentine bursts into tears. The Lover cannot stand this: he falls on his knees in front of her and asks forgiveness. This plea is for the most part composed independently of the French source, where the Lover tries to soften the guardians after they have locked up Bel Acueil.

In this episode the lady thus assumes a central position in the narrative action, replacing especially Bel Acueil. Scone Ontfange is not removed completely but now appears only in the initial greetings. To some extent Florentine takes over the role of the guardians as well. But the lady cannot do without them entirely: in her defense, the guardians seize the Lover violently, and of course a lady cannot act so aggressively herself.

There are indications that Florentine also played the part of Bel Acueil in other episodes of the Flemish *Rose* that have not come down to us. The episode discussed above contains several references to earlier parts of the story. From the way in which these references are reproduced in the translation, we may infer that Florentine played an important part elsewhere as well. In the *Roman de la Rose*, Bel Acueil thanks the Lover for the chaplet he sent (v. 14773), and the guardians refer to the appeal of la Vieille to allow the Lover into the tower (vv. 14887–88). Both statements refer to the same episode, known only from the French source: la Vieille, on behalf of the Lover, presented the chaplet to Bel Acueil and asked whether he was willing to receive its donor (vv. 12541–739). Then la Vieille delivered her lengthy discourse to Bel Acueil, who finally agreed to see the Lover. In the Flemish *Rose*, as we have seen, it is Florentine rather than Scone Ontfange who thanks the Lover for the chaplet (Bl 3: 73–76), and later on she refers to the fact that the Quene [la Vieille] asked her to grant the Lover a meeting. From such allusions it may be argued that the entire exchange between la Vieille and Bel Acueil is revised in the Flemish *Rose* to take place between the Quene and Florentine.[17] If this is true, then Florentine figures in a significant portion of the poem.

The above-mentioned conversation between the Lover and Florentine also reveals that there must have been at least one earlier encounter. This can be inferred from the motivation the narrator ascribes to the Lover's efforts to seize Florentine's Rose: he does so because he has the impression that she has changed her mind.[18] Furthermore, in the *Roman de la Rose*, the guardians claim that the Lover means to cause Bel Acueil harm: "E vous tendez a son domage" [and you are inclined to injure him (v. 14897)]. In the Flemish *Rose*, this is altered in a revealing manner: Florentine tells the Lover that he wants to do her harm *as he tried before* (Bl 3: 247–48). This and other allusions show that in the Flemish *Rose*, an earlier meeting of Florentine and the Lover took place, during which he also tried to seize her Rose.[19]

This episode of the Flemish *Rose* has not survived, but it is likely that it was the adaptation of vv. 2779–970 of the *Roman de la Rose*, where the Lover met Bel Acueil and was allowed through the hedge in order to smell the roses. On that occasion the Lover requested the Rose; Bel Acueil was shocked, and Dangier intervened. Probably Florentine replaced Bel Acueil in this episode. Chances are that the second encounter in the *Roman de la Rose* between the Lover and Bel Acueil (vv. 3325–60) was recast as an encounter with Florentine as well. In the French source, this encounter ended with the imprisonment of Bel Acueil; in the Flemish adaptation, Florentine and Scone Ontfange become locked up together.

Indeed, it is most likely that Florentine plays the part of Bel Acueil throughout the Flemish *Rose*. The rose metaphor is not affected by this transfer, while at the same time a strong attachment is suggested between Florentine and her Rose; I shall return to this point below. This interpretation of the differences between original and adaptation sheds light on the episode I discussed above, in which the protagonist falls in love with the Rose. Here the adapter adopted the rose symbol unaltered. Bel Acueil does not figure in this episode, and therefore the lady does not yet play an important part. The allusion to her presence near the roses behind the thorny hedge can be regarded as preparation for a later episode: the adaptation of *Roman de la Rose*, vv. 2779–970. In the Old French text, Bel Acueil led the Lover through the hedge; in the Flemish *Rose*, Florentine probably does this.

That Florentine should take over the role of Bel Acueil is not surprising. Scholars have noted that Bel Acueil coincides with the beloved lady in large parts of the *Roman de la Rose*. Langlois, for example, speaks of "Bel-Accueil personnifié en un jeune et beau 'vallet' [. . .], qui dispose de la rose convoitée et finit par être identifié avec la jeune fille aimée."[20] The Middle Dutch poet interpreted Bel Acueil in the same way and drew the obvious conclusion: he would make *la jeune fille* herself appear in the story.

As stated above, the rose metaphor is preserved: the Lover falls in love with the Rose, he wants to pick Florentine's Rose, and so on. The adapter evidently wants to exploit the rich and long-standing symbolism surrounding this flower: from an early time, the rose is associated with such qualities as virginity, beauty, love, and sexuality. In the *Roman de la Rose*, the entire range of meanings is present: in the part by Guillaume de Lorris, the Rose especially has connotations of love and of the virginity of the lady; with Jean de Meun, it increasingly becomes a sexual metaphor. In the *Roman de la Rose*, a game of veiling and unveiling is played, a game in which it is often not possible to identify exactly what the Rose stands for; precisely this enigma must have been one of the greatest attractions of the allegory. I would argue that the adapter wished to participate in this game revolving around the ambiguity of the Rose when he preserved the rose symbolism of his source. The symbol enabled him to portray the erotic side of the Lover's feelings for Florentine, without having to call a spade a spade. The need to speak in veiled terms about sexuality became all the greater now that the lady was explicitly present.

In short, the adapter of the Flemish *Rose* changed parts of the text radically, especially the narrative episodes in which the love story is recounted. However, the discourses of the allegorical characters were rendered more faithfully. Parts of the discourses of Amor, Ami, Richesse, and la Vieille have survived. These monologues were partly translated and partly adapted, and the Middle Dutch adapter did take many liberties with the source, but the changes were never as radical as in the narrative sections.

Why has the Flemish adapter changed the *Roman de la Rose* as he did? The alteration of the allegorical structure can be regarded as a reaction to the narrative method of the French text. The *Roman de la Rose* was an innovative text, the first major work in the vernacular in which an allegorical tale of love is recounted in the form of a dream-vision.[21] The new framework of the Flemish *Rose* was probably added in order to introduce the allegorical mode to the audience and to arouse curiosity about the instructive story that will follow. In the extended frame narrative, one first gets to know the sympathetic, unhappy "I." He says in passing that he is of Flemish origin: he is one with his audience. The happy couple Jolijs and Florentine is seen through his eyes. Everything serves to make the audience share his admiration for Jolijs, the supremely successful lover, and to regard Florentine as the ideal woman. Jolijs and Florentine are highly favorable characters: they are aristocratic, behave in a courtly manner, and are perfectly happy in love.[22] The narrator appeals to a public interest in love. In several instances, it is stressed that Jolijs can serve as a model for all lovers. Jolijs states that he has reached the very highest that lovers possibly can, and he expresses the hope that "alle die met trouwen minnen" [everyone who loves faithfully (Ab 1: 187)] will be similarly rewarded. *Minre met groter Quale* too remarks that Jolijs has endured what "Elken man die wille ghewinnen / Ere ende vrome van siere minnen" [every man who wants to derive benefit from his love (Ab 1: 197–98)] must endure. In this way the general validity of Jolijs's experiences is suggested: he can function as a model, not only for Minre, but for all lovers.

In this context the manner in which Minre asks Jolijs to tell the story of his love is significant. Minre says that he hopes to learn from the story:

Wat minne si ende hare maniren
Ende hoe jcse sal anthieren
Dat ick bliscap af gewinne
An hare die jc met trouwen minne.
(Ab 1: 203–6)

[What love is and what its characteristics are, and how I must act in order to obtain joy from her whom I love faithfully.]

I would suggest that these verses provide a subtle clue about how the story should be interpreted, or rather, how the allegorical form should be interpreted. From the story of these two ideal lovers not only can general lessons about love be deduced ("what love is"), but also a working knowledge can be inferred ("how I must act"). Before he begins his story, Jolijs says to Minre, and implicitly to the audience, "Nu vernemt mine tale / Jc hope het sal v wesen goet / Keerdi dar ane vwen moet" [now listen to my story; I hope it will do you good if you adhere to it (Ab 1: 214–16)]. It seems that the Middle Dutch poet took the *Roman de la Rose* as an instructive text from which general and practical lessons about love could be derived.

In the frame narrative of the Flemish *Rose*, the interest of the audience is thus aroused by the introduction of the ideal lovers Jolijs and Florentine, with whom one can identify with great admiration. The character of the lady then reappears in the text. In this way one remembers the idyllic situation from the opening sequence while hearing or reading the text, and one keeps on wondering how Jolijs will win Florentine, in spite of all adversity.

Not all parts of the *Roman de la Rose* were modified to this extent: as I have said, the adapter did not introduce such sweeping changes in the discourses of the allegorical characters. From this it can be inferred that in the eyes of the adapter, the monologues of the various personifications were the most important part of the Old French text. The major discourses offered a wealth of information, being full of examples and citations of authorities. It was the duty of the adapter to make the learning contained in these discourses accessible to a new audience. He thus refrained from significantly altering the authoritative substance of the monologues, feeling freer to introduce modifications in the narrative portions of the text. His free adaptation of the narrative serves to motivate the audience to take the didactic discourses to heart.

In sum, the poet of the Flemish *Rose* was an attentive and nearly contemporary reader of the *Roman de la Rose*. He saw the text as a story with a favorable protagonist, Jolijs. For his audience, a more lengthy introduction to the allegorical form was appropriate. And for this adapter, the most important parts of the poem were the discourses of the allegorical characters.

Notes

1. It is conceivable that the existence of no less than three Middle Dutch adaptations of the prose *Lancelot*—a faithful prose translation, a verse translation, and a verse adaptation—can be explained with reference to their respective audiences. These translations may have been written each for a different public: the prose translation for a public with more progressive tastes, the verse translations for publics with more conservative tastes. See Orlanda S. H. Lie, *The Middle Dutch Prose Lancelot: A Study of the Rotterdam Fragments and Their Place in the French, German, and Dutch "Lancelot en prose" Tradition, with an edition of the text* (Amsterdam/Oxford/New York: Noord-Hollandsche Uitgevers Maatschappij, 1987), pp. 175–78. A major part of Middle Dutch literature consists of adaptations of all kinds. Considerable research has been devoted to the technique of adaptation; see for example Willem P. Gerritsen, "Les Relations littéraires entre la France et les Pays-Bas au Moyen Âge: quelques observations sur la technique des traducteurs," in *Actes du septième congrès national de la Société Française de Littérature Comparée, Poitiers, 27–29 mai 1965* (Paris, 1967): 28–46; Gerritsen's "L'Episode de la guerre contre les Romains dans *La Mort Artu* néerlandaise," in *Mélanges de langue et de littérature du Moyen Âge et de la Renaissance offerts à Jean Frappier*, Publications Romanes et Françaises 112 (Geneva: Droz, 1970), vol. 1: 337–49; Hans van Dijk, "Les Chansons de geste en Moyen Néerlandais," in *Essor et fortune de la chanson de geste dans l'Europe et l'Orient latin. Actes du IXe Congrès International de la Société Rencesvals pour l'Étude des Épopées Romanes* (Modena: Mucchi, 1984), vol. 1: 369–74.

2. This is not exceptional: from about 1260 onward many important works were translated quite soon after they appeared, such as the *Vita Lutgardis* of Thomas of Cantimpré, the *Chastelaine de Vergi*, and the *Voeux du paon* of Jacques de Longuyon. See Frits P. van Oostrom, "Hoe snel dichtten middeleeuwse dichters? Over de dynamiek van het literaire leven in de middeleeuwen," *Literatuur* 1 (1984): 327–35.

3. This Heinric has sometimes been identified as Heinric van Aken, to whom an adaptation of the fabliau *L'Ordene de chevalerie*, entitled *Van den coninc Saladijn ende van Hughen van Tabaryen*, is also attributed. The current edition of

the *Rose* translation is Heinric van Aken, *Die Rose*, ed. Eelco Verwijs (The Hague 's-Gravenhage: Nijhoff, 1868; rpt. Utrecht: Hes, 1976).

4. The translation omits vv. 15891–20682. Only vv. 16323–706, a digression about women's lack of discretion, are retained.

5. *De fragmenten van de tweede Rose (avec un résumé en français)*, ed. Klaas Heeroma (Zwolle: W. E. J. Tjeenk Willink, 1958).

6. I give a more detailed account of the techniques of translation and adaptation employed by the two poets in my *De Vlaamse* Rose *en* Die Rose *van Heinric: Onderzoekingen over twee Middelnederlandse bewerkingen van de* Roman de la Rose *(avec un résumé en français)* (Hilversum: Verloren, 1989).

7. The fragments of the Flemish *Rose* correspond with these parts of the Old French text:

Flemish Rose	Roman de la Rose *(ed. Langlois)*
fragment Ab 1	vv. 45–141
fragment Ab 2	vv. 1439–1734
fragment Bj	vv. 2492–2628
fragment Bu 1	vv. 4843–4960
fragment Bu 2	vv. 7525–7608
fragment Al, vv. 1–162	vv. 16589–700
fragment Al, vv. 163–1200	vv. 9421–10740
fragment Bl 2	vv. 13869–14226
fragment Bl 3	vv. 14697–970

In addition, there is a fragment Bl 1 (160 lines) in which a character shows someone else how to declare his love for a lady. There is no analogue for this in the Old French text, but for several reasons (content, style, and codicological data) it is not unlikely that fragment Bl 1 is a part of the Flemish *Rose*, in particular a section of the discourse of Cupid. If so, it would have been added by the adapter.

8. In the study of adaptation technique it is of course necessary to use a version of the Old French text that is as close as possible to the version that the translator used. Therefore, studies of the manuscript traditions of French texts are essential for the investigation of adaptation techniques. Fortunately, we know quite a bit about the manuscript tradition of the *Roman de la Rose*, thanks to the work of Ernest Langlois, *Les Manuscrits du* Roman de la Rose: *Description et classement* (Lille: Tallandier/Paris: Champion, 1910). I cite the *Rose* in the edition by Langlois, Guillaume de Lorris and Jean de Meun, *Le Roman de la Rose*, Société des Anciens Textes Français, 5 vols. (Paris: Firmin-Didot/Champion, 1914–24). Langlois's critical apparatus provides considerable information about the *Rose* manuscript tradition.

9. E. Verwijs and J. Verdam, *Middelnederlandsch Woordenboek* (The Hague 's-Gravenhage: M. Nijhoff, 1885–1952), give the following meanings for the word 'jolijs': *vroolijk, opgewekt, aangenaam gestemd, galant, vatbaar voor liefde, van eene verliefde natuur* (vol. 3, 1057).

10. *Roman de la Rose* vv. 1439–1734 correspond to Flemish *Rose* fragment Ab 2.

11. Ab 2: 195–205, an adaptation of *Roman de la Rose*, vv. 1615–18.

12. *Roman de la Rose* vv. 1634–36 correspond to Flemish *Rose* Ab 2: 226–30. As a result of the fragmentary transmission, it is impossible to determine Déduit's role in the overall narrative.

13. Flemish *Rose* Ab 2: 232–38 are a translation and amplification of *Roman de la Rose* vv. 1673–74.

14. *Roman de la Rose* vv. 14697–790 correspond to Flemish *Rose* Bl 3.

15. *Roman de la Rose* vv. 14774–807 correspond to Flemish *Rose* Bl 3: 77–128.

16. *Roman de la Rose* v. 14848 becomes Flemish *Rose* Bl 3: 179.

17. One could argue that la Vieille's bawdy discourse could hardly have been meant for the courtly Florentine. From Bel Acueil's reaction in the *Roman de la Rose*, however, it appears that he really did not want to learn from what la Vieille told him (see vv. 14604–62); and, earlier, the narrator asserts that Bel Acueil did not intend to put her teachings into practice (vv. 12987–13000). It would have fitted her character if Florentine had reacted in this way.

18. Bl 3: 137–39 translate *Roman de la Rose* vv. 14815–16 in a variant reading from the *B* manuscripts: "Que ce fust fait legierement, / Mais il m'avint tout autrement" [that that was done lightly, but it happened to me quite otherwise].

19. Other allusions are Bl 3: 149–50 (*Roman de la Rose*, v. 14829); Bl 3: 230–32 (*Roman de la Rose*, vv. 14883–85); Bl 3: 284–85 (*Roman de la Rose*, v. 14923).

20. Langlois, ed., *Roman de la Rose*, vol. 5, p. 333. See also, among others, Daniel Poirion, *Le "Roman de la Rose"* (Paris: Hatier, 1973), p. 59.

21. See Marc-René Jung, *Etudes sur le poème allégorique en France au Moyen Âge*, Romanica Helvetica, 82 (Bern: Francke, 1971).

22. According to John Fleming, the Lover in the *Rose* is ironically portrayed as a typical *fol amoureux*; see his *The* Roman de la Rose*: A Study in Allegory and Iconography* (Princeton, NJ: Princeton University Press, 1969). However, the adapter of the Flemish *Rose* presents Jolijs as a role model and clearly did not disapprove of the behavior of the Lover in the garden. See Dieuwke van der Poel, "The *Romance of the Rose* and I: Narrative Perspective in the *Roman de la Rose* and Its Two Middle Dutch Adaptations," in Keith Busby and Erik Kooper, eds., *Courtly Literature: Culture and Context. Selected Papers from the Fifth Triennial Congress of the International Courtly Literature Society, Dalfsen, The Netherlands, 9–16 Aug. 1986.* Utrecht Publications in General and Comparative Literature 25 (Amsterdam/Philadelphia: John Benjamins, 1990), pp. 573–83.

Lee Patterson

13. Feminine Rhetoric and the Politics of Subjectivity: La Vieille and the Wife of Bath

If the Middle Ages is a culture of the book, then for vernacular writers its central text is the *Roman de la Rose*: to trace the *Roman*'s influence is virtually to write the history of late-medieval poetry. And of no writer is this more true than Geoffrey Chaucer. When about 1385 Eustache Deschamps praised Chaucer as a "grant translateur," he was referring, we may surmise, to more than the Chaucerian authorship of an English *Romaunt of the Rose* (although whether the one that survives is Chaucer's is less certain).[1] For in saying that it was Chaucer who first "planted the rosebush" of the *Roman* in England, Deschamps reminds us that the entire corpus of Chaucer's writing is saturated with allusions to the *Roman*; indeed, in a 1914 dissertation Dean Fansler listed more than seven hundred separate passages that witness to its influence, passages included in texts as unlikely as the *Boece* and the *Parson's Tale*.[2] Of course, the influence of the *Roman* on Chaucer's kind of poetry cannot be understood quantitatively, and it was not until 1957, with Charles Muscatine's still indispensable *Chaucer and the French Tradition*, that the meaning of Chaucer's indebtedness began to be understood.[3] For Muscatine, the *Roman*'s bequest to Chaucer was twofold: it set what he defined as the two main traditions of French writing, the courtly/idealist and bourgeois/realist, into clear and cogent relation, and it achieved, especially in the figures of Ami and la Vieille, a monologue form that allowed for the dramatic representation of a complex inwardness.[4]

Certainly it is true that Chaucerian poetics depends heavily upon juxtapositioning, most visibly in the *quiting* game of the *Canterbury Tales* but

This essay was originally published in *Speculum* 58 (1983): 656–95, and reprinted in revised form as chapter 6 of *Chaucer and the Subject of History* (Madison: University of Wisconsin Press, 1991), 280–321. It appears here after some further revision.

also in other, less dramatic works, where various registers—and especially the courtly and the noncourtly—are played off against each other. So too, Chaucer consistently grounds discourse in a speaking subject that becomes itself the object of poetic attention. In this general sense, Chaucer's poetry can be aptly described—to reinvoke Deschamps's metaphor—as a transplant from the *Roman*. Following Muscatine, I wish to argue here that the binary oppositions of the *Roman* provided Chaucer with a rhetorical structure, a *disposition*, that organizes both the *Wife of Bath's Prologue and Tale* and much of the *Canterbury Tales* as a whole; and to argue further that the *Roman* provided Chaucer with a precedent for his privileging of the subject at a crucial moment in the development of the *Tales*. But I will also develop Muscatine's fundamental perceptions in terms of gender issues that were not part of the critical repertoire of the 1950s. Neither discursive structures nor subjectivity itself is, we now understand, a socially neutral phenomenon: both are constructed, and constructed in thoroughly gendered ways. Specifically, it is the sexualized femininity with which these male poets invested their poetic constructions that is the focus of my attention, especially since this strategy entails an analogous definition of the poet as himself endowed with an oddly labile gender identity.

*   *   *

One of the more notorious of Alison of Bath's wanderings by the way is her digression into the realm of classical scholarship. In the midst of an Arthurian romance she interposes an Ovidian epyllion, a version of the tale of Midas and his ass's ears. Her stated purpose is to show that "we wommen konne no thyng hele" or hide (v. 950), but despite this laudable attempt at self-criticism her telling is both inaccurate and incomplete.[5] The male servant of the original becomes Midas's wife, and the crucial conclusion, in which the reeds whisper Midas's secret abroad, is suppressed. No wonder, then, that modern commentators have seen the Wife's Ovidianism as evidence of her irrepressible loquacity, her bad scholarship, even her moral turpitude.[6] But the very unanimity of these conclusions tempts a counterthought: does not the Wife here, as elsewhere, mean more than she says?

When Ovid's *famulus* revealed his lord's shameful secret he did so, paradoxically, by hiding it. He dug a hole and buried his *parva vox*, his whisper; his words were literally covered over (*obruta verba*).[7] In Alison's version the hiddenness of the wife's disclosure is imaged differently:

> And sith she dorste telle it to no man,
> Doun to a mareys faste by she ran—
> Til she cam there hir herte was a-fyre—
> And as a bitore bombleth in the myre,
> She leyde hir mouth unto the water doun.
>   (vv. 969−73)[8]

Kneeling by the edge of the swamp and bumbling her message into the mire, Midas's wife provides an image of feminine speaking that suggests both obscurity and uncleanness. The metaphor governs, disturbingly, what we are also told, that the very ardor that impels her to speak is peculiarly feminine: the "conseil" swells within her as if she were with child; her heart is on fire as if she were in love. Her sense of relief is similarly physical: "Now is myn herte al hool, now is it oute" (v. 977). Her speaking, in short, is coextensive with her nature as a woman and apparently as compulsive and untrustworthy as her sexuality. The obscurity of her speech is thus a function of the passion that urges her; its indecency a function of the carnality that characterizes her as a woman.

But the habits—or compulsions—of the Wife's almost entirely male audience may be equally suspect.[9] As she is at pains to point out, the climax of Ovid's story is, in her version, not denied but strategically deferred: "The remenant of the tale if ye wol heere, / Redeth Ovyde, and ther ye may it leere" (vv. 981−82). This withholding ought to encourage her audience to remember Ovid's version, and to recall that the tattletale there is not a woman at all but the trusted, male servant; that the secret of Midas's ears is no secret at all—the wind in the reeds has wafted abroad the telltale sound *aures aselli*; and, most important, that the ears have a crucial significance. They are Midas's punishment for his foolish incapacity as a listener: called upon to judge between Pan's satyr songs and Apollo's divine hymns, he all too eagerly chose the carnal before the spiritual, the body before the mind. In discovering the full dimensions of Ovid's original, the reader comes to understand the Wife's strategy. The deferred conclusion explains both the misogynist surface with which she has covered over a tale of male deficiency and the need for the covering in the first place. For her telling argues that men, their listening obstructed by the carnality symbolized by their ass's ears, will naturally prefer the immediate self-gratifications of antifeminism to the severer pleasures of self-knowledge. The initial image of feminine speaking appears now to have been only an enticement, the deferral a test of the reader's patience: if men are really committed to a disinterested quest for truth they will avoid a surface misogyny in favor of the wisdom offered by the full story. Masculine listening can be as compelled as feminine speaking, a conclusion that rebounds with fine appropriateness upon the current critical responses to the Wife's digression. But can a man learn the lesson of his ass's ears when he has ass's ears? The Wife of Bath's text, here and elsewhere, solicits both body and mind, and it requires for its explication both an erotics and a hermeneutic. Who is equal to its demands? "Yblessed be God that I have wedded fyve! / Welcome the sixte, whan that evere he shal" (vv. 44–45).

The tale of Midas is a digression that exemplifies the characteristic method of the Wife's rhetoric. Most commentaries on the *Prologue and Tale* assume that the Wife has no rhetorical strategy at all: her garrulous ramblings are taken as a process of continual, unmotivated self-disclosure: she speaks, apparently, only that we may know her.[10] To demonstrate that this is not the case, I wish to analyze not only the *Prologue and Tale* themselves but a number of other texts, most available to Chaucer, in which the special status of feminine rhetoric had already been explored. The larger purpose is to show that Chaucer, conceiving of the Wife's performance as an act of deliberate self-fashioning, sought to establish the construction of subjectivity—the representation of character—as itself a topic worthy of serious literary practice. It is in this sense that the Wife's performance provided Chaucer with an opportunity to represent and defend his own poetic activity.

The language of poetry, as enacted by the poet and received by the reader, was often conceived in the Middle Ages in sexual, and specifically in feminine, terms. The voice of the poet is inescapably aligned with that of women: his rhetoric is, to an important degree, always feminine. Jean de Meun, for instance, draws a continuous parallel between the lover's "art d'amors" and the poet's art of writing about love: "whoever writes about the thing—if he doesn't wish to turn aside from the truth—ought to make the words resemble the deeds; for sounds, neighbors to their things, ought to be cousins to the facts."[11] Cousins to their deeds, Jean's words enact the reality they represent, a glossing that is at once explanatory and obfuscating, pedagogic and seductive. Similarly, when the Wife of Bath interrupts the Parson, she substitutes in no uncertain terms her carnal enticements for his moralistic preaching. "Nay, by my fader soule," she says,

> schal he nat preche;
> He schal no gospel glosen here ne teche.
> · · · · · · · · · · · · · · · · · · ·
> My joly body schal a tale telle.
> (vv. 1178–85)

The Wife's analogy between her "joly body" and the corpus of her text invokes a powerful medieval connection between sexuality and reading. The locus classicus for this connection is Augustine's misreading of the *Aeneid*, when he was seduced into weeping for the death of Dido while remaining unmoved by the dying of his own soul. This monitory scene recurs throughout the later Middle Ages: Paolo and Francesca (and Dante) relive it, Boccaccio anxiously argues against it, Chaucer, in the *House of Fame* and in the *Troilus*, reenacts it.[12] For each of these writers, the relationship between the lovers *in* the text becomes a warning figure for the relationship that might develop between the reader *and* the text. What Dido did to Aeneas the *Aeneid* did to Augustine: how can the reader protect himself against the "joly body" of the text?[13]

✳   ✳   ✳

Antifeminist literature presents woman as an inveterate and interminable talker, wagging her tongue like the clapper on a bell. And for much of this literature, a woman's voice is not merely part of her weaponry but the very mode of her existence, the substance from which she is constituted as well as the means by which she is made manifest. This poetry is a mimesis not of character but of language, a domestic counterpart to those texts, such as Rutebeuf's *Dit de l'herberie*, that record the patter of the street vendor.[14] A good example of a poem in which feminine speaking is virtually aligned with the poetic function is the *Liber lamentationum Matheoluli*.[15] Written at the end of the thirteenth century in Latin, this brilliant and vitriolic poem was translated into French in the 1370s by Jean Lefèvre, and it is doubtless this version that Chaucer knew.[16] While Matheolus includes explicit attacks on the potent feminine voice, his most telling strategy is to travesty the feminine idiom directly, and his poem includes large chunks of wifely nagging. But it shortly becomes ironically clear that the verbal energy that motivates his poem derives from just this feminine copiousness. Once having entered the poem, his wife's voice comes to possess it and even subverts the poet's attempts to regain control: in complaining about her endless nagging Matheolus repeats himself verbatim and at length, just like a woman.[17]

In one of his additions to Matheolus's text, Jean Lefèvre furnishes a suggestive image of the feminine idiom that makes explicit several of the anxieties behind the misogynist tradition as a whole. He tells the story of Carfania, a Roman matron who displayed her verbal mastery by arguing cases before the courts. But at the moment of crisis, Carfania would reveal her true nature: "Carfania bent way over—she was a greater jangler than a magpie, for she didn't plead wisely—she showed her ass in court" (2.183–86).[18] Women try to hide behind masculine respectability but their carnality will out. A woman will say anything, the more embarrassing the better. Hence her wicked delight in ferreting out masculine secrets that she may publish abroad—a theme that is compulsively repeated throughout misogynist literature.[19] This fear of woman's shamelessness is at the domestic heart of medieval misogyny, a central source of the power that invests a speaker like the Wife of Bath. As she promises, "My joly body schal a tale telle." This is a verbal licentiousness that is at once frightening and exciting. When Carfania shows her *cul* in court she is mocking her male judges with both her carnality and theirs, simultaneously ridiculing their judicial solemnity and arousing their secret desires. For the male audience, feminine speaking is never wholly divested of the titillating ambivalences of eroticism. Christine de Pizan, who doubtless knew better than most, speaks (apparently apocryphally) of the learned daughter of an Italian professor whose beauty forced her to lecture with a veil before her face.[20]

The double bind of antipathy and allure precipitated by feminine speech is wound more tightly when the woman happens to be old. The old woman has a double existence in medieval literature, as the randy widow searching for a new husband or as the practiced *entremetteuse* presiding over someone else's affair. The randy widow is virtually always a figure of mockery, but she is mocked less in fun than in outrage and even horror. The male fear of vidual sexuality appears throughout misogynist literature and is so profound a part of medieval life that it has left a mark even on the fugitive record of social history. The half-mocking, half-menacing village cavalcade known in France as the charivari and in England as the "skimmington" or "rough music" was one of the central ways by which the medieval community could bring its norms to bear upon the domestic life of the individual. Typical targets for these processions were child-beaters, adulterers, domineering wives, and widowers and—especially—widows who remarried. Of all the offenders, domineering wives and widows who remarried a much younger man were by far the most common target of community disapproval.[21]

A taboo witnesses to a potency that is desired as well as feared, and the randy widow has her attractions. Matheolus suggests what these are in a passage that begins to move us from the widow to the *entremetteuse*. He offers us a commentary on Genesis 18, the account of Sarah's response to the news that she will bear Abraham a son:

> Sarah was old and toothless, and didn't seem lively enough for a coupling. But quickly enough she could make herself supple ("Mais asses tost se rendi souple"); when she knew that she was going to have a child the spear of pleasure pierced her. The old woman laughed when she thought that someone would make *la bonne chose* with her. It's an old woman's custom, when age overtakes her, she knows how to induct young folk and introduce them to the *jeu d'amour*. By her sayings and her words ("Par ses dis et par sa parole") she makes them dance to her tune.[22]

There are two kinds of teaching here, by the notorious feminine tongue ("Par ses dis et par sa parole") and by the old woman's well-practiced body ("Mais asses tost se rendi souple"). She is truly a go-between: a way of at once preparing for and getting to the young girl who is every young man's fancy. As the passage to female sexuality she is endowed with both its terrors and its delights. Too old to be a permanent mate, she can be enjoyed with the abandon accorded the merely temporary lover; but her age also renders her a monitory prefiguration of the fate that awaits all lovers, a *memento temporis*. She is both beginning and end, and encloses the young man both temporally and psychologically. She ushers her son/lover into manhood, but her very support demonstrates his childish dependence.

These dark matters can also be illuminated by reference to the folk rituals embodied in the wooing play. In its fullest form the wooing play enacts the process of courtship for both youth and maiden, and the crucial action for both is the rejection of an unseemly mate. But while the maiden's rejected alternative is simply an old man, the youth is challenged by an old woman who carries a baby. She is both mother and sexual partner, and witnesses both to his past (as her son and perhaps lover) and to his future (as the young woman's husband and father to her family). While in the action of the play the maiden simply rejects the old man, the youth is more violent: he beats and sometimes even kills the old woman, suppressing the past that has made him capable of grasping the future. These anthropological concerns are perhaps not as remote from the Wife of Bath's discourse as might at first appear: in both *Prologue* and *Tale* age gives way to youth, and her rhetoric also invokes a festive and nuptial context.[23]

Alison of Bath also combines the roles of widow and go-between: she is an *entremetteuse* who prepares the way to herself. The most important of Chaucer's literary precedents for this conflation of roles is the pseudo-Ovidian *De vetula*, composed in the mid-thirteenth century, probably by Richard of Fournival, and translated in the 1370s as *La Vieille* by Jean Lefèvre.[24] The story of *La Vieille* can help us to understand how the ambivalences embodied in the old woman can be explicated into narrative, and it provides as well an important example of the eroticism of feminine discourse. The poem is a vast elaboration on the story of Dipsas in *Amores* 1, 8; it recounts "Ovid's" humiliation at the hands of an *anus* or *vetula* and his conversion from love to philosophy and finally to a saving adoration of none other than the Virgin Mary. Having fallen in love with a young girl, the middle-aged poet hires la Vieille as "une moienneresse" (2.2831) to smooth his way, with disastrous results. Teased by her long-winded descriptions of the lady's beauty into a frenzy of anticipation, the lustful poet makes furious love to the woman awaiting him in the assigned bed, only to discover that he has lavished his attentions on the old woman herself. This sudden transformation of the virgin he was expecting into the "vielle chauve ridée" he has found is all too ironically apt, introducing into Ovid's own life the metamorphic principle he had previously recognized only in its effects on others:

> Those mutations that I have told about—which are written in my large book—there is no mutation like to that which came to me, miraculously, when in so short a time it happened that she was old, ugly, and gray.[25]

Here metamorphosis is nothing more nor less than aging, a process that applies to Ovid more immediately than he is at this point prepared to acknowledge. Consequently, he closes this episode with a vengeful description of la Vieille's withered body and with a truly horrible, excremental curse.

But the story is not over yet, and sixteen years later the lesson he had earlier evaded now confronts him. With the help of a chambermaid, Ovid succeeds in seducing his long-sought-for beloved, and although she is now a wife and mother he discovers that her body is still all he could desire. But her character holds unsuspected and disquieting depths. For he learns that the trick played upon him sixteen years earlier had originated not with la Vieille but with the young girl herself: she had been trying to teach him, he now realizes, the bitter lesson that middle age should turn not back to its youthful past but forward to its inevitable if dismaying future. That this is a precept that she has herself now learned is shown by her own middle-aged choice of the elderly Ovid as a lover. The sixteen-year delay that his beloved has forced upon him has brought him not merely to age, then, but to the consciousness of age; and la Vieille, in having led him to herself, is now revealed to have been a "moienneresse" not to beauty but, inevitably if slowly, to wisdom. The human being he confronted when the sun rose on his bed of shame those many years ago was an image of his own future: an aged but unabated sexuality veiled by garrulity and nostalgia. That he did not recognize her wisdom until it was proffered to him by a desirable woman is of course a comment on Ovid's own, masculine limitations. For, as the Wife of Bath's tale of Midas points out, men do not easily learn distasteful lessons about themselves, and as her *Tale* demonstrates, they often have to be taught twice.

Jean Lefèvre's *La Vieille* thus provides suggestive precedents for the *Wife of Bath's Prologue and Tale*, if we think primarily in terms of narrative and theme: the dialectic of youth and age; the quest for beauty that discovers wisdom; sexuality as the bait with which women lure men toward self-knowledge; the old woman as a surrogate or veil for the maiden; the harsh lesson that is learned only when repeated in a milder form. But while part of my purpose in discussing the *Prologue and Tale* will be to show how Chaucer disposes these elements into his own configuration, my immediate interest remains the rhetoric of the Wife's discourse. From this narrower perspective, the most relevant of *La Vieille*'s strategies is its exploitation of the erotic possibilities of the old woman's garrulity. The ambivalent sexuality that invests the old woman is here expressed in *La Vieille*'s interlacing of delectable accounts of the young girl's body with self-pitying laments for her own age and poverty. Titillation and tedium alternate in her discourse, successfully arousing Ovid to a state of all too blind lust. Admittedly, however, this rhetorical strategy is elementary. The verbal sporting by which Chaucer creates the Wife of Bath is far more sophisticated, and we must look elsewhere, to the *Roman de la Rose*, for his precedent.

*   *   *

Guillaume de Lorris abandoned the *Roman de la Rose* when it became apparent that the outcome of the Lover's quest was dependent not upon his invention but upon the lady's generosity. Far from achieving the visionary authority to which he laid claim at the outset, Guillaume retreated to a graceful submission to the inevitability of history. Indeed, the literary embarrassment of an unfinished poem became in the context of extra-literary courtship a virtue: by not presuming to project the end of his story he demonstrates a *politesse* that marks him as worthy of his lady's favors. In part the impasse to which Guillaume brings the poem is a function of his reliance upon the formal strategy of personification allegory, and to understand fully how la Vieille's discourse offers a solution requires us to explore this point in some detail. It is a point important as well to our understanding of the Wife of Bath and her role in the *Canterbury Tales*. Both the *Canterbury Tales* and the *Roman de la Rose* begin with incomplete fragments and both engage in progressively more intricate processes of self-reflection. That la Vieille plays a crucial role in these processes is what I now hope to demonstrate and so to suggest why the old woman should reappear when Chaucer's poem reaches its own revisionary moment.

The personification allegory adopted by Guillaume inevitably promises the clarified understanding of vision. Within the enclosure of the garden, so says the form of the discourse, the origin and essence of love can be known and possessed: "l'art d'Amors est tote enclose" (v. 38). The poem's dreamtime is the "tens enmoreus" (v. 48) of an apparently perpetual youthfulness: Vieillesse is kept outside the walls, and the time of which she is at once mistress and victim is exorcised with a curse (vv. 361–92). The gate is opened by a Oiseuse who "mout avoit bon tens et bon mai" (v. 569), for the garden world has time to grow up but no time to grow old, the special if all too temporary immortality of the young. That the garden is also a *prison amoreuse* is the burden of the Narcissus episode. The will to possession, whether by plucking the beloved or by codifying love, derives from egoistic overreaching and issues in a bemused admiration for one's own creation. The crystals in the fountain reproduce the garden with precisely the unmediated clarity and completeness to which the poem itself aspires:

> Just as a mirror shows the things which are set over against it and one sees there without covering both their color and their shape, in the same way I tell you truthfully that the crystal without deception reveals the whole of the garden to him who gazes in the water.... There is no little thing, be it however hidden or shut, of which a demonstration is not made there, just as if it were portrayed in crystal.[26]

In the depths of the Fontaine d'Amour glimmers the lure of poetic inclusiveness, allegory's enticing promise to strip off the veil of the accidental to allow us to see the essence of things *facie ad faciem*. Many others have written of this fountain, says Guillaume, "But never will you hear the truth of the matter described better after I have set forth the mystery."[27] But the truth, as Narcissus has already discovered, is that the revealed essences are mere shadows (vv. 1484, 1492), that our vision remains always *per speculum in aenigmate*. In the autobiographical passage that shortly follows the description of the fountain, the whole of Guillaume's poem is revealed as a shadow, belatedly dependent upon a history that has not yet fully taken place. It is written as an offering to the very Rose that it represents, hoping by its representation or shadowing to earn a happy ending (vv. 3481–92). At the outset Guillaume told us that he believed "that a dream is significant of the good and the harm of people, that most people dream many things in a hidden way that they later see openly."[28] It now appears that this revelation will be accomplished not by allegory but by history, by the time that was so conclusively excluded from the garden in the frozen image of Vieillesse.

The entry of time into a poem posited upon its exclusion is a reversal radical enough to account for Guillaume's abrupt if apt withdrawal: his Lover reaches an impasse that can be resolved only by the extrinsic decision of the lady. Jean de Meun, however, has higher ambitions, aspiring to bring both poem and amorous quest to simultaneous climax. He wants not to set his poem against or above history but to make temporality itself a key structural component. Love is not a timeless object, codified in a set of rules and enclosed within a *hortus conclusus*, but a process that must be enacted within the multivalent context of experience itself. But to introduce time into the poem—so sedulously excluded by Guillaume—is to introduce old age, with its penitential retrospections, and history, with its promised apocalyptic finale. It is, in short, to introduce into the poem larger perspectives that will inevitably call into question the amorous quest itself.

Jean's romance is built on the structural irony of a knight errant whose success depends upon not listening to the guides who direct him. These guides offer him commentaries on human experience that take a longer and larger view than his single-minded concentration on the rose—what Jean calls his "enterins corages" (v. 10361)—will permit him to encompass. Each presents him with an image of his future that, were he to take it seriously, would dissuade him from his present course. Raison praises the wisdom of a Vieillesse who regards with scorn and remorse the follies of youth, and so offers the Lover a prospect from which his sought-for end is revealed to be only a squalid means. Amis returns the poem to its narrower amorous concerns but provides two equally distasteful portraits of the future that awaits the experienced Lover: either his own corrosive cynicism or the obsessions of the *mari jaloux*. The next pair of speakers repeats this pattern of expansion and contraction. Where Raison broadened the poem's perspective by invoking the Platonism of Boethius and Cicero, Faus Semblant turns to the chiliasm of William of St.-Amour. He introduces not merely the mendicant controversy, in other words, but the mendicant controversy as seen in an apocalyptic perspective. He opens the poem not merely to its historical context but to history as seen from the prospect of eternity, dwarfing the Lover's petty concerns by comparison.

Then, like Amis, la Vieille returns the poem to the erotic life. But she does so in terms that are by no means as wholly negative as his. True to her lineage and function, she plays a role in the drama of the Lover's quest that is genuinely ambivalent. She is an *entremetteuse* whose cynical teachings seem to make love impossible; a celebrant of carnality who witnesses to the devastations of a lifetime of love; a remorseful penitent reinvigorated by the memory of her sins; a guardian of the lady's virtue who betrays her charge. But her primary function, and the source of her ultimate affirmation, is to introduce the ambivalences of *temporality* into the poem in a fully human form. The temporality to which she witnesses is time as experienced and experience as time—the experience, in fact, of a lifetime. That she has a biography at all, rather than just a set of typifying habits, marks her off from the other interlocutors. But that she can dispose it before us as *autobiography* shows how fully self-possessed she is. The very existence of this self requires and justifies the imperfections of temporality. As for the Lover, her autobiography supports his passion and subjects it to ironies of which he is, quite appropriately, unaware. When young she loved as he loves, now old she has fallen into bitter regret. Youth and age, beauty and wisdom, means and end are enacted in the same personality. In sum, the antagonistic elements of the Lover's world are at once joined and held apart by being disposed upon a temporal continuum and located within a single self.

La Vieille's autobiography is not, however, offered to us in linear sequence, with a beginning, middle, and end. Her discourse includes seven distinguishable themes, and these are presented as a series of interlocking subordinations. La Vieille's personal history begins and ends her discourse, providing a frame that contains and ameliorates her cynical Ovidian pedagogy. And this is true, in turn, of each of the succeeding six themes. The result is an overall structure of interlocking boxes, an *emboîtement*, as a diagram makes clear: [29]

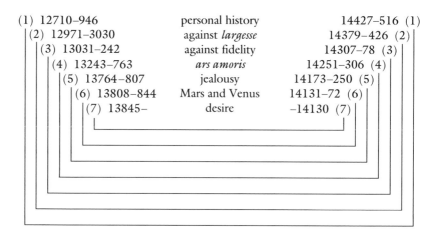

As well as its subordinating function, this *emboîtement* structure has a figurative intention. It imitates the poem's climactic action, the gradual exfoliation of the rose that the final lines of the poem so graphically and embarrassingly describe. La Vieille's verbal dilation upon her themes, in other words, is organized so as to match the rose's floral dilation. This means that her discourse is erotic in perhaps the most immediate way possible. In deferring the poem's longed-for conclusion, la Vieille's discourse stands as a barrier that tests the Lover's patience and perseverance. And yet by being figured in the shape of the goal he seeks, her discourse lures him on; it reminds him of his rose at the very moment that it defers the rose. The structure of dilation translates the ambivalence of the old woman into the rhetoric of romance: it is the form of courtship. Jean's achievement, then, is not merely to exploit the meanings contained in the rhetorical term *dilatio*, a process that Chaucer will carry even further in the Wife of Bath's discourse. In a larger sense he manages to translate the central Ovidian principle of amorous delay into stylistic terms and to show with impressive specificity how rhetorical structure can bear erotic value.[30]

The way in which la Vieille's discourse provides Jean with a *formal* solution to Guillaume's impasse may best be grasped by comparing her to the figures who precede and follow. Faus Semblant is the truthful hypocrite, motivated by an "entencion double" that Jean attempts to present by a simple but unsuccessful version of interlace. Sincere self-denunciations are interleaved with outrageous braggings, an almost mechanical alternation that repeats itself throughout the discourse.[31] These crude juxtapositions make it impossible for Jean to portray either the ethos or the language of hypocrisy. As a speaking subject, Faus Semblant dissolves before the pressure of the inherited rhetorics that jostle side by side in his discourse, dissipating any coherence of character before it can coalesce. La Vieille's autobiographical mode, on the other hand, subordinates language to character. She possesses and even incorporates—embodies—her significance: she is what she means.

That la Vieille provides the strategy by which the impasse of the poem's inheritance can be resolved is suggested, finally, by the way her discourse provides a model for the decisive statement now offered by Nature. Nature's message of universal generation and her explicitly feminine tone are first introduced into the poem by la Vieille. At times, indeed, Nature sounds like little more than la Vieille in a philosophical mood, and she herself defines her discourse as a typically feminine indiscretion: "I am a woman, so I can't keep quiet but always want to reveal everything: a woman can hide nothing."[32] As we might expect, then, la Vieille's *emboîtement* also controls the structure of Nature's discourse—indeed, here the form proliferates into a plenitude of interlocking boxes.[33] Nature articulates the language of natural philosophy in the structures of erotic pursuit, providing a rhetorical synthesis of the poem's disparate materials that implies a larger, cultural reconciliation.

The total effect is to ground the poem's presiding personification in the specifics of human experience and to give that experience its fullest philosophical extension. Fulfilled by Nature, la Vieille's dilations are now seen as both a penetration into the self and an expansion outward to encompass the whole of created nature. In temporal terms, la Vieille's erotic dialectic between delay and fulfillment becomes in Nature's discourse the greater dialectic between human action and providential vision. In both cases, deferral is a controlling concept. For man's participation in history to retain its significance, God's providential order must remain inscrutable, hidden until the end of time; for the meaning of erotic action to be fully explored, the plucking of the rose must be similarly delayed. The amorous quest and the pilgrimage of human life are at once insignificant and crucial: although their value depends entirely upon their conclusions, they are themselves the only means by which conclusions can be reached.[34]

In sum, la Vieille's autobiographical mode introduces temporality into the poem in a form that aligns the Lover's amorous obsessions with the poem's larger, more severe perspectives. Her mediation is accomplished, as we have seen, through the construction of subjectivity in language. The conflicting pressures that inevitably afflict the pilgrim's journey through the world are, if not resolved, at least contained within the capacious embrace of her selfhood, an embrace that is imaged in the *emboîtement* of her discourse. This is not to say, of course, that in disclosing her full dimensions la Vieille provides an unambiguous encouragement to Amanz's quest. On the contrary, she reveals that his goal is not a gradually dilating rose but a human being, and that the penetration he seeks to accomplish is not into a flower or even a body but into the labyrinths of personality. That this complicating knowledge would disable the intensity of Amanz's pursuit we may gather from his absence at her lecture. As I have said, each of his interlocutors offers advice he cannot afford to take, and the romance is built on the irony of a knight errant who can succeed only by ignoring his guides. But the threat posed by la Vieille is disarmed with special care: her words of feminine wisdom are mediated to the lover by a masculine Bel Acueil, who himself listens to her only after first deciding not to hear. As the Wife of Bath well knows, such are the vicissitudes of feminine speaking in a masculine world.

*   *   *

The last text we need to consider before returning our attention to the Wife of Bath is Roger de Collerye's *Sermon pour une nopce*.[35] Jean de

Meun had labeled la Vieille's discourse a sermon, implicitly linking it with the genre of the *sermon joyeux*.[36] Conversely, de Collerye's sermon is delivered by a (presumably male) preacher "habillé en femme," and like the Wife of Bath "she" celebrates carnality in terms derived from Jean de Meun.[37] At the conclusion of the *sermon joyeux* the preacher rehearses her text or *thema*: "Listen, daughter, and hearken—which will be, without dilation, the conclusion to our sermon, and sleep well, just as I have taught you."[38] The reference to dilation in de Collerye's text recalls the opening of Jean de Meun's rose and invokes the rhetoric of preaching to which the term is primarily relevant. The *ars praedicandi* teaches that sermonizing is a process of revelation and illumination. Each scriptural text or *thema* contains the truth in all its fullness, a truth that the preacher is to explicate and spread abroad (*dilatare*). To this end he is endowed with certain keys (*claves*), techniques of dividing the text into elements that can be dilated upon to reveal the full significance hidden within the verbal form.[39] Faced with an opened text, the listener is then moved to a corresponding openness. "Delate my herte in thy love," says a fourteenth-century mystic, and the metaphor harks back to Augustine's classic formulation: "My heart is too narrow for you to enter: let it be dilated by you."[40]

De Collerye's explicit invocation of *dilatio* adds a special decorum to his disposition of Jean's erotic motifs. The ambivalence that characteristically invests the discourse of the old woman is here enforced by the sermon's occasion: as an entertainment for the wedding feast it is at once preparation and deferral. Appropriately, then, this la Vieille provides titillation with an account of the delightful sufferings that await the bride and dissuasion with a grim reminder that the pleasures of the marriage bed will shortly become the harassments of family life. The structure of the discourse similarly enacts the pattern of enticement and delay, and it does so with a special attention to the rhetorical meaning of *dilatio*. The "old woman's" method of analysis is to broach a series of discontinuous matters but then to develop each so that the focus of attention returns always to herself. She opens by begging the groom not to hurt his bride but soon pauses to demand a drink; restarts with an account of the horrors of domestic life and adds an encomium to the bride but then shifts to an extended defense of her own preaching; proffers more advice to the new husband but interrupts with self-regarding pleas to the "seigneurs d'église" to have mercy on fallen women; then justifies her own role as being to instruct "fillettes" in the art of profitable love; and finally concludes with an extended autobiographical account of the experience that authorizes her words.

The total effect is a mix of frustration and enticement. As each element of the sermon is introduced only to be discarded we experience a growing irritation; but in devaluing her words the preacher promotes an all the more fascinating self. Her dilations are a series of openings into the same psychological space: the conclusion that is constantly deferred is the self that is constantly offered, the mystery that is at once veiled and unveiled. The saving knowledge is thus contained not in the *thema* ("Audi, filia, et vide"), but in the subject to which the *thema* points, and it is this subject that is opened by the keys of the *divisio* and spread abroad. In sum, this *sermon joyeux* brilliantly blends the random garrulity of la Vieille with the premeditated manifestations of the preacher. In terms of literary history, it shows us how a later writer could adapt Jean de Meun's amorous rhetoric to the generic requirements of the *sermon joyeux*; and it does so in a way remarkably like the one that had earlier been devised by Chaucer in the Wife of Bath's *Prologue*. Indeed, the likeness of these two independent rewritings of Jean de Meun argues for a tradition of such rewritings, a tradition of which these texts are among the few surviving vestiges.[41]

*   *   *

As everyone knows, the Wife of Bath's *Prologue* is divided into three parts, the first being the discussion of marriage versus virginity, the second the account of husbands one through three, and the last the account of husbands four and five.[42] I have no wish to quarrel with this self-evident disposition, but I do want to define more carefully than usual the kind of matter that is distributed among these three parts. Part one is a brief version of a *sermon joyeux*. The Wife's text is from 1 Corinthians 7.28: "If however you take a wife, you do not sin. And if a maiden marries, she does not sin: *but they will have trouble in the flesh because of this*" ("Si autem acceperis uxorem, non peccasti. Et si nupserit virgo, non peccavit: *tribulationem tamen carnis habebunt huiusmodi*").[43] She frames her sermon with two citations of this text, invoking it at the start as the "wo that is in marriage" and at the end in a direct quotation:

An housbonde I wol have—I wol nat lette—
Which shal be bothe my dettour and my thral,
And have his tribulacion withal
Upon his flessh, whil that I am his wyf.

(vv. 154–57)

By *tribulatio carnis*, St. Paul meant the inevitable and unwelcome temptations that marriage imposes upon the flesh. For the Wife, these temptations are to be embraced and celebrated, and her *sermon joyeux* explicates Paul's text to show that it means the opposite of what a more orthodox exegete would claim it says.[44] She does this by manipulating one of the most common of the *modi dilatandi* taught by the *ars praedicandi*, the citation of scriptural authorities.[45] She draws upon both Old and New Testaments but returns over and over again to the crucial seventh chapter of 1 Corinthians, citing it no fewer than eight separate times.[46] Her alternative reading of verse 28 can thus be supported even by the exegetical principle of intertextuality, taking one passage from a text to gloss another.[47] And as we would expect from a *sermon joyeux*, she unlocks the letter to discover an irreducible carnality. In other words, her exegetical method is not, as is usually argued, a sign of her moral limitations but a knowing strategy appropriate to her chosen genre.

With the Pardoner's interruption, the Wife's discourse takes a new turn, although without abandoning the principles of sermon rhetoric. Responding to her as both professional colleague and sexual challenge, the Pardoner suggests a new dimension to her *explication de texte*:

> Ye been a noble prechour in this cas.
> I was aboute to wedde a wyf; allas!
> What sholde I bye it on my flesh so deere?
>   (vv. 165−67)[48]

Guided by the Pardoner's suggestion, the Wife now explicates Paul's *tribulatio carnis* not as sexual temptation but as domestic tyranny, and the festivity of the *sermon joyeux* takes a darker turn. There are, to be sure, appealing moments in her account of her mastery over the three old husbands: the very intimacy of her revelations assures her male audience that they are not old and foolish, that they might even be one of those with whom she has shared "many a myrthe" (v. 399). Nonetheless, the total effect cannot help but be appalling: she presents herself as a nightmare of the misogynist imagination, a woman who not only exemplifies every fault of which women have been accused but preempts the very language of accusation.

The first two parts of the Wife's *Prologue*, then, offer a characteristically ambivalent self-image: the *sermon joyeux* is at once exciting and troubling in its vigorous sexuality and mastery of masculine modes of argument; the account of her first three marriages at once appalling and entertaining. And while the male listener might decide that this image of femininity is, on balance, more chilling than heating, these off-puttings are shortly to be revealed as preliminaries to a come-on. Like the Wife's tale of Midas with its veiled revisions and deferred conclusion, the self-images of the first two parts are ways of testing the patience and persistence of the masculine audience. The account of husband number four begins the process of opening up, in content and, more tellingly, in form. "Now wol I speken of my fourthe housbonde" (v. 452), she begins, and then allows an entrance into the poem of a twenty-seven line passage of nostalgic self-definition, only to close it off with a repetition of virtually the same line: "Now wol I tellen of my fourthe housbonde" (v. 480).

This passage provides a structural image of dilation, an opening into the subject that is framed by a delayed narrative movement, and it stands as a paradigm for the rest of the *Prologue*, which consists of small narrative movements intercalated and retarded with increasingly detailed self-revelations. These digressions are not, as Geoffrey de Vinsauf would say, leaps off to the side of the road, but motivations for the very narrative they retard.[49] Not only, in other words, does the interleaving of digressive meditations within the narrative provide an image of dilation, but the narrative itself is both an opening up and a standing still, a deepening explication of that which is already known.[50] The three parts of the *Prologue*, as the principles of sermon rhetoric prescribe, deal with the same text at three different levels of analysis: in part one *tribulatio carnis* is sexual temptation; in part two it is domestic tyranny; and now in part three it is the suffering of the unloved spouse. As the Wife says about herself, commenting upon Jankin's antifeminist mockings, "Who wolde wene, or who wolde suppose, / The wo that in myn herte was, and pyne?" (vv. 786–787).

The sequence of the *Prologue* is thus both temporal, its three parts matching the stages of a woman's sexual life, and analytic. As an analysis, the *Prologue* is a progressive series of glosses on a text, the gradual moralization of the letter *tribulatio*. The account of the first three husbands presents the Wife as object rather than subject: whatever internal reality she may possess is hidden behind the carapace of antifeminist rhetoric, and whatever human cost her mercenary marriages may have exacted remains uncomputed, at best a speculation in the mind of the sympathetic reader. The story of Jankin, however, renders these implications explicit, manifesting them in the expositions of narrative: the Wife becomes the victim of the antifeminism she previously manipulated, and the money she earlier extorted for her own sexual favors she now pays out for another's attentions. Beyond these ironic reversals, however, is a deeper revelation. In telling us about Jankin, she discloses a range of previously unacknowledged human feelings that include both a genuinely marital affection and a sense of disappointment, even discouragement. For in revealing the "wo . . . and pyne" of the early days of her marriage to Jankin, she shows that she is capable of love as well as desire, that she covets his affection at least as much as his well-turned legs. Hence she is willing to abandon *maistrie* once she learns that he cares enough to grant it:

> God help me so, I was to hym as kynde
> As any wyf from Denmark unto Ynde,
> And also trewe, and so was he to me.
> (vv. 823–25)

At the heart of the Wife's dilated discourse, then, rests the subjectivity that it both masks and discloses. The ambivalences of her old woman's identity are carefully anatomized and disposed on the narrative line of her rhetoric. The *sermon joyeux* presents a theatrical exaggeration of female sexuality, the account of the first three husbands an equally exaggerated feminine combativeness. The story of Jankin returns her to the human level on which her audience can meet and accept her. The complexities of this strategy, and its erotic value, are neatly ideogrammed in the episode that concludes her narrative, the tearing of the book. Initially, this episode eagerly offers itself to a misogynist reading, for the Wife behaves in what appears to be a typically feminine way, responding to Jankin's learned authority with irrational aggression and then using affection, even sexuality ("yet wol I kisse thee" [v. 802]) to lure the unsuspecting husband within striking distance. But like so many of the other antifeminist readings elicited throughout both *Prologue* and *Tale*, this one proves to be merely preliminary. A more patient analysis reveals this episode to be a symbolic reenactment of both the Wife's life and her rhetoric. A violent assault precipitates an equally violent rejection; but then a more subtle approach disarms the opposition and allows for the beginnings of accommodation. The male listener is assaulted by the license and violence of the first two parts of the *Prologue*, and inevitably responds by turning away; but the immediacy of autobiographical disclosure lures him back, and he is finally, perhaps to his surprise, prepared to admit that the Wife deserves her happiness. For both Jankin and for him, conditioned by the "booke of wikked wives" that is their (and our) common cultural inheritance, this recognition of the Wife's moral superiority is indeed a blow upon the cheek. But in both cases, once having achieved *maistrye*, the Wife abandons it in the interests of a larger purpose, whether it be marital harmony or the pleasure of the reader. As a wife she withdraws into gentle submission; as a speaker she replaces the complex self-promotions of her *Prologue* with a *Tale* that offers itself as pure entertainment.

To show that the canons of the *ars praedicandi* remain in force throughout the *Prologue*, it is the Friar who gives formal notice of its conclusion. As well as his sexual interest, he shares with the Pardoner a professional concern with the Wife's preaching, as he snidely implies by criticizing the disposition of her discourse—"'Now dame,' quod he, 'so have I joye or blis, / This is a long preamble of a tale!'" (vv. 830–31)—just as later he will criticize its invention ("scole-matere" [v. 1272]). The Wife's response to this critique demonstrates her uncontrite ingenuity. She allows the Friar a place in her tale by devising yet another preamble in which the Friar's malevolence is disarmed by the fairy-tale norms of her Arthurian fable. The "lymytours and othere hooly freres" are invited into the tale, in other words, only to be held in abeyance, suspended "as thikke as motes in the sonne-beem" (v. 868) while the magic of her story fulfills itself. Far from violating her story, they too succumb to its charms, just as her sly allusion to the Friar's sexual conquests is both an insult and a compliment, a counterattack that is in the event a good-humored caress.

This sense of raising the mean and squalid into a higher, cleansing action, of transforming a petty desire by absorbing it into a larger, more generous motion, is characteristic of the *Tale* as a whole. The *Tale* presents a series of quests that are displaced into progressively more inclusive movements. The initial quest after a "maydenheed" succeeds only to reveal a new quest after the knight's own "heed," a movement that is in turn displaced into the primary action of the tale, a quest after the "thyng . . . that wommen moost desiren." An assault on beauty has thus been absorbed into a hard-earned approach to wisdom, a displacement that is then repeated in the narrative itself: the questing knight rushes toward a group of dancing maidens only to see them vanish, leaving behind the old "wyf." That they vanish in order to reveal the saving figure of the hag is a function of his motives in approaching them. "He drow ful yerne, / In hope that som wysdom sholde he lerne" (vv. 993–94), a sharp contrast to his earlier approach to women; and not surprisingly, the hag delivers her advice in a manner strikingly reminiscent of Midas's wife: "Tho rowned she a pistel in his ere" (v. 1021). The wisdom that the old wife purveys (that women desire mastery above all else) apparently concludes his efforts, but of course he then discovers that this quest was only preliminary to a further journey, the internalized quest of his marriage. Now the barrier becomes the moral severity of the bedtime sermon and the temptation the magical offer to have a wife who is either beautiful or faithful, a choice that ungenerously assumes that fidelity is possible only for the woman who has no alternative.[51] In rejecting this offer altogether and in allowing his wife to choose for herself, the knight is submitting to the *maistrie* of her wisdom. Now he can cast aside the veil of his own misogyny and achieve the ultimate goal of clarified vision: "Cast up the curtyn, looke how that it is" (v. 1249). The deferrals of both *Prologue* and *Tale* have thus prepared for and authorized a final opening up that is truly a revelation. This is a climactic, all-inclusive movement that joins wisdom to beauty to allow for the proper matching of male and female: "And thus they lyve unto hir lyves ende / In parfit joye" (vv. 1257–58).

Yet the perfection at which the *Tale* arrives is marked with unreality, as the Wife well knows. Both *Prologue* and *Tale* playfully demonstrate the truth of the kind of proposition that a logician such as the Clerk would call an *impossible*—a proposition whose contrary is self-evident. The Wife's particular proposition, moreover, has as its subject matter clerks themselves, as she herself points out: "For trusteth wel it is an impossible / That any clerk wol speke good of wyves" (vv. 688–89). Both *Prologue* and *Tale* are of course just such a speaking: in the *Prologue* clerical misogyny is appropriated by a woman's voice in order to articulate feminist truths, while in the *Tale* the presumably feminine genre of Arthurian romance gives way to a fully authentic clerical *topos—nobilitas est virtus non sanguis*—that is not only spoken by a woman but that challenges the patriarchal ideology of property and inheritance.[52] Nonetheless, this success marks the limits of the Wife's achievement. Her accommodations and resolutions are more verbal than actual—she is herself, after all, on the lookout for husband number six—and her very verbalizations remain unavoidably dependent, feminine respeakings of a resolutely masculine idiom. Try as she (and Chaucer) might, she remains confined within the prison house of masculine language; she brilliantly rearranges and deforms her authorities to enable them to disclose new areas of experience, but she remains dependent on them for her voice. Her performance is a kind of transvestism, and she speaks "habillé en homme."

This dependence is at the very heart of the Wife's *Tale* and of the feminine desire that it at once defines and exemplifies. The *Tale*'s project is to answer the question Freud made notorious—"What thyng is it that wommen moost desiren?" (v. 905)—and the *Tale* is itself motivated by what the Wife calls a "queynte fantasye" (v. 516). Feminine wishfulness is then initially defined, in a deliberately superficial way, as the simple desire for "maistrie" (v. 1040). But as in the *Prologue*, mastery is sought only that it may be surrendered, an abnegation that allows both spouses to escape from the economy of domination that blights marriage. The hag's answer to the knight's question is thus of a piece with the other, more explicitly but no less thoroughly misogynist answers he has been given in the course of his quest (vv. 925–51), and it serves as a misleading half-truth to cover over a larger understanding of the feminine personality. Yet while this dynamic neatly enacts for the *Tale* the *Prologue*'s pattern of a misogynist preliminary followed by a more authentic revelation, the truth that is finally revealed is itself disturbingly irresolute in its sexual valence. For the point is not simply that the hag's transformation into a wife "bothe fair and good" (v. 1241) expresses the Wife of Bath's secret hankering to trade her hard-won wisdom for more conventional pleasures, but that the feminine wishes that are here fulfilled are themselves a function of *masculine* desire. The *Tale* tells us, first, that the husband who abandons *maistrye* will receive in return a wife who will fulfill his every wish ("And she obeyed hym in every thyng / That myghte doon hym pleasuance or likyng" [vv. 1255–56]), and second, that what women most desire is to be just this sort of obedient wife. The feminine desire that is anatomized throughout the *Tale* is here revealed to be, in its authentic form, determined by a desire that is not only masculine but is beyond scrutiny. The Wife's "queynte fantasye," in short, is a masculine wish-fulfillment, and one in which she appears to be fully complicit.

That the *Wife of Bath's Tale* serves finally to articulate a fundamental orthodoxy is, to be sure, a not unexpected Chaucerian conclusion, but what *is* surprising is that this is not in fact the Wife's conclusion. When the hag had finished her account of *gentillesse*, she closed with a high-minded invocation of divine grace:

> Yet may the hye God, and so hope I,
> Grante me grace to lyven vertuously.
> Thanne am I gentil, whan that I bigynne
> To lyven vertuously and weyve synne.
>
> (vv. 1173–76)

But when the Wife comes to conclude the whole of her performance she not only respeaks the hag's prayer in very different tones but actually allows it to modulate into its opposite, a curse:

> and Jhesu Crist us sende
> Housbondes meeke, yonge, and fressh abedde,
> And grace t'overbyde hem that we wedde;
> And eek I praye Jhesu shorte hir lyves
> That nought wol be governed by hir wyves;
> And olde and angry nygardes of dispence,
> God sende hem soone verray pestilence!
> (vv. 1258–64)

Coming hard upon the description of the "blisse" (v. 1253) and "parfit joye" (v. 1258) of the knight and his "new" wife, these discordant lines are deeply dismaying, and they constitute a final gesture as challenging and contradictory as, for instance, the Pardoner's offer of his relics. In part, certainly, the Wife is here reenacting the ambivalence that motivates her entire performance, luring the listener on with a seductive vision of feminine docility and then abruptly reminding him that the goal is not won without a struggle, that lasting peace emerges only from testing marital wars.[53] But beyond this, we are I think right to hear in the Wife's impenitent abrasiveness a subversion of her *Tale*'s wish-fulfilling promises, a jesting but nonetheless severe ("*verray* pestilence") judgment upon the masculine enterprise that has been constituted as her *Prologue* and *Tale*. For not only does her conclusion remind us that masculine consciousness is, in some of its forms, irredeemable—"olde and angry nygardes" will never be converted into "housbondes meeke, yonge, and fressh abedde"—it more tellingly suggests that the economy of domination will inevitably continue if the only alternative is a supervening, hegemonic masculinity. The Wife's conclusion, in short, undoes the very resolution at which she has herself arrived by suggesting that it may be merely the latest, most insidious move in an endless battle of the sexes.

✳ ✳ ✳

The Wife of Bath, like la Vieille, is not just one voice among many in a roundtable conversation but serves to articulate a new course for the tale-telling's critical path. After the Knight had finished the "noble storie" with which he had begun the game, the Host calls upon the monk to tell "somwhat to quite with the Knightes tale" (v. 3119). In turning to the Monk, Harry Bailly was trying to organize his tale-telling game according to the ideology of the three orders, a formal organization that had already underwritten, albeit in a revised form, the *General Prologue*: first the *miles*, then his clerical counterpart, the *monachus*.[54] But the Miller would have none of it, and his intervention challenged the "noble" values of Knight and Monk in terms that were, as I have argued elsewhere, aggressively and proudly political.[55] The Miller's challenge was devastating in its effect, and yet for all its local success it introduced into the pilgrimage a spirit of hostility, of class antagonism, that could be sustained by neither the taletelling game nor, apparently, Chaucer. For the Miller's political defiance was immediately stigmatized as unacceptable by the tales it inspired, those told by the social-climbing Reeve and *Lumpenproletariat* Cook that debased the "game and pley" (v. 4335) of tale telling into "harlotrie" (v. 3184) and "ribaudye" (v. 3866). With the breaking off of the *Cook's Tale*, the first movement of the *Canterbury Tales*, which editors have come to call Fragment I, collapsed in ruins.

Not surprisingly, then, the next movement of the tales, Fragments II and III, begins as if the Miller had never interrupted: it opens with a chronographia (II, vv. 1–15) that repeats, and replaces, the one that originally introduced the *General Prologue* (I, vv. 1–18).[56] "Lordynges," says the Host (II, 16), using a title that signals the highly placed male audience to whom he thinks it worthwhile to direct his attention,

> Wel kan Senec and many a philosophre
> Biwaillen tyme moore than gold in cofre;
> For "los of catel may recovered be,
> But los of tyme shendeth us," quod he.
> (vv. 25–28)

This language of bourgeois parsimony reinvokes the sober respectability that the churls of Fragment I had so scandalously flouted, a respectability then given a legalistic force in the language with which the Host solicits the next tale from the Man of Law. "Ye been submytted, thurgh youre free assent, / To stonden in this cas at my juggement," he says, "*Acquiteth* yow now of youre biheeste" (vv. 35–37)—a phrase that seeks to relocate the Miller's fabliau *quiting* in an institutional and regulatory context. The Man of Law replies in kind: "Biheste is dette, and I wol holde fayn / Al my biheste" (vv. 41–42). Then he casts about for a "thrifty tale" (v. 46), one that is "profitable" or "rewarding," that will now fulfill the prescription that the Host tried vainly to invoke when the Miller had first interrupted ("Abyd," he had said to the Miller, "and lat us werken thriftily" [v. 3131]). The pressures of social and legal constraint are thus poised to return the tale-telling game to the authoritarian orthodoxy that the Miller had originally challenged. And given the very substantial wealth of a sergeant of the law, the social ambitiousness of lawyers generally, and their role in enforcing the status quo, the Man of Law is an excellent choice to fill this role.[57]

Perhaps surprisingly, Fragments II and III replay the pattern of fragment I: social authority is invoked by the Man of Law and countered by the Wife of Bath, a rebellion that is then dangerously exaggerated in the two *quiting* tales that follow, especially in the scurrilous *fabliau* with which the Summoner concludes this four-tale movement. But the terms of contention are in fact very different: we move from political opposition generated by class inequality to ideological antithesis determined by gender. Not that important class distinctions are not at work here as well. The highly placed Man of Law tells a story he learned from wealthy merchants about an empress of Rome—a story originally written by a cleric (Nicholas Trevet) for a royal nun (Mary of Woodstock, daughter of Edward I).[58] The Wife of Bath is a rural commodity producer and tradeswoman whose economic independence challenges the traditional order of feudal society and whose *Tale* concludes with a sermon on *gentillesse* that defines nobility in terms of virtue, not birth.[59] But these social determinants provide not the topic of the confrontation, which is gender, but its context.

Moreover, gender itself is conceived largely, although not entirely, in metaphoric terms. What the Wife champions, as perhaps we should expect from a male author, is less the rights of her sex, much less those of her class, than the rights of selfhood. It is subjectivity per se that she promotes, a subjectivity that Chaucer, by no means uniquely, here associates with women. Throughout the Middle Ages, women were denied social conceptualization and even existence as social, and historical, beings. In the estates lists by which medieval society imagined itself, lay women were categorized not by economic, social, or political function but either by social status as determined by their male relatives or by marital status.[60] Hence it is not surprising that when Marsilius of Padua defined the *populus*, he said that it included everybody but children, slaves, aliens—and women.[61] But perhaps this exclusion also carried with it (or so men thought) a sense of freedom, a liberation from the constraints of a highly regulatory social system. If women were denied social definition, did this not mean that the realm of the *asocial*—of the internal, the individual, the subjective—was peculiarly theirs? Men, as befitted historical beings, had social responsibilities; women, as befitted the socially invisible, had private lives. Men had careers; women had character.

This familiar ideology of gender is deeply inscribed in Chaucer's representation of the feminine in the *Wife of Bath's Prologue and Tale*. What Chaucer's Wife wants is not political or social change; on the contrary, the traditional order is quite capable of providing the marital happiness she desires. To be sure, to acknowledge that the basic unit of social life is a socially undetermined selfhood entails important consequences that themselves carry the possibility (although by no means the certainty) of political change. And to see that the bearers of this message are women is also a political statement. But the implications of the politics of individualism are very different from the class-determined dissent articulated by the Miller. After all, the selfhood privileged by individualism is by definition already common property. Thus the Wife avoids the kind of antagonistic political issues invoked by the Miller and offers in their place a less activist, more congenial message.

The revisionary process initiated by the Wife of Bath can be successfully completed, therefore, because her opposition is generated from a position that does *not* correspond to the most visible and politically specific oppositional forces at work in Chaucer's historical world. On the contrary, her invocation of the rights of the subject derives its force, as we have seen, from a dense and widespread web of precedents found in earlier medieval writing, and especially in the notoriously misogynist *Roman de la Rose*. Precisely the familiarity of her challenge, however brilliantly innovative the form in which it is articulated, makes it appealing and useful to Chaucer. Moreover, Chaucer uses the opposition between the Man of Law and Wife of Bath to explore yet again the problematic of authorship that preoccupied him throughout his career. And here too the terms of representation are directed less toward the political specificities of writing within a class-bound context than with a highly generalized notion of cultural authority understood in terms of gender.

Not only does the Man of Law represent the attitudes and values of the governing classes, but he immediately identifies Chaucer with his own orthodoxy. He is, he claims, bereft of thrifty tales because Chaucer has exhausted the store—"And if he have nought seyed hem, leve brother, / In o book, he hath seyd hem in another" (vv. 51–52). In fact, the Man of Law's survey of what he calls Chaucer's "sermons" (v. 87) is restricted to the poems of Ovidian pathos: the Ceyx and Alcyone episode in the *Book of the Duchess* and the tales of "noble wyves . . . and loveris" (v. 59) included in the *Legend of Good Women*. But in aligning his *Tale* with this kind of writing, the Man of Law places it, as we have seen, in opposition to the developing *Canterbury Tales*.[62] And when Chaucer counters it with the *Wife of Bath's Prologue and Tale*, he makes it clear that the specific term of opposition is the representation of women.

In the *Prologue* to the *Legend of Good Women*, Queen Alceste reveals herself to be a victim who has internalized her own subjection. When the poet attempts to correct the God of Love's reductive reading of his poetry, Alceste denies him voice: "Lat be thyn arguynge," she says, "For Love ne wol nat countrepleted be / In ryght ne wrong; and lerne that at me!" (F, vv. 475–77)—learn it, that is, from my imposition on you of the tyranny of which I am myself a victim. This economy of suffering is repeated throughout the legends, as the dogged poet imposes upon his protagonists the tyranny under which he himself groans and so generates the virtuous female suffering he is condemned to celebrate. Each of the legends thematizes the effacement of the subject that is the condition of its production. Just as the poet becomes an agent for Alceste's monolithic message, so does each of the good women bow before male tyranny in order to make manifest their virtue. And the condition of this self-defeating display of female superiority is that it always be seen from the outside, as object rather than subject. Consequently the individual legends mute their protagonists: they continually gesture toward the Ovidian letters in which these women expressed, at least fictively, their own experience; but they never allow them, nor the female subjects they inscribe, presence in the poem. In this sense the most typical of the legends is that of the definitively muted Philomela. But the female "tonge" that Tereus severed (v. 2334) reappears in the vigorous "tonge" of that "verray jangleresse" (III, v. 638) the Wife of Bath—a reappearance that measures the distance between the *Legend* and the *Canterbury Tales* precisely in terms of the recuperation of the speaking subject.

The *Tale* told by the orthodox Man of Law is a Christianized version of the Ovidian tales of pathos told by Chaucer in the *Legend*—the dutiful author with whom the Man of Law identifies but whom the *Canterbury Tales* show to be in the process of supersession. As a foil to the *Wife of Bath's Prologue and Tale*, it offers a feminine virtue brought into existence by male authority. As Constance herself acknowledges, her redemptive mission is an effect of her father's tyranny:

> I, wrecche womman, no fors though I spille!
> Wommen are born to thraldom and penance,
> And to been under mannes governance
>   (vv. 285–87)

At the end of her career she pathetically begs her father to "sende me namoore unto noon hethenesse" (v. 1112). This governance extends, moreover, to Alla's marital demands (vv. 708–14) and to Constance's pitiless exile by this "housbonde routhelees" (v. 863). However edifying Constance's suffering may be, it is a function of the sexual authority of men, just as, at the level of narrative form, her exemplary role is a function of the generic authority of hagiography. Indeed, the disturbing instrumentality of her role in the *Tale* extends to the *Tale* itself: the Syrian merchants first pass on their "tidynges" of Constance's beauty to the Sultan along with their other wares, just as more recent merchants, "fadres of tidynges / And tales" (vv. 129–30), later passed them on to the Man of Law, who finally transmits them to us. The tale is a mercantile "wynnynge" (v. 127) with which the Man of Law will pay his "dette" (v. 41) to the Host, a transaction that bears a striking similarity to the model of patronage described in the Prologue to the *Legend*, where the poet pays his "dette" (F, v. 541) to Alceste first with his balade, then with the Legends themselves. In sum, then, the *Legend* and the *Tale* both describe and exemplify the way men traffic in women.

With the completion of the *Man of Law's Tale*, the Host calls upon the Parson, the counterpart to the Monk whom he had invited to follow the Knight in Fragment I. The Wife interrupts, setting aside the "lerned men of lore" (v. 1168) whom the Host so much admires. Her tale, she tells us, "schal not ben of philosophie, / Ne phislyas, ne termes queinte of lawe" (vv. 1188–89): with these designations she is rejecting the kind of tales told by the Clerk, the Physician, and the Man of Law himself, all of them tales of good women (Griselda, Virginia, and Constance). But her brilliant manipulations of the authority of male learning are not accomplished, as we have seen, merely for purposes of parody. On the contrary, she seeks to find a means for the expression of the female subjectivity that the *Legend* and the *Man of Law's Tale* effaced. Her program thus requires her to revise the model that prescribed her intervention in the first place, the *Miller's Tale*. The *Miller's Tale* is a narrative staging of the natural vitality and resourcefulness embodied in the "yonge wyf" Alison—values that reappear, with a sharply different valence, in the narrative told by Alison of Bath.

The vernal innocence and beauty of the Miller's Alison served to elicit the male desire that motived the tale. And in the last analysis, Alison evaded both the possessiveness of male desire and the severity of male judgment: the elegant plot spun its webs around her without actually entangling her, and she provided not only the model for the tale's climactic joke but also, and against all expectation, the norm by which we were invited to understand her world. Her inarticulate "Tehee!" (v. 3740) fulfilled itself in the festivity first of the neighbors—"every wight gan laughen at this stryf" (v. 3849)—and then of the pilgrims themselves, who "laughen at this nyce cas" (v. 3855). Alison was not merely the heroine of the *Miller's Tale* but its presiding spirit.

And as such she partook of its limitations. She was, finally, no *more* articulate than her "Tehee," and her preeminence was never anything more than ludic: the political dynamic that motivated the *Tale* as a whole took place entirely apart from her. However ungraspable, she remained an object, "a prymerole, a piggesnye" (v. 3268). Like the victimized maiden of the *Wife of Bath's Tale*, she elicited overmastering desire from the men of her world, but despite (or even because of) her resistance we cannot imagine her either leading them to enlightenment or herself purveying a saving wisdom. But of course this is not true of Alison of Bath, and when the feminine principle reinterrupts the tale-telling game, it appears in a sharply expanded form. The Wife's *Prologue and Tale*, unlike the *Miller's Tale*, do not bespeak "Alison-ness" but are on the contrary spoken by it. No longer merely the protagonist of a fictive narration, the female is a force that both controls her own verbal world and the tale-telling game itself. And in this she becomes a model for the poet.

In the Man of Law and his *Tale*, Chaucer has dramatized the aspect of authorship that he seems to have found most problematic. This is the tyranny of orthodox authority, a force that, whether it be embodied in the patron, in the source, or in the poet himself, is at once inhibiting and enabling, oppressive and supportive. Moreover, in both the *Legend* and the *Man of Law's Tale* that authority is conceived in terms of gender, as male dominion over women, an ascendancy that is sanctimoniously assumed in the name of feminine virtue. With the *Man of Law's Tale*, Chaucer at once acknowledges and disclaims this authority: the Man of Law tells a tale that is Chaucerian and yet not, he claims, by Chaucer, an affirmation of the central Chaucerian commitment to the narrative of affective piety and yet a laying bare of its less than pious motivations.[63]

When the Wife first appears, she challenges her audience by first dis-

placing the Parson's severe, Lollard-like moralism with her own osten-
tatiously unorthodox carnal rhetoric: "My joly body schal a tale telle." As
we have seen, the Wife's analogy between her "joly body" and the *corpus*
of her text is elaborately staged in both the form and the content of her
performance, and with it she solicits a reading that is itself unorthodox in
the terms of medieval hermeneutics. It is, nonetheless, a kind of reading
that is a prerequisite for the understanding of Chaucer's kind of poetry.
For the orthodox reader, the "joly body" of the Wife's text can be disarmed
by interpretation. Every text, according to Augustine, can and must be
read so that it teaches the single lesson of the law of charity.[64] What is
important about this hermeneutic is that it is preemptive: the reader
knows before he approaches the text what will be the result of his reading,
and his interpretive task is not to discover *what* the text means but its way
of signifying the meaning it must have. Armed with the strength of the
spirit, he is immune to the solicitations of the letter, for he knows that the
letter is a mere covering, a veil to be torn aside and discarded in pursuit of
the truth. Interpretation, in other words, is a way of mastering the text.

   Maistrie and *acorde*, *auctoritee* and *experience*, the *joly body* and the *curtyn* that darkens it—these terms define the polarized values of the Wife of
Bath's marital world. They are also terms that define alternative ways of
reading her text. We can either master the text with the *auctoritee* of preemptive interpretation, or we can *acorden* with it through the negotiations
of experience; we can display its carnality by hastily ripping off the *curtyn*
of its rhetorical strategies, or we can patiently allow it to reveal itself to us.
By offering a redefinition of reading, a way to make meaning that avoids
the preemptions of Augustinian hermeneutics, the Wife of Bath is engaged
in a project that is central to the poetic of the *Canterbury Tales* as a whole.
For she offers a mode of reading that is at once literal and moral; and she
insists that interpretation must be deferred, that meaning (whether literary
or personal) is available only at the end (whether of a narrative or a life).

   When the Wife of Bath preempts the Parson, she displaces a voice
that will provide a conclusion to the tale telling so authoritative that it
comes to include the tones of the author himself. The *Parson's Tale*, when
it is finally allowed audience, is a treatise on confession that in turn preempts all discourse that is not conducted in the authorized language of
penance. In rejecting "fables and swich wrecchednesse," the Parson rejects
the whole of the *Canterbury Tales*, a rejection that Chaucer authorizes in
the Retractions he appends to the *Parson's Tale*. For the *Canterbury Tales*
to exist at all, then, the *Parson's Tale* must be deferred; and who could be

a more appropriate agent of deferral than the Wife of Bath? The "joly body" of the Wife's text is thus a paradigm for the *Canterbury Tales* as a whole: just as her speaking is a dilation that defers her conclusion, so too are the *Tales* a "game" or "pleye" that postpones the penance of Canterbury. But as we have seen, this is a postponement and not a dismissal, and a digression that leads inevitably if eventually to the goal. Her rhetoric has as its goal not mere delectation but the higher pleasures of ethical understanding, an understanding that may properly be seen as preparatory to the Parson's absolutism. By introducing a rhetoric that is at once carnal and moral, in other words, the Wife of Bath ameliorates the harsh polarizations of Augustinian theory and opens up a space in which what we have come to call literature can find its home. And when we do finally arrive at the *Parson's Tale*, we discover to our surprise that both penitential pilgrimage and playful tale telling have reached a simultaneous conclusion, that the Parson will now both "knitte up al this feste and make an ende." The longest way round has proved to be the shortest way home.

This is a conclusiveness that is profoundly satisfying and thoroughly medieval; but I am reluctant to deny to Chaucer's Wife either the nobility of her innovations or the last word. "Welcome the sixte, whan that evere he schal," she says; and we must admire her stamina. But if we really imagine an endless series, the pleasure of the text will quickly diminish. If we truly understand the Wife of Bath as a traditional figure, we will remember that the tradition she articulates depends for its own vitality on the threat of temporality. More, by making us wait so patiently for the right ending—or the right interpretation—it comes to seem, when it comes, so much the more right. She makes us ourselves desire an ending, and she herself insists that there is an ending to be desired:

"Now wol I dye, I may no lenger speke."
But atte laste, with muchel care and wo,
We fille acorded by us selven two.
(vv. 810–12)

Notes

1. Deschamps's ballade is printed, with a useful translation, by Derek Brewer, ed., *Chaucer: The Critical Heritage, I: 1385–1837* (London: Routledge and Kegan Paul, 1978), 39–42.

2. Dean Spruill Fansler, *Chaucer and the* Roman de la Rose (New York: Columbia University Press, 1914).

3. *Chaucer and the French Tradition* (Berkeley: University of California Press, 1957).

4. For later, valuable discussions of the general influence of the *Roman* on Chaucer, see James I. Wimsatt, "Chaucer and French Poetry," in *Geoffrey Chaucer: Writers and their Background*, ed. Derek Brewer (London: Bell, 1974), 109–36; Wimsatt, *Allegory and Mirror: Tradition and Structure in Middle English Literature* (New York: Pegasus, 1970); Wimsatt, "Medieval and Modern in Chaucer's *Troilus and Criseyde*," *PMLA* 92 (1977): 203–16; and David Wallace, "Chaucer and the European Rose," in *Studies in the Age of Chaucer, Proceedings, No. 1, 1984: Reconstructing Chaucer*, ed. Paul Strohm and Thomas J. Heffernan (Knoxville, TN: New Chaucer Society, 1985), 61–67.

5. All citations from Chaucer's works are from Larry Benson, gen. ed., *The Riverside Chaucer*, 3rd ed. (Boston: Houghton-Mifflin, 1987).

6. See, for example, Judson Boyce Allen and Patrick Gallacher, "Alisoun through the Looking Glass: Or Every Man His Own Midas," *Chaucer Review* 4 (1970): 99–105; and Richard Hoffman, *Ovid and the* Canterbury Tales (Philadelphia: University of Pennsylvania Press, 1966), 145–49.

7. *Metamorphoses* 11, 187, 193.

8. The "bitore" or bittern was known as the "myredromylle" because, in the words of John Trevisa, it "is a bridde þat makeþ soun and voys in watir. . . . And he . . . is a bridde of greet glotonye and puttiþ þe bille down into þe watir and makeþ an horrible noyse and is enemye namliche to eles" (M. C. Seymour et al., eds., *On the Properties of Things: John Trevisa's Translation of Bartholomaeus Anglicus, De proprietatibus rerum*, vol. 1 [Oxford: Clarendon Press, 1975], 635–36); see also Sidney J. H. Herrtage, ed., *Catholicon Anglicum*, EETS OS 75 (London: Trübner, 1881), 50, 240. The Wife's use of the bittern image is appropriately antifeminist: reputed to have two stomachs or "wombes," as does a woman, its gluttony parallels the uncontrolled devouring that characterizes the feminine appetite. Chaucer probably got the image from Guillaume Deguileville's portrait of Gluttony, who has "com butor / deuz ventres" that are labeled "ivrece" and "Goufres, . . . Qui se mengier touz jours est prest" (*Le pélerinage de la vie humaine*, ed. J. J. Stürzinger [London: Roxburghe Club, 1893], 325).

9. There are only two other women on the pilgrimage, the Prioress and her companion, the Second Nun. As for the immediate audience comprised of Chaucer's "literary circle," there is no evidence of women having been included: see Paul Strohm, "Chaucer's Audience," *Literature and History* 5 (1977): 26–41; Derek Pearsall, "The *Troilus* Frontispiece and Chaucer's Audience," *Yearbook of English Studies* 7 (1977): 68–74; and V. J. Scattergood, "Literary Culture at the Court of Richard II," in *English Court Culture in the Later Middle Ages* (London: Duckworth, 1983), 29–43. That the maleness of the Wife's implied audience creates a problem for modern feminist readers is shown by Elaine Tuttle Hansen, "Fearing for Chaucer's Good Name," *Exemplaria* 2 (1990): 23–36.

10. The powerlessness of the Wife before her own language is an assumption shared by those who read her iconographically, as "a literary personification of ram-

pant 'femininity' or carnality," in D. W. Robertson's well-known phrase (*A Preface to Chaucer* [Princeton, NJ: Princeton University Press, 1963], 321) or ethically, as a complex human character (see E. T. Donaldson, *Speaking of Chaucer* [London: Athlone Press, 1970], 174). The only real exception to this assumption is Theodore Silverstein, "The Wife of Bath and the Rhetoric of Enchantment," *Modern Philology* 58 (1961): 153–73, but see also Charles Koban, "Hearing Chaucer Out: The Art of Persuasion in the *Wife of Bath's Tale*," *Chaucer Review* 5 (1970–71): 225–39.

> 11. quiconques la chose escrit,
> se du voir ne vous velt ambler,
> li diz doit le fet resambler;
> car les voiz aus chose voisines
> doivent estre a leur fez cousines.
>   (vv. 15158–62)

All references to the *Roman de la Rose* are to the edition of Félix Lecoy, Classiques Français du Moyen Âge 92, 95, 98 (Paris: Champion, 1965–70), unless otherwise noted.

12. Augustine, *Confessions* 1, 13; Dante, *Inferno* 5; Boccaccio, *Genealogia deorum gentilium* 14, 18. In the *House of Fame*, the Chaucerian reading of the *Aeneid* in the Temple of Venus is so compromised by the seductiveness of Dido that it reproduces not Virgil's epic of *pietas* but an Ovidian epistle; the narrator's seduction by Criseyde in the *Troilus* is well known.

13. The phrase "joly body" also occurs in the *Shipman's Tale*, which was almost certainly written originally for the Wife of Bath: "Ye shal my joly body have to wedde" (v. 423), the wife says to her merchant husband. For the appearance of the phrase "au cuer joli, au cors inel" in the *Roman de la Rose*, and its punning on Jean de Meun's surname "Clopinel," see Daniel Poirion, ed., *Roman de la Rose* (Paris: Garnier-Flammarion, 1974), v. 10566 and Poirion's note.

14. Edmond Faral and Julia Bastin, eds., *Oeuvres complètes de Rutebeuf* (Paris: Picard, 1960), 2:268–71; Faral and Bastin mention other instances on p. 267. For further discussion, see Mikhail Bakhtin, *Rabelais and His World*, trans. Hélène Iswolsky (Cambridge, MA: MIT Press, 1968), 181ff. and bibliography cited there. A Chaucerian poem that draws on this tradition is the *Canon's Yeoman's Prologue* (misleadingly printed as *Pars prima* of his tale in the *Riverside Chaucer*).

15. *Les lamentations de Matheolus et le Livre de leesce de Jehan Le Fèvre de Resson*, ed. A. G. Van Hamel, Bibliothèque de l'École des Hautes Études, fasc. 95, 96 (Paris: Bouillon, 1892–1905). Lefèvre also translated the pseudo-Ovidian *De vetula* as *La vielle* (see below, note 24) and several other works, including the unpublished *Epistre sur les misères de la vie* (MS B.N. fr. 19137), apparently a version of Innocent III's *De miseria humanae conditionis*, a treatise that Chaucer himself claimed to have translated.

16. On Chaucer and Matheolus, see Zacharias P. Thundy, "Matheolus, Chaucer, and the Wife of Bath," in *Chaucerian Problems and Perspectives: Essays Presented to Paul E. Beichner*, ed. Edward Vasta and Zacharias P. Thundy (Notre Dame, IN: University of Notre Dame Press, 1979), 24–58.

17. In the Latin original, Matheolus frames his long and chaotic complaint with a repeated couplet: "Est horologium quod nulla cessat in hora / Uxor litigium dans, cujus lingua sonora" (1, 331–32; cf. 1, 519–20, and also lines 322 and 545). Another brilliant mimicry of the feminine idiom is Gautier Le Leu's *La Veuve*, a poem that captures femininity as it bespeaks the three crises of widowhood: first the lament for the dead husband, then the chattering with a gossip that initiates the search for a new mate, and finally the inevitable harangue of sexual disappointment that follows upon remarriage. This poem has been discussed by Charles Muscatine, "The Wife of Bath and Gautier's *La veuve*," in *Romance Studies in Honor of Edward Billings Ham*, ed. Urban T. Holmes, California State College Publication 2 (Hayward: California State College, 1967).

18.   Cafurne͞en fu bien accroupie,
      Plus jangleresse qu'une pie,
      Car pas ne plaida sagement;
      Son cul moustra en jugement.

On Carfania or Afrania, see Claudine Herrmann, *Le Rôle judicaire et politique des femmes sous la République romaine*, Collection Latomus 67 (Brussels: Latomus, 1964), 107–08.

19. Perhaps nowhere more fervently than in the *Roman de la Rose*, for example, vv. 16317–676. The Wife of Bath brags of how, if her husband had "pissed on a wal, / Or doon a thyng that sholde han cost his lyf" (vv. 534–35), she would have tattled on him to her gossips, but other texts detail far more intimate revelations. One wife recounts how, when she returns from confession, her husband wants to know "si j'ay pissé en ma chemise," but this scatological curiosity in fact hides a yet more shameful fascination with her adulterous acts with the priest. See "Sermon joyeux de la patience des femmes obstinées contre leurs maris," in *Recueil de poésies françaises de XVe et XVIe siècles*, ed. Anatole de Montaiglon, vol. 3 (Paris: P. Jannet, 1856), 261–67.

20. The story is told about Novella d'Andrea at the University of Bologna in Christine's *Cité des dames*; see *The Book of the City of Ladies*, trans. Earl Jeffrey Richards (New York: Persea Books, 1982), 154. For a more recent instance of this way of understanding feminine writing, Nathaniel Hawthorne's comments on the pseudonymous and very popular Fanny Fern are exemplary: "The woman writes as if the Devil was in her; and that is the only condition under which a woman ever writes anything worth reading. Generally women write like emasculated men, and are only to be distinguished from male authors by greater feebleness and folly; but when they throw off the restraints of decency, and come before the public stark naked, as it were—then their books are sure to possess character and value" (cited by Beverly Voloshin, "A Historical Note on Women's Fiction," *Critical Inquiry* 2 [1975–76], 818).

21. See Edward P. Thompson, "'Rough Music': Le charivari anglais," *Annales* 27 (1972): 285–312; C. Gauvard and A. Gokalp, "Les conduites de bruit et leur signification à la fin du moyen âge: Le charivari," *Annales* 29 (1974): 693–704; Jacques Le Goff and Jean-Claude Schmitt, eds., *Le Charivari*, Ecole des Hautes

Etudes en Sciences Sociales, Civilisation et Sociétés, 67 (The Hague: Mouton, 1981); and Natalie Zemon Davis, *Society and Culture in Early Modern France* (Stanford: Stanford University Press, 1975), 97–151. The fear of widows is visible throughout the entire corpus of misogynist texts; one of the most extensive treatments of the theme is Boccaccio's *Il Corbaccio*, translated by Anthony K. Cassell (Urbana: University of Illinois Press, 1975).

> 22. Sarre fu vieille et esdentee,
> Ne sembloit pas entalentée
> De recevoir charnele couple.
> Mais assés tost se rendi souple;
> Quand elle sçot qu'enfant avroit,
> Dart de leëse la navroit
> Vieille rit quant elle suppose
> Qu'on li fera la bonne chose;
> C'est coustume de vieille femme,
> Que, puis que vieillesce l'entame,
> Elle seult les jeunes induire
> Et au jeu d'amours introduire.
> Par ses dis et par sa parole
> Les fait dancer a sa karole.
>   (2, vv. 1823–36)

This is by no means Matheolus's only expedition into biblical exegesis: among other interpretations, he also suggests that the risen Christ revealed himself to women because he knew that they would spread the word. Chaucer's Dame Prudence, in the *Tale of Melibee*, cites this example as well, although for her it is a sign of the high regard in which Christ held women (VII, v. 1075).

23. On the wooing play, see the two articles by Charles Read Baskerville, "Dramatic Aspects of Medieval Folk Festivals in England," *Studies in Philology* 17 (1920): 19–87, and "Mummers' Wooing Plays in England," *Modern Philology* 21 (1924): 225–72.

24. The *De vetula* has been edited by Paul Klopsch, Mittellateinische Studien und Texte 2 (Leiden: Brill, 1967), and by Dorothy M. Robathan (Amsterdam: Hakkert, 1968). Jean Lefèvre's adaptation, *La Vieille, ou les dernières amours d'Ovide*, has been edited by Hippolyte Cocheris (Paris: A. Aubry, 1861). Its relevance to Chaucer is also discussed by William Matthews, "The Wife of Bath and All Her Sect," *Viator* 5 (1974): 413–43.

> 25.   Ces mutacions que j'ay dictes,
> Qui sont en mon grand livre escriptes,
> N'a point mutacion pareille
> Dont ce, me vint à grant merveille,
> Qu'en si pou de temps devenue
> Fut vielle, hideuse et chanue.
>   (1, vv. 3175–80)

26.   ausi con li mireors montre
les choses qui sont a l'encontre
et i voit l'en sanz coverture
et lor color et lor figure,
tot autresi vos di por voir
que li cristaus sanz decevoir
tot l'estre dou vergier encuse
a celui qui en l'eve muse;
. . . .
si n'i a si petite chose,
tant soit reposte ne enclose,
dont demontrance ne soit feite
con s'ele ert ou cristal portrete.
                    (vv. 1553–68)

27.   Mes ja mes n'oroiz mielz descrivre
la verité de la matere,
quant j'avré apost le mistere.
                    (vv. 1598–1600)

28.   que songes est senefiance
des biens as genz et des anuiz,
que li plusor songent de nuiz
maintes choses covertement
que l'en voit puis apertement.
                    (vv. 16–20)

29. My diagram follows the suggestion of Daniel Poirion, who identified this rhetorical structure in his *Le "Roman de la Rose"* (Paris: Hatier, 1973), 125. Poirion actually designs a similar diagram for Ami's discourse, and suggests that one could also be constructed for Nature: see below, n. 33. This kind of structure, known in studies of the epic as "ring composition," is a favorite Homeric ordering principle (Cedric H. Whitman, *Homer and the Heroic Tradition* [Cambridge, MA: Harvard University Press, 1958], 249–84, 288–91, and 367–70) and is also visible in *Beowulf* (John D. Niles, "Ring Composition and the Structure of *Beowulf*," *PMLA* 94 [1979]: 924–35). Within the tradition in which Jean de Meun and Chaucer are working, however, the crucial precedent for chiastic structure is Ovid's *Metamorphoses* (Brooks Otis, *Ovid as an Epic Poet*, 2d ed. [Cambridge: Cambridge University Press, 1970], 45–90, and the diagrams passim). This is not to say that Ovid is the only Roman poet to avail himself of chiastic structure—see, e.g., Gordon Williams, *Technique and Ideas in the Aeneid* (New Haven, CT: Yale University Press, 1983), 75–78; Mario Di Cesare, *The Altar and the City: A Reading of Virgil's Aeneid* (New York: Columbia University Press, 1974), 90; and David Vessey, *Statius and the Thebaid* (Cambridge: Cambridge University Press, 1973), 317–28—but he is the most persistent and, for the Middle Ages, the most influential. Within the twelfth-century romance, we find this structure enacted, for example, in Thomas's *Tristan* (Joan M. Ferrante, *The Conflict of Love and Honor*

[The Hague: Mouton, 1973], 74–78) and in the two linked romances of Chrétien de Troyes, the *Chevalier de la Charrette* (F. Douglas Kelly, *Sens and Conjointure in the* Chevalier de la charrette [The Hague: Mouton, 1966], 166–84) and, most explicitly and importantly, the *Chevalier au Lion* (a preliminary account of the structure is offered in the diagram appended to Erich Köhler's *Ideal und Wirklichkeit in der höfischen Epik*, 2d ed. [Tübingen: Niemeyer, 1970]). Chrétien's use of *emboîtement* for thematic purposes both here and elsewhere provides an important precedent for its definition as a narrative *topos* specific to romance; indeed, narratives that have previously been identified as "interlaced" might be more properly described as chiastic. See, for example, Dale B. J. Randall, "A Note on Structure in *Sir Gawain and the Green Knight*," *MLN* 72 (1959): 161–63), Larry Benson, *Malory's Morte Darthur* (Cambridge, MA: Harvard University Press, 1976), 34–35; James Nohrnberg, *The Analogy of the Faerie Queene* (Princeton, NJ: Princeton University Press, 1976).

30. Delay is of course, a *sine qua non* of courtship: "delay is a great bawd," says Ovid (*Ars amatoria* 3, 752: "maxima lena mora est"; see also 3, 473–74: "mora semper amantes / Incitat, exiguum si modo tempus habet"; and 2, 717–18: "Crede mihi, non est veneris properanda voluptas, / Sed sensim tarda prolicienda mora"). The same advice is repeated throughout Andreas Capellanus's *De Amore*, ed. and trans. P. G. Walsh (London: Duckworth, 1982), 94, 154, 176, 178, 194, and 196. Andreas does use the Ovidian term *mora* but prefers *dilatio* and its cognates, and may well be the source of the implied pun; for similar Andrean jesting, see Betsy Bowden, "The Art of Courtly Copulation," *Medievalia et humanistica* 9 (1979): 67–85. The connection between dilation as delay and as opening is implicit throughout the *Roman*: Guillaume's failure in Part 1 leads him to describe the gradually opening rose in terms that make it clear that more time must pass before possession (or penetration) can be accomplished—the whole time of the poem in fact (3339–60). A masculine version of this pun may be found in *Li consaus d'amours* by Richard of Fournival, in which courtship is called *prolongance* (Gian Battista Speroni, ed., *Medioevo romanzo* 1 [1974]: 217–78). I am indebted for my initial interest in dilation as the structural *topos* of romance to Patricia Parker, *Inescapable Romance: Studies in the Poetics of a Mode* (Princeton, NJ: Princeton University Press, 1979).

31. As the following outline makes clear, in which the five separate movements of Faus Semblant's discourse, each marked by an interjection by Amors, are divided according to their alternating pattern of judgment and collusion. In each of the A speeches, Faus Semblant expresses a sense of moral outrage at current ecclesiastical abuse, while in each of the B speeches, he delights in his own complicity.

I:	10997–1006 —A	V:	11499–568 —B
	11007–52 —B		11569–606—A
II:	11061–132 —A		11607–756 —B
	11133–92 —B		11757–814 —A
III:	11211–38 —A		11815–66 —B
	11239–376 —A		11867–87 —A
IV:	11383–478 —A		11888–922 —B
	11479–94 —B		11923–38 —A

Verses 11947–84 function as a conclusion and assert that the paradox of the truthful hypocrite allows of no solution.

32. "Fame sui, si ne me puis tere, / ainz veill des ja tout reveler, / car feme ne peut riens celer" (vv. 19188–90).

33. The basic structure is:

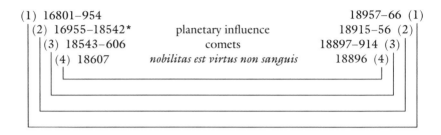

This relatively simple structure is amplified, however, by a series of further *emboîtements* that are embedded within the extended first half of the second movement (asterisked above):

34. The sharp disjunction between Genius's *sermon joyeux* on generation and his predication about the "parc du champ joli" presided over by "li filz de la Vierge" (vv. 19905–08) perhaps calls Nature's reconciliation into question; but it remains true that even Genius recognizes that the relationship between the two gardens is temporal as well as hierarchical and that entrance to the higher garden is accorded only after service in the lower: see verses 19877–909 and 20597–629.

35. Charles d'Héricault, ed., *Les oeuvres de Roger de Collerye* (Paris: P. Jannet, 1885), III–22. The sermon was written around 1500.

36. This genre was first identified by Emile Picot, "Le monologue dramatique dans l'ancien théatre français," *Romania* 15 (1886), 358–422; *Romania* 16 (1887), 438–542; *Romania* 17 (1888), 207–75. Particularly relevant to this discussion

are the sermons listed by Picot as numbers 14–28, 44–56, and especially 94: "Sermon joyeux des femmes" (ca. 1420). Picot's edition has been superseded by Jelle Koopmans, ed., *Recueil de sermons joyeux* (Geneva: Droz, 1988). Very similar to this text is the dialogue *Gilote et Johane*, extant in MS Harley 2253 and dated 15 September 1293; see Achille Jubinal, ed., *Nouveau recueil de contes, dits, fabliaux, et autres pièces inédites des XIIIe, XIVe et XVe siècles* (Paris: Pannier, 1842), 2:28–39, and Carter Revard, "*Gilote et Johane*: An Interlude in B. L. MS. Harley 2253," *Studies in Philology* 79 (1982): 122–46. In *The Mediaeval Stage* (Oxford, 1903), E. K. Chambers briefly discusses the *sociétés joyeuses* that seem to have been the secular inheritors of the defunct feast of fools (1:383–84); see also Jelle Koopmans and Paul Verhuyck, *Sermon joyeux et truanderie (Villon-Nemo-Ulespiègle)* (Amsterdam: Rodopi, 1987). For Latin and German material, see Sander L. Gilman, *The Parodic Sermon in European Perspective*, Beiträge zur Literatur des XV. bis XVIII. Jahrhunderts 6 (Wiesbaden: Steiner, 1974). Genius's first sermon on generation in the *Roman de la Rose* (vv. 19433–900) is a fine example of the genre, as are Gautier Le Leu's *Du con* and the sermon in praise of sexuality delivered by Bernart the Ass in the *Roman de Renart*; for the last of these, see Charles Muscatine, *Chaucer and the French Tradition*, 78.

37. Compare, for instance, the opening of the *Sermon pour une nopce* with Genius's discussion in verses 19763–66.

38. *Audi, filia, et vide,*
   Qui sera, sans dilation,
   De nostre predication
   L'achevement, et bien couché
   Ainsy que je vous ay touché.
   (vv. 261–65)

39. Of the many discussions of sermon theory, see especially Jean Leclercq, "Le magistère du prédicateur au XIIe siècle," *Archives d'histoire doctrinale et littéraire du moyen âge* 15 (1946): 105–47, and Étienne Gilson, "M. Menot et la technique du sermon médiéval," in *Les Idées et les lettres* (Paris: J. Vrin, 1932), 93–154. *Dilatio* (or *dilatatio*) is a term relevant primarily to preaching theory: rhetoricians prefer *amplificatio*, although the verbal form *dilato* and its cognates are used. Heinrich Lausberg, *Handbuch der literarischen Rhetorik*, 2 vols. (Munich: Hueber, 1960), contains only a single reference to *dilatio*. On the other hand, a key text for the development of preaching theory is Richard of Thetford's *Ars dilatandi sermones*: for bibliography, see James J. Murphy, *Rhetoric in the Middle Ages* (Berkeley: University of California Press, 1974), 326–29. For *dilatio* and *divisio* in preaching theory, see also Simon Alcok's *De modo dividendi thema pro materia sermonis dilatanda*, ed. Mary F. Boynton in the *Harvard Theological Review* 34 (1941): 201–16; Ranulph Higden, *Ars componendi sermones*, in MS Bodley 316, fol. 176r, in Margaret Jennings, ed., *The Ars componendi sermones of Ranulph Higden* (Leiden: Brill, 1987); and T. M. Charland, *Artes praedicandi*, Publications de l'Institut d'Études médiévales d'Ottawa 7 (Paris-Ottawa: Presses de l'Université d'Ottawa, 1936), 194–211.

40. William Atkynson, trans., *The earliest English Translation of . . . the De*

imitatione Christi, ed. John K. Ingram, EETS ES 63 (London: K. Paul, Trench, and Trübner, 1893), 201; Augustine, *Confessions* 1, 5: "Angusta est domus animae meae, quo venias ad eam: dilatetur abs te."

41. See, for instance, J. Morawski, "Parodie d'un passage du *Roman de la Rose* dans un *Sermon Joyeux*," *Romania* 52 (1926): 159–60.

42. These natural divisions have been further authorized by Robert Pratt's analysis of Chaucer's use of different sources for these three parts, an analysis that nicely defines the disparate tones of the *Prologue* without requiring us to accept Pratt's complicated speculations about the order of composition: "The Development of the Wife of Bath," in *Studies in Medieval Literature in Honor of Professor Albert Croll Baugh*, ed. MacEdward Leach (Philadelphia: University of Pennsylvania Press, 1961), 45–79.

43. The importance of this text to the Wife's *Prologue*, and its medieval interpretation, are well discussed by Britton J. Harwood, "The Wife of Bath and the Dream of Innocence," *Modern Language Quarterly* 33 (1972): 257–73. That the Wife delivers a sermon in the first 162 verses is of course well known, but that it is a *sermon joyeux* has not, to my knowledge, been suggested before.

44. That the Wife's exegesis is heterodox is thoroughly demonstrated by Robertson, *Preface to Chaucer*, 317–31, and Harwood, "Wife of Bath," 258–63. Nonetheless, the specific advice that she offers in her sermon (insofar as she offers any) is less flagrantly illegitimate than some commentaries might lead us to think: see Howard, *Idea of the* Canterbury Tales, 250. The *sermon joyeux* as a genre, it should be pointed out, inverts the spirit of medieval orthodoxy but not its structure or its content: the Wife is not urging us to sin but to enjoy our inevitable limitations. Another reference to 1 Cor. 7:28 and its exegetical meaning may be found in the "Envoy to Bukton," where Chaucer also invokes the Wife as an authority on marriage: "Bet ys to wedde than brenne in worse wise. / But thow shal have sorwe on thy flessh, thy lyf, / And ben thy wives thral, as seyn these wise" (vv. 18–20).

45. See, for instance, Thomas Walys's treatment, in Charland, ed., *Ars praedicandi*, 390.

46. Verses 46–52, 64–65, 79–84, 87, 102–4, 129–30, 147–48, 154–60.

47. On intertextuality, see Augustine, *De doctrina Christiana* 3, 26–27; trans. D. W. Robertson (Indianapolis: Bobbs-Merrill, 1958), 101–02; and Woodburn O. Ross, ed., *Middle English Sermons*, EETS OS 209 (London: Oxford University Press, 1940), xlvi–xlvii.

48. That there is a shift here in the subject of the Wife's discourse was first noted by Arthur K. Moore, "Alysoun's Other Tonne," *MLN* 59 (1944): 481–83, and "The Pardoner's Interruption of the *Wife of Bath's Prologue*," *MLQ* 10 (1949): 49–57.

49. Geoffrey of Vinsauf, *Poetria nova*, trans. Margaret F. Nims (Toronto: Pontifical Institute of Mediaeval Studies, 1967), 35.

50. On this as a principle of medieval poetics, see, for example, Ernest Gallo's comment on the teachings of the rhetoricians: "*Everything is already known from the beginning*: that which follows is an unfolding, a *manifestatio*, of a nature, a type, an essence" ("Matthew of Vendome: Introductory Treatise on the Art of

Poetry," *American Philosophical Society Proceedings* 118 [1974], 60). Also relevant here is the important definition in the *Rhetorica ad Herennium* of *expolitio* as "standing in the same place:" "Expolitio est cum in eodem loco manemus et aliud atque aliud dicere videmur" (Harry Caplan, ed. and trans. [Cambridge, MA: Harvard University Press, 1954], 364).

51. This is an assumption that is central to the misogynist attitude and so provides the knight with an opportunity to transcend his earlier consciousness. See Ovid, *Amores* 1, 8, 43: "she is chaste because no one asked" ("casta est, quam nemo rogavit"). In closing the Wife's discourse with a sermon, Chaucer neatly imitates Jean's *emboîtement* structure. He also provides a revision of Genius's two sermons, with the temporality that is compressed in Genius's version here given its full extension.

52. The source of the discussion of *gentillesse* in the sermon is John of Wales's preaching handbook, the *Communiloquium*; see Robert A. Pratt, "Chaucer and the Hand that Fed Him," *Speculum* 41 (1966): 624–27. It would be quite wrong to think that the topos that nobility derives from virtue rather than lineage was by definition antiaristocratic. On the contrary, it is cited by chivalric writers in order to argue not only that inherited nobility demands the exercise of virtue but that high lineage predisposes one to virtuous deeds. See, for example, Ghillebert de Lannoy's *Enseignements paternels*, in *Œuvres de Ghillebert de Lannoy*, ed. Charles Potvin, Académie Impériale et Royale des Sciences et Belles-Lettres (Louvain: Lefever, 1878), 460–61; and Malcolm Vale, *War and Chivalry: Warfare and Aristocratic Culture in England, France and Burgundy* (London: Duckworth, 1981), 22–28.

53. From this perspective, the conclusion to the *Tale* is analogous to the tearing of the book that serves to bring to a climax the struggle with Jankin, and specifically to the blow upon the cheek with which Alisoun greets Jankin's response to her apparent vulnerability.

54. For the *General Prologue* and the three estates, see Jill Mann, *Chaucer and Medieval Estates Satire* (Cambridge: Cambridge University Press, 1973); for the relation of Knight to Monk, see Robert A. Kaske, "The Knight's Interruption of the *Monk's Tale*," *ELH* 24 (1957): 249–68.

55. See *Chaucer and the Subject of History* (Madison: University of Wisconsin Press, 1991), 244–79.

56. For the *Man of Law's Prologue* as establishing a new beginning to the *Canterbury Tales*, see V. A. Kolve, *Chaucer and the Imagery of Narrative* (Stanford: Stanford University Press, 1984), 293–94.

57. For the very large income of a sergeant-at-law (£300 annually), see Christopher Dyer, *Standards of Living in the Later Middle Ages* (Cambridge: Cambridge University Press, 1989), 47; for the social advancement of lawyers, M. M. Postan, *The Medieval Economy and Society* (Harmondsworth: Penguin Books, 1975), 175; and for the interpenetration of the legal and mercantile classes, Sylvia Thrupp, *The Merchant Class of Medieval London, 1300–1500* (Ann Arbor: University of Michigan Press, 1962), 246. As the rage toward lawyers and legal records expressed by the rebels of 1381 shows, the legal system was widely perceived as serving the governing class.

58. On Trevet's *Chronicles* and their suitability for their patroness, see Ruth Dean, "Nicholas Trevet, Historian," in *Medieval Learning and Literature; Essays Presented to Richard William Hunt,* ed. J. J. G. Alexander and M. T. Gibson (Oxford: Clarendon Press, 1976), 328–52.

59. See Mary Carruthers, "The Wife of Bath and the Painting of Lions," *PMLA* 94 (1979): 209–22, and D. W. Robertson, Jr., "'And for my land thus hastow mordred me?': Land Tenure, the Cloth Industry, and the Wife of Bath," *Chaucer Review* 14 (1979–80): 403–20. For the importance of the workers in the cloth industry in the Rising of 1381, see Rodney Hilton, *Class Conflict and the Crisis of Feudalism* (London: Hambledon Press, 1985), 152. The independent commodity producer is postfeudal not because he or she produces commodities (which is true to some extent of virtually all agrarian production thoughout the Middle Ages) but because the mode of production is *independent*, the defining characteristic of the feudal mode of production being its dependency (Postan, *Medieval Economy and Society*, 88).

60. For the "overwhelmingly private nature" ascribed to medieval womankind which allowed them to be conceived "in iconic rather than narrative terms"— that is, without a history—see Diane Owen Hughes, "Invisible Madonnas? The Italian Historiographical Tradition and the Women of Medieval Italy," in *Women in Medieval History and Historiography,* ed. Susan Mosher Stuard (Philadelphia: University of Pennsylvania Press, 1987), 25–26.

61. Shulamith Shahar, *The Fourth Estate: A History of Women in the Middle Ages* (London: Methuen, 1983), 2–3; Marsilius of Padua, *The Defender of the Peace (Defensor pacis)*, trans. Alan Gewirth (New York: Harper, 1967), 12, 4.

62. An excellent guide to these issues is provided by Alfred David, *The Strumpet Muse: Art and Morals in Chaucer's Poetry* (Bloomington: Indiana University Press, 1976), 118–34.

63. In the *Key of Remembrance* (New Haven, CT: Yale University Press, 1963), Robert Payne points out that "the dead-center aesthetic orthodoxy of the God of Love in the Prologue to the *Legend of Good Women* receives five-fold obeisance in the one-dimensional elaboration of morality into sentimentality by the Man of Law, the Clerk, the Physician, the Second Nun, and the Prioress" (163).

64. *De doctrina Christiana* 3, 15, trans. Robertson: "what is read should be subjected to diligent scrutiny until an interpretation contributing to the reign of charity is produced" (93). See also 1, 36 and 3, 7 (30, 86).

Lori Walters

Appendix: Author Portraits and Textual Demarcation in Manuscripts of the *Romance of the Rose*

David Hult argues convincingly that the author portraits that occur in manuscripts of the *Romance of the Rose*, far from constituting mechanical reminiscences of classical writers or the four Evangelists, develop the theme of the dual authorship of the work.[1] I believe that the use of the author portrait is related to specific literary techniques employed by Jean de Meun. The nature and position of the visual representation was inspired by Jean's creation of written portraits of both himself (vv. 10535ff, Lecoy edition) and his predecessor Guillaume de Lorris (vv. 10496ff) in a justly famous passage situated near the middle of the combined *Rose* texts (vv. 10465–650; henceforth referred to as the conjoined *Rose* midpoint passage). Exact quotations of the last six verses of Guillaume's text (vv. 10525–30) and the first two lines of Jean's continuation (vv. 10565–66) accompany the two literary portraits. The quotations, like the written portraits, refer back to the point of intersection of the two texts, the exact spot where Jean took up the task of continuing the work he chose to view as incomplete. As shown in Part I of the accompanying chart, in the majority of cases a miniature that portrays one of the authors (usually Jean de Meun) appears between the two texts. Variations on this standard practice include a double author portrait that we can reasonably assume shows Guillaume de Lorris opposite Jean de Meun or an author portrait positioned rather at the conjoined *Rose* midpoint. At a certain moment in time a manuscript planner, taking a cue from Jean de Meun who wished to emphasize his role as Guillaume's legitimate continuator despite his radical transformation of the givens of Guillaume's text, started a mode which found a secure place in the manuscript tradition of the *Romance of the Rose*.[2]

Part I of the chart shows the placement of author portraits (and other references to authorship) in manuscripts dated 1400 or earlier.[3] By and large I have accepted the datings given by Langlois unless there was good reason to question them. In most cases I have also adopted Langlois's designation of the manuscript. In the last column of the chart, I reproduce the sigla provided by Langlois.[4] The sigla designate the manuscript family of each section of the text. A blank space in the final column of the chart indicates that Langlois did not give sigla for a particular manuscript, either because he was unaware of its existence or did not have access to it.

Part II of the chart concerns textual demarcation in manuscripts containing the anonymous continuation of the *Romance of the Rose*.[5] In only one case do we find anything approaching the typical visual author portrait (Manchester, Rylands FR. 66). Some manuscripts contain elaborate rubrication that sets off the anonymous continuation; others give few signals or none whatsoever that the continuation is about to begin.[6]

I have eliminated from the study manuscripts in a poor state of preservation (for example, Paris, B.N. fr. 1571; Paris, B.N. fr. 12587; and Paris, B.N. fr. 799). I assumed that a manuscript contained miniatures even if these had been removed at a later date or if spaces had been left for them to be executed. Unless historiated, I did not count ornamental letters as miniatures.[7] When an author portrait was not physically present, I assumed it would have been placed in an empty space if a rubric or gloss indicated it was meant to go there.

Here is a list of manuscripts in which the *Rose* has no miniatures:

1. Bruxelles, Bib. roy. 11019
2. Cambridge, MA, Harvard B
3. Cambridge, Univ. Lib. Add. 2993
4. Chalon-sur-Saône, Bib. Mun. 33
5. New Haven, Yale A
6. Paris, B.N. fr. 1568
7. Paris, B.N. fr. 1573
8. Paris, B.N. fr. 2194
9. Paris, B.N. fr. 2195
10. Paris, B.N. fr. 12594
11. Paris, B.N. fr. 25524

These manuscripts do not contain author portraits:

1. Copenhague, Bib. roy. Fr. LV (also known as Gl Kgl.S.2061)
2. The Crawford MS
3. Dijon, Bib. mun. 525

4. London, Brit. Lib. Egerton 881
5. London, Brit. Lib. Roy. 19B xiii
6. New York, Pierpont Morgan M 372
7. Paris, Arsenal 3337
8. Paris, Arsenal 5210
9. Paris, B.N. fr. 803
10. Paris, B.N. fr. 1559
11. Paris, B.N. fr. 1566
12. Paris, B.N. fr. 1567
13. Paris, B.N. fr. 1575
14. Paris, B.N. fr. 2196
15. Paris, B.N. fr. 12589
16. Paris, B.N. fr. 15109
17. Paris, B.N. fr. 24391
18. Paris, B.N. fr. 25523
19. Paris, B.N. Nouv. Acq. fr. 9252
20. Paris, Mazarine 3874
21. Rome, Vatican Urb. 376

(Note: Many of the manuscripts figuring in the above list include rubrics that make reference to authorship.)

At the end of the chart I treat six manuscripts that, although listed above (nos. 2, 10, 13, 18, 19, 21) as having no author portrait, do contain miniatures and/or rubrics that may refer to authorship.

Manuscripts without miniatures	11
Manuscripts without author portraits	21
Manuscripts represented in the chart (excluding entries 60–65)	59
Total manuscripts in the study	91
Manuscripts with author portraits per se (at the end of Rl and/or at the combined *Rose* midpoint)	59
Percentage of total 59/91 = 65%	

The 91 manuscripts sampled in this study represent more than half of the approximately 130–140 extant manuscripts of the *Romance of the Rose* that predate 1400. About two thirds of the group in the survey contain an author portrait, and possible references to authorship appear in several other manuscripts. Two related facts indicate the importance of the notion of authorship in the manuscript tradition of the *Rose*. First of all, the author portrait became an acknowledged feature of manuscripts of the work, a recognized element in the tradition. Second, planners of manuscripts felt free to vary the way in which they made reference to the idea of authorship, using double portraits, rubrication, or novel representations of the notion. The most impressive rendition of the transfer of literary authority from one clerk to another appears in Paris, B.N. fr. 1569. In a miniature found at the conjoined *Rose* midpoint, Guillaume de Lorris is shown passing the *Romance of the Rose* to Jean de Meun. Apparently the only example of its kind, it illustrates in a striking way the continuity of the poetic tradition despite the radical differences in the texts of the two authors.

PART I: AUTHOR PORTRAITS AND OTHER REFERENCES TO AUTHORSHIP IN THE MANUSCRIPT TRADITION OF THE *ROMANCE OF THE ROSE*

Manuscript and date	End of Guillaume's Rose		The Rose Midpoint		Sigla
	Miniatures	Rubrics	Miniatures	Rubrics	
Miniatures of both authors at end of Guillaume's Rose					
1. London Brit. Lib. Stowe 947; mid-14th century	Yes	Yes	No	The God of Love's prayer for Jean's birth	Lm³ Lm³
2. Munich Bib. roy. Gall 17; 2nd third of 14th century	Yes	Yes	No	No	Ky Ky
3. Paris, B.N. fr. 24390; 2nd third of 14th century	Yes	Yes	No	The prayer	Ke Ke
Author portraits at end of Guillaume's Rose *and* Rose *midpoint*					
4. Paris, B.N. fr. 1569; end 13th, beg. 14th century	Yes	Guillaume de St. Amor and Jean de Meun	One writer passes his book to second writer	Yes	Jo Jo
5. Paris, B.N. fr. 19157; 2nd third of 14th century	Yes	Jean de Meun	Yes	None with this min.; the prayer on fol. 66v.	Fe Fe

Manuscript and date	End of Guillaume's Rose		The Rose Midpoint		
	Miniatures	*Rubrics*	*Miniatures*	*Rubrics*	*Sigla*
Author portrait only at Rose *midpoint*					
6. Arras, Bib. mun. 897; 1370	Lover laments outside garden walls	No, but gloss in similar hand: "Here begins Master Jean de Meun"	Yes, found before verses dealing with Guillaume's tomb	No	Ra Bê
7. Brussels, Bib. roy. 9574–75; beg. 14th (Langlois) ca. 1340 (B.R. cat.)	Jealousy's tower	No	Yes	Jean de Meun	Lt Lt
8. Chantilly, Musée Condé 483 (1480); mid-14th century	No	No	Yes	Jean de Meun	Jl Jl
9. Oxford, Bodl. Add. A 22; 14th century	No	No	Yes (on fol. 97)	The prayer (on fol. 97v.)	$\phi\iota$ $\lambda\upsilon$
Author portraits only at end of Guillaume's Rose					
10. Brussels, Bib. roy. 9576 14th century (Langlois); ca. 1320 (B.R. cat.)	Yes	Jean de Meun	No	The prayer	$\gamma\alpha$ $\gamma\alpha$
11. Brussels, Bib. roy. 9577; 1st half of 14th century (Langlois); 1360–1370 (B.R. cat.)	Yes	Jean de Meun	No	No	$\mu\iota$ $\mu\iota$
12. Cambridge, Fitzwilliam Museum 168; 14th century (1398?)	Yes (removed)	Jean de Meun	Info. incomplete	Info. incomplete	Lm[4] Lm[4]

Manuscript and date	End of Guillaume's Rose		The Rose Midpoint		Sigla
	Miniatures	Rubrics	Miniatures	Rubrics	
13. Chantilly, Musée Condé 479 (911); early 14th century	Space left	Both authors	Info. incomplete	Info incomplete	φα By
14. Chantilly, Musée Condé 481 (664); 3rd quarter of 14th century	Yes	Jean de Meun	No	No	Ni Ni
15. Chantilly, Musée Condé 482 (665); mid-14th century	Yes	Jean de Meun	No	No	No No
16. Draguignan Bib. mun. 17; first half 14th century	Yes	No	No	No	Lu Lu
17. Florence, Bib. Laurentienne Acq. et Dons 153; beg. of 14th century	Yes	Jean de Meun	No	No	Jê Lv
18. London, Brit. Lib. Addit. 31840; 14th century	Yes, but falsely identified as Reason	Other rubrics announce the coming of Jean de Meun	No	No	Jb Jb
19. London, Brit. Lib. Addit. 42133; 2nd half of 14th century	Yes	Jean de Meun	No	The prayer	
20. London, Brit. Lib. Roy. 20A xvii; 14th century	Yes; he has just written his name, "Jehan."	Jean de Meun	No	The prayer	λο λο
21. Lyon, Bib. mun. 763; mid-14th century	Yes	Jean de Meun	No	Info. incomplete	Lm⁶ Lm⁶
22. Lyon, Bib. mun. 764; 2nd half 14th century	Space left	Jean de Meun	Space left	The prayer	Mo Mo

Manuscript and date	End of Guillaume's Rose		The Rose Midpoint		Sigla
	Miniatures	Rubrics	Miniatures	Rubrics	
23. Lyon, Palais des Arts 23; 14th century	Yes	Guillaume de St.-Amor and Guillaume de Lorris	No	Info. incomplete	με Mo
24. Lyon, Palais des Arts 24; 1300	Yes	"Here Bel Acueil is in prison."	No Info. incomplete	Lh Lh	
25. Montpellier, Fac. Med. H 245; 3rd quarter of 14th century	Yes	Jean de Meun	No	No	Nb Nb
26. New York Pierpont Morgan M 48; 2nd half of 14th century	Yes	Jean de Meun	No	The prayer	
27. New York Pierpont Morgan M 120; ca. 1370	Space left	No	No	No	
28. New York Pierpont Morgan M 132; ca. 1380	Yes	Jean de Meun	No	No	
29. New York Pierpont Morgan M 185; 14th century	Yes	Jean de Meun	No	No	
30. New York Pierpont Morgan M 324; mid-14th century	Yes	Jean de Meun	No	The prayer	
31. New York Pierpont Morgan M 503; ca. 1370	Yes	Jean de Meun	No	The prayer	

| Manuscript and date | End of Guillaume's Rose | | The Rose Midpoint | | Sigla |
	Miniatures	Rubrics	Miniatures	Rubrics	
32. Oxford, Bodl. Selden supra 57; 14th century	Yes	Jean de Meun	Nun talks to a tonsured man. On fol. 118 we see the God of Love; a rubric identifies the figure as Nature.	No	Sel Sel
33. Oxford, Bodl. Rawlinson C537; 2nd quarter 14th century	Space left	No	No	No	Lm⁷ Lm⁷
34. Paris, B.N. fr. 378; end 13th century	Yes	Both authors	No	The prayer	θα θα
35. Paris, B.N. fr. 802; 3rd quarter 14th century	Yes	Jean de Meun	No	The prayer	μα My
36. Paris, B.N. fr. 1558; 1st third 14th century	Yes	Jean de Meun	No	No	Ll Kb
37. Paris, B.N. fr. 1560; mid-14th century	Yes	Jean de Meun	No	No	Me Me
38. Paris, B.N. fr. 1561; 1st half 14th century	Yes	Jean de Meun	The God of Love seated at lectern reads book to Jean de Meun and disciples	Yes, and the prayer	Lb Lb
39. Paris, B.N. fr. 1564; 1st half 14th century	Yes	Jean de Meun	No	No	Lg Lg
40. Paris, B.N. fr. 1565; 1352	Yes	Jean de Meun	No	No	Nd Nd

Manuscript and date	End of Guillaume's Rose		The Rose Midpoint		Sigla
	Miniatures	Rubrics	Miniatures	Rubrics	
41. Paris, B.N. fr. 1574; 14th century	Space left	Rubrics written in a later hand announce both writers	No	Info. incomplete	Je Lw
42. Paris, B.N. fr. 12588; 1st half 14th century	Yes	No	No	The prayer	Lc Lc
43. Paris, B.N. fr. 19154; 14th century	Space left	Jean de Meun	No	A gloss in another hand speaks of both writers	Gê Bô
44. Paris, B.N. fr. 19156; 1st half 14th century	Yes	Jean de Meun	No	The prayer	τα τα
45. Paris, B.N. fr. 24388; 14th century	Yes	Jean de Meun	No	The prayer	Nf Nf
46. Paris, B.N. fr. 24389; 14th century	Yes	Both authors (See Hult, *Prophecies*, p. 58).	No	No	Gu Bî
47. Paris, B.N. fr. 25526; mid-14th century	Yes	Jean de Meun	Min. shows Lover kneeling before God of Love; man and woman shown making book in marginalia	No rubric about authorship	Mi Mi
48. Paris, B.N. Rothschild 2801; mid-14th century	Yes	Jean de Meun	No	The prayer	Nv Nv
49. Paris, Arsenal 2988; 3rd quarter 14th century	Yes	Jean de Meun	No	The prayer	Gé Bó

Manuscript and date	End of Guillaume's Rose		The Rose Midpoint		Sigla
	Miniatures	Rubrics	Miniatures	Rubrics	
50. Paris, Arsenal 3338; 14th century	Yes	The Lover's lament	No	No	Kl Nh
51. Paris, Arsenal 5209; 2nd third 14th century	Yes	Jean de Meun	No	The prayer	Ng Ng
52. Paris, Arsenal 5226; 3rd quarter 14th century	Yes	Both authors	No	Two rubrics mention Jean de Meun	γλ Lp
53. Paris, Mazarine 3872; 2nd quarter 14th century	Yes	Jean de Meun	No	No	
54. Paris, Mazarine 3873; 2nd quarter 14th century	Yes	Guillaume de St.-Amor and Jean de Meun	No	No	Ki Ki
55. Paris, St. Geneviève 1126; mid-14th century	Yes	Jean de Meun	No	Two sets of rubrics state that the God of Love is talking about Jean de Meun	Ny Ny
56. Paris, Chambre des Députés 1230; 2nd third 14th century	Yes	Jean de Meun	No	The prayer	Lm² Lm²
57. Princeton, Garrett 126; mid-14th century	Yes	Jean de Meun	No	The prayer	
58. Rome, Vatican Reg. 1522; beg. of 14th century	Yes	The prayer rubric usually seen at Rose midpoint.	Man lectures a large group of seated people.	No	Le Le

Manuscript and date	End of Guillaume's Rose		The Rose Midpoint		
	Miniatures	Rubrics	Miniatures	Rubrics	Sigla
59. San Marino, CA, Hunting-ton MS 902; 1st half 14th century	Space left	Both writers	Info. incomplete	Info. incomplete	

Manuscripts with possible references to authorship

60. The Crawford MS; private col-lection; Haigh Hall, County Lancaster	Info. incomplete	Info. incomplete	Guillaume's funeral	Notes added in Latin mention the change in author-ship	B
61. Paris, B.N. fr. 1559; end of 13th century	A man speaks to a woman	Ref. to Jean de Meun added later?	No	The prayer	La La
62. Paris, B.N. fr. 1575; 1st half of 14th century	A man speaks to a woman	No	The God of Love as-sembles his barons	Yes	λι Zi
63. Paris, B.N. fr. 25523; 1330	No	No	Man reads a book	No	Za Za
64. Paris, B.N. Nouv. Acq. fr. 9252; 1st half 14th century	The God of Love in front of altar	The prayer	This section of text missing; other min. may be misplaced		γω Zε
65. Rome, Vati-can Urb. 376; 14th century	A seated man addresses an audi-ence of five men	No	The God of Love and his troops	The prayer before v. 10586; ini-tial letter shows the God of Love pray-ing while God's face appears out of the clouds	Urb Urb

PART II: TEXTUAL DEMARCATION IN MANUSCRIPTS CONTAINING THE
ANONYMOUS CONTINUATION OF THE *ROMANCE OF THE ROSE*

Manuscript, date and sigla	End of Guillaume's Rose	End of anonymous continuation	Rose midpoint
1. Amiens, Bib. mun. 437; 2nd half 14th century; Sigla: Ce/Ce.	No miniatures or rubrics.	No miniatures, but the anonymous continuation is set off by painted letters.	No miniatures or rubrics.
2. Cambridge, Harvard A Rg. 3.40; 1st half 14th century; Sigla: both parts related to Ca.	No miniatures or rubrics.	No miniatures or rubrics.	No miniatures or rubrics.
3. Manchester, Rylands Fr. 66; end of 14th century.	No miniatures, but rubrics introduce anonymous continuation.	No miniatures; rubrics indicate where Guillaume ended and Jean began. The planner considers the anonymous continuation to have been written by Guillaume de Lorris.	On fol. 87, the God of Love speaks to his barons. On fol. 87v, the God of Love dictates to a clerk who writes his name, "Jehan Chopinel." Rubrics accompany each min.; the 2nd min. is of the God of Love's prophecy that Jean de Meun will continue the *Rose*.

Manuscript, date and sigla	*End of Guillaume's* Rose	End of anonymous continuation	Rose *midpoint*
4. Paris, B.N. Rothschild 2800 (IV.2.24). Transcribed in 1329 by Robechounet de Goumecourt; Sigla: γo/Eb	Guillaume's poem is followed by the first 2 verses of Jean's contin., then 2 verses that tell us that Jean's text is continued in "the other book." Then we find a min. of a man lecturing to six people followed by a 72-verse rendition of the anonymous contin. whose first verse is set off by a painted initial.	A rubric that reads "Explicit primus/ Incipit secundus." A min. of the Lover sitting despondently on a hill is followed by Jean's continuation minus the first two verses.	On fol. 66v, the God of Love lectures to a group of people; no rubric. This illustration appears in a series of eight mins. dealing with the God of Love.
5. Tournai MS (MS 101 of the Mun. Library of Tournai, Belgium); 1330; Sigla: Tou/ Tou.	Heading of Chapter 28 (in red) introduces anonymous continuation identified as the end of the text of Guillaume de Lorris. Following the chapter heading, a min. shows the Lover speaking to Pitié, Biautez, Bel Acueil, Simplece and Douz Regard. Marginal images also present. The 72-verse continuation comes after the miniature.	Heading of Chapter 29 (in red) introduces Gui's colophon in verse. Long rubric that also functions as heading of Chapter 30, followed by miniature of Bel Acueil in Jealousy's Castle (plus marginalia). After the miniature we find the last six verses of Guillaume's text followed by Jean's continuation.	Literary portrait of Gui de Mori added to those of Guillaume de Lorris and Jean de Meun.

Manuscript, date and sigla	End of Guillaume's Rose	End of anonymous continuation	Rose *midpoint*
6. Rouard MS; 14th century; this MS, containing some of the changes made by Gui de Mori, has passed out of sight.	Guillaume's text followed immediately by the anonymous continuation in 72 verses.	Rubric in prose; text in verse adapts Gui's colophon without mentioning Gui's name; text in prose introduces Jean's continuation.	No information given.
7. Tersan MS; 1290; MS now lost.	No miniatures, anonymous continuation probably begins immediately.	Rubric in prose; Gui's colophon in verse includes riddle to determine his name; prose interpolation includes the name, "Gui"; repetition of last 12 verses of Guillaume's text; rubric in prose; Jean's continuation.	No miniatures; no information on rubrication.
8. Paris, B.N. 12786; early 14th century; Sigla: Da/ξα	No miniatures or rubrics.	No miniatures or rubrics.	Jean's text not included.

Notes

1. David Hult, *Self-Fulfilling Prophecies: Readership and Authority in the First "Roman de la Rose,"* (Cambridge: Cambridge University Press, 1986), pp. 74–93. The reader should consult these pages for a more complete study of the use of the author portrait in manuscripts of the *Romance of the Rose*. Hult's book includes reproductions of significant examples of the author portrait.

2. For a fuller treatment of the relationship between visual and written author portraits in the *Rose*, consult my article, "A Parisian Manuscript of the *Romance of the Rose*," *The Princeton University Library Chronicle* 51 (Autumn 1989): 31–55.

3. Here is where information can be found on manuscripts not described by Langlois that I include in Part I of the chart: #12: Catalogue of the Fitzwilliam Museum Library; #59: R. Dean, "A 14th century MS of *Le Roman de la Rose* and a Fragment of *Le Compot*"; Huntington MS 902: *Medium aevum* 12 (1943): 18–24; #60: R. Fawtier, "Deux Manuscrits du *Roman de la Rose*," *Romania* 58 (1932): 265–70.

4. Ernest Langlois, *Les Manuscrits du "Roman de la Rose"*, (1910; Geneva: Slatkine Reprints, 1974), pp. 238–40.

5. The anonymous continuation is printed in Ernest Langlois's edition of the *Roman de la Rose*, 5 vols. (Paris: Firmin-Didot, 1914), 2: 330–33. Langlois makes a mistake in his notes on p. 332. Although he claims that vv. 47 and 48 (De beles roses de rosiers / Fumes convert e de baisiers.) are missing from MS Paris, B.N. fr. 12786, these verses are present. It is rather vv. 49–50 (A grant solaz, a grant deduit / Fumes trestoute cele nuit.) that are absent from that manuscript.

6. Consult the following references for information on manuscripts not described by Langlois that I include in Part II of the chart: #2: Richmond Laurin Hawkins, "The Manuscripts of the *Roman de la Rose* in the Libraries of Harvard and Yale Universities," *Romanic Review* 19 (Jan.–Mar. 1928): 1–24; #3: R. Fawtier, "Deux Manuscrits du *Roman de la Rose*," *Romania* 58 (1932): 270–73; #5: Ernest Langlois, "Gui de Mori et le *Roman de la Rose*," *Bibliothèque de l'École des Chartes* 68 (1907): 249–71: Marc-René Jung, "Gui de Mori et Guillaume de Lorris," *Vox Romanica* 27 (1968): 106–37; #6: M. Rouard, "D'un manuscrit inconnu du *Roman de la Rose*," *Bulletin du Bibliophile* (1860): 976–87; Ernest Langlois, *Les Manuscrits*, pp. 207–09 (in the section he calls "Manuscrits dont le domicile actuel est inconnu"); #7: M. Meon's edition of the *Rose* (Paris: 1814), intro. to vol. 1; Langlois, "Gui de Mori," 250–51; Hult's reconstruction (based on the transcriptions of Meon and Langlois) of the passage situated between the texts of Guillaume de Lorris and Jean de Meun found on pp. 36–39 of *Prophecies*.

7. For instance, in Paris, B.N. fr. 2195, the *Rose*, *Fauvel*, and the *Testament* all include ornamental initials; in addition, a large miniature decorates the initial page of *Fauvel*.

Index

Contributors

Pierre-Yves Badel teaches at the University of Paris VIII (Vincennes-St. Denis). He is the author of *Le* Roman de la Rose *au XIVe siècle: Étude de la réception de l'oeuvre* (1980), and editor of *Le Dit du prunier* (1985).

Emmanuèle Baumgartner is Professor at the University of Paris III (Sorbonne Nouvelle). She is the author of *Le Tristan en prose* (1975), *L'Arbre et le pain: Essai sur la* Queste del saint graal (1981), and *La Harpe et l'épée: Tradition et renouvellement dans le* Tristan en prose (1990).

Kevin Brownlee is Professor of Romance Languages at the University of Pennsylvania. He is the author of *Poetic Identity in Guillaume de Machaut* (1984) and co-editor, with Stephen Nichols and Marina Scordilis Brownlee, of *The New Medievalism* (1991). He is currently completing a book on Christine de Pizan.

John V. Fleming is Professor of English and Comparative Literature at Princeton University. He has published extensively on the *Roman de la Rose*, including *The* Roman de la Rose: *A Study in Allegory and Iconography* (1969) and *Reason and the Lover* (1984), and is also the author of *From Bonaventure to Bellini: An Essay in Franciscan Exegesis* (1983).

Robert Pogue Harrison is Associate Professor of Italian at Stanford University. He is a specialist on Dante and medieval Italian lyric, and the author of *The Body of Beatrice* (1988).

David F. Hult is Associate Professor of French at the University of Virginia, Charlottesville. The author of *Self-fulfilling Prophecies: Readership and Authority in the First* Roman de la Rose (1986), he has also published on issues in textual criticism, and is working on an edition of Chrétien de Troyes' *Chevalier au lyon*.

Sylvia Huot is Associate Professor of French at Northern Illinois University. She is the author of *From Song to Book: The Poetics of Writing in Old French Lyric and Lyrical Narrative Poetry* (1987) and *The* Romance of the Rose *and Its Medieval Readers* (forthcoming). She is currently writing a book on thirteenth-century French motets.

Stephen G. Nichols is the Edmund J. Kahn Distinguished Professor of Humanities at the University of Pennsylvania. He is the author of *Romanesque Signs: Early Medieval Narrative and Iconography* (1983), which won the Modern Language Association's James Russell Lowell Prize; editor of *The New Philology, Speculum* 65.1 (January 1990); and co-editor, with Marina Scordilis Brownlee and Kevin Brownlee, of *The New Medievalism* (1991).

Lee Patterson is Professor of English at Duke University. A specialist on Chaucer and late medieval literature, he is the author of *Negotiating the Past: The Historical Understanding of Medieval Literature* (1987) and *Chaucer and the Subject of History* (1991).

Daniel Poirion is Professor of French at Yale University and Professor Emeritus of the University of Paris IV (Sorbonne). His publications include *Le Poète et le prince: La Poésie lyrique de Guillaume de Machaut à Charles d'Orléans* (1965), *Le* Roman de la Rose (1973), and *Résurgences: Mythe et littérature à l'âge du symbole (XIIe siècle)* (1986).

Karl D. Uitti is the John N. Woodhull Professor of Modern Languages at Princeton University. He is the author of *Linguistics and Literary Theory* (1969) and *Story, Myth, and Celebration in Old French Narrative Poetry, 1050–1200* (1973). In collaboration with Alfred Foulet he has published an edition and translation of Chrétien de Troyes' *Chevalier de la charrette* (1989).

Dieuwke E. van der Poel teaches at the University of Utrecht. She is a specialist in medieval Dutch and Flemish literature and the author of *De Vlaamse* Rose *en* Die Rose *van Heinric* (1989).

Lori Walters is Associate Professor of French at Florida State University. She has published articles on medieval romance and its manuscript tradition and, with Keith Busby and M. Alison Stones, is editing a collection of essays on the manuscripts of Chrétien de Troyes. She is also writing a book on the text and illustrations of Gui de Mori's *remaniement* of the *Roman de la Rose*.

University of Pennsylvania Press
MIDDLE AGES SERIES
Edward Peters, General Editor

F. R. P. Akehurst, trans. *The* Coutumes de Beauvaisis *of Philippe de Beaumanoir.*
1992
Peter Allen. *The Art of Love: Amatory Fiction from Ovid to the* Romance of the Rose.
1992
David Anderson. *Before the Knight's Tale: Imitation of Classical Epic in Boccaccio's*
Teseida. 1988
Benjamin Arnold. *Count and Bishop in Medieval Germany: A Study of Regional*
Power, 1100–1350. 1991
Mark C. Bartusis. *The Late Byzantine Army: Arms and Society, 1204–1453.* 1992
J. M. W. Bean. *From Lord to Patron: Lordship in Late Medieval England.* 1990
Uta-Renate Blumenthal. *The Investiture Controversy: Church and Monarchy from the*
Ninth to the Twelfth Century. 1988
Daniel Bornstein, trans. *Dino Compagni's* Chronicle *of Florence.* 1986
Betsy Bowden. *Chaucer Aloud: The Varieties of Textual Interpretation.* 1987
James William Brodman. *Ransoming Captives in Crusader Spain: The Order of Mer-*
ced on the Christian-Islamic Frontier. 1986
Kevin Brownlee and Sylvia Huot, eds. *Rethinking the* Romance of the Rose*: Text,*
Image, Reception. 1992
Otto Brunner (Howard Kaminsky and James Van Horn Melton, eds. and trans.).
Land *and Lordship: Structures of Governance in Medieval Austria.* 1992
Robert I. Burns, S. J., ed. *Emperor of Culture: Alfonso X the Learned of Castile and*
His Thirteenth-Century Renaissance. 1990
David Burr. *Olivi and Franciscan Poverty: The Origins of the* Usus Pauper *Contro-*
versy. 1989
Thomas Cable. *The English Alliterative Tradition.* 1991
Anthony K. Cassell and Victoria Kirkham, eds. and trans. *Diana's Hunt/Caccia di*
Diana: Boccaccio's First Fiction. 1991
Brigitte Cazelles. *The Lady as Saint: A Collection of French Hagiographic Romances*
of the Thirteenth Century. 1991
Anne L. Clark. *Elisabeth of Schönau: A Twelfth-Century Visionary.* 1992
Willene B. Clark and Meradith T. McMunn, eds. *Beasts and Birds of the Middle*
Ages: The Bestiary and Its Legacy. 1989
Richard C. Dales. *The Scientific Achievement of the Middle Ages.* 1973
Charles T. Davis. *Dante's Italy and Other Essays.* 1984
Katherine Fischer Drew, trans. *The Burgundian Code.* 1972
Katherine Fischer Drew, trans. *The Laws of the Salian Franks.* 1991
Katherine Fischer Drew, trans. *The Lombard Laws.* 1973

Nancy Edwards. *The Archaeology of Early Medieval Ireland.* 1990

Margaret J. Ehrhart. *The Judgment of the Trojan Prince Paris in Medieval Literature.* 1987

Richard K. Emmerson and Ronald B. Herzman. *The Apocalyptic Imagination in Medieval Literature.* 1992

Felipe Fernández-Armesto. *Before Columbus: Exploration and Colonization from the Mediterranean to the Atlantic, 1229–1492.* 1987

Robert D. Fulk. *A History of Old English Meter.* 1992

Patrick J. Geary. *Aristocracy in Provence: The Rhône Basin at the Dawn of the Carolingian Age.* 1985

Peter Heath. *Allegory and Philosophy in Avicenna (Ibn Sînâ), with a Translation of the Book of the Prophet Muḥammad's Ascent to Heaven.* 1992

J. N. Hillgarth, ed. *Christianity and Paganism, 350–750: The Conversion of Western Europe.* 1986

Richard C. Hoffmann. *Land, Liberties, and Lordship in a Late Medieval Countryside: Agrarian Structures and Change in the Duchy of Wrocław.* 1990

Robert Hollander. *Boccaccio's Last Fiction: Il Corbaccio.* 1988

Edward B. Irving, Jr. *Rereading* Beowulf. 1989

C. Stephen Jaeger. *The Origins of Courtliness: Civilizing Trends and the Formation of Courtly Ideals, 939–1210.* 1985

William Chester Jordan. *The French Monarchy and the Jews: From Philip Augustus to the Last Capetians.* 1989

William Chester Jordan. *From Servitude to Freedom: Manumission in the Sénonais in the Thirteenth Century.* 1986

Ellen E. Kittell. *From Ad Hoc to Routine: A Case Study in Medieval Bureaucracy.* 1991

Alan C. Kors and Edward Peters, eds. *Witchcraft in Europe, 1100–1700: A Documentary History.* 1972

Barbara M. Kreutz. *Before the Normans: Southern Italy in the Ninth and Tenth Centuries.* 1992

E. Ann Matter. *The Voice of My Beloved: The Song of Songs in Western Medieval Christianity.* 1990

María Rosa Menocal. *The Arabic Role in Medieval Literary History.* 1987

A. J. Minnis. *Medieval Theory of Authorship.* 1988

Lawrence Nees. *A Tainted Mantle: Hercules and the Classical Tradition at the Carolingian Court.* 1991

Lynn H. Nelson, trans. *The Chronicle of San Juan de la Peña: A Fourteenth-Century Official History of the Crown of Aragon.* 1991

Charlotte A. Newman. *The Anglo-Norman Nobility in the Reign of Henry I: The Second Generation.* 1988

Joseph F. O'Callaghan. *The Cortes of Castile-León, 1188–1350.* 1989

William D. Paden, ed. *The Voice of the Trobairitz: Perspectives on the Women Troubadours.* 1989

Edward Peters. *The Magician, the Witch, and the Law.* 1982

Edward Peters, ed. *Christian Society and the Crusades, 1198–1229*: Sources in Translation, including The Capture of Damietta by Oliver of Paderborn. 1971

Edward Peters, ed. *The First Crusade: The* Chronicle of Fulcher of Chartres *and Other Source Materials.* 1971

Edward Peters, ed. *Heresy and Authority in Medieval Europe.* 1980

James M. Powell. *Albertanus of Brescia: The Pursuit of Happiness in the Early Thirteenth Century.* 1992

James M. Powell. *Anatomy of a Crusade, 1213–1221.* 1986

Michael Resler, trans. Erec *by Hartmann von Aue.* 1987

Pierre Riché (Michael Idomir Allen, trans.). *The Carolingians: A Family Who Forged Europe.* 1993.

Pierre Riché (Jo Ann McNamara, trans.). *Daily Life in the World of Charlemagne.* 1978

Jonathan Riley-Smith. *The First Crusade and the Idea of Crusading.* 1986

Joel T. Rosenthal. *Patriarchy and Families of Privilege in Fifteenth-Century England.* 1991

Steven D. Sargent, ed. and trans. *On the Threshold of Exact Science: Selected Writings of Anneliese Maier on Late Medieval Natural Philosophy.* 1982

Sarah Stanbury. *Seeing the* Gawain-*Poet: Description and the Act of Perception.* 1992

Thomas C. Stillinger. *The Song of Troilus: Lyric Authority in the Medieval Book.* 1992

Susan Mosher Stuard. *A State of Deference: Ragusa/Dubrovnik in the Medieval Centuries.* 1992

Susan Mosher Stuard, ed. *Women in Medieval History and Historiography.* 1987

Susan Mosher Stuard, ed. *Women in Medieval Society.* 1976

Jonathan Sumption. *The Hundred Years War: Trial by Battle.* 1992

Ronald E. Surtz. *The Guitar of God: Gender, Power, and Authority in the Visionary World of Mother Juana de la Cruz (1481–1534).* 1990

Patricia Terry, trans. *Poems of the Elder Edda.* 1990

Frank Tobin. *Meister Eckhart: Thought and Language.* 1986

Ralph V. Turner. *Men Raised from the Dust: Administrative Service and Upward Mobility in Angevin England.* 1988

Harry Turtledove, trans. *The* Chronicle *of Theophanes: An English Translation of Anni Mundi 6095–6305 (A.D. 602–813).* 1982

Mary F. Wack. *Lovesickness in the Middle Ages: The* Viaticum *and Its Commentaries.* 1990

Benedicta Ward. *Miracles and the Medieval Mind: Theory, Record, and Event, 1000–1215.* 1982

Suzanne Fonay Wemple. *Women in Frankish Society: Marriage and the Cloister, 500–900.* 1981

This book has been set in Linotron Galliard. Galliard was designed for Mergenthaler in 1978 by Matthew Carter. Galliard retains many of the features of a sixteenth-century typeface cut by Robert Granjon but has some modifications that give it a more contemporary look.

Printed on acid-free paper.